8. Presentation graphics that save you hours of explanation

9. Daily performance measurement results through AIMR-compliant system

10. Taxable and tax-exempt bond indices from all the leading providers modeled in their entirety

BONDEDGE STREAMLINES INVESTMENT MANAGEMENT

11. Inventory management to quickly identify where securities are held

12. What-if analytics to fully understand the implications of proposed trades

13. Custom report writer for simplified management and client reporting

14. Electronic trade tickets that eliminate time-consuming, hand-written forms

15. Connectivity with other systems to easily import data and export calculations

WE'RE THERE WHEN YOU NEED US

16. Keep your costs down by subscribing only to the applications you need

17. Independent, unbiased research that lets you consider the facts without the sales pitch

18. Choose between a flexible 30-day contract or an annual contract

19. Frequent enhancements help you keep up with new market developments

20. Full training and continual support makes using BondEdge productive and cost effective

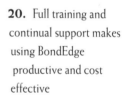

PRESENTING TWO NEW FEATURES

The Compliance Module: Designed to alert you to conditions in a portfolio that violate constraints set by management, clients or regulators

Performance Attribution: An OAS-based bond-by-bond approach to attribution for portfolios and indices updated daily to capture the effects of trading

For more information call Lisa Herbert at
310.479.9715

 CAPITAL MANAGEMENT SCIENCES

A DATA BROADCASTING CORPORATION COMPANY

Advances in Fixed Income Valuation Modeling and Risk Management

Edited by

Frank J. Fabozzi, CFA

Adjunct Professor of Finance
School of Management
Yale University
and
Editor
Journal of Portfolio Management

Published by Frank J. Fabozzi Associates

© 1997 By Frank J. Fabozzi Associates
New Hope, Pennsylvania

This publication is designed to provide accurate and authoritative information in regard to the subject matter covered. It is sold with the understanding that the publisher is not engaged in rendering legal, accounting, or other professional services.

ISBN: 1-883249-17-1

Printed in the United States of America

Table of Contents

Preface

The purpose of *Advances in Fixed Income Valuation Modeling and Risk Management* is twofold. First, the state-of-the-art models for valuing fixed income securities and derivatives are explained and illustrated. The general principles and issues associated with valuation modeling are explained and applied to all cash market sectors — Treasuries, corporate bonds, mortgage-backed securities (both residential and commercial mortgage-backed securities), and international bonds (including Brady bonds). Second, various measures of interest rate risk are covered along with strategies for controlling the many dimensions of interest rate risk.

There are 20 chapters in the book contributed by highly regarded practitioners and academicians. In the remainder of this preface I provide an overview of the 20 chapters.

In the book's first chapter, Oren Cheyette discusses interest rate models. An interest rate model is a probabilistic description of the future evolution of interest rates. He begins the chapter with a discussion of the principles of valuation algorithms and then provides an overview of the features differentiating interest rate models that have been proposed in the literature. Cheyette recommends the use of the mean reverting Gaussian model because it is easy to implement valuation algorithms for both path independent and path dependent securities.

While models of the term structure of interest rates are critical in valuation modeling, there is sometimes a misinterpretation of the proper uses of particular models that can lead to significant errors in application. In Chapter 2, Peter Fitton and James McNatt attempt to clear up some of the most commonly misconstrued aspects of interest rate models — the choice between an arbitrage-free or equilibrium model, and the choice between risk neutral or realistic parameterizations of a model. Fitton and McNatt describe and explain the use of each model.

In Chapter 3, Thomas Ho and Michael Chen present a new methodology for canonical decomposition of bonds and asset-liability strategies. For analyzing complex securities such as collateralized mortgage obligations (CMOs) and designing complex strategies like those for single premium deferred annuities, traditional tools such as option-adjusted spread, duration, and convexity do not capture all of the important complexities. Ho and Chen present a more comprehensive framework based on a methodology developed by Ho which considers all paths through an arbitrage-free binomial lattice of the term structure of interest rates. For practical applications, Ho draws on the linear path space, which provides a tractable structured sample of the space of all paths through the lattice. Ho and Chen illustrate the methodology by analyzing a CMO support tranche.

Path dependence is a major source of complexity in the implementation of recursive lattice-based valuation models. In Chapter 4, Douglas Howard explains the notion of "path dependence" and analyzes two path-dependent fixed income securities. He uses both the more common Monte Carlo approach and an efficient recursive procedure that involves coupling a non-stochastic state variable with the underlying stochastic interest rate process. Some numerical techniques are discussed that render recursive models more tractable.

Yiannos Pierides proposes in Chapter 5 a valuation methodology that can be used to value any interest rate derivative. This methodology is applied to the valuation of two such derivatives, one plain vanilla (a call on the bond price) and the other exotic (a lookback put on the bond price). In the case of the plain vanilla derivative, Pierides shows that the price is insensitive to the modeler's choice of stochastic process for the short-term interest rate as long as a consistency condition is met. However, in the case of the exotic derivative, the price is very sensitive to the modeler's choice of stochastic process for the short-term interest rate even if the consistency condition is met. Unfortunately, there is widespread disagreement as to which stochastic process for the short-term interest rate provides a better fit to market data. For this reason, different practitioners will, in general, disagree on the price they obtain for complex interest rate derivatives because each practitioner will prefer to use a different stochastic process for the short-term interest rate.

Louis Gagnon, William Hurley, and Lewis Johnson detail some of the recent advances in the valuation of corporate bonds. In Chapter 6, they examine the formal pricing of default risk. They begin by reviewing the literature on corporate bond performance and mortality to provide a sense of the magnitude of the default risk premium. They then explain the two approaches to corporate bond valuation: equilibrium-contingent claim approaches and various non-equilibrium approaches. An illustration and a discussion of the difficulties of these approaches are then provided. The comparison of these approaches that Gagnon, Hurley, and Johnson present provides the intuition behind and the complexities associated with corporate bond valuation models.

As with corporate bond buyers, investors in commercial mortgages and commercial mortgage-backed securities are exposed to credit risk. In addition, investors in these instruments are exposed to prepayment risk. Much of the valuation modeling developed for corporate bonds and securities backed by residential mortgages has not been applied to commercial mortgages and commercial mortgage-backed securities. In Chapter 7, David Jacob, Ted Hong, and Laurence Lee provide an option-based approach to valuing default risk and prepayment risk for these instruments.

There are several equilibrium term structure models proposed in the literature and employed in practice. In the broadest terms, there are one-factor models and multi-factor models. Empirical evidence indicates that one-factor models do not capture the historical variability of interest rates and do a poor job of fitting observed yield curves. Ren-Raw Chen and Louis Scott in Chapter 8 discuss multi-factor models and develop a multi-factor version of the well-known Cox-Ingersoll-Ross term structure model. They also demonstrate how their model can be used in hedging strategies.

In Chapter 8, Soren Nielsen and Ehud Ronn present a consistent and arbitrage-free two-factor model for the valuation of the two most important options embedded in the Treasury bond futures contract: the quality option and the timing option. They accomplish this objective by assuming the two factors to be the 3-month and 2-year zero-coupon interest rates, with a (risk-neutral) lognormal distribution centered about their respective forward rates. Nielsen and Ronn infer the state-specific realizations of all other interest rates from the realizations of these two zero-coupon interest rates. They estimate the discount function using Treasury C-STRIPS prices, while also explicitly recognizing the market-observed price-deviation of Treasury bonds from the discounted present values of their cash flows. Their valuation uses a trinomial lattice to generate state-specific prices for all deliverable bonds, and hence the value of the Treasury bond futures contract.

Over the last few years, adjustable-rate mortgage securities (ARMs) have appealed to a variety of new investors, ranging from money managers to international financial institutions. As investor understanding and analytical techniques have improved, so too has demand for these securities. In Chapter 10, Satish Mansukhani explains the structural characteristics of ARMs, and how these characteristics affect the value and risk profile of ARMs. In addition, he discusses various traditional and state-of-the-art tools used to discern relative value within the sector.

In Chapter 11, Stavros Zenios describes the state-of-the-art models used to value mortgage-backed securities. He describes Monte Carlo simulation procedures to estimate the fair value of a security, as well as the sensitivity of this value to changes in interest rates. Option-adjusted duration and convexity measures are also developed, together with scenarios of holding-period returns. Zenios then goes on to describe how these measures can be incorporated into portfolio optimization models. These models allow the manager of a portfolio of mortgage securities to control the portfolio's risk exposure. The application of these models in two diverse institutional settings is discussed, so that readers get a view of the effectiveness of the developed methodologies.

A framework for constructing a valuation model for international fixed income securities is provided in Chapter 12 by Lisa Goldberg and Roveen Bhansali. The model is a multi-factor risk model that quantifies various sources of risk, taking into account factors such as interest rates, currencies, and spread that contribute to risk in a multi-currency fixed income portfolio. Using observed returns to these sources of risk, a covariance matrix is constructed that embodies the volatilities and correlations. The approach presented by Goldberg and Bhansali enables portfolio managers to formulate strategies by separating local market decisions from currency decisions.

The Tax Reform Acts of 1984 and 1986 introduced important new changes in the tax treatment of discount and premium bonds, respectively. Congress grandfathered tax provisions for bonds issued before the cutoff dates specified in these Acts. The differential tax treatment allows researchers to perform new tests for the existence or absence of tax effects in U. S. government bond markets. In Chapter 13, Ehud Ronn and Yongai Shin report the result of their empirical tests. They find a statistically significant difference in the valuation of grandfathered and non-grandfathered bonds, implying that taxes matter: the tax-exempt clientele cannot be the dominating price determining tax bracket in the market for government bonds.

In Chapter 14, Ronald Kahn discusses the various definitions of risk and describes some key characteristics of risk. While the total risk can be defined by the standard deviation of returns, portfolio managers care mainly about relative risk. For a portfolio manager whose performance is measured relative to a performance benchmark, the crucial risk is the standard deviation of the difference between the portfolio's return and the benchmark's return. Kahn calls this measure "active risk" and it is sometimes called "tracking error" by market players. Structural risk models provide insightful analysis by decomposing risk into total risk and active risk. By doing so, a portfolio manager can identify those bets that are inherent, those that are intentional, and those that are incidental. These models include the major sources of risk allowing for (1) the analysis of present risks and bets in a portfolio, (2) the forecast of future risk as part of the portfolio construction process, and (3) the analysis of past risk to facilitate performance analysis.

Since fixed income markets are primarily concerned with interest rate risk, most risk measures (such as option-adjusted durations) describe a security's exposure to changes in interest rates. However, there are other sources of risk which affect a fixed income security's return, such as changes in volatility, changes in market risk premia, and risks associated with the accuracy of various models, such as prepayment models used for mortgage-backed security valuation. Teri Geske and Gunnar Klinkhammer describe risk measures which quantify a security's price sensitivity to these additional sources of risk. In Chapter 15, they also discuss how the concept of a zero-volatility spread explains the importance of volatility in measuring option risk.

Yield curve risk management refers to the general discipline of controlling the sensitivity of a fixed income portfolio to one or more interest rate changes or yield curve shifts. As explained by Robert Reitano in Chapter 16, the purpose of control can be for defensive or offensive purposes. However, in virtually all such cases, the sensitivity of the given portfolio is being controlled relative to the sensitivity of a second "target" fixed income portfolio. In defensive yield curve risk management, the primary objective is to control interest rate risk so as to protect against losses relative to the target portfolio. The primary objective of offensive or opportunistic management, in contrast, is to capitalize on perceived opportunities for gain.

Risk measurement of fixed income investments is a complex process due to the asymmetry of return distributions. Gifford Fong and Oldrich Vasicek demonstrate that by utilizing value at risk and stress testing, a manager has the ability to evaluate non-symmetric return outcomes. In Chapter 17, they show that value at risk calculated by a Gamma distribution approximation gives expected loss under normal conditions. Stress testing determines how the portfolio would perform under abnormal conditions. Together, these two techniques offer the type of complete analysis necessary to understand the risks behind portfolios containing complex structures or a high degree of interrelatedness.

Practitioners have observed that discrete-time lattice valuation models wreak havoc on the derived duration and convexity measures. In Chapter 18, Howard Douglas discusses this "lattice effect" and the numerical pitfall. He finds that the lattice effect is even more pronounced for convexity calculations.

Brady bonds come in several forms: collateralized and uncollateralized, fixed and floating, and short and long term. In Chapter 19, Steven Dym presents price sensitivity measures for Brady bonds. The analysis presented provides a basis for comparing the price sensitivity of Brady bonds to that of other bonds.

Modeling and forecasting interest rate volatility plays an important role in pricing and hedging interest rate-sensitive securities. In Chapter 20, Wai Lee and John Yin introduce the use of probably the most extensively applied family of volatility models in finance, Generalized AutoRegressive Conditional Heteroskedasticity (GARCH) models. Lee and Yin discuss how mean reversion in interest rate level and volatility can be incorporated into the model, as well as other underlying properties. Estimation, model diagnostics, and volatility forecasting are illustrated with the weekly 3-month Treasury bill rate as an example. Extensions and limitations of GARCH models are also discussed.

Frank J. Fabozzi

Contributing Authors

Roveen Bhansali	BARRA, Inc.
Michael Z. H. Chen	Global Advanced Technology Corporation
Ren-Raw Chen	Rutgers University
Oren Cheyette	BARRA, Inc.
Steven Dym	Steven I. Dym & Associates
Peter Fitton	SS&C Technologies, Inc.
H. Gifford Fong	Gifford Fong Associates
Louis L. Gagnon	Queen's University
Teri Geske	Capital Management Sciences
Lisa Goldberg	BARRA, Inc.
Thomas S. Y. Ho	Global Advanced Technology Corporation
Ted C.H. Hong	Nomura International Securities, Inc.
C. Douglas Howard	Polytechnic University
William J. Hurley	Royal Military College of Canada
David P. Jacob	Nomura International Securities, Inc.
Lewis D. Johnson	Queen's University
Ronald N. Kahn	BARRA, Inc.
Gunnar Klinkhammer	Capital Management Sciences
Laurence H. Lee	Nomura International Securities, Inc.
Wai Lee	J.P. Morgan Investment Management, Inc.
Satish M. Mansukhani	Bear, Stearns & Co.
James F. McNatt	SS&C Technologies, Inc.
Soren S. Nielsen	University of Texas at Austin
Yiannos A. Pierides	University of Cyprus
Robert R. Reitano	John Hancock Mutual Life Insurance Company
Ehud I. Ronn	University of Texas at Austin
Louis O. Scott	University of Georgia
Yongjai Shin	Merrill Lynch & Co.
Oldrich A. Vasicek	Gifford Fong Associates
Stavros A. Zenios	University of Cyprus
John Yin	J.P. Morgan Investment Management, Inc.

Index of Advertisers

Chapter 1

Interest Rate Models

Oren Cheyette, Ph.D.
Manager, Fixed Income Research
BARRA, Inc.

INTRODUCTION

An interest rate model is a probabilistic description of the future evolution of interest rates. Based on today's information, future interest rates are uncertain: an interest rate model is a characterization of that uncertainty. Quantitative analysis of securities with rate dependent cash flows requires application of such a model in order to find the present value of the uncertainty. Since all fixed-income securities other than option-free bonds have interest rate sensitive cash flows, this matters to most fixed-income portfolio managers, as well as to traders and users of interest rate derivatives.

For security valuation and risk estimation one wants to use only models that are arbitrage free and matched to the currently observed term structure of interest rates. "Arbitrage free" means just that if one values the same cash flows in two different ways, one should get the same result. For example, a 10-year bond putable at par by the holder in 5 years can also be viewed as a 5-year bond with an option of the holder to extend the maturity for another 5 years. An arbitrage-free model will produce the same value for the structure viewed either way. This is also known as the *law of one price*. The term structure matching condition means that when a default-free straight bond is valued according to the model, the result should be the same as if the bond's cash flows are simply discounted according to the current default-free term structure. A model that fails to satisfy either of these conditions cannot be trusted for general problems, though it may be usable in some limited context.

For equity derivatives, lognormality of prices (leading to the Black-Scholes formula for calls and puts) is the standard starting point for option calculations. In the fixed-income market, unfortunately, there is no equally natural and simple assumption. Wall Street dealers routinely use a multiplicity of models based on widely varying assumptions in different markets. For example, an options desk most likely uses a version of the Black formula to value interest rate caps and floors. This use assumes a lognormal distribution of bond prices (since, e.g., a caplet is a put on a 3-month discount bond), which in turn implies a normal distribution of interest rates. A few feet away, the mortgage desk may use a lognormal interest rate model to evaluate their passthrough and CMO effective durations.

It may seem that one's major concern in choosing an interest rate model should be the accuracy with which it represents the empirical volatility of the term structure of rates, and its ability to fit market prices of vanilla derivatives such as at-the-money caps and swaptions. These are clearly important criteria, but they are not decisive. The first criterion is hard to pin down, depending strongly on what historical period one chooses to examine. The second criterion is easy to satisfy for most commonly used models, by the simple (though unappealing) expedient of permitting predicted future volatility to be time dependent. So, while important, this concern doesn't really do much to narrow the choices.

A critical issue in selecting an interest rate model is, instead, ease of application. For some models it is difficult or impossible to provide efficient valuation algorithms for all securities of interest to a typical investor. Given that one would like to analyze all assets using the same underlying assumptions, this is a significant problem. At the same time, one would prefer not to stray too far from economic reasonableness — such as by using the Black-Scholes formula to value callable bonds. These considerations lead to a fairly narrow menu of choices among the known interest rate models.

The organization of this chapter is as follows. In the next section I provide a (brief) discussion of the principles of valuation algorithms. This will give a context for many of the points made in the third section, which provides an overview of the various characteristics that differentiate interest rate models. Finally, in the fourth section I describe the empirical evidence on interest rate dynamics and provide a quantitative comparison of a family of models that closely match those in common use. I have tried to emphasize those issues that are primarily of interest for application of the models in practical settings. There is little point in having the theoretically ideal model if it can't actually be implemented as part of a valuation algorithm.

VALUATION

Valuation algorithms for rate dependent contingent claims are usually based on a risk neutral formula, which states that the present value of an uncertain cash flow at time T is given by the average over all interest rate scenarios of the scenario cash flow divided by the scenario value at time T of a money market investment of $1 today.[1] More formally, the value of a security is given by the expectation (average) over interest rate scenarios

$$P = E\left[\sum_i \frac{C_i}{M_i}\right] \tag{1}$$

[1] The money market account is the *numeraire*.

where C_i is the security's cash flows and M_i is the money market account value at time t_i in each scenario, calculated by assuming continual reinvestment at the prevailing short rate.

The probability weights used in the average are chosen so that the expected rate of return on any security over the next instant is the same, namely the short rate. These are the so-called "risk neutral" probability weights: they would be the true weights if investors were indifferent to bearing interest rate risk. In that case, investors would demand no excess return relative to a (riskless) money market account in order to hold risky positions — hence equation (1).

It is important to emphasize that the valuation formula is not dependent on any *assumption* of risk neutrality. Assets are valued by equation (1) *as if* the market were indifferent to interest rate risk *and* the correct discount factor for a future cash flow were the inverse of the money market return. Both statements are false for the real world, but the errors are offsetting: a valuation formula based on probabilities implying a nonzero market price of interest rate risk and the corresponding scenario discount factors would give the same value.

There are two approaches to computing the average in equation (1): by direct brute force evaluation, or indirectly by solving a related differential equation. The brute force method is usually called the Monte Carlo method. It consists of generating a large number of possible interest rate scenarios based on the interest rate model, computing the cash flows and money market values in each one, and averaging. Properly speaking, only path generation based on random numbers is a Monte Carlo method. There are other scenario methods — e.g., complete sampling of a tree — that do not depend on the use of random numbers. Given sufficient computer resources, the scenario method can tackle essentially any type of security.[2]

A variety of schemes are known for choosing scenario sample paths efficiently, but none of them are even remotely as fast and accurate as the second technique. In certain cases (discussed in more detail in the next section) the average in equation (1) obeys a partial differential equation — like the one derived by Black and Scholes for equity options — for which there exist fast and accurate numerical solution methods, or in special cases even analytical solutions. This happens only for interest rate models of a particular type, and then only for certain security types, such as caps, floors, swaptions, and options on bonds. For securities such as mortgage passthroughs, CMOs, and index amortizing swaps, simulation methods are the only alternative.

MODEL TAXONOMY

The last two decades have seen the development of a tremendous profusion of models for valuation of interest rate sensitive securities. In order to better understand these models, it is helpful to recognize a number of features that characterize and distin-

---

[2] This is true even for American options. For a review see P. Boyle, M. Broadie, and P. Glasserman, "Monte Carlo Methods for Security Pricing," working paper, 1995, to appear in the *Journal of Economic Dynamics and Control*.

guish them. These are features of particular relevance to practitioners wishing to implement valuation algorithms, as they render some models completely unsuitable for certain asset types.[3] The following subsections enumerate some of the major dimensions of variation among the different models.

One Versus Multi-Factor

In many cases, the value of an interest rate contingent claim depends, effectively, on the prices of many underlying assets. For example, while the payoff of a caplet depends only on the reset date value of a zero coupon bond maturing at the payment date (valued based on, say, 3month LIBOR), the payoff to an option on a coupon bond depends on the exercise date values of all of the bond's remaining interest and principal payments. Valuation of such an option is in principle an inherently multi-dimensional problem.

Fortunately, in practice these values are highly correlated. The degree of correlation can be quantified by examining the covariance matrix of changes in spot rates of different maturities. A principal component analysis of the covariance matrix decomposes the motion of the spot curve into independent (uncorrelated) components. The largest principal component describes a common shift of all interest rates in the same direction. The next leading components are a twist, with short rates moving one way and long rates the other, and a "butterfly" motion, with short and long rates moving one way, and intermediate rates the other. Based on analysis of weekly data from the Federal Reserve H15 series of benchmark Treasury yields from 1983 through 1995, the shift component accounts for 84% of the total variance of spot rates, while twist and butterfly account for 11% and 4%, leaving about 1% for all remaining principal components.

The shift factor alone explains a large fraction of the overall movement of spot rates. As a result, valuation can be reduced to a one factor problem in many instances with little loss of accuracy. Only securities whose payoffs are primarily sensitive to the shape of the spot curve rather than its overall level (such as dual index floaters, which depend on the difference between a long and a short rate) will not be modeled well with this approach.

In principle it is straightforward to move from a one-factor model to a multi-factor one. In practice, though, implementations of multi-factor valuation models are complicated and slow, and require estimation of many more volatility parameters than are needed for one-factor models, so there is substantial benefit to using a one-factor model when possible. The remainder of this chapter will focus on one-factor models.

Exogenous Versus Endogenous Term Structure

The first interest rate models were not constructed so as to fit an arbitrary initial term structure. Instead, with a view towards analytical simplicity, the Vasicek[4] and Cox-

---

[3] There is, unfortunately, a version of Murphy's law applicable to interest rate models, which states that the computational tractability of a model is inversely proportional to its economic realism.

[4] O. Vasicek, "An Equilibrium Characterization of the Term Structure," *Journal of Financial Economics* (November 1977).

Ingersoll-Ross[5] (CIR) models contain a few constant parameters that define an endogenously specified term structure. That is, the initial spot curve is given by an analytical formula in terms of the model parameters. These are sometimes also called "equilibrium" models, as they posit yield curves derived from an assumption of economic equilibrium based on a given market price of risk and other parameters governing collective expectations.

For *dynamically* reasonable choices of the parameters — values that give plausible long-run interest rate distributions and option prices — the term structures achievable in these models have far too little curvature to accurately represent typical empirical spot rate curves. This is because the mean reversion parameter, governing the rate at which the short rate reverts towards the long-run mean, also governs the volatility of long-term rates relative to the volatility of the short rate — the "term structure of volatility." To achieve the observed level of long-rate volatility (or to price options on long-term securities well) requires that there be relatively little mean reversion, but this implies low curvature yield curves. This problem can be partially solved by moving to a multi-factor framework — but at a significant cost as discussed earlier. These models are therefore not particularly useful as the basis for valuation algorithms — they simply have too few degrees of freedom to faithfully represent real markets.

To be used for valuation, a model must be "calibrated" to the initial spot rate curve. That is, the model structure must accommodate an exogenously determined spot rate curve, typically given by fitting to bond prices, or sometimes to futures prices and swap rates. All models in common use are of this type.

There is a "trick" invented by Dybvig that converts an endogenous model to a calibrated exogenous one.[6] The trick can be viewed as splitting the nominal interest rate into two parts: the stochastic part modeled endogenously, and a non-stochastic drift term, which compensates for the mismatch of the endogenous term structure and the observed one. (BARRA uses this technique to modify the CIR model to match the observed term structure in its fixed income analytics.) The price of this method is that the volatility function is no longer a simple function of the nominal interest rate, because the nominal rate is not the one that governs the level of volatility.

Short Rate Versus Yield Curve

The risk neutral valuation formula requires that one know the sequence of short rates for each scenario, so an interest rate model must provide this information. For this reason, many interest rate models are simply models of the stochastic evolution of the short rate. A second reason for the desirability of such models is that they have the *Markov property*, meaning that the evolution of the short rate at each instant depends

[5] J.C. Cox, J.E. Ingersoll, Jr., and S.A. Ross, "A Theory of the Term Structure of Interest Rates," *Econometrica* (March 1985).

[6] P. Dybvig, "Bond and Bond Option Pricing Based on the Current Term Structure," working paper, 1989, forthcoming in *Mathematics of Derivative Securities*, M. A. H. Dempster and S. Pliska, (eds.), Cambridge University Press.

only on its current value — not on how it got there. The practical significance of this is that, as alluded to in the previous section, the valuation problem for many types of assets can be reduced to solving a partial differential equation, for which there exist efficient analytical and numerical techniques. To be amenable to this calculation technique, a security's cash flow at time t must depend only on the state of affairs at that time, not on how the evolution occurred prior to t, or it must be equivalent to a portfolio of such securities (for example, a callable bond is a position long a straight bond and short a call option).

Short-rate models have two parts. One specifies the average rate of change ("drift") of the short rate at each instant; the other specifies the instantaneous volatility of the short rate. The conventional notation for this is

$$dr(t) = \mu(r, t)dt + \sigma(r, t)dz(t) \tag{2}$$

The left-hand side of this equation is the change in the short rate over the next instant. The first term on the right is the drift multiplied by the size of the time step. The second is the volatility multiplied by a normally distributed random increment. For most models, the drift component must be determined through a numerical technique to match the initial spot rate curve, while for a small number of models there exists an analytical relationship. In general, there exists a no-arbitrage relationship linking the initial forward rate curve, the volatility $\sigma(r,t)$, the market price of interest rate risk, and the drift term $\mu(r,t)$. However, since typically one must solve for the drift numerically, this relationship plays no role in model construction. Differences between models arise from different dependences of the drift and volatility terms on the short rate.

For assets whose cash flows don't depend on the interest rate history, the expectation formula (1) for present value obeys the Feynman-Kac equation

$$\frac{1}{2}\sigma^2 P_{rr} + (\mu - \lambda)P_r + P_t - rP + c = 0 \tag{3}$$

where, for example, P_r denotes the partial derivative of P with respect to r, c is the payment rate of the security, and λ, which can be time and rate dependent, is the market price of interest rate risk.

The terms in this equation can be understood as follows. In the absence of uncertainty ($\sigma = 0$), the equation involves four terms. The last three assert that the value of the security increases at the risk-free rate (rP), and decreases by the amount of any payments (c). The term $(\mu - \lambda)P_r$ accounts for change in value due to the change in the term structure with time, as rates move up the forward curve. In the absence of uncertainty it is easy to express ($\mu - \lambda$) in terms of the initial forward rates. In the presence of uncertainty this term depends on the volatility as well, and we also have the first term, which is the main source of the complexity of valuation models.

The Vasicek and CIR models are models of the short rate. Both have the same form for the drift term, namely a tendency for the short rate to rise when it is below the long-term mean, and fall when it is above. That is, the short-rate drift has the form $\mu = \kappa(\theta - r)$, where r is the short rate and κ and θ are the mean reversion and long-term rate constants. The two models differ in the rate dependence of the volatility: it is constant (when expressed as points per year) in the Vasicek model, and proportional to the square root of the short rate in the CIR model.

The Dybvig-adjusted Vasicek model is the mean reverting generalization of the Ho-Lee model,[7] also known as the mean reverting Gaussian (MRG) model or the Hull-White model.[8] The MRG model has particularly simple analytical expressions for values of many assets — in particular, bonds and European options on bonds. Like the original Vasicek model, it permits the occurrence of negative interest rates with positive probability. However, for typical initial spot curves and volatility parameters, the probability of negative rates is quite small.

Other popular models of this type are the Black-Derman-Toy[9] (BDT) and Black-Karasinski[10] (BK) models, in which the volatility is proportional to the short rate, so that the ratio of volatility to rate level is constant. For these models, unlike the MRG and Dybvig-adjusted CIR models, the drift term is not simple. These models require numerical fitting to the initial interest rate and volatility term structures. The drift term is therefore not known analytically. In the BDT model, the short-rate volatility is also linked to the mean reversion strength (which is also generally time dependent) in such a way that — in the usual situation where long rates are less volatile than the short rate — the short-rate volatility decreases in the future. This feature is undesirable: one doesn't want to link the observation that the long end of the curve has relatively low volatility to a forecast that in the future the short rate will become less volatile. This problem motivated the development of the BK model in which mean reversion and volatility are delinked.

All of these models are explicit models of the short rate alone. It happens that in the Vasicek and CIR models (with or without the Dybvig adjustment) it is possible to express the entire forward curve as a function of the current short rate through fairly simple analytical formulas. This is not possible in the BDT and BK models, or generally in other models of short-rate dynamics, other than by highly inefficient numerical techniques. Indeed, it is possible to show that the only short-rate models consistent with an arbitrary initial term structure for which one can find the whole forward curve analytically are in a class that includes the MRG and Dybvig-adjusted CIR models as special cases, namely where the short-rate volatility has the form[11]

$$\sigma(r, t) = \sqrt{\sigma_1(t) + \sigma_2(t)r}.$$

[7] T.S.Y. Ho and S.B. Lee, "Term Structure Movements and Pricing Interest Rate Contingent Claims," *Journal of Finance* (December 1986); and, J. Hull and A. White, "Pricing Interest Rate Derivative Securities," *The Review of Financial Studies*, 3:4 (1990).

[8] This model was also derived in F. Jamshidian, "The One-Factor Gaussian Interest Rate Model: Theory and Implementation," Merrill Lynch working paper, 1988.

[9] F. Black, E. Derman and W. Toy, "A One Factor Model of Interest Rates and its Application to Treasury Bond Options," *Financial Analysts Journal* (January/February 1990).

[10] F. Black and P. Karasinski, "Bond and Option Prices when Short Rates are Lognormal," *Financial Analysts Journal* (July/August 1992).

[11] A. Jeffrey, "Single Factor Heath-Jarrow-Morton Term Structure Models Based on Markov Spot Interest Rate Dynamics," *Journal of Financial and Quantitative Analysis*, 30:4 (December 1995).

While valuation of certain assets (e.g., callable bonds) does not require knowledge of longer rates, there are broad asset classes that do. For example, mortgage prepayment models are typically driven off a long-term Treasury par yield, such as the 10-year rate. Therefore a generic short-rate model such as BDT or BK is unsuitable if one seeks to analyze a variety of assets in a common interest rate framework.

An alternative approach to interest rate modeling is to specify the dynamics of the entire term structure. The volatility of the term structure is then given by some specified function, which most generally could be a function of time, maturity, and spot rates. A special case of this approach (in a discrete time framework) is the Ho-Lee model mentioned earlier, for which the term structure of volatility is a parallel shift of the spot rate curve, whose magnitude is independent of time and the level of rates. A completely general continuous time, multi-factor framework for constructing such models was given by Heath, Jarrow and Morton (HJM).[12]

It is sometimes said that all interest rate models are HJM models. This is technically true: in principle, every arbitrage-free model of the term structure can be described in their framework. In practice, however, it is impossible to do this analytically for most short-rate Markov models. The only ones for which it is possible are those in the MRG-CIR family described earlier. The BDT and BK models, for instance, cannot be translated to the HJM framework other than by impracticable numerical means. To put a model in HJM form, one must know the term structure of volatility at all times, and this is generally not possible for short-rate Markov models.

If feasible, the HJM approach is clearly very attractive, since one knows now not just the short rate but also all longer rates as well. In addition, HJM models are very "natural," in the sense that the basic inputs to the model are the initial term structure of interest rates and a term structure of interest rate volatility for each independent motion of the yield curve.

The reason for the qualification in the last paragraph is that a generic HJM model requires keeping track of a potentially enormous amount of information. The HJM framework imposes no structure other than the requirement of no-arbitrage on the dynamics of the term structure. Each forward rate of fixed maturity evolves separately, so that one must keep track of each one separately. Since there are an infinite number of distinct forward rates, this can be difficult. This difficulty occurs even in a one factor HJM model, for which there is only one source of random movement of the term structure. A general HJM model does not have the Markov property that leads to valuation formulas expressed as solutions to partial differential equations. This makes it impossible to accurately value interest rate options without using huge amounts of computer time, since one is forced to use simulation methods.

In practice a simulation algorithm breaks the evolution of the term structure up into discrete time steps, so one need keep track of and simulate only forward rates for the finite set of simulation times. Still, this can be a large number (e.g., 360 or more for a mortgage passthrough), and this computational burden, combined with the

---

[12] D. Heath, R. Jarrow, and A. Morton, "Bond Pricing and the Term Structure of Interest Rates: A New Methodology for Contingent Claims Valuation," *Econometrica*, 60:1 (January 1992).

inefficiency of simulation methods has prevented general HJM models from coming into more widespread use.

Some applications require simulation methods because the assets' structures (e.g., mortgage-backed securities) are not compatible with differential equation methods. For applications where one is solely interested in modeling such assets, there exists a class of HJM models that significantly simplify the forward rate calculations.[13] The simplest version of such models, the "two state Markov model," permits an arbitrary dependence of short-rate volatility on both time and the level of interest rates, while the ratio of forward-rate volatility to short-rate volatility is solely a function of term. That is, the volatility of $f(t,T)$, the term T forward rate at time t takes the form

$$\sigma_f(r, t, T) = \sigma(r, t)e^{-\int_t^T k(u)\,du} \tag{4}$$

where $\sigma(r,t) = \sigma_f(r,t,t)$ is the short-rate volatility and $k(t)$ determines the mean reversion rate or equivalently, the rate of decrease of forward rate volatility with term. The evolution of all forward rates in this model can be described in terms of two state variables: the short rate (or any other forward or spot rate), and the slope of the forward curve at the origin. The second variable can be expressed in terms of the total variance experienced by a forward rate of fixed maturity by the time it has become the short rate. The stochastic evolution equations for the two state variables can be written as

$$d\tilde{r}(t) = (V(t) - k(t)\tilde{r})dt + \sigma(r, t)dz(t)$$
$$V_t(t) = \sigma^2(r, t) - 2k(t)V(t) \tag{5}$$

where $\tilde{r}(t) \equiv r(t) - f(0, t)$ is the deviation of the short rate from the initial forward rate curve. The state variable $V(t)$ has initial value $V(0)=0$; its evolution equation is non-stochastic and can be integrated to give

$$V(t) = \int_0^t \sigma_f^2(r, s, t)\,ds = \int_0^t \sigma^2(r, s)e^{-2\int_s^t k(u)\,du}\,ds \tag{6}$$

In terms of these state variables, the forward curve is given by

$$f(t, T) = f(0, T) + \phi(t, T)\left(\tilde{r} + V(t)\int_t^T \phi(t, s)\,ds\right) \tag{7}$$

---

[13] O. Cheyette, "Term Structure Dynamics and Mortgage Valuation," *Journal of Fixed Income* (March 1992). The two state Markov model was also described in P. Ritchken and L. Sankarasubramanian, "Volatility Structure of Forward Rates and the Dynamics of the Term Structure," *Mathematical Finance*, 5(1) (1995), pp. 55-72.

where

$$\phi(t, T) = \sigma_f(r, t, T)/\sigma_f(r, t, t) = e^{-\int_t^T k(s)\,ds}$$

is a deterministic function.

Instead of having to keep track of hundreds of forward rates, one need only model the evolution of the two state variables. Path independent asset prices also obey a partial differential equation in this model, so it appears possible at least in principle to use more efficient numerical methods. The equation, analogous to equation (3), is

$$\frac{1}{2}\sigma^2 P_{\tilde{r}\tilde{r}} + (V - k\tilde{r})P_{\tilde{r}} + (\sigma^2 - 2kV)P_V + P_t - rP + c = 0. \tag{8}$$

Unlike equation (3), for which one must use the equation itself applied to bonds to solve for the coefficient $\mu-\lambda$, here the coefficient functions are all known in terms of the initial data: the short-rate volatility and the initial forward curve. This simplification has come at the price of adding a dimension, as we now have to contend also with a term involving the first derivative with respect to V, and so the equation is much more difficult to solve efficiently by standard techniques.

In the special case where $\sigma(r,t)$ is independent of r, this model is the MRG model mentioned earlier. In this case, V is a deterministic function of t, so the P_V term disappears from equation (8), leaving a two dimensional equation that has analytical solutions for European options on bonds, and straightforward numerical techniques for valuing American bond options. Since bond prices are lognormally distributed in this model, it should be no surprise that the formula for options on pure discount bounds (PDB's) looks much like the Black-Scholes formula. The value of a call with strike price K, exercise date t on a PDB maturing at time T is given by

$$C = P(T)N(h_1) - KP(t)N(h_2), \tag{9}$$

where

$$h_1 = \frac{k}{(1 - e^{-k(T-t)})\sqrt{V(t)}} \ln\frac{P(T)}{KP(t)} + \frac{\sqrt{V(t)}}{2},$$

$$h_2 = h_1 - \sqrt{V(t)},$$

$N(x)$ is the Gaussian distribution, and $P(t)$ and $P(T)$ are prices of PDB's maturing at t and T. (The put value can be obtained by put-call parity.) Options on coupon bonds can be valued by adding up a portfolio of options on PDBs, one for each coupon or principal payment after the exercise date, with strike prices such that they are all at-the-money at the same value of the short rate. The Dybvig-adjusted CIR model has similar formulas for bond options, involving the non-central χ^2 distribution instead of the Gaussian one.

If $\sigma(r,t)$ depends on r, the model becomes similar to some other standard models. For example, $\sigma(r,t)=a\sqrt{r}$ has the same rate dependence as the CIR model, while choosing $\sigma(r,t)=br$ gives a model similar to BK, though in each case the drift and term structure of volatility are different.

Unless one has some short- or long-term view on trends in short-rate volatility, it is most natural to choose $\sigma(r,t)$ to be time independent, and similarly $k(u)$ to be constant. This is equivalent to saying that the shape of the volatility term structure — though not necessarily its magnitude — should be constant over time. (Otherwise, as in the BDT model, one is imposing an undesirable linkage between today's shape of the forward rate volatility curve and future volatility curves.) In that case, the term structure of forward-rate volatility is exponentially decreasing with maturity, and the integrals in equations (6) and (7) can be computed, giving for the forward curve

$$f(t, T) = f(0, T) + e^{-k(T-t)}\left(\tilde{r} + V(t)\,\frac{1-e^{-k(T-t)}}{k}\right). \tag{10}$$

Finally, if the volatility is assumed rate independent as well, the integral expression for $V(t)$ can be evaluated to give

$$V(t) = \sigma^2\,\frac{1-e^{-2kt}}{2k}, \tag{11}$$

and we obtain the forward curves of the MRG model.

Empirically, neither the historical volatility nor the implied volatility falls off so neatly. Instead, volatility typically increases with term out to between 1 and 3 years, then drops off. The two state Markov model cannot accommodate this behavior, except by imposing a forecast of increasing then decreasing short-rate volatility, or a short run of negative mean reversion. There is, however, an extension of the model that permits modeling of humped or other more complicated volatility curves, at the cost of introducing additional state variables.[14] With five state variables, for example, it is possible to model the dominant volatility term structure of the U.S. Treasury spot curve very accurately.

Recently, a model of bond price dynamics was devised[15] that does not fit the dichotomy of this section, for the simple reason that it is not a model of interest rates, but is instead a model of discount factors (PDB prices). Rather than using a valuation formula based on risk-neutral rate movements and a money-market numeraire, the model is based on another probability distribution and numeraire with many nice properties. The developers of the model call their approach the "positive interest" framework, since it has the attractive feature that all models in the framework have positive interest rates at all times. In addition, the interest rate process is guaranteed not to explode. Like the HJM approach, this model is really a framework for constructing specific models, as it imposes no structure other than that dictated by the

---

[14] O. Cheyette, "Markov Representation of the HJM Model," working paper, 1995.

[15] B. Flesaker and L. P. Hughston, "Positive Interest," *Risk Magazine* (January 1996) and "Dynamic Models for Yield Curve Evolution," working paper (January 1996).

requirements of arbitrage freedom, calibration, and positivity of rates. Unfortunately, the only published model based on this approach (the "rational lognormal model"[16]) suffers from some fairly serious financial defects.[17] First, interest rates are bounded below at a level that approaches the forward rate curve, so floors with strikes below the bound are valued at zero, as are long calls on bonds with low but nonzero coupons. Second, the short-rate volatility decreases over time and eventually approaches zero. So, while the model provides closed form solutions for many types of derivatives, its defects seem to render it unusable.

EMPIRICAL AND NUMERICAL CONSIDERATIONS

Given the profusion of models, it is reasonable to ask whether there are empirical or other considerations that can help motivate a choice of one model for applications. One might take the view that one should use whichever model is most convenient for the particular problem at hand — e.g., BDT or BK for bonds with embedded options, Black model for caps and floors, a two state Markov model for mortgages, and a ten state, two factor Markov-HJM model for dual index amortizing floaters. The obvious problem with this approach is that it can't be used to find hedging relationships or relative value between assets valued according to the different models. I take as a given, then, that we seek models that can be used effectively for valuation of most asset types with minimum compromise of financial reasonableness. The choice will likely depend on how many and what kinds of assets one needs to value. A trader of vanilla options may be less concerned about cross-market consistency issues than a manager of portfolios of callable bonds and mortgage-backed securities.

The major empirical consideration — and one that has produced a large amount of inconclusive research — is the assumed dependence of volatility on the level of interest rates. Different researchers have reported various evidence that volatility is best explained (1) as a power of the short rate[18] ($\sigma \propto r^\gamma$) — with γ so large that models with this volatility have rates running off to infinity with high probability ("explosions"), (2) by a GARCH model with very long (possibly infinite) persistence,[19] (3) by some combination of GARCH with a power law dependence on rates,[20] (4) by none of the above.[21] All of this work has been in the context of short-rate Markov models.

---

[16] Ibid.

[17] O. Cheyette and L. Goldberg, unpublished note, and L. Goldberg, "An Examination of the Rational Lognormal Model," working paper, 1996.

[18] K.C. Chan, G.A. Karolyi, F.A. Longstaff, and A.B. Sanders, "An Empirical Comparson of Alternative Models of the Short Rate," *Journal of Finance* 47:3 (1992).

[19] See R.J. Brenner, R.H. Harjes, and K.F. Kroner, "Another Look at Alternative Models of the Short-Term Interest Rate," University of Arizona working paper (1993), and references therein.

[20] Ibid.

[21] Y. Aït-Sahalia, "Testing Continuous Time Models of the Spot Interest Rate," *Review of Financial Studies*, 9:2 (1996).

Here I will present some fairly straightforward evidence in favor of choice (4) based on analysis of movements of the whole term structure of spot rates, rather than just short rates, from U.S. Treasury yields over the period 1977 to early 1996.

The result is that the market appears to be well described by "eras" with very different rate dependences of volatility, possibly coinciding with periods of different Federal Reserve policies. Since all the models in common use have a power law dependence of volatility on rates, I attempted to determine the best fit to the exponent (γ) relating the two. My purpose here is not so much to provide another entrant in this already crowded field, but rather to suggest that there may be no simple answer to the empirical question. No model with constant parameters seems to do a very good job. A surprising result, given the degree to which the market for interest rate derivatives has exploded and the widespread use of lognormal models, is that the period since 1987 is best modeled by a nearly *normal* model of interest rate volatility.

The data used in the analysis consisted of spot rate curves derived from the Federal Reserve H15 series of weekly average benchmark yields. The benchmark yields are given as semiannually compounded yields of hypothetical par bonds with fixed maturities ranging from 3 months to 30 years, derived by interpolation from actively traded issues. The data cover the period from early 1977, when a 30-year bond was first issued, through March of 1996. The spot curves are represented as continuous, piecewise linear functions, constructed by a root finding procedure to exactly match the given yields, assumed to be yields of par bonds. (This is similar to the conventional bootstrapping method.) The two data points surrounding the 1987 crash were excluded: the short and intermediate markets moved by around ten standard deviations during the crash, and this extreme event would have had a significant skewing effect on the analysis.

A parsimonious representation of the spot curve dynamics is given by the two state Markov model with constant mean reversion k and volatility that is time independent and proportional to a power of the short rate: $\sigma(r)=\beta r^{\gamma}$. In this case, the term structure of spot rate volatility, given by integrating equation (4), is

$$\sigma(r_t)v(T) \;=\; \beta r_t^{\gamma}\,\frac{1-e^{-kT}}{kT} \tag{12}$$

where T is the maturity and r_t is the time t short rate. The time t weekly change in the spot rate curve is then given by the change due to the passage of time ("rolling up the forward curve") plus a random change of the form $v(T)x_t$, where for each t, x_t, is an independent normal random variable with distribution $N(\mu, \sigma(r_t)\sqrt{52})$. (The systematic drift μ of x_t, over time was assumed to be independent of time and the rate level.) The parameters β, γ, and k are estimated as follows. First, using an initial guess for γ, k is estimated by a maximum likelihood fit of the maturity dependence of $v(T)$ to the spot curve changes. Then, using this value of k, another maximum likelihood fit is applied to fit the variance of x_t to the power law model of $\sigma(r_t)$. The procedure is then iterated to improve the estimates of k and γ, but it turns out that the best fit value of k is quite insensitive to the value of γ, and vice versa.

Exhibit 1: Parameter Estimates for the Two State Markov Model with Power Law Volatility over Various Sample Periods*

Sample Period	Exponent (γ)	Mean Reversion (k)	Comments
3/1/77 - 3/29/96	1.04 ± 0.07	0.054 ± 0.007	Full data set
3/1/77 - 1/1/87	1.6 ± 0.10	0.10 ± 0.020	Pre-Greenspan
3/1/77 - 1/1/83	1.72 ± 0.15	0.22 ± 0.040	"Monetarist"policy
1/1/83 - 3/29/96	0.45 ± 0.07	0.019 ± 0.005	Post high-rate period
1/1/87 - 3/29/96	0.19 ± 0.09	0.016 ± 0.004	Greenspan

* The uncertainties are one standard deviation estimates based on bootstrap Monte Carlo resampling.

One advantage of looking at the entire term structure is that we avoid modeling just idiosyncratic behavior of the short end, e.g., that it is largely determined by the Federal Reserve. An additional feature of this analysis is proper accounting for the effect of the "arbitrage-free drift" — namely, the systematic change of interest rates due purely to the shape of the forward curve at the start of each period. Prior analyses have typically involved fitting to endogenous short-rate models with constant parameters not calibrated to each period's term structure. The present approach mitigates a fundamental problem of prior research in the context of one-factor models, namely that interest rate dynamics are poorly described by a single factor. By re-initializing the drift parameters at the start of each sample period and studying the volatility of changes to a well-defined term structure factor, the effects of additional factors are excluded from the analysis.

The results for the different time periods are shown in Exhibit 1. (The exhibit doesn't include the best fit values of β, which are not relevant to the empirical issue at hand.) The error estimates reported in the exhibit are derived by a bootstrap Monte Carlo procedure that constructs artificial data sets by random sampling of the original set with replacement and applies the same analysis to them.[22] It is apparent that the different subperiods are well described by very different exponents and mean reversion. The different periods were chosen to include or exclude the monetarist policy "experiment" under Volcker of the late 1970s and early 1980s, and also to sample just the Greenspan era. For the period since 1987, the best fit exponent of 0.19 is significantly different from zero at the 95% confidence level, but not at the 99% level. However, the best fit value is well below the threshold of 0.5 required to guarantee positivity of interest rates, with 99% confidence. There appears to be weak sensitivity of volatility to the rate level, but much less than is implied by a number of models in widespread use — in particular, BDT, BK, and CIR.

The estimates for the mean reversion parameter k can be understood through the connection of mean reversion to the term structure of volatility. Large values of k imply large fluctuations in short rates compared to long rates, since longer rates reflect the expectation that changes in short rates will not persist forever. The early 1980s saw just such a phenomenon, with the yield curve becoming very steeply inverted for a brief period. Since then, the volatility of the short rate (in absolute terms of points per year) has been only slightly higher than that of long-term rates.

[22] B.J. Efron and R.J. Tibshirani, *An Introduction to the Bootstrap*, (New York: Chapman & Hall, 1993).

Exhibit 2: 52 Week Volatility of Term Structure Changes Plotted Against the 3-Month Spot Rate at the Start of the Period

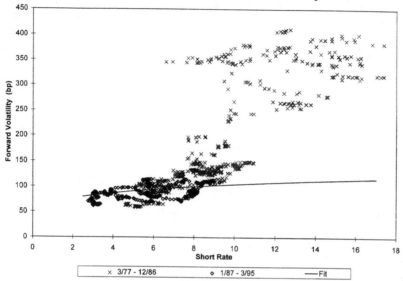

The x's are periods starting 3/77 through 12/86. The diamonds are periods starting 1/87 through 3/95. The data points are based on the best fit k for the period 1/87-3/96, as described in the text. The solid curve shows the best fit to a power law model. The best fit parameters are β=91 bp, γ=0.19. (This is *not* a fit to the points shown here, which are provided solely to give a visual feel for the data.)

Exhibit 2 gives a graphical representation of the data. There is clear evidence that the simple power law model is not a good fit and that the data display regime shifts. The exhibit shows the volatility of the factor in equation (12) using the value of k appropriate to the period January 1987 - March 1996 (the "Greenspan era"). The vertical coordinate of each dot represents the volatility of the factor over a 52-week period; the horizontal coordinate shows the 3-month spot rate (a proxy for the short rate) at the start of the 52-week period. (Note that the maximum likelihood estimation is not based on the data points shown, but on the individual weekly changes.) The dots are broken into two sets: the x's are for start dates prior to January 1987, the diamonds for later dates. Divided in this way, the data suggest fairly strongly that volatility has been nearly independent of interest rates since 1987 — a time during which the short rate has ranged from around 3% to over 9%.

From an empirical perspective, then, no simple choice of model works well. Among the simple models of volatility, the MRG model most closely matches the recent behavior of U.S. Treasury term structure.

There is an issue of financial plausibility here, as well as an empirical one. Some models permit interest rates to become negative, which is undesirable, though how big a problem this is isn't obvious. The class of simple models that provably have positive interest rates without suffering from explosions and match the initial term structure is quite small. The BDT and BK models satisfy these conditions, but don't provide information about future yield curves as needed for the mortgage problem. The Dybvig-adjusted CIR model also satisfies the conditions, but is somewhat hard to work with. There is a lognormal HJM model that avoids negative rates, but it is analytically intractable and suffers from explosions.[23] The lognormal version of the two state Markov model also suffers from explosions, though, as with the lognormal HJM model, these can be eliminated by capping the volatility at some large value. The rational lognormal model has positive rates without explosions, but unreasonable long-term volatility.

It is therefore worth asking whether the empirical question is important. It might turn out to be unimportant in the sense that, properly compared, models that differ only in their assumed dependence of volatility on rates actually give similar answers for option values.

The trick in comparing models is to be sure that the comparisons are truly "apples to apples," by matching term structures of volatility. It is easy to imagine getting different results valuing the same option using the MRG, CIR, and BK models, even though the initial volatilities are set equal — not because of different assumptions about the dependence of volatility on rates, but because the long-term volatilities are different in the three models even when the short-rate volatilities are the same. There are a number of published papers claiming to demonstrate dramatic differences between models, but which actually demonstrate just that the models have been calibrated differently.[24]

The two state Markov framework provides a convenient means to compare different choices for the dependence of volatility on rates while holding the initial term structure of volatility fixed. Choosing different forms for $\sigma(r)$ while setting k to a constant in expression (4) gives exactly this comparison. We can value options using these different assumptions and compare time values. (Intrinsic value — the value of the option when the volatility is zero — is of course the same in all models.) To be precise, we set $\sigma(r, t)=\sigma_0(r/r_0)^\gamma$, where σ_0 is the initial annualized volatility of the short rate in absolute terms (e.g., 100 bp/year) and r_0 is the initial short rate. Choosing the exponent $\gamma=\{0, 0.5, 1\}$ then gives the MRG model, a square root volatility model (not CIR), and a lognormal model (not BK), respectively.

The results can be summarized by saying that a derivatives trader probably cares about the choice of exponent γ, but a fixed-income portfolio manager probably doesn't. The reason is that the differences in time value are small, except when the time value itself is small — for deep in- or out-of-the-money options. A derivatives trader may be required to price a deep out-of-the-money option, and would get very different results across models, having calibrated them using at-the-money options. A portfolio manager, on the other hand, has option positions embedded in bonds, mortgage-backed securities, etc., whose time value is a small fraction of total portfolio

---

[23] Heath, Jarrow, and Morton, *op. cit.*

[24] For a recent example, see M. Uhrig and U. Walter, "A New Numerical Approach to Fitting the Initial Yield Curve," *Journal of Fixed Income* (March 1996).

value. So differences that show up only for deep in- or out-of-the-money options are of little consequence. Moreover, a deep out-of-the-money option has small option delta, so small differences in valuation have little effect on measures of portfolio interest rate risk. An in-the-money option can be viewed as a position in the underlying asset plus an out-of-the-money option, so the same reasoning applies.

Exhibit 3 shows the results of one such comparison for a 5-year quarterly pay cap, with a flat initial term structure and modestly decreasing term structure of volatility. The time value for all three values of γ peaks at the same value for an at-the-money cap. Caps with higher strike rates have the largest time value in the lognormal model, because the volatility is increasing for rate moves in the direction that make them valuable. Understanding the behavior for lower strike caps requires using put-call parity: an in-the-money cap can be viewed as paying fixed in a rate swap and owning a floor. The swap has no time value, and the floor has only time value (since it is out-of-the-money). The floor's time value is greatest for the MRG model, because it gives the largest volatility for rate moves in the direction that make it valuable. In each case, the square root model gives values intermediate between the MRG and lognormal models, for obvious reasons. At the extremes, 250 bp in or out of the money, time values differ by as much as a factor of 2 between the MRG and lognormal models. At these extremes, though, the time value is only a tenth of its value for the at-the-money cap.

Exhibit 3: Time Values for Five Year Quarterly Pay Caps for Gaussian, Square Root and Lognormal Two State Markov Models with Identical Initial Term Structure of Volatility and a 7% Flat Initial Yield Curve *

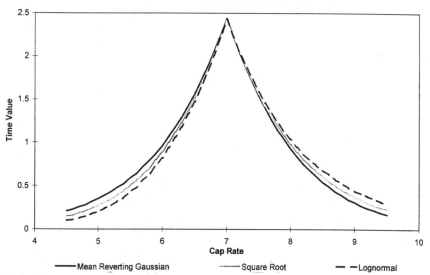

* The model parameters (described in the text) are σ_0=100 bp/yr., k=0.02/yr., equivalent to an initial short-rate volatility of 14.8%, and a 10-year yield volatility of 13.6%.

Exhibit 4: Sensitivity of Cap Value to Change in Rate Level as a Function of Cap Rate*

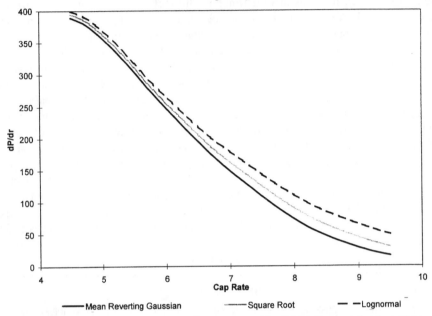

* The cap structure and model parameters are the same as used for Exhibit 3, except that the initial term structure is the (positively sloped) US Treasury curve as of 5/13/96. The short rate volatility is 19.9% and the ten year yield volatility is 14.9%.

If the initial term structure is not flat, the model differences can be larger. For example, if the term structure is positively sloped, then the model prices match up for an in-the-money rather than at-the-money cap. Using the same parameters as for Exhibit 3, but using the actual Treasury term structure as of 5/13/96 instead of a flat 7% curve, the time values differ at the peak by about 20% — about half a point — between the MRG and lognormal models. Interestingly, as shown in Exhibit 4, even though the time values can be rather different, the option deltas are rather close for the three models. (The deltas are even closer in the flat term structure case.) In this example, if a 9.5% cap were embedded in a floating-rate note priced around par, the effective duration attributable to the cap according to the lognormal model would be 0.49 year, while according to the MRG model it would be 0.17 year. The difference shrinks as the rate gets closer to the cap. This ⅓ year difference isn't trivial, but it's also not large compared to the effect of other modeling assumptions, such as the overall level of volatility or, if mortgages are involved, prepayment expectations.

These are just two numerical examples, but it is easy to see how different variations would affect these results. An inverted term structure would make the MRG model time value largest at the peak and the lognormal model value the smallest. Holding σ_0 constant, higher initial interest rates would yield smaller valuation differences across models since there would be less variation of volatility around the mean. Larger values of the mean reversion k would also produce smaller differences between models, since the short-rate distribution would be tighter around the mean.

Finally, there is the question raised earlier as to whether one should be concerned about the possibility of negative interest rates in some models. From a practical standpoint, this is an issue only if it leads to a significant contribution to pricing from negative rates. One simple way to test this is to look at pricing of a call struck at par for a zero coupon bond. Exhibit 5 shows such a test for the MRG model. For reasonable parameter choices (here taken to be $\sigma_0 = 100$ bp/year, $k = 0.02$/year, or 20% volatility of a 5% short rate), the call values are quite modest, especially compared to those of a call on a par bond, which gives a feel for the time value of at-the-money options over the same period. The worst case is a call on the longest maturity zero coupon bond which, with a flat 5% yield curve, is priced at 0.60. This is just 5% of the value of a par call on a 30-year par bond. Using the actual May 1996 yield curve, all the option values — other than on the 30-year zero — are negligible. For the 30-year zero the call is worth just 1% of the value of the call on a 30-year par bond. In October 1993, the U.S. Treasury market had the lowest short rate since 1963, and the lowest 10-year rate since 1967. Using that yield curve as a worst case, the zero coupon bond call values are only very slightly higher than the May 1996 values, and still effectively negligible for practical purposes.

Again, it is easy to see how these results change with different assumptions. An inverted curve makes negative rates likelier, so increases the value of a par call on a zero coupon bond. (On the other hand, inverted curves at low interest rate levels are rare.) Conversely, a positive slope to the curve makes negative rates less likely, decreasing the call value. Holding σ_0 constant, lower interest rates produce larger call values. Increasing k produces smaller call values. The only circumstances that are really problematic for the MRG model are flat or inverted yield curves at very low rate levels, with relatively high volatility.

Exhibit 5: Valuation of a Continuous Par Call on Zero Coupon and Par Bonds of Various Maturities in the MRG Model

Model parameters are:

$$\sigma_0 = 100 \text{ bp/year}$$
$$k = 0.02\text{/year}$$

The value of the call on the zero coupon bond should be zero in every case, assuming non-negative interest rates.

Term	5% Flat Curve Zero Cpn	5% Flat Curve Par Bond	7% Flat Curve Zero Cpn	7% Flat Curve Par Bond	5/96 US Tsy Yields Zero Cpn	5/96 US Tsy Yields Par Bond	10/93 US Tsy Yields Zero Cpn	10/93 US Tsy Yields Par Bond
3 Year	<0.01	0.96	<0.01	0.93	<0.01	0.65	<0.01	0.62
5	<0.01	1.93	<0.01	1.83	<0.01	1.43	<0.01	1.27
10	0.06	4.54	<0.01	4.07	<0.01	3.47	0.02	3.06
30	0.60	11.55	0.10	8.85	0.08	7.86	0.09	7.26

CONCLUSIONS

For portfolio analysis applications, the mean reverting Gaussian model has much to recommend it. For this model, it is easy to implement valuation algorithms for both path independent securities such as bond options, and path dependent securities such as CMOs. It is one of the simplest models in which it is possible to follow the evolution of the entire yield curve (à la HJM), making it especially useful for valuing assets like mortgage-backed securities whose cash flows depend on longer term rates. The oft raised bogeyman of negative interest rates proves to have little consequence for option pricing, since negative rates occur with very low probability for reasonable values of the model parameters and initial term structure.

Option values are somewhat (though not very) sensitive to the assumed dependence of volatility on the level of rates. The empirical evidence on this relationship is far from clear, with the data (at least in the United States) showing evidence of eras, possibly associated with central bank policy. The numerical evidence shows that, for a sloped term structure, different power law relationships give modestly different at-the-money option time values, and larger relative differences for deep in- or out-of-the-money options. These differences are unlikely to be significant to fixed-income portfolio managers, but are probably a concern for derivatives traders.

Chapter 2

The Four Faces of an Interest Rate Model

Peter Fitton
Senior Analyst and Consultant
SS&C Technologies, Inc.

James F. McNatt, CFA
Managing Director
SS&C Technologies, Inc.

INTRODUCTION

Models of the term structure of interest rates are becoming increasingly important in the practice of finance and actuarial science. However, practitioner understanding of these models has not always kept pace with the breadth of their application. In particular, misinterpretation of the proper uses of a particular model can lead to significant errors. In this chapter, we attempt to clear up some of the most commonly misconstrued aspects of interest rate models: the choice between an arbitrage-free or equilibrium model, and the choice between risk neutral or realistic parameterizations of a model. These two dimensions define four classes of model forms, each of which has its own proper use.

Much of the confusion has arisen from overuse and misuse of the term "arbitrage-free." Virtually all finance practitioners believe that market participants quickly take advantage of any opportunities for risk-free arbitrage among financial assets, so that these opportunities do not exist for long; thus, the term "arbitrage-free" sounds as if it would be a good characteristic for any model to have. Simply based on these positive connotations, it almost seems hard to believe that anyone would not want their model to be arbitrage-free. Briefly, in the world of finance this expression has the associations of motherhood and apple pie.

The authors would like to thank David Becker of Lincoln National Life for asking the questions that motivated this chapter, and for the many helpful comments that were applied herein. Any remaining errors are the authors' alone.

Unfortunately, this has led some users (and even builders) of interest rate models to link uncritically the expression "arbitrage-free" with the adjective "good." One objective of this chapter is to show that arbitrage-free models are not appropriate for all purposes. Further, we show that just because a model uses the arbitrage-free approach does not mean that it is necessarily good, even for the purposes for which arbitrage-free models are appropriately used.

Another common confusion ensues from implicitly equating the terms "arbitrage-free" and "risk neutral." This arises partly from the fact that, in the academic and practitioner literature, there have been very few papers which have applied the arbitrage-free technique to a model that was not in risk neutral form. We explain the reason for this below. The natural result is that the terms have sometimes been used interchangeably. In addition, since quantitative risk management is a relatively new concept to the finance community, most well-known papers have focused only on the application of interest rate models to simple valuation and hedging problems. These have not required either the realistic or equilibrium approaches to modeling. This lack of published work has led to a mistaken belief that an arbitrage-free, risk neutral model is the only valid kind of term structure model. In this chapter, we intend to dispel that notion.

CATEGORIZATION OF APPROACHES TO TERM STRUCTURE MODELING

Arbitrage-Free Modeling

Arbitrage-free models take certain market prices as given, and adjust model parameters in order to fit the prices exactly. Despite being called "term structure" models, they do not in reality attempt to emulate the dynamics of the term structure. Instead, they assume some computationally convenient, but essentially arbitrary, random process underlying the yield curve, and then add time dependent constants to the drift (mean) and volatility (standard deviation) of the process until all market prices are matched. To achieve this exact fit, they require at least one parameter for every market price used as an input to the model.

For valuation, it is possible to produce reasonable current prices for many assets without having a realistic term structure model, by using arbitrage-free models for interpolation among existing prices. To this end, the trading models used by most dealers in the over-the-counter derivatives market employ enormous numbers of time dependent parameters. These achieve an exact fit to prices of assets in particular classes, without regard to any differences between the behaviors of the models and the actual behavior of the term structure over time. Placed in terms of a physical analogy, the distinction here is between creating a robot based on a photograph of an animal, and creating a robot based on multiple observations of the animal through time. While the robot produced using only the photograph may *look* like the animal, only the robot built based on behavioral observations will *act* like the animal. An arbitrage-free model is like the former robot, constructed with reference to only a single point in time; that is, a snapshot of the fixed-income marketplace.

As an example of an arbitrage-free model, at *RISK Magazine's* "Advanced Mathematics for Derivatives" conference in New York on October 26 and 27, 1995, Merrill Lynch's Greg Merchant presented a linear normal model that used time dependent drifts, volatilities, and correlations to reproduce prices in the Eurodollar, cap, and swaption markets, respectively. It is important to realize that an arbitrage-free model such as this one is just an interpolation system, which reads prices off some complicated hyper-surface that passes through each of the points at which prices are known.

Equilibrium Modeling

In contrast to arbitrage-free models, equilibrium term structure models are truly models of the term structure process. Rather than interpolating among prices at one particular point in time, they attempt to capture the behaviors of the term structure over time. An equilibrium model employs a statistical approach, assuming that market prices are observed with some statistical error, so that the term structure must be *estimated*, rather than taken as given. Equilibrium models do not exactly match market prices at the time of estimation, because they use a small set of state variables (fundamental components of the interest rate process) to describe the term structure. The models do not contain time dependent parameters; instead they contain a small number of statistically estimated constant parameters, drawn from the historical time series of the yield curve.

Risk Neutral Probabilities:
The Derivative Pricing Probability Measure

When we create a model for pricing interest rate derivatives, the "underlying" is not the price of a traded security, as it would be in a model for equity options. Instead, we specify a random process for the instantaneous, risk-free spot interest rate, the rate payable on an investment in default-free government bonds for a very short period of time. For convenience, we call this interest rate "the short rate." Financial analysts have chosen to create models around the short rate because it is the only truly riskless interest rate in financial markets. An investment in default-free bonds for any non-instantaneous period of time carries *market risk*, the chance that the short rate will rise during the term of the investment, leading to a decline in the investment's value.

As with any risky investment, an investor in bonds subject to market risk expects to earn a risk-free return (that is, the return from continuously investing at the short rate, whatever that may be) plus a risk premium. Thus, the spot rate for a particular term is composed of the return expected under the random process for the short rate up to the end of that term, plus a *term premium*, an additional return to compensate the investor for the market risk of the investment. The term premium offered in the market depends on the aggregate risk preference of market participants; the more risk averse investors are, the higher the term premium will be.

Let r_t be the short rate at time t. Let $D(t, T)$ be the price, at time t, of a discount bond paying one dollar at time T. Let $s(t, T)$ be the spot rate at time t for the term $(T-t)$. Finally, let $\phi(T-t)$ be the term premium (expressed as an annual excess rate of return) required by investors for a term of $(T-t)$. All rates are continuously compounded. We can then write,

$$D(t, T) = \frac{1}{e^{s(t, T) \times (T-t)}} = \frac{1}{e^{\phi(T-t) \times (T-t)}} E \left[\frac{1}{e^{\int_t^T r_s ds}} \right] \tag{1}$$

The second term in the two-term expression above is a discount factor that reflects the expected return from investing continuously at the short rate for the term $(T-t)$. The first term is the additional discount factor that accounts for the return premium that investors require to compensate them for the market risk of investing for a term of $(T-t)$. The use of an integral in the expression for the expected short rate discount factor is necessary because the short rate is continuously changing over the bond's term.

From this description and formula, it may seem necessary to know the term premium for every possible term, in addition to knowing the random process for the short rate, in order to value a default-free discount bond. This is not the case, however. As in the pricing of a forward contract or option on a stock, we can use the mathematical sleight-of-hand known as *risk neutral valuation* to find the relative value of a security that is derivative of the short rate.

The principle of risk neutral valuation as it applies to bonds and other interest rate derivatives is that, regardless of how risk averse investors are, we can identify a set of spot rates that values discount bonds correctly relative to the rest of the market. We do not have to identify separately the term premium embedded in each spot rate in order to use it to discount future cash flows. This fact can be used to make the valuation of all interest rate derivatives easier by *risk adjusting* the term structure model; that is, by changing the probability distribution of the short rate so that the spot rate of every term is, under the new model, equal to the expected return from investing at the short rate over the same term. This is accomplished by redefining the model so that, instead of being a random process for the short rate, it is a random process for the short rate plus a function of the term premium. If we specify the process for r_t^* in such a way that

$$r_s^* = r_s + \phi(s - t) + \phi'(s - t) \times (s - t) \tag{2}$$

at every future point in time s (accomplished by adjusting the rate of increase of r_t upward) then we can write,

$$D(t, T) = \frac{1}{e^{s(t, T) \times (T-t)}} = E \left[\frac{1}{e^{\int_t^T (r_s + \phi(T-t))ds}} \right] = E \left[\frac{1}{e^{\int_t^T r_s^* ds}} \right] \tag{3}$$

By transforming the short rate process in this manner, we have created a process for a random variable which, when used to discount a certain future cash flow, gives an expected present value equal to the present value obtained by discounting that cash flow at the appropriate spot rate. It is important to note that this random variable is no longer the short rate, but something artificial that we might refer to as the *risk adjusted short rate.*[1]

The resulting *risk neutral model* might be construed as a model for the true behavior of the short rate in an imaginary world of risk neutral market participants, where there is no extra expected return to compensate investors for the extra price risk in bonds of longer maturity. This impression, while accurate, is not very informative. The important aspect of the risk neutral model is that the term premia, whatever their values, that exist in the marketplace are embedded in the interest rate process itself, so that the expected discounted value of a cash flow at the risk adjusted short rate is equal to the discounted value of the cash flow at the spot rate. A useful implication of this is that the expected present value of a future spot rate under the risk neutral model is equal to the present value of the current implied forward rate.[2]

The value of the *risk neutral probability measure* is that, under this parameterization, an interest-sensitive instrument's price can be estimated by averaging the present values of its cash flows, discounted at the short term interest rates along each path of the short rate under which those cash flows occur. In contrast, valuing assets under the model before it was risk adjusted would require a more complicated discounting procedure which applied additional discount factors to the short rate paths to compensate for market risk; however, the price obtained under both approaches would be the same. For this reason, we use randomly generated scenarios from risk neutral interest rate models for pricing.

To sum up, there is nothing magical about risk neutrality. There are any number of changes of variables we could make to a short rate process that would retain the structure of the model, but have a different (but equivalent) probability distribution for the new variable. We could change the measure to represent imaginary worlds in which market participants were risk seeking (negative term premia), or more risk

---

[1] This is not the way that risk neutrality is usually presented. Typically, writers have focused on the stochastic calculus, using Girsanov's Theorem to justify a change of probability measure to an *equivalent* (i.e., an event has zero probability under one measure if and only if it has zero probability under the other measure) *martingale measure*. This complexity and terminology can obscure the simple intuition that we are making a change of variables in order to restate the problem in a more easily solvable form. For this approach to explaining risk neutral valuation, see G. Courtadon, "The Pricing of Options on Default-free Bonds," *Journal of Financial and Quantitative Analysis* (March 1982), pp. 301-29, or J. Harrison and S. Pliska, "Martingales and Stochastic Integrals in the Theory of Continuous Trading," *Stochastic Processes and their Applications* (1981), pp. 215-260.

[2] Note that this is *not* the same as the expectations hypothesis of the term structure, which holds that the term structure's shape is determined solely by the market's expectations about future rates. The expectations hypothesis is a theory of the real term structure process, whereas the risk neutral approach is an analytical convenience which takes no position about the truth or falsity of any term structure theory. For a brief, cogent discussion of the expectations hypothesis in contrast to risk neutral pricing, see Don Chance, "Theories of the Term Structure: Part I," *Derivatives 'R Us* (May 13, 1996), pp. 1-3.

averse than in the real world; regardless, as long as we structured the discounting procedure properly we would always determine the same model price for an interest rate derivative. The specific change of variables that produces a risk neutral model simply makes the algebra easier than the others, because one can ignore risk preferences.

Realistic Probabilities:
The Estimated Market Probability Measure

We have described why risk neutral interest rate scenarios are preferred for pricing bonds and interest rate derivatives. However, it is important to note that risk neutral scenarios are not appropriate for all purposes. For example, for scenario-based evaluation of portfolio strategies, realistic simulation is needed. And a computerized system for stress testing asset/liability strategies under adverse movements in interest rates is to actuaries what a wind tunnel is to aerospace engineers. The relevance of the information provided by the testing depends completely on the realism of the simulated environment. Stated differently, the test environment must be like the real environment; if not, the test results are not useful.

The realistic term structure process desired for this kind of stress testing must be distinguished from the risk neutral term structure process used for pricing. The risk neutral process generates scenarios in which all term premia are zero. This process lacks realism; in the real world, term premia are clearly not zero, as evidenced by the fact that the implied spot curve from Treasuries has been upward sloping 85% of the time in the 1955-94 period.[3] Either investors do a very poor job of anticipating the future (they constantly think interest rates are going to rise, only to be disappointed) or this upward slope reflects an expected return premium for bonds of longer maturity.

Thus, the user of an interest rate model must be careful. When generating scenarios for reserve adequacy testing, where the purpose is to examine the effect on a company's balance sheet of changes in the real (risk averse) world, he must not use the scenarios from a risk neutral interest rate model.

WHEN DO I USE EACH OF THE MODELING APPROACHES?

The two dimensions, risk neutral versus realistic and arbitrage-free versus equilibrium, define four classes of modeling approaches. Each has its appropriate use.

Risk Neutral and Arbitrage-Free

The risk neutral and arbitrage-free model is the most familiar form of an interest rate model for most analysts. The model has been risk adjusted to use for pricing interest

---

[3] This fact is one of the many useful observations about the realistic term structure process appearing in David Becker, *Stylized Historical Facts Regarding Treasury Interest Rates from 1955 to 1994* (Fort Wayne, IN: Technical report, Lincoln National Life, 1995). See also David Becker, "The Frequency of Inversions of the Yield Curve, and Historical Data on the Volatility and Level of Interest Rates," *Risks and Rewards* (October 1991), pp. 3-5.

rate derivatives, and its parameters have been interpolated from a set of current market prices rather than being statistically estimated from historical data. It is appropriately used for current pricing when the set of market prices is complete and reliable.

It is worth noting that, just because two models are each both risk neutral and arbitrage-free, we cannot conclude that they will give the same price for a particular interest rate derivative. Two arbitrage-free models will produce the same prices only for the instruments in a subset common to both sets of input data. The form of the model, and particularly the number of random factors underlying the term structure process, can make a large difference to valuations of the other instruments.

When the market data is sparse, the behavior of the model becomes important. For example, the value of a Bermudan or American swaption depends on the correlations among rates of different maturities. The swaption market is not liquid, nor are its prices widely disseminated, so there is no way to estimate a "term structure of correlations" that would allow a simple arbitrage-free model to interpolate reasonable swaption prices. In this case, a multi-factor model which captures the nature of correlations among rates of different maturities, including the way that those correlations are influenced by the shape of the term structure, will perform better for pricing swaptions than will a one-factor model. Models with good statistical fit to historical correlation series are needed for Bermudan or American options on floating-rate notes, caps, and floors for the same reason. Model behavior is also important for long-dated caps and floors, where there is a lack of reliable data for estimating the "term structure of volatilities" beyond the 5-year tenor.

Risk Neutral and Equilibrium

There are a number of sources of "error" in quotations of the market prices of bonds, so that the discount rates that exactly match a set of price quotations may contain bond-specific effects, corrupting the pricing of other instruments. These sources, defined as any effects on a bond's market price apart from the discount rates applying to all market instruments, include differences in liquidity, differential tax effects, bid-ask spreads (the bid-ask spread defines a range of possible market prices, implying a range of possible discount rates), quotation stickiness, timeliness of data, the human element of the data collection and reporting process, and market imperfections.

Since arbitrage-free models accept all input prices as given, without reference to their reasonability or comparability to other prices in the input data, they impound in the pricing model any bond-specific effects. In contrast, equilibrium models capture the global behavior of the term structure over time, so security-specific effects are treated in the appropriate way, as noise. For this reason, risk neutral equilibrium models can have an advantage over arbitrage-free models in that equilibrium models are not overly sensitive to outliers. Also, for current pricing (as distinguished from horizon pricing, described below), equilibrium models can be estimated from historical data when current market prices are sparse. Thus, a risk neutral and equilibrium model can be used for pricing when the current market prices are unreliable or unavailable.

For most standard instruments, circumstances rarely prevail such that the current market prices needed for estimating an arbitrage-free model are not available. However, such circumstances always prevail for horizon pricing, where the analyst calculates a price for an instrument in some assumed future state of the market. Since arbitrage-free models require a full set of market prices as input, arbitrage-free models are useless for horizon pricing, the future prices being unknown. Thus, the horizon prices obtained under the different values of the state variables in an equilibrium model provide an analytical capability that arbitrage-free models lack.

Using Models of Borrower Behavior with a Risk Neutral Interest Rate Model

Often, an interest rate model is not enough to determine the value of a fixed income security or interest rate derivative. To value mortgage-backed securities or collateralized mortgage obligations, one also needs a prepayment model. To value bonds or interest rate derivatives with significant credit risk, one needs a model of default and recovery. To value interest-sensitive annuities and insurance liabilities, one needs models of lapse and other policyholder behaviors. In all of these behavioral models, the levels of certain interest rates are important explanatory variates, meaning that, for example, the prepayment speeds in a CMO valuation system are driven primarily by the interest rate scenarios.

Common practice has been to estimate parameters for prepayment, default, and lapse models using regression on historical data about interest rates and other variables. Then, in the valuation process, the analyst uses the interest rates from a set of risk neutral scenarios to derive estimates for the rates of prepayment, default, or lapse along those scenarios. This borrower behavior information is combined with the interest rates to produce cash flows and, ultimately, prices. Unfortunately, this practice leads to highly misleading results.

The primary problem here is that the regressions have been estimated using historical data, reflecting the *real* probability distributions of borrower behavior, and then used with scenarios from a risk neutral model, with an *artificial* probability distribution. The risk neutral model is not a process for the short rate; rather, it is a process for the risk adjusted short rate. Since the real world is risk averse, the risk adjusted short rate has an expected value much higher than the market's forecast of the short rate; the extra premium for interest rate risk permits one to value optionable default-free bonds by reference to the forward rate curve.

The same procedure can be applied to corporate bonds. Corporate bonds are exposed to default risk in addition to interest rate risk. One may construct a behavioral model of failure to pay based on historical data about default rates and recovery, perhaps using bond ratings as explanatory variates in addition to interest rates. One can then attempt to compute the present value of a corporate bond by finding the expected value of the discounted cash flows from the two models in combination: a risk neutral model of the Treasury curve, and a realistic model of default behavior as a function of interest rates and other variables. Because the cash flows of the bond, adjusted for default, will be less than the cash flows for a default-free bond, the model will price the corporate bond at a positive spread over the Treasury curve.

This spread will almost certainly be substantially too low in comparison to the corporate's market price. The reason for this is that, just as investors demand a return premium for interest rate risk, they demand an additional return for default risk. The application of an econometrically estimated model of default to pricing has ignored the default risk premium encapsulated in the prices of corporate bonds. Market practice has evolved a simple solution to this; one adjusts the default model to fit (statistically, in the equilibrium case; exactly, in the arbitrage-free case) the current prices of active corporates in the appropriate rating class. By using the market prices of active corporates to imbed the default risk premium in the model, the analyst is really applying the principle of risk neutral valuation to the default rate. The combined model of risk adjusted interest rates and risk adjusted default rates now discounts using the corporate bond spot rate curve instead of the Treasury spot curve.

The same technique of risk neutralizing a model by embedding information about risk premia derived from current market prices, can be applied to prepayment models as well. The results of a prepayment model can be risk adjusted by examining the prices of active mortgage backed securities. Unfortunately, one can only guess at the appropriate expected return premium for insurance policy lapse risk or mortality risk. Nevertheless, these quantities should be used to "risk neutralize" these models of behavior to the extent practical. The integrity of risk neutral valuation depends on risk adjusting all variables modeled; otherwise, model prices will be consistently overstated.

A final note can be made in this regard about option adjusted spread (OAS). OAS can be understood in this context as a crude method to risk adjust the pricing system to reflect all risk factors not explicitly modeled.

Realistic and Arbitrage-Free

A realistic, arbitrage-free model starts by exactly matching the term structure of interest rates implied by a set of market prices on an initial date, then evolves that curve into the future according to the realistic probability measure. This form of a model is useful for producing scenarios for evaluation of hedges or portfolio strategies, where it is important that the initial curve in each scenario exactly matches current market prices. The difficulty with such an approach lies in the estimation; realistic, arbitrage-free models are affected by *confounding*, where it is impossible to discriminate between model misspecification error and the term premia. Since the model parameters have been set to match market prices exactly, without regard to historical behavior, too few degrees of freedom remain to estimate both the term premia and an error term. Unless the model perfectly describes the true term structure process (that is, the time dependent parameters make the residual pricing error zero at all past and future dates, not just on the date of estimation), the term premia cannot be determined. The result is that realistic, arbitrage-free models are not of practical use.

Exhibit 1: When to Use Each of the Model Types

Model Classification	Risk Neutral	Realistic
Arbitrage-free	• Current pricing, where input data (market prices) are reliable	• Unusable, since term premium cannot be reliably estimated
Equilibrium	• Current pricing, where inputs (market prices) are unreliable or unavailable • Horizon pricing	• Stress testing • Reserve and asset adequacy testing

Realistic and Equilibrium

Since the arbitrage-free form of a realistic model is not available, the equilibrium form must be used for stress testing, Value at Risk (VAR) calculations, reserve and asset adequacy testing, and other uses of realistic scenarios.

Some analysts express concern that, because the *predicted* initial curve under the equilibrium model does not perfectly match observed market prices, then the results of scenario testing will be invalid. However, the use of an equilibrium form does not require that the predictions be used instead of the current market prices as the first point in a scenario. The scenarios can contain the observed curve at the initial date and the conditional predictions at future dates. This does not introduce inconsistency, because the equilibrium model is a statistical model of term structure behavior; by taking this approach we explicitly recognize that its predictions will deviate from observed values by some error. In contrast, the use of an arbitrage-free, realistic model implicitly assumes that the model used for the term structure process is absolutely correct.

Summary of the Four Faces

Exhibit 1 summarizes the uses of the four faces of an interest rate model. Exhibit 2 shows the mathematical form of a commonly used interest rate model, disseminated by Black and Karasinski,[4] under each of the modeling approaches and probability measures. In each equation, u is the natural logarithm of the short rate.

In the above models, σ is the instantaneous volatility of the short rate process, κ is the rate of mean reversion, θ is the mean level to which the natural logarithm of the short rate is reverting, and λ represents the term premium demanded by the market for holding bonds of longer maturity. The value of the state variable u at the time of estimation is represented by u_0.

The realistic model forms can be distinguished from the risk neutral forms by the presence of the term premium function λ. The difference between the arbitrage-free forms and the equilibrium forms can be discerned in that the parameters of the arbitrage-free forms are functions of time.

---

[4] Fischer Black and Piotr Karasinski, "Bond and Option Pricing when Short Rates are Lognormal," *Financial Analysts Journal* (July-August 1991), pp. 52-59.

Exhibit 2: Four Forms of the Black-Karasinski Model

Model Classification	Risk Neutral	Realistic
Arbitrage-free	$du = \kappa(t)\,(\theta(t) - u)\,dt + \sigma(t)\,dz$ • u_0 and $\theta(t)$ matched to bond prices • $\kappa(t)$ and $\sigma(t)$ matched to cap or option prices	$du = \kappa(t)\,(\theta(t) - \lambda(u,t) - u)\,dt + \sigma(t)\,dz$ • u_0 and $\theta(t)$ matched to bond prices • $\kappa(t)$ and $\sigma(t)$ matched to cap or option prices • $\lambda(u,t)$ cannot be reliably estimated
Equilibrium	$du = \kappa(\theta - u)\,dt + \sigma\,dz$ • u_0 statistically fit to bond prices • κ, θ, σ historically estimated	$du = \kappa(\theta - \lambda(u) - u)\,dt + \sigma\,dz$ • u_0 statistically fit to bond prices • κ, θ, σ, $\lambda(u)$ historically estimated

Chapter 3

Arbitrage-Free Bond Canonical Decomposition

Thomas S. Y. Ho, Ph.D.
President
Global Advanced Technology Corporation

Michael Z. H. Chen, Ph.D.
Research Analyst
Global Advanced Technology Corporation

INTRODUCTION

The development of bond valuation models in the past 20 years has had a dramatic impact on the bond market. Pricing models provide market participants with the necessary tools to measure relative values and manage risks. For example, we use arbitrage-free models to develop an option-adjusted spread (OAS) approach for measuring a bond's value relative to other bonds. We also use these models to calculate duration measures in formulating hedging strategies. As a result, traders, portfolio managers, risk managers, asset/liability strategists, and research analysts find applications for these pricing models.

As fixed-income securities become more complex and bond markets become more volatile, the applicability of both the OAS approach and duration methodologies becomes questionable. OAS is the additional spread (or yield) the bond offers above the Treasury yields, net of the cost of the embedded options. However, the OAS approach does not offer any description of the "embedded options." Indeed, any uncertainty of cash flows is often referred to as embedded options. If two bonds differ significantly in their embedded options, there is no simple interpretation of their relative values by their OASs. We cannot assert that the bond that offers a higher return has a better value, primarily because the bonds are incomparable. It follows we must precisely identify the embedded options before we can measure their relative values.

The authors thank Pamela Hyder, David Pfeffer, Fred H.T. Eng, and Sanjay Mazumdar for their comments, suggestions and assistance.

Duration measures (or key rate durations) are also limited in their applications for complex securities in risk management. Durations are price sensitivity measures for small movements of interest rates. Therefore, durations offer a dynamic hedging strategy for controlling interest rate risks. Hedgers need to continually revise the hedging portfolio. Further, they must respond to the market in that they must trade when rates rise or fall. Such dynamic hedging strategies can be costly, especially when the market is less liquid. Most bond markets are not perfectly liquid. As a result, a more static hedging strategy is needed for managing interest rate risks when the market is illiquid.

This chapter proposes a new methodology for determining relative values of bonds and in managing interest rate risks. The methodology is called *arbitrage-free bond canonical decomposition* (ABCD). ABCD proposes a standardized ("canonical") way of decomposing any bond into its basic parts. This decomposition is based on an objective relative valuation ("arbitrage-free") and not on the investor's subjective views. Further, these basic parts are standard securities that are traded in the market. If we know the prices of these basic securities, we can determine the cost of the bond according to the decomposition.

In this chapter we will prove theoretically that such a decomposition is possible. A practical procedure in decomposing a collateralized mortgage obligation (CMO) is then presented. As will be shown, ABCD can offer many applications in the bond market, avoiding the limitations of the OAS approach and the duration measures. More specifically, ABCD offers the following advantages:

- a standardized and specific description of the bond risk, avoiding ambiguous terminologies such as "embedded option;"
- a more precise hedging technique using caps and floors against changes in volatilities, comparable to the use of "vega;"
- a hedging methodology that avoids continual revision of the hedging positions in response to the changes in the market;
- since bond value is determined by the observed prices of the basic securities that compose the bond, the bond value is less dependent on the choice of the pricing model (for example, the choice of a normal versus a lognormal model); and
- a practical approach to cash flow matching strategies for option embedded bond portfolios.

For these reasons, ABCD should find broad applications from arbitrage operations to asset-liability management.

BASIC FRAMEWORK

The model assumptions are the same as those proposed in arbitrage-free valuation in Ho and Lee, a perfect capital market over discrete time.[1] The assumptions are:

---

[1] Thomas S. Y. Ho and Sang-Bin Lee, "Term Structure Movements and Pricing of Interest Rate Contingent Claims," *Journal of Finance*, 41 (1986).

Exhibit 1: Binomial Lattice Method

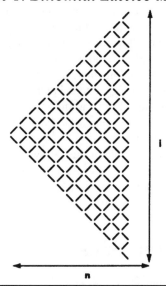

1. *The market is frictionless.* There are no taxes and no transaction costs, and all securities are perfectly divisible.
2. *The market clears at regular time intervals.* There is unlimited riskless borrowing and lending at each interval.
3. *A discount bond of maturity T is defined to be a bond that pays $1 at the end of T years, with no other payments to its holders.* The bond market is complete in that there exists a discount bond for all maturities. Let $P(T)$ denote the price of the discount bond with maturity T, with $P(.)$ being called the discount function.
4. *There is no arbitrage opportunity at any time.*
5. *The discount function moves stochastically in a binomial lattice.* A one-factor model where all interest rates are perfectly correlated is assumed. Denoting the i-th state, (i) is used, and (n) denotes the n-th period on the lattice. The binomial lattice is shown in Exhibit 1.

Given the initial discount function $P(T)$, an arbitrage-free movement of the discount function on the binomial lattice can be determined. Specifically, the 1-period interest rate at each time n and state i can be determined. We denote this one period rate by $r(i,n)$ and the discount factor $d(i,n)=(1/(1+r(i,n)))$. An interest rate path $p(k)$ is a path taken from the binomial lattice. It follows that there are 2^N distinct paths in a binomial lattice with N intervals. The complete set of interest rate paths of a binomial lattice is called the *path space*.

Along each interest rate path, we can assign a cash flow. A bond (or even a bond strategy) is an unambiguous assignment of cash flows to each of the possible paths. For example, a 10-year zero-coupon bond assigns $100 at the end of the tenth year for all interest rate paths. In general, a bond is "option embedded" if the cash flows may differ depending on the interest rate path taken. We say that two bonds are the same when the bonds' cash flows are the same along each interest rate path. Ho describes the construction of bonds in more detail.[2]

For a particular bond, option embedded or otherwise, select an interest rate path and the cash flows that are assigned to the path. The cash flow along the interest rate path can then be discounted. The resulting present value is called the *pathwise value* of that particular interest rate scenario of the bond, and it is denoted by $pwv(k)$, where k is the index of the scenario.

Ho reported that the average of the pathwise values of all the interest rate paths of a bond is the arbitrage-free bond value.[3] In this chapter we will show that the pathwise values of a bond contain significant information about the bond. The information is, in fact, sufficient to determine a decomposition of a bond.

DECOMPOSITION THEOREMS

ABCD is based on two analytical results. The first result applies to option-free bonds (bonds with no embedded options), and the second extends the previous result to the path-independent bonds.

> *Proposition 1.* Given an option-free bond, the bond cash flows are uniquely determined by the pathwise values. That is, given two option-free bonds, if their pathwise values are the same, then their cash flows are identical.[4]

This result shows that if we know the bond has no embedded option, and if we find a bond portfolio with no embedded option that can match the bond's pathwise values (hence implementing a pathwise immunization), we have in essence accomplished a cash flow matching. Pathwise values have complete information about an option-free bond. But how about an option-embedded bond? First, we must consider one significant option-embedded bond type: a path-independent bond.

A *path-independent bond* is a bond whose cash flows depend only on the time (n) and state (i) on the binomial lattice and not on the path that it has taken. For example, all option-free bonds and European options are path-independent bonds.

> *Proposition 2.* Suppose there are two path-independent bonds having the same pathwise values. If their cash flows are identical along one interest

---

[2] Thomas S. Y. Ho, "Primitive Securities: Portfolio Building Blocks," *Journal of Derivatives,* 1:2 (Winter 1993).

[3] Thomas S. Y. Ho, "Managing Illiquid Bonds and the Linear Path Space," *Journal of Fixed Income,* 2:1 (June 1992).

[4] For a complete proof of Proposition 1, see Appendix A.

rate scenario (any one scenario from the binomial lattice), then the two bonds are identical. Further, all path-independent bonds are a portfolio of option-free bonds, caps, and floors.[5]

This result shows that a path-independent bond using Treasury securities, caps, and floors which have liquidity in the market, can be decomposed. Consequently, an inability to decompose the bond by the Treasuries, caps, and floors enables the measuring of the impact of the path dependency.

CANONICAL DECOMPOSITION

This section presents the canonical decomposition procedure using the above analytical results. ABCD follows a three-step procedure, referred to as the primary, secondary, and tertiary decompositions. Each step extracts the basic components of a given bond.

Primary Decomposition

The first step is primary decomposition. Given a bond, the primary decomposition determines the bond cash flows along the forward curve. That is, the cash flows of the bond are determined if the interest rate volatility is zero. The cash flow is called the "Treasury equivalent" (TE).

Let T_n denote the zero-coupon Treasury with maturity n years. The Treasury equivalent cash flows can then be represented by the following equation, where X_n represents the dollar value of a position in the zero-coupon Treasury bond with maturity n year.

$$TE = \Sigma(X_n \, T_n) \tag{1}$$

It is important to note that the primary decomposition is, in general, not the total hedge position of a swap desk or other bond desks. Typically, these trading desks monitor their exposures to the changing shape of the yield curve by calculating their required Treasury positions to immunize their risks. These exposures are calculated by simulating the sensitivity of their portfolio value to the change of each key rate, and not using the forward curve. Treasury equivalent provides the correct hedging only in the case where there are no embedded options in the portfolio.

Secondary Decomposition

For the second step, secondary decomposition, the pathwise values of the Treasury equivalent are calculated and the difference between the pathwise values of the bond and those of the Treasury equivalent is considered. That is,

$$Y_i = pwv_i(\text{bond}) - pwv_i(\text{TE}) \text{ for } i = 1... \, 2^N \tag{2}$$

---

[5] Refer to Appendix B, for a complete proof of Proposition 2.

According to Proposition 2, if the bond is path independent, then Y uniquely determines the set of caps and floors which, together with the Treasury equivalent, have the same cash flows as the bonds for all the interest rate paths. The caps and the floors have their strikes above and below the forward rates effectively.

In bond analytics, "option cost" is often referred to the difference between the bond value and the Treasury equivalent value. The option cost is the price change in the presence of interest rate volatility. Proposition 2 shows that this option cost can in fact be uniquely represented by caps and floors, if the scenario referred to in Proposition 2 is the forward curve. Therefore, secondary decomposition is the specification of the embedded options of a bond.

A forward cap with strike of $x\%$ and window between calendar years a and b is represented by $C_{x\%,a-b}$. For example, a forward cap of strike 8%, and with window 2000 - 2005 is denoted by $C_{8\%,00\text{-}05}$. A forward floor is analogously denoted by $F_{x\%,a-b}$. Then a bond decomposition can be represented by the following equation where Y_i and Z_i are the market values of the caps and floors, respectively, in the decomposition:

$$B = \text{TE} + \Sigma(Y_i\, C_i) + \Sigma(Z_i\, F_i) \tag{3}$$

Proposition 2 asserts that equation (3) is unambiguously determined if the bond is path independent.

Tertiary Decomposition

Now we turn to step 3, tertiary decomposition. Equation (3) is correct only if the conditions of Proposition 2 are met. Generally, they are not met. In this case, the right side of equation (3) is the portfolio that provides the best fit of the bond pathwise values, and not the exact matching of the pathwise values. The standard minimization of mean squared errors without probability weighting may be used. The difference between the pathwise values of the bond and the pathwise values of the right hand side of equation (3) is the residual values. These residual values are then subject to further decomposition.

According to the analysis, the residual values arise from four possible sources: path dependency, model risk premium, liquidity premium, and arbitrage profit.

Path Dependency The residuals of pathwise values can identify the impact of the path dependency of the bond. As the result of the fitting procedure, some residuals are positive and others negative. If the pathwise value of the bond exceeds that of the primary/secondary decomposition, then the bond outperforms in that scenario. Conversely, if the residual pathwise value is negative, then the bond underperforms in that scenario. Thus, it is found that the residuals of the decomposition provide an effective insight into the bond's performance across all the important scenarios.

Model Risk Premium The decomposition is based on the robustness of the model. However, the model may not capture all the risk sources such as credit risk for corporate issues and prepayment risks for mortgage-backed securities. As the pathwise values are calculated along the Treasury interest rate path, it is not possible to capture the credit spread and the spread to compensate for the prepayment risks involved.

For this reason, the decomposition has to be applied to a sample of bonds with similar credit risks or prepayment risks to identify comparable premiums. These risk sources are beyond the model's specifications. However, the decomposition does isolate all the interest rate factors, enabling the comparison of the credit and prepayment premiums.

Liquidity Premiums Liquidity risk differs from credit and prepayment risks in that the liquidity risk depends not only on the bond but also on the market. For this reason, the class of bonds that is exposed to similar liquidity risks of the market must be identified before the premium for such risks can be isolated.

Arbitrage Profit Arbitrage profit is the value of the bond net of the primary/secondary decomposition and the risk/liquidity premiums. In essence, the ABCD approach translates the option-adjusted spread from yield measures in basis points to values in dollars. The arbitrage profits identify the discrepancy between the bond's quoted price and the cost of replicating the bond from the basic components.

A NUMERICAL EXAMPLE

In this section we apply ABCD to a collateralized mortgage obligation (CMO) to illustrate the use of the decomposition procedure. To implement the procedure, we need to make some simplifying assumptions. In practice, the binomial lattice of a pricing model is often based on a one-month step size, and the bond maturity may be up to 30 years. Therefore, the number of paths (or the number of pathwise values) will be 2^{360}, which is astronomical.

Linear Path Space

One approach is to construct a set of paths that spans the path space. Here, *linear path space* (LPS) as described in Ho is used.[6] LPS is a probability weighted structured sampling technique to condense a binomial lattice with many periods into a lattice of manageable size.

Begin with the full binomial lattice with 1-month time steps, and partition the path space into term segments at 1, 3, 5, 7, 10, 20, and 30 years. At each term, partition the full set of interest rate levels into much smaller sets of "gates." A path can now be classified by the sequence of gates through which it travels. Define an equiva-

---

[6] Ho, "Managing Illiquid Bonds and the Linear Path Space."

lence class. The number of paths in a given equivalence class as a proportion of the total number of paths is the "probability weight" for that class.

For each class, a representative path (the one going through the midpoints of each of its gates) is chosen. These representative paths are then used to determine the pathwise values of the decomposition.

Canonical Basis of Caps and Floors

In theory, the decomposition requires the basis of the caps and floors to have strikes at each node of the binomial lattice. In practice, we construct the basis that can sufficiently span the scenarios without requiring too many caps and floors.

Only the caps and floors with strikes above and below the forward rates are chosen. Their windows are determined by the term segments of the LPS. Therefore there are seven windows: 0-1 year, 1-3 years, 3-5 years, 5-7 years, 7-10 years, 10-20 years, and 20-30 years. The strikes of the forward caps and floors of a window are determined by the rate levels of the LPS and representative paths at the beginning of each window. The reset rate of all the caps and floors is specified to be the 6-month rate.

Decomposition of FH1747:Q

The next procedure is to decompose a CMO. FH1747:Q is a fixed 8% coupon bond maturing on December 2003. The bond is a support tranche bearing much prepayment risk allocated from the PAC tranches. The collaterals are FHLMC 30-year with a net weighted average coupon of 8%. On the analysis date, January 9, 1995, the price is $92.09. The option cost is calculated to be 41 basis points and the option adjusted spread is 64 basis points.

The bond has unstable cash flows. At 100 PSA, the window of the bond's principal payments is 2015-2018. However, at PSA 200, the bond window shortens to 1995-1998. This shortening of the weighted average life of the bond with the fall in interest rates (with the rise of prepayment speed) is referred to as the *call risk*. When the prepayment speed slows to PSA 75, the window is extended. The lengthening of the weighted average life with the rise in interest rates is called *extension risk*. To explicitly model these call and extension risks, the decomposition is continued.

Exhibit 2 is the scattered plot graph of the pathwise values of the CMO against pathwise values of the bond's Treasury equivalent. If the bond has no call and extension risks, the scattered plots would assume a 45° line. Exhibit 2 clearly depicts the call risks when the Treasury equivalent pathwise values rise above $110, as the scattered points fall below the 45° line. The result shows that the loss under a worst-case scenario could exceed 20%.

In contrast, since the bond has a long weighted average life along the forward curve, the extension risk is limited. Exhibit 2 shows that the cost of extension appears for those scenarios where the Treasury equivalent pathwise values fall below par. However the cost is limited, not exceeding 5% for all the scenarios.

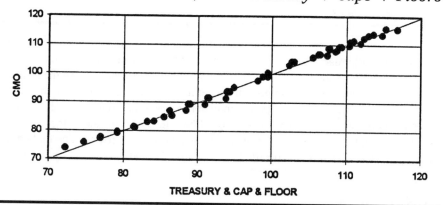

Exhibit 2: Pathwise Values, CMO: Treasury Equivalent

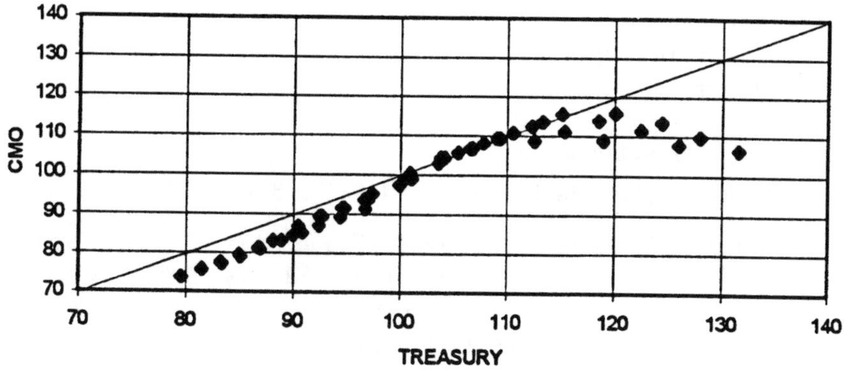

Exhibit 3: Pathwise Values, CMO: Treasury + Caps + Floors

Analytical Results of the Decomposition

Exhibit 3 depicts the scattered plots of the pathwise values of the CMO against those of the bond's Treasury, caps, and floors decomposition. Even though the CMO bond is path dependent, the fit is high, with an R^2 equal to 0.9688. The positions of the points above and below the 45° line shows the impact of path dependency on the bond.

The ABCD equation shown in Exhibit 4 presents the exact decomposition of the bond of $100 value. The cash flow value of the bond is $109.08 ($110.343–$1.258). The cost of call risk is $1.874 and the cost of the extension risk is $1.485. The cost of extension risk is high because of the caps being close to "in the money," but the potential loss is limited, as discussed earlier. In contrast, the potential loss of call risk is much higher, but the floors are more "out of the money." The sum of the cost of the call risk and extension risk, amortized over the life of the bond, is the option cost.

Exhibit 4: ABCD Equation

Ca = Cash
T = Treasury
C = Cap
F = Floor
RP = Risk Premium

$$\text{CMO} = -1.258\ Ca + 110.343\ T - 1.485\ C - 1.874\ F - 5.726\ RP$$

$$\begin{aligned}
\text{FHLMC 1747 Q} = -1.258\ Ca &+ 9.815\ T_1 + 7.688\ T_2 + 7.110\ T_3 + 6.574\ T_4 \\
&+ 6.079\ T_5 + 5.619\ T_6 + 5.194\ T_7 + 4.801\ T_8 + 4.436\ T_9 \\
&+ 4.098\ T_{10} + 3.784\ T_{11} + 10.298\ T_{12} + 9.412\ T_{13} \\
&+ 8.903\ T_{14} + 7.114\ T_{15} + 5.774\ T_{16} + 3.642\ T_{17} \\
&- 1.485\ C_{95\text{-}18,\ 8.17\%} - 8.335\ F_{95\text{-}08,\ 6.54\%} \\
&+ 6.461\ F_{95.08,\ 6.87\%} - 5.726\ RP
\end{aligned}$$

$R^2 = 0.9688$

According to the ABCD equation, the premium for the prepayment risk, the liquidity, and arbitrage profit is $5.726 on the $100 bond value. This premium, amortized over the life of the bond, is the option-adjusted spread. Considering the unstable nature of the bond, it may be ambiguous in defining the amortization of the premium. For this reason, a measure of the premium in dollar terms can offer a more appropriate comparison of values. The ABCD equation shows the cash flow along the base case (the forward rate scenario) by the positions in Treasury securities. The embedded options are represented by the positions in forward caps and floors.

CONCLUSIONS

This chapter presents the analytical framework for decomposing a bond into its basic components, Treasuries, caps, and floors. Further, it provides an implementable procedure and illustrates the methodology with a numerical example. This decomposition methodology has broad applications in the bond market. The followings are some of its applications.

A Standardized Risk Measure

To date, we use bond sensitivities to describe bond risks. These sensitivities include duration, convexity, and option cost. When bonds become more complicated, these measures become less adequate in representing bond risks. Further, they become inaccurate measures. For example, duration numbers become sensitive to model assumptions for some of the "risky" bonds. Or, option cost may be negligible because the cost of call risks cancels the cost of extension risks. In contrast, if we represent the bond by its basic components, the description of the bond structure is relatively stable. From the decomposition, we can then infer whether the bond sensitivity measures are appropriate.

Volatility Hedging

In hedging securities with significant embedded options, managing the change in volatility is important. Yet to date, the use of vega is prevalent, though clearly inadequate. The decomposition shows exactly the caps and floors that the hedge requires in managing the volatility risks. In essence, the decomposition describes exactly where the embedded options are and not just the volatility sensitivity.

Static Hedging versus Dynamic Hedging

The decomposition enables a manager to implement a static hedging versus a dynamic hedging. Dynamic hedging requires a manager to continually rebalance the portfolio, reacting to the changes of the market. This hedging approach subjects the portfolio to high trading or liquidity risks. In contrast, static hedging is more stable. The hedging is constructed in such a way that the hedging portfolio anticipates the changes in duration, convexity, and other measures as the market changes. As a result, we do not need to be continually fine tuning. More importantly, the portfolio can be rebalanced at times to minimize the cost of trading.

Valuation by Observed Prices

Since the Treasuries, cap and floor prices are observable, we can determine the bond price from these observed prices. The valuation model is used to determine the decomposition of the bond, specifying the sizes and types of the caps and floors. If we use the observed prices of the basic components of the bond decomposition, we can avoid some inaccuracies of the pricing model. For example, a lognormal interest rate model may overweigh the scenarios where interest rate are high. As a result, the model may overstate the cost of the extension risk.

Also such a model may also overstate the cap values. However, by applying the observed cap prices, the misspecification of the model would not appear in the pricing of the bond. This decomposition approach is consistent with the pricing of bonds at trading desks, where traders continually monitor the combination and recombination value of bonds. This decomposition procedure offers them a systematic way to implement this pricing operation.

Cash Flow Matching by Scenarios

In asset/liability management, managers are concerned with the behavior of the surplus cash flows under different scenarios. When the assets and liabilities are significantly option embedded, the behavior of the surplus cash flows becomes complicated to analyze. This chapter suggests that the manager can decompose the surplus and identify the embedded caps and floors in the surplus. This approach greatly simplifies the asset/liability analysis. If there is success in eliminating the embedded caps and floors, the cash flows of the asset and liability may be quite well matched under all the scenarios. Further, this decomposition approach suggests that the optimal asset and liability management is not immunization of all risk exposures, but that decomposition should be used to depict the risk exposure.

There are many avenues to extend this research. This decomposition has more applications when it is used to compare a sample of bonds. While this chapter has only analyzed one bond, the research can be extended to classify bonds according to the decomposition. Another important extension is to better understand the path dependent nature of bonds. While analytical results for path independent bonds have been furnished, it is possible to gain more insight into the tertiary decomposition if we have an analytical decomposition of path dependent bonds.

APPENDIX A: PROOF OF PROPOSITION 1

Proposition 1: Given two option-free bonds, if their pathwise values are the same, then their cash flows are identical.

Proof: The above proposition is equivalent to proving that if a given option-free bond B has zero pathwise value along each path, then the bond B has zero cash flow along each path also.

Since bond B is option free, its cash flow at time n is a function only of time (n), denoted by $B(n)$. The bond B is completely determined by the numbers $B(n)$, $n = 1,2,...,N$.

Let the k-th scenario on the interest rate lattice $r(i,n)$ be represented by the underlying interest rates $r(1)$, $r(2)$,..., $r(N)$. Discounting the cash flow of the bond B along the path, we have $pwv(k)$ as follows:

$$pwv(k) = B(1)e^{-r(1)} + B(2)e^{-r(1)-r(2)} + ... + B(N)e^{-r(1)-...-r(N)} \tag{1}$$

Let path p and path q be two paths which are identical except for the last period. Path p ends at $r(i,N)$ and path q ends at $r(i+1,N)$. Following the assumption that bond B has zero pathwise value along each path, we have equations $pwv(p)= 0$ and $pwv(q) = 0$. Subtracting one equation from the other, we have equation $pwv(p)-pwv(q) = 0$, i.e.,

$$B(N)e^{-R-r(i,N)} - B(N)e^{-R-r(i+1,N)} = 0 \tag{2}$$

where R is the summation of the interest rates along path p (or path q) from period 1 to period $N-1$. Equation (2) can be rewritten as:

$$B(N)(e^{-r(i,N)} - e^{-r(i+1,N)}) = 0 \tag{3}$$

Since $r(i,N)$ is not equal to $r(i+1,N)$, we have $B(N)=0$. Henceforth, bond B will be considered as a bond with maturity of $N-1$ periods. By the same argument it can be proved that B has zero cash flow at end of period $N-1$, i.e., $B(N-1) = 0$. Consequently from the same argument, we have $B(t)= 0$, for $t = 1,2,...,N$. Thus, bond B has zero cash flow along each path.

APPENDIX B: PROOF OF PROPOSITION 2

Proposition 2: Given two path independent bonds having the same pathwise value, if their cash flows are identical along one interest rate scenario, then the two bonds are identical. Further, all path independent bonds are a portfolio of option-free bonds, caps, and floors.

Proof: The proposition is equivalent to proving that if a given path independent bond B has zero pathwise value along each path, and its cash flow is zero along one scenario, then bond B has zero cash flow along all the paths.

Since bond B is path-independent, its cash flow at time n depends only on time (n) and state (i), and not the historical interest rate paths it took to reach there. Its cash flow can be labeled on the nodes of the binomial interest rate lattice, denoted by $B(i,n)$, where $i = 1,..., n$, $n = 1,..., N$. Since there are a total of $N(N+1)/2$ nodes in the lattice, bond B is completely determined by the expression $B(i,n)$.

Let path p and path q be two paths which are identical except for the last period. Path p ends at $r(i,n)$ and path q ends at $r(i+1,N)$. By the assumption that bond B has zero pathwise value along each path, we have equations $pwv(p)=0$ and $pwv(q)=0$. Subtracting one equation from the other, we have equation $pwv(p)-pwv(q)=0$.

$$B(i,N)e^{-R-r(i,N)}-B(i+1,N)e^{-R-r(i+1,N)} = 0 \tag{1}$$

(For example, where R is the summation of interest rates along path p or path q from period 1 to period $N-1$.)

Following our assumption that bond B has zero cash flow along one scenario, we can safely assert one of $B(1,N),...,B(N,N)$ is zero. Without loss of generality, let $B(1,N) = 0$. For the special case of Equation (1), $i = 1$, it follows that repeating our argument, $B(i,n)$ must be zero for $i = 1, 2,...,N$.

$$B(2,N) - B(1,N)e^{r(2,N)-r(1,N)} = 0 \tag{2}$$

Now, bond B can be considered as a bond with maturity of $N-1$ periods. By the same argument it can proven that B has zero cash flow at the end of period $N-1$. Then, by induction, bond B has zero cash flow at every period and along every path.

Now it will be proven that all path independent bonds are a portfolio of option-free bonds, caps, and floors. At first, it is easy to see that a given path independent bond is a portfolio of some simple bonds having zero cash flow at all lattice points except one node. Thus, it can be proven that these simple bonds are a portfolio of option-free bonds, caps, and floors. Assume that at the N-th column of the interest rate lattice, we have $r(i,N)$ which satisfies the expression $r(N,N) > r(N-1,N) > ... > (1,N)$. Constructing a sequence of forward cap C_i which is in the N-th period with a strike rate of $[r(i,n)+r(i-1,N)]/2$, $i= N,N-1,...,2$. The linear combination of C_i will give us all simple bonds in the column which have zero cash flow at all lattice points except for one node. For example, bond C_N will strike at only the top node of the column. The bond $C_{N-1} - (2r(N,N) - r(N-1,N) - r(N-2,N))/(r(N,N) + r(N-1,N))C_N$ will only strike at the node $r(N-1,N)$. Similarly, we can construct all the other simple bonds from the linear combinations of C_i. However, it is desirable to choose a basis which makes sense in financial theory. Therefore, it is natural that the zero-coupon Treasury with maturity N periods was chosen. Selection of the caps and floors was made by placing them above and below the forward curve. See Appendix C for an example.

APPENDIX C: LPS LATTICE AND THE CANONICAL BASIS OF CAPS AND FLOORS

Exhibit 5 is a linear path space (LPS) lattice of 6-month rates. That part of the lattice representing extremely high and low interest rates has been eliminated.

The following is a list of caps and floors chosen to form a canonical basis for the pathwise value space of path-independent bonds on an empirical level:

		Window (years)	Strike Rate (%)
1	Cap	1-3	8.5
2	Floor	1-3	7.0
3	Cap	3-5	10.0
4	Cap	3-5	8.5
5	Floor	3-5	7.0
6	Floor	3-5	5.0
7	Cap	5-7	10.0
8	Cap	5-7	8.5
9	Floor	5-7	7.0
10	Floor	5-7	5.0
11	Cap	7-10	10.0
12	Cap	7-10	8.5
13	Floor	7-10	7.0
14	Floor	7-10	5.0
15	Cap	10-20	10.5
16	Cap	10-20	8.5
17	Floor	10-20	7.0
18	Floor	10-20	5.0
19	Cap	20-30	11.0
20	Cap	20-30	9.5
21	Floor	20-30	8.0
22	Floor	20-30	5.5

Exhibit 5: Linear Path Space Lattice of 6-Month Rates

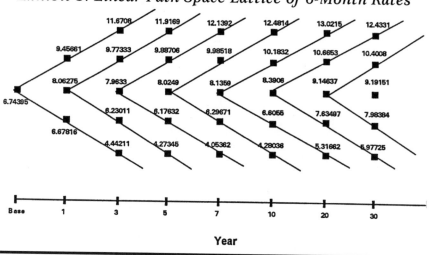

In accordance with this theory, the set of simple bonds, which has a zero cash flow at all lattice points except one node, form the basis of the path-independent bond space. Consequently, this basis generates the pathwise value space of all path-independent bonds. The following procedure was adhered to in determining the caps and floors.

The lattice was dissected into seven segments, namely: 0-1 year, 1-3 years, 3-5 years, 5-7 years, 7-10 years, 10-20 years, and 20-30 years. In every period, different strike rates were used separating every lattice node, choosing strike rates above and below the forward curve for caps and floors respectively. The entire set of caps and floors and zero-coupon Treasuries with different maturities (used in the primary decomposition) formed the basis for path-independent bond space. Whenever the basis is fixed, the decomposition of a given bond is unique. In other words, this is the canonical way to decompose any bond.

Chapter 4

Valuing Path-Dependent Securities:
Some Numerical Examples

C. Douglas Howard, Ph.D.
Department of Applied Mathematics and Physics
and
The Center for Finance and Technology
Polytechnic University

INTRODUCTION

Lattice-based valuation techniques are today commonly used to value a host of financial instruments. The procedure typically involves modeling the random behavior of a relevant market observable (often called the "factor"). If the application involved valuing a stock option, for example, the factor would be the underlying stock price. To value a collateralized mortgage obligation (CMO), some proxy for the general level of interest rates would be more relevant. The underlying lattice usually represents a discrete version of a continuous stochastic process that the factor is presumed to follow over time. With some securities, the stock option for example, the procedure is quite straightforward. With other securities, however, the methodology becomes quite cumbersome. The CMO is an extreme example of this latter category.

A major source of complexity arises from "path dependence." This occurs when knowing the value $F(t^*)$ of the factor at some time $t^*>0$ (our convention is that time 0 corresponds to today) does not provide sufficient information to calculate the cash flow generated by the security at time t^*. Rather, in the case of path dependence, the time t^* cash flow also depends in some manner on $F(t)$ for all or some of $0 \leq t < t^*$, i.e., how the value of F got to $F(t^*)$ is important.

Research for this chapter was supported by Andrew Kalotay Associates, Inc. The author thanks Lee Bittengle for surveying the literature on this topic.

Consider again a stock option, a European call to be precise. Path dependence is not present in this example. Let $F(t)$ denote the underlying stock price at time t. Suppose the option is exercisable at time T at a strike of K. At any time prior to T, a European option generates no cash flow regardless of what happens to F, thus exhibiting path independence for times $t^*<T$. At time T, the cash flow generated is given by max $(0, F(T) - K)$ — how F got to $F(T)$ is again irrelevant. Note that path dependence *does not* mean simply that the security's cash flow depends on the factor's path. Indeed, the stock option's time T payoff depends on the path of the underlying stock — but *only* through the underlying's value at time T.

A CMO, on the other hand, is heavily path-dependent. Among many other things, we must certainly know the amount of the underlying mortgage pool still outstanding at time t^* to calculate the time t^* cash flow of the CMO. This, unfortunately, is a function of the prepayment experience from time 0 to time t^* which, in turn, is a function of the path of interest rates over this entire period — not just the rate environment at time t^*.

In this chapter we examine closely two fixed-income securities exhibiting intermediate degrees of path dependence. The first, an indexed amortizing note (IAN), is simply a bond that makes principal payments prior to its stated maturity that are a prescribed function of the prevailing level of interest rates: principal payments are structured to accelerate in low rate environments. As with the much more complicated CMO, path dependence arises because the amount of the IAN outstanding at any point in time (and hence the IAN's cash flow at that time) depends on prior interest rates. The second example, an interest rate derivative, is a periodic cap on a short-term rate. Specifically we study a floating-rate note (FRN) with the feature that its coupon rate, which adjusts yearly, is permitted to increase only a limited amount from one year to the next. If market rates decrease from one year to the next, the FRN's coupon rate decreases accordingly unaffected by the periodic cap. Periodic caps are commonly found embedded along with a host of other option-like features in adjustable-rate mortgages.

This chapter is organized as follows. In the next section we review the basic methodology of lattice-based arbitrage-free pricing, first abstractly and then with a concrete example. We outline the difference between recursive and Monte Carlo (path sampling) methodologies. This section also develops the notation we use in subsequent sections. Following this, we value a simple IAN first via Monte Carlo and then, with the introduction of a necessary non-stochastic "state" variable, via a recursive procedure. In the last section we subject the periodic cap to the same analysis and discuss some numerical procedures that make problems of this sort more tractable. In this second example a different state variable is called for.

To the author's knowledge, recursive techniques using coupled non-stochastic state variables first appeared in practice in the late 1980's to value sinking fund bonds[1] whose complicated package of embedded options exhibit substantial

---

[1] Salomon Brothers Inc. developed such a model.

path-dependence. Hull and White[2] describe the use of this procedure in a different context. Prior to the advent of the state variable technique, less efficient Monte Carlo procedures were commonly used to value path-dependent securities.[3]

ARBITRAGE-FREE PRICING

The Single-Period Case

Consider the following single-period setup. At some future time $\Delta t > 0$, m different "states of the world" are possible. We label these possible outcomes 1, 2, ..., m. For the moment we leave the notion of what exactly a state of the world is as an abstraction. However, let's suppose that this notion contains sufficient information to know the payoff of any security C at time Δt once the outcome is specified. We denote these state-dependent (future) payoffs by $C(1), C(2), ..., C(m)$ and we presume there is no cash flow prior, nor subsequent, to time Δt . Let $aC + bC'$ denote the security that pays $aC(j)+bC'(j)$ in state j (i.e., $aC+bC'$ is a portfolio comprising a units of security C and b units of security C'). Any reasonable method $V(\cdot)$ of ascribing value to securities based on these future payoffs should satisfy:

$$V(aC + bC') = aV(C) + bV(C') \tag{1}$$

$$\text{if } C(j) > 0 \text{ for } 1 \leq j \leq m \text{ then } V(C) > 0 \tag{2}$$

Condition (1) says that a portfolio may be valued by summing the values of its constituent securities weighted by amounts held in the portfolio, while condition (2) is the "arbitrage-free" condition that any security generating positive payoff in every future outcome has positive value today. One can show that any such $V(\cdot)$ must be of the form:

$$V(C) = e^{-r\Delta t}(p_1 C(1) + p_2 C(2) + ... + p_m C(m)) \tag{3}$$

where $p_1, p_2, ..., p_m$ satisfy

$$\text{each } p_j \geq 0 \text{ and } \sum_{j=1}^{m} p_j = 1 \tag{4}$$

---

[2] See J. Hull and A. White, "Efficient Procedures for Valuing European and American Path-Dependent Options," *Journal of Derivatives* (Fall 1993), pp. 21-31. For other numerical examples and a good list of further references, see Chapter 18 in J. Hull, *Options, Futures, and Other Derivatives* (Englewood Cliffs, NJ: Prentice Hall, 1997).

[3] See, for example, W.C. Hunter and D.W. Stowe, "Path-Dependent Options: Valuation and Applications," *Economic Review*, Federal Reserve Bank of Atlanta, 77:2 (1992), pp. 29-34.

Note, in particular, that the p_j behave like probabilities (they are referred to as *arbitrage probabilities*). For any security C, this calculation represents the expected payoff of C at time Δt discounted back to today at the continuously compounding annual risk-free rate r.

The Multi-Period Case

Most securities generate a sequence of cash flow over time — not just one future payoff. The single-period model generalizes to accommodate this fact. Suppose our security C generates cash flow at a sequence of times $0 = t < t_1 < t_2 < ... < t_n = T$. Between the t_i and after T there is no possibility of cash flow. At the i-th period there are $m(i)$ possible states of the world which, again, we label $1, 2, ..., m(i)$. When $i=0$, of course, there is only one state so $m(0)=1$. We assume that the description of the states at period i contains any information necessary to calculate the state-dependent period i cash flow $CF_i(j)$ for each state $1 \leq j \leq m(i)$. In the multi-period model, an "outcome" corresponds to a sequence of states

$$\omega = (j_1, ..., j_n) \text{ where } 1 \leq j_i \leq m(i)$$

representing how the world unfolds over time. We let Ω represent the space of all such outcomes.

We shall refer to a pair (i,j), where i is a time period $(0 \leq i < n)$ and j is a state $(1 \leq j \leq m(i))$, as a "node." Assume that at each node there resides a single-period arbitrage-free pricing (AFP) model specified by the node-dependent risk-free rate r_{ij} and arbitrage probabilities $p_i(j \rightarrow j')$ for each j' with $1 \leq j' \leq m(i + 1)$. This latter expression represents the probability of a transition from state j in period i to state j' in period $i+1$.

Suppose that at time t_i we are in state j. The aggregate payoff of C one period forward (at time t_{i+1}) comes from two sources: (1) the cash flow $CF_{i+1}(j')$ generated by C at time t_{i+1} (which depends on the period $i+1$ state j'); and (2) the value, which we denote $V_{i+1}(j')$, assigned at node $(i+1,j')$ to the *subsequent* cash flow that C may generate at times $t_{i+2}, ..., t_n$. Using equation (3), we deduce that we must have

$$V_i(j) = e^{-r_{ij}(t_{i+1} - t_i)} \sum_{j'=1}^{m(i+1)} p_i(j \rightarrow j')[CF_{i+1}(j') + V_{i+1}(j')] \qquad (5)$$

if our model is to satisfy conditions (1) and (2) at each node. Since we know the state dependent cash flow $CF_{i+1}(j')$, this procedure makes sense if we know the $V_{i+1}(j')$'s. But we know that $V_n(j') = 0$ for $1 \leq j' \leq m(n)$: this is merely the statement that there *is no* cash flow subsequent to time t_n. This allows us to apply equation (5) when $i=n-1$ to calculate the $V_{n-1}(j)$'s. But then we can apply equation (5) to $i=n-2$ and so forth, backwards (recursively) through the lattice, until we have calculated $V_0(1)$. But $V_0(1)$ represents the value today of all future cash flow — precisely what we are interested in.

A Simple Example

We make this concrete with a simple example. In the subsequent sections, we will expand upon this same example for purposes of valuing the IAN and periodic cap. Suppose each $t_i = i$ (so cash flow can occur only annually) and consider the lattice shown in Exhibit 1. The arbitrage probabilities are prescribed as follows:

$$p_i(j \to j') = \begin{cases} 0.5 \text{ if } j' = j \text{ or } j' = j+1 \\ 0 \quad \text{otherwise} \end{cases}$$

and only those transitions with positive probability are shown in Exhibit 1. The numbers at each node correspond to the r_{ij} stated as rates compounded *annually* so as to correspond, for convenience, to the time increments. With the r_{ij} quoted in this manner and noting that $t_{i+1} - t_i = 1$, equation (5) must be rewritten as

$$V_i(j) = \frac{1}{1 + r_{ij}} \sum_{j'=1}^{m(i+1)} p_i(j \to j')[CF_{i+1}(j') + V_{i+1}(j')] \tag{6}$$

and setting into this the values for our arbitrage probabilities yields

$$V_i(j) = \frac{1}{1 + r_{ij}}[0.5(CF_{i+1}(j) + V_{i+1}(j))$$
$$+ 0.5(CF_{i+1}(j+1) + V_{i+1}(j+1))] \tag{7}$$

Exhibit 1: State-Dependent 1-Year Risk-Free Rate

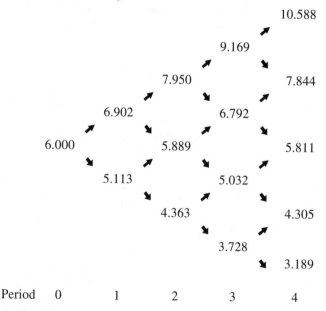

| Period | 0 | 1 | 2 | 3 | 4 |

Exhibit 2: State-Dependent $C_i(\cdot)$ and $V_i(\cdot)$ for the 3-Year Note

Period 0	Period 1	Period 2	Period 3	Period 4
				106.000
				0.000
			6.000	
			97.097	
		6.000		106.000
		96.505		0.000
	6.000		6.000	
	97.610		99.258	
		6.000		106.000
100.000		100.190		0.000
	6.000		6.000	
	102.390		100.922	
		6.000		106.000
		103.060		0.000
			6.000	
			102.190	
				106.000
				0.000

Period	0	1	2	3	4

We use this setup to value a (risk-free) bond that pays $6 in years 1, 2, and 3, and $106 in year 4 irrespective of the states in those periods. Exhibit 2 shows the values of $C_i(j)$ and $V_i(j)$ that equation (7) produces in this setting. For example, letting $\langle 6.902 \rangle$ denote the state (in period 1) in which the 1-year rate is 6.902%, the calculation of $V_1(\langle 6.902 \rangle)$ is

$$V_1(\langle 6.902 \rangle) = \frac{1}{1.06902}[0.5(6.0+100.190) + 0.5(6.0+96.505)] = 97.610$$

We note that this bond is valued today at 100.0. In fact, the four bonds paying a 6% annual coupon maturing in 1, 2, 3, and 4 years are all valued at 100.0. This lattice was *constructed* to explain a flat 6% term structure. One can also confirm that the local volatility of the 1-year rate is 15% throughout the lattice (e.g., ½ log(6.902/ 5.113) = 0.15).

There is another algorithm that arrives at the 100.0 value of the 4 year 6% bond. Specifically: (1) calculate the period-by-period cash flow corresponding to each of the (sixteen) 4 year paths through the lattice; (2) discount each of those flows back to today using the earlier path-dependent r_{ij} to arrive at a "path-dependent present value" $PV(\omega)$; (3) calculate the expected PV over the sixteen paths ω. We represent a path ω by a sequence of +'s and −'s depending on whether at each juncture we move up or down, respectively. Then, for this 4 year 6% bond, we have, for example:

$$PV(+ + + +) = 106.0/1.09169/1.0795/1.06902/1.06$$
$$+ \ 6.0/1.0795/1.06902/1.06$$
$$+ \ 6.0/1.06902/1.06$$
$$+ \ 6.0/1.06$$
$$= 95.237$$

Note also that $PV(+ + + -) = 95.237$ also. This is because neither the year 4 cash flow nor the discounting process depend on the year 4 interest rate. This holds in this case for all paths ω: $PV(\omega)$ is independent of the last $+$ or $-$ step. Notationally, we write this as $PV(+ + + \pm) = 95.237$. Calculating an expected value over the eight equally likely pairs of paths $(+ + + \pm)$, $(+ + - \pm)$, $(+ - + \pm)$, $(+ - - \pm)$, $(- + + \pm)$, $(- + - \pm)$, $(- - + \pm)$, and $(- - - \pm)$ (respectively) gives:

$$V_0(1) = (95.237 + 97.004 + 98.678 + 100.064$$
$$+ 100.261 + 101.671 + 102.997 + 104.088) \, / \, 8 \qquad (8)$$
$$= 100.000$$

This procedure works for general securities in the setting of equation (6). In fact, letting

$$p(\omega) = \prod_{i=0}^{n-1} p_i(j_i \rightarrow j_{i+1})$$

denote the probability of observing the path $\omega = (j_1, ...j_n)$, (where $j_0 = 1$ — today's state) we have in general that

$$V_0(1) = \sum_{\omega \in \Omega} PV(\omega)p(\omega) = \sum_{\omega \in \Omega} \left[\sum_{i=1}^{n} CF_i(j_i)d_i(\omega) \right] p(\omega) \qquad (9)$$

where

$$d_i(\omega) = \prod_{k=0}^{i-1} \frac{1}{1 + r_{kj_k}}$$

is the path-dependent discount factor that discounts a period i cash flow to today. (Equation (9) can be proved by induction on the length of the lattice and partitioning Ω on the value of j_1.)

We refer to equation (9) as the Monte Carlo approach. This is somewhat of a misnomer since equation (9) samples *every* path ω through the lattice and calculates the average of $PV(\omega)$ weighted by the probability of observing each path ω. In practice, the scale of the problem will be much larger and there will be too many paths through the lattice to perform an exhaustive sampling. Usually, therefore, Monte Carlo simulation involves *estimating* $V_0(1)$ by randomly sampling paths through the lattice in a manner such that the probability of selecting any particular path ω is precisely $p(\omega)$. In general (and depending on the variance of $PV(\omega)$ across paths), accurate estimates require a large number of sample paths making the method computationally inefficient.

INDEXED AMORTIZING NOTES

Presently we apply these two approaches to the IAN — our first example of a path-dependent security. The stochastic factor is the one year risk-free rate, which follows the stochastic process in the previous example (Exhibit 1). Recall that this means 6% is a market yield for risk-free bonds maturing in 1, 2, 3, and 4 years. The security is a 4-year IAN paying interest annually at a fixed rate of 6% per year. Regardless of what happens to interest rates, there is no principal payment the first year (the "lock-out" period). In years two and three, the amount of principal paid depends on the level of the 1-year rate via the "amortization schedule": if the 1-year rate is below 5%, 75% of the remaining balance is repaid; if the rate is between 5% and 6%, 50% of the balance is repaid; if the rate exceeds 6%, there is no principal payment. If a principal payment made in accordance with this formula brings the outstanding balance below 20% of the amount originally issued (which we take to be 100.0), the entire bond is retired immediately (the "clean-up" provision). At maturity in year 4 any remaining principal is amortized. Instruments with these qualitative features are quite common, both as stand-alone notes and, more frequently, as the fixed-pay side of interest rate swaps. We observe that the amortization schedule accelerates principal payment in low rate environments and thus behaves like a partial par call. We expect, therefore, that this note will be valued below 100.0 since a note with the same coupon but no principal acceleration is valued at 100.0.

Valuation Via Monte Carlo

First we value the IAN via Monte Carlo, where it is again feasible to sample every path and calculate exactly the expected value of $PV(\omega)$. Again, we describe paths by a sequence of + or − signs, so, for example $\omega = (----)$ corresponds to the following progression of the 1-year yield:

year 1		year 2		year 3		year 4
6.000%	→	5.113%	→	4.363%	→	3.728%	→	3.189%

producing the following sequence of principal payments:

year 1	year 2	year 3	year 4
0.0	75.0	25.0	0.0

This particular path illustrates the lock-out period (year 1: there is no amortization even though 5.113 < 6.0), the amortization schedule (year 2: the payment is 75.0 because 4.363 < 5.0), and the clean-up provision (year 3: the payment *would be*

0.75 × 25.0 but this would leave only 6.25 outstanding which is less than the clean-up provision). When interest payments on the outstanding principal are added, the following sequence of cash flow results:

year 1	year 2	year 3	year 4
6.0	81.0	26.5	0.0

The resulting *PV* is calculated as

$$PV(----) = 26.5/1.04363/1.05113/1.06$$
$$+ 81.0/1.05113/1.06$$
$$+ 6.0/1.06$$
$$= 101.148$$

Repeating this exercise for each of the 16 paths through the lattice yields the table of cash flow and *PV* shown in Exhibit 3. Since each path through this lattice has equal probability, we may calculate the expected value of $PV(\omega)$ by simply averaging the final column in this table. This yields 99.311. Any recursive procedure, of course, must agree with this calculation of value.

The path dependence of the IAN can be observed in this table. For example, consider the paths (+ + − −), (+ − + −), (− + − +), and (− − + +). In each case, the state in year 4 corresponds to a 1-year rate of 5.811%, i.e., each of these paths ends up in state ⟨5.811⟩. However, the year 4 cash flow corresponding to these paths is 106.0, 53.0, 26.5, and 0.0, respectively. Hence the cash flow in year 4 cannot be deduced from the state in year 4 — it is influenced also by how one gets to that state.

Exhibit 3: Path-by-Path Analysis of the IAN

ω	Year 1	Year 2	Year 3	Year 4	$PV(\omega)$
(+ + + +)	6.000	6.000	6.000	106.000	95.237
(+ + + −)	6.000	6.000	6.000	106.000	95.237
(+ + − +)	6.000	6.000	6.000	106.000	97.004
(+ + − −)	6.000	6.000	6.000	106.000	97.004
(+ − + +)	6.000	56.000	3.000	53.000	98.941
(+ − + −)	6.000	56.000	3.000	53.000	98.941
(+ − − +)	6.000	56.000	28.000	26.500	99.442
(+ − − −)	6.000	56.000	28.000	26.500	99.442
(− + + +)	6.000	56.000	3.000	53.000	100.528
(− + + −)	6.000	56.000	3.000	53.000	100.528
(− + − +)	6.000	56.000	28.000	26.500	101.038
(− + − −)	6.000	56.000	28.000	26.500	101.038
(− − + +)	6.000	81.000	26.500	0.000	101.148
(− − + −)	6.000	81.000	26.500	0.000	101.148
(− − − +)	6.000	81.000	26.500	0.000	101.148
(− − − −)	6.000	81.000	26.500	0.000	101.148

Recursive Valuation

To value the IAN recursively, we partition the interest rate states (like $\langle 5.811 \rangle$) by further specifying how much of the IAN is outstanding *before* the principal payment of that year. The state $\langle 5.811 \rangle$, for example, is partitioned into $\langle 5.811, 100 \rangle$, $\langle 5.811, 50 \rangle$, $\langle 5.811, 25 \rangle$, and $\langle 5.811, 0 \rangle$. This additional variable, whose values partition the state as specified by the value of the stochastic variable, is referred to as a non-stochastic state variable and its range of attainable values is referred to as the state space. (It is easy in this example to verify that the state space is {0, 25, 50, 100}, i.e., at all times one of these amounts must be outstanding. More about this later.) Notice that some states, $\langle 3.189, 100 \rangle$ for example, are impossible to reach. This phenomenon will not make our calculations incorrect, it just means that we will do some unnecessary calculations.

Once the time t 1-year rate and amount outstanding (prior to current-period amortization) are *both* specified as, say, $\langle r, P \rangle$, the time t cash flow can easily be calculated: the interest component is just $0.06P$; the principal component is deduced from the value of P, the lock-out period, the amortization table, and the clean-up provision by the formula

$$\text{time } t \text{ principal payment } = \begin{cases} 0 & \text{if } t = 1 \\ 0.75P & \text{if } t = 2 \text{ or } 3,\ r < 5\%,\ \text{and } 0.25P > 20 \\ 0.5P & \text{if } t = 2 \text{ or } 3,\ 5\% \le r < 6\%,\ \text{and } 0.5P > 20 \\ 0 & \text{if } t = 2 \text{ or } 3,\ \text{and } r \ge 6\% \\ P & \text{otherwise} \end{cases}$$

and the state-dependent cash flow is the sum of interest and principal. We begin our recursive calculations at the end of the lattice, just as we do when there is no path dependence. Exhibit 4 shows for periods 1 through 4 the cash flow $CF_i(\langle r, P \rangle)$ calculated as just described (and shown as principal and interest combined) as well as the value of subsequent cash flow $V_i(\langle r, P \rangle)$ (shown just below the cash flow) for each combination of r and P.

We reiterate that $V_4(\langle r, P \rangle)=0$ for all r and P since there is no cash flow after year 4. Since the IAN matures in period 4, the cash flow is simply the sum of the amount outstanding and interest on that amount — a calculation that is independent of the 1-year rate at period 4. For example, the period 4 cash flow corresponding to state $\langle 4.305,25 \rangle$ is 25.0+1.5=26.5.

The situation is more complicated in period 3. Here the amortization schedule and the amount outstanding interact to determine the cash flow. Consider, for example, the calculations corresponding to state $\langle 5.032,50 \rangle$. The interest payment of 3 is calculated as 0.06×50.0. Also, since $5.0 \le 5.032 < 6.0$, 50% of the outstanding amount is prepaid in period 3. This principal payment of 25.0 leaves 25.0 still outstanding — an amount which exceeds the clean-up provision. The state $\langle 5.032,50 \rangle$ cash flow is therefore 25.0+3.0=28.0. Next we calculate $V_3(\langle 5.032,50 \rangle)$. From a rate of 5.032% in year 3, the stochastic interest rate process moves to either 4.305% or 5.811% in year 4 — each possibility with probability ½ (see Exhibit 1).

Since 50.0 of principal was outstanding (before the period 3 payment) and 25.0 is paid off in period 3, the amount outstanding changes to 25.0. Thus, from state $\langle 5.032, 50 \rangle$ in period 3, one moves to either $\langle 4.305, 25 \rangle$ or $\langle 5.811, 25 \rangle$ in year 4 with each possibility having probability ½. We therefore have, using equation (6) and the period 4 results in Exhibit 4,

$$V_3(\langle 5.032, 50 \rangle) = \frac{1}{1.05032}[0.5(26.5 + 0.0) + 0.5(26.5 + 0.0)] = 25.230$$

Exhibit 4: $CF_i(\cdot)$ and $V_i(\cdot)$ for the IAN

| | | Amount Outstanding | | | |
		0	25	50	100
Period 1	6.902%	0.000	1.500	3.000	6.000
		0.000	24.381	48.732	97.515
	5.113	0.000	1.500	3.000	6.000
		0.000	25.211	50.393	101.024
Period 2	7.950	0.000	1.500	3.000	6.000
		0.000	24.127	48.253	96.506
	5.889	0.000	26.500	28.000	56.000
		0.000	0.000	24.939	49.986
	4.363	0.000	26.500	53.000	81.000
		0.000	0.000	0.000	25.392
Period 3	9.169	0.000	1.500	3.000	6.000
		0.000	24.274	48.549	97.097
	6.792	0.000	1.500	3.000	6.000
		0.000	24.815	49.629	99.258
	5.032	0.000	26.500	28.000	56.000
		0.000	0.000	25.230	50.461
	3.728	0.000	26.500	53.000	81.000
		0.000	0.000	0.000	25.548
Period 4	10.588	0.000	26.500	53.000	106.000
		0.000	0.000	0.000	0.000
	7.844	0.000	26.500	53.000	106.000
		0.000	0.000	0.000	0.000
	5.811	0.000	26.500	53.000	106.000
		0.000	0.000	0.000	0.000
	4.305	0.000	26.500	53.000	106.000
		0.000	0.000	0.000	0.000
	3.189	0.000	26.500	53.000	106.000
		0.000	0.000	0.000	0.000

Compare this with the analogous calculations for state $\langle 5.032,25 \rangle$ in period 3. The interest cash flow is $0.06 \times 25.0 = 1.5$. The principal payment specified by the amortization schedule is again 50% of the amount outstanding which results in a payment of $12.5 = 0.5 \times 25.0$. This would leave only 12.5 remaining outstanding, however, so the clean-up provision requires that the entire amount of 25.0 be retired leaving nothing outstanding. Thus, from state $\langle 5.032,25 \rangle$ in period 3, one moves to either $\langle 4.305,0 \rangle$ or $\langle 5.811,0 \rangle$ in period 4, with probability ½. Hence

$$V_3(\langle 5.032, 25 \rangle) = \frac{1}{1.05032}[0.5(0.0 + 0.0) + 0.5(0.0 + 0.0)] = 0.0$$

The calculations in period 2 are analogous. For example, in state $\langle 5.889,100 \rangle$, the principal payment is 50.0 generating a cash flow of $6.0+50.0=56.0$ and leaving 50.0 remaining outstanding. Hence one moves from state $\langle 5.889,100 \rangle$ in period 2 to either $\langle 5.032,50 \rangle$ or $\langle 6.792,50 \rangle$ in period 3, each with equal likelihood. Thus

$$V_2(\langle 5.889, 100 \rangle) = \frac{1}{1.05889}[0.5(28.0 + 25.230) + 0.5(3.0 + 49.629)]$$

$$= 49.986$$

Similarly, in period 1, one moves from state $\langle 5.113,100 \rangle$ to either $\langle 4.363,100 \rangle$ or $\langle 5.889,100 \rangle$ in period 2, each with equal likelihood. Thus, $CF_1(\langle 5.113,100 \rangle) = 0.06 \times 100.0$ (plus 0 principal) and

$$V_1(\langle 5.113, 100 \rangle) = \frac{1}{1.05113}[0.5(81.0 + 25.392) + 0.5(56.0 + 49.986)]$$

$$= 101.024$$

Finally, at time 0 (not shown in Exhibit 4), there is only today's state $\langle 6.000, 100 \rangle$ to calculate. From this state we move to either $\langle 5.113,100 \rangle$ or $\langle 6.902,100 \rangle$, each with probability ½. We therefore have

$$V_0(1) = V_0(\langle 6.000, 100 \rangle) = \frac{1}{1.06}[0.5(6.0 + 101.024) + 0.5(6.0 + 97.515)]$$

$$= 99.311$$

This agrees, as required, with the result obtained via the Monte Carlo analysis.

Selecting the Necessary State Space

As we previously observed, only the amounts in the list $\{0,25,50,100\}$ can be outstanding at any point in time. This is because the IAN starts with 100.0 outstanding and this list is closed under the rules of principal amortization (the amortization schedule and the clean-up provision). (For example, if we amortize 50% of 50.0 we get 25.0 outstanding, another number in the list.) In general, it may not be so easy to construct an exhaustive list of possible states or, commonly, the list of possible states may be very large. A very effective numerical procedure is to partition the range of the state space (in this case, the range is from 0 to 100 outstanding) into a manageable number of "buckets," for example: 0, 20-30, 30-40,..., 90-100. Sometimes a surprisingly small number of buckets can lead to a very good approximation of the precise answer. We illustrate this technique with the periodic cap in the next section.

Notice also that not all the states in each period can be reached. For example, in periods 1 and 2 only those states with 100.0 outstanding are reached. This is because the lock-out provision prevents any amortization until year 2. Thus, even in year 2, the amount outstanding prior to that year's amortization must be 100.0. In Exhibit 4 we have highlighted the region of each period's state space that is actually reachable.

From the standpoint of computational efficiency, it may be better to first pass *forward* through the lattice to determine which states are actually reachable. Then, during the recursive process described above, it is only necessary to calculate the CF_i and V_i values for those states that are flagged as reachable in the first pass. In our IAN example, this would result in substantial savings. On the other hand, in some situations, this forward pass may take more time than it saves. It may be better to compromise and avoid only some of the unused state space by (non-time-consuming) ad hoc reasoning. In the case of the IAN, for example, the unnecessary states in periods 1 and 2 could be avoided simply by recognizing the effects of the lock-out provision. The best computational strategy will certainly depend on the application.

PERIODIC CAPS

In this final section we subject a floating-rate note with an embedded periodic cap to similar analyses. We illustrate with this application both the bucketing and forward pass numerical procedures described above. Specifically, consider a 4-year FRN that, for ease of exposition, pays interest annually. Its initial rate of interest is 6% — today's 1-year risk-free rate. Each year, the note's rate of interest resets to the new 1-year risk-free rate subject to the constraint that the rate is not permitted to increase (a very strong periodic cap!). In year 4, the note makes a final interest rate payment (of at most 6% due to the periodic cap) and returns the original principal (which we again take to be 100.0). We study this instrument in the same yield environment as before: a flat 6% term structure with a 15% volatility. Exhibit 1 again represents the underlying interest rate process.

Valuation via Monte Carlo

Consider again the interest rate path $\omega = (----)$ through the lattice in Exhibit 1:

	year 1		year 2		year 3		year 4
6.000%	$\rightarrow$	5.113%	$\rightarrow$	4.363%	$\rightarrow$	3.728%	$\rightarrow$ 3.189%

Since the 1-year yield decreases steadily along this path, the periodic cap has no impact. The capped FRN behaves just as an uncapped FRN producing the following sequence of cash flow:

year 1	year 2	year 3	year 4
6.000	5.113	4.363	103.728

resulting in the PV calculation:

$$PV(----) = 103.728/1.03728/1.04363/1.05113/1.06$$
$$+ 4.363/1.04363/1.05113/1.06$$
$$+ 5.113/1.05113/1.06$$
$$+ 6.0/1.06$$
$$= 100.000$$

It is not surprising that for this choice of ω we have a path-dependent present value of exactly 100.000 since the security is always paying a rate of interest equal to the discount rate.

In the scenario corresponding to $\omega = (+ + + +)$, which unfolds as follows:

year 1	year 2	year 3	year 4
6.000% →	6.902% →	7.950% →	9.169% →	10.588%

the situation is very different. In each year, the periodic cap is binding, preventing the interest rate from increasing. The resulting sequence of cash flow is therefore:

year 1	year 2	year 3	year 4
6.000	6.000	6.000	106.000

which produces the result $PV(\omega) = 95.237$.

Exhibit 5 shows the same analysis for all 16 paths through the lattice. Since the paths are all equally likely, the arithmetic average of the path-dependent present values yields the value of the capped FRN. This number is 98.343. Noting that the value of the uncapped FRN is 100.000 (this follows since, in every path, the uncapped FRN is always paying an interest rate equal to the discount rate), we deduce that the value of the periodic cap (to the issuer) is $100.000 - 98.343 = 1.657$. As with the IAN, this is an exact calculation representing an exhaustive sampling of the 16 paths through the lattice. In practice, of course, an exhaustive sampling would be impossible and valuing a periodic cap with this approach would require true Monte Carlo path sampling.

Exhibit 5 reveals the path-dependent nature of the capped FRN. In particular, the six paths that end in year 4 at the interest rate state $\langle 5.881 \rangle$ (i.e., paths with two +'s and two −'s) produce five different cash flow amounts corresponding to that state. Notice also that the periodic cap behaves very differently from a straight cap at 6% (see, for example, the path $\omega = (- + - +)$).

Exhibit 5: Path-by-Path Analysis of the Capped FRN

ω	Year 1	Year 2	Year 3	Year 4	$PV(\omega)$
$(+ + + +)$	6.000	6.000	6.000	106.000	95.237
$(+ + + -)$	6.000	6.000	6.000	106.000	95.237
$(+ + - +)$	6.000	6.000	6.000	106.000	97.004
$(+ + - -)$	6.000	6.000	6.000	106.000	97.004
$(+ - + +)$	6.000	6.000	5.889	105.889	98.499
$(+ - + -)$	6.000	6.000	5.889	105.889	98.499
$(+ - - +)$	6.000	6.000	5.889	105.032	99.204
$(+ - - -)$	6.000	6.000	5.889	105.032	99.204
$(- + + +)$	6.000	5.113	5.113	105.113	98.010
$(- + + -)$	6.000	5.113	5.113	105.113	98.010
$(- + - +)$	6.000	5.113	5.113	105.032	99.342
$(- + - -)$	6.000	5.113	5.113	105.032	99.342
$(- - + +)$	6.000	5.113	4.363	104.363	99.452
$(- - + -)$	6.000	5.113	4.363	104.363	99.452
$(- - - +)$	6.000	5.113	4.363	103.728	100.000
$(- - - -)$	6.000	5.113	4.363	103.728	100.000

Recursive Valuation

Finally, we use a recursive procedure to value the capped FRN and hence the peri-odic cap itself. In this example, the non-stochastic state variable that we couple with the stochastic process governing the 1-year risk-free rate is simply the current inter-est rate that the capped FRN is paying, a number which we call C. At any period a state is denoted by $\langle r, C \rangle$, where C takes on values in

$$C = \{3.728, 4.363, 5.032, 5.113, 5.889, 6.000\}$$

and r is the state-dependent 1-year risk-free rate. We remark that only in year 4 are all six possibilities for C attainable. In our simple example, C is quickly obtained from a glance at Exhibit 5. As previously mentioned, in general it may be impracti-cal to explicitly calculate the state space or its size may render the calculations intractable. A numerical shortcut is necessary.

Bucketing and the Forward Pass We illustrate the bucketing procedure described above by crudely *assuming* that C takes on one of the four values in

$$\hat{C} = \{3.000, 4.000, 5.000, 6.000\}$$

a numerical simplification that will result in obtaining only an approximate solu-tion. (We think of these numbers as buckets into which intermediate values are placed.) In period 4, for example, r assumes one of five possible values each of which is partitioned by the four states of C, yielding 20 states of the world.

Exhibit 6 shows the forward pass analysis that is used to flag the subset of states in each period that are actually reachable. The period 0 analysis is straightforward. Referring to today's state simply as $\langle 6.000 \rangle$ (today's value of r), the value of r moves from 6.000 to either 5.113 or 6.902 (refer again to Exhibit 1) and in either case the period 1 value of C will be 6.000 (the capped FRN's initial interest rate). Hence only the states $\langle 5.113, 6.000 \rangle$ and $\langle 6.902, 6.000 \rangle$ are reachable in period 1. The period 1 analysis illustrates a ramification of the bucketing approximation. From state $\langle 5.113, 6.000 \rangle$ the value of r moves to either 4.363 or 5.889. The value of C, however, should change to 5.113 (because the FRN is permitted to reset downward) which is a number not present in $\hat{C}$. Numerically, we will interpolate between what happens when $C=5.000$ and $C=6.000$ in period 2. Therefore, to calculate values in state $\langle 5.113, 6.000 \rangle$ in period 1 we must have already calculated values in states $\langle 4.363, 5.000 \rangle$, $\langle 4.363, 6.000 \rangle$, $\langle 5.889, 5.000 \rangle$, and $\langle 5.889, 6.000 \rangle$ in period 2. We therefore flag these four states as reachable. From state $\langle 6.902, 6.000 \rangle$ in period 1, in contrast, the value of C is not permitted to reset upward to 6.902 and only states $\langle 5.889, 6.000 \rangle$ and $\langle 7.950, 6.000 \rangle$ are reachable in period 2. We collect the (five) states in period 2 that it is possible to reach from the reachable states in period 1 and repeat the analysis at each of these states. Moving forward period-by-period confirms that we need only calculate values for the portion of the state space in Exhibit 7 where numbers are displayed.

The Recursive Valuation Pass Finally, we move backward through the lattice calculating the relevant values of $CF_i(\cdot)$ and $V_i(\cdot)$ (see Exhibit 7 — calculations start at the bottom).

In period 4 (at maturity), $V_4(\cdot)=0$ as usual. The cash flow at maturity is just 100.000 (the return of principal) plus C (the current interest rate that the FRN is paying). This produces the period 4 results. For example: $CF_4(\langle 7.844, 5.000 \rangle) = 100.0 + 5.0 = 105.0$. In periods 1 through 3, $CF_i(\langle r, C \rangle)=C$ since the FRN repays principal only at maturity.

We verify three calculations of $V_i(\cdot)$. First, from state $\langle 5.032, 5.000 \rangle$ in period 3, the value of r moves to either 4.305 or 5.811 with equal likelihood. The value of C does not change in this case since $5.032 > 5.000$. So from state $\langle 5.032, 5.000 \rangle$ in period 3, we branch to either $\langle 4.305, 5.000 \rangle$ or $\langle 5.811, 5.000 \rangle$ in period 4 with equal likelihood and we have

$$V_3(\langle 5.032, 5.000 \rangle) = \frac{1}{1.05032}[0.5\,(CF_4(\langle 4.305, 5.000 \rangle) + V_4(\langle 4.305, 5.000 \rangle))$$

$$+ 0.5(CF_4(\langle 5.881, 5.000 \rangle) + V_4(\langle 5.881, 5.000 \rangle))]$$

$$= \frac{1}{1.05032}[0.5(105.000 + 0.0) + 0.5(105.000 + 0.0)]$$

$$= 99.970$$

Exhibit 6: State Transitions for the Capped FRN

Period	From	To
Today	$\langle 6.000\rangle$	$\langle 5.113,\ 6.000\rangle$, $\langle 6.902,\ 6.000\rangle$
1	$\langle 5.113,\ 6.000\rangle$	$\langle 4.363,\ 5.000\rangle$, $\langle 4.363,\ 6.000\rangle$, $\langle 5.889,\ 5.000\rangle$, $\langle 5.889,\ 6.000\rangle$
	$\langle 6.902,\ 6.000\rangle$	$\langle 5.889,\ 6.000\rangle$, $\langle 7.950,\ 6.000\rangle$
2	$\langle 4.363,\ 5.000\rangle$	$\langle 3.728,\ 4.000\rangle$, $\langle 3.728,\ 5.000\rangle$, $\langle 5.032,\ 4.000\rangle$, $\langle 5.032,\ 5.000\rangle$
	$\langle 4.363,\ 6.000\rangle$	$\langle 3.728,\ 4.000\rangle$, $\langle 3.728,\ 5.000\rangle$, $\langle 5.032,\ 4.000\rangle$, $\langle 5.032,\ 5.000\rangle$
	$\langle 5.889,\ 5.000\rangle$	$\langle 5.032,\ 5.000\rangle$, $\langle 6.792,\ 5.000\rangle$
	$\langle 5.889,\ 6.000\rangle$	$\langle 5.032,\ 5.000\rangle$, $\langle 5.032,\ 6.000\rangle$, $\langle 6.792,\ 5.000\rangle$, $\langle 6.792,\ 6.000\rangle$
	$\langle 7.950,\ 6.000\rangle$	$\langle 6.792,\ 6.000\rangle$, $\langle 9.169,\ 6.000\rangle$
3	$\langle 3.728,\ 4.000\rangle$	$\langle 3.189,\ 3.000\rangle$, $\langle 3.189,\ 4.000\rangle$, $\langle 4.305,\ 3.000\rangle$, $\langle 4.305,\ 4.000\rangle$
	$\langle 3.728,\ 5.000\rangle$	$\langle 3.189,\ 3.000\rangle$, $\langle 3.189,\ 4.000\rangle$, $\langle 4.305,\ 3.000\rangle$, $\langle 4.305,\ 4.000\rangle$
	$\langle 5.032,\ 4.000\rangle$	$\langle 4.305,\ 4.000\rangle$, $\langle 5.811,\ 4.000\rangle$
	$\langle 5.032,\ 5.000\rangle$	$\langle 4.305,\ 5.000\rangle$, $\langle 5.811,\ 5.000\rangle$
	$\langle 5.032,\ 6.000\rangle$	$\langle 4.305,\ 5.000\rangle$, $\langle 4.305,\ 6.000\rangle$, $\langle 5.811,\ 5.000\rangle$, $\langle 5.811,\ 6.000\rangle$
	$\langle 6.792,\ 5.000\rangle$	$\langle 5.811,\ 5.000\rangle$, $\langle 7.844,\ 5.000\rangle$
	$\langle 6.792,\ 6.000\rangle$	$\langle 5.811,\ 6.000\rangle$, $\langle 7.844,\ 6.000\rangle$
	$\langle 9.169,\ 6.000\rangle$	$\langle 7.844,\ 6.000\rangle$, $\langle 10.588,\ 6.000\rangle$

Next, from state $\langle 4.363, 5.000\rangle$ in period 2, the value of r moves to either 3.728 or 5.032, each with probability ½. The value of C should change to 4.363 since $4.363 < 5.000$, but this number is not in $\hat{C}$. If it *were*, we would calculate

$$V_2(\langle 4.363, 5.000\rangle) = \frac{1}{1.04363}[0.5\,(CF_3(\langle 3.728, 4.363\rangle) + V_3(\langle 3.728, 4.363\rangle)$$

$$+ 0.5(CF_3(\langle 5.032, 4.363\rangle) + V_3(\langle 5.032, 4.363\rangle))\,]\ (10)$$

However, we have calculated neither $V_3(\langle 3.728, 4.363\rangle)$ nor $V_3(\langle 5.032, 4.363\rangle)$ nor the corresponding values for $CF_3(\langle\cdot,\ 4.363\rangle)$, so we estimate them by interpolating between values that we have calculated. In particular,

$$V_3(\langle 3.728, 4.363\rangle) \approx 0.637 V_3(\langle 3.728, 4.000\rangle) + 0.363 V_3(\langle 3.728, 5.000\rangle)$$

$$= 100.000$$

Exhibit 7: $CF_i(\cdot)$ and $V_i(\cdot)$ for the Capped FRN

| | | Current Coupon Rate | | | |
		3.000	4.000	5.000	6.000
Period 1	6.902%				6.000 / 97.334
	5.113				6.000 / 99.139
Period 2	7.950				6.000 / 96.505
	5.889			5.000 / 98.354	6.000 / 99.599
	4.363			5.000 / 99.695	6.000 / 99.695
Period 3	9.169				6.000 / 97.097
	6.792			5.000 / 98.322	6.000 / 99.258
	5.032		4.000 / 99.017	5.000 / 99.970	6.000 / 100.000
	3.728		4.000 / 100.000	5.000 / 100.000	
Period 4	10.588				106.000 / 0.000
	7.844			105.000 / 0.000	106.000 / 0.000
	5.811		104.000 / 0.000	105.000 / 0.000	106.000 / 0.000
	4.305	103.000 / 0.000	104.000 / 0.000	105.000 / 0.000	106.000 / 0.000
	3.189	103.000 / 0.000	104.000 / 0.000		

and

$$V_3(\langle 5.032, 4.363 \rangle) \approx 0.637\, V_3(\langle 5.032, 4.000 \rangle) + 0.363\, V_3(\langle 5.032, 5.000 \rangle)$$

$$= 99.363$$

while both interpolated values for $CF_3(\langle \cdot, 4.363 \rangle)$ are, not surprisingly, 4.363. Setting these estimates into equation (10) gives $V_2(\langle 4.363, 5.000 \rangle) = 99.695$.

Finally, today's value of the capped FRN is calculated from the period 1 values by

$$V_0(\langle 6.000 \rangle) = \frac{1}{1.06}[0.5(6.0 + 99.139) + 0.5(6.0 + 97.334)] = 98.336$$

which puts the value of the periodic cap at $100.000 - 98.336 = 1.664$. As predicted, this is not in precise agreement with the exhaustive path-by-path analysis that produced the value of 98.343 for the capped FRN and 1.657 for the periodic cap. This is because we bucketed the state space of C into the four quantities in $\hat{C}$. By increasing the number of states (using more, and smaller, buckets), the degree of error is reduced. For example, when we take

$$\hat{C} = \{3.000, 3.500, 4.000, 4.500, 5.000, 5.500, 6.000\}$$

the recursive process yields 98.341 (1.659 for the periodic cap).

CONCLUSION

We have worked through two simple numerical examples that illustrate how non-stochastic state variables may be coupled with a stochastic interest rate process to value path-dependent fixed-income securities using recursive techniques. In our 4-period examples, of course, this technique offers little, if any, improvement over exhaustive path sampling. In more realistic settings, however, recursion is generally much more efficient than Monte Carlo path sampling.

Path dependence occurs in many forms and with varying degrees of complexity. Sometimes it is necessary to couple more than one state variable to the stochastic process. Consider, for example, a hybrid of the IAN and capped FRN. Such a note would pay down principal in accordance with a rate sensitive amortization schedule, while paying a rate of interest that resets periodically but that is permitted to increase only a limited amount with each reset. Generalizing the notation of our previous sections, a state would be described as $\langle r, P, C \rangle$ where r is the stochastic risk-free rate, P is the amount of the note currently outstanding, and C is its current coupon rate.

Chapter 5

Problems Encountered in Valuing Interest Rate Derivatives

Yiannos A. Pierides, Ph.D.
Assistant Professor of FInance
Department of Public and Business Administration
University of Cyprus

INTRODUCTION

In this chapter we describe the procedure involved in valuing any interest rate derivative. We then apply this valuation procedure to two interest rate derivatives, one plain vanilla and the other exotic, in order to explain some of the practical problems involved.

STATE OF THE ART VALUATION OF INTEREST RATE DERIVATIVES

The pricing of any interest rate derivative involves the following three stage procedure:

> *Stage 1:* Adopt an assumption about the evolution (or probability distribution) of the short-term interest rate.
>
> *Stage 2:* Specify the payoff to the derivative at its maturity.
>
> *Stage 3:* Calculate the price of the derivative as its discounted expected payoff.

Below we describe the three stages.

Stage 1: Adopt an Assumption about the Evolution of the Short-Term Interest Rate

The first stage is perhaps the most crucial one in the whole procedure. Several researchers have proposed different assumptions. The pioneering ones are Vasicek,[1] Cox, Ingersoll, and Ross[2] (henceforth CIR), and Hull and White[3] (henceforth HW). The interest rate stochastic process proposed by each researcher is shown below:

Model	Stochastic Process
Vasicek	$dr(t) = (a + br(t))dt + \sigma dW(t)$
CIR	$dr(\mathrm{t}) = \kappa(\theta - r(t))dt + \sigma(r(t))^{0.5}\, dW(t)$
HW	$dr(\mathrm{t}) = (\theta(t) + a(t)(b - r(t)))dt + \sigma(t)\, dW(t)$

The Vasicek model assumes that the interest rate follows an Ornstein-Uhlenbeck process: a, b and σ are the parametetrs of the process and $W(t)$ is a standard Brownian motion under a probability measure P. This is a Gaussian process which leads to relatively simple closed form solutions for the price of Treasury bonds and for the price of plain vanilla options on such bonds. Its main drawbacks are (1) it implies that the interest rate may become negative and (2) it implies that the volatility of the interest rate is independent of the level of the interest rate.

CIR proposed a stochastic process for the interest rate that does not suffer from the drawbacks of the Vasicek process. As in the case of the Vasicek process κ, θ, and σ are the parametetrs of the process and $W(t)$ is a standard Brownian motion under a probability measure P. This process became known as the *square root process* because it implies that the volatility of the interest rate is not independent of the interest rate; instead it is proportional to the square root of the interest rate. Also, the interest rate cannot become negative. CIR showed that this process leads to closed form solutions for the price of Treasury bonds and for the price of plain vanilla options on such bonds

HW point out that a major drawback of both the Vasicek model and the CIR model is that they are not consistent with any initial term structure of interest rates and interest rate volatilities that are observed in the market. In other words, these models do not imply a perfect fit to the initial term structure of interest rates and interest rate volatilities that are observed in the market.

HW proposed an extension to the Vasicek process that provides a perfect fit to the initial term structure of interest rates and interest rate volatilities that are observed in the market. The process became known as the *extended Vasicek* or *Hull and White (HW) process*. In this process $a(t)$, $\theta(t)$, b and $\sigma(t)$ are the parametetrs of the process and $W(t)$ is a standard Brownian motion under a probability

[1] Oldrich Vasicek, "An Equilibrium Characterization of the Term Structure," *Journal of Financial Economics* Vol. 5 (1977), pp. 177-188.

[2] John Cox, Jonathan Ingersoll, and Stephen Ross, "A Theory of the Term Structure of Interest Rates," *Econometrica* Vol. 53, No. 2 (1985), pp 385-407.

[3] John Hull and Alan White, "Pricing Interest Rate Derivatives," *Review of Financial Studies* Vol. 3, No. 4 (1990), pp. 573-592.

measure P. Note that unlike the Vasicek and CIR processes, three of the four parameters of this process are time dependent and this enables one to estimate these parameters in a way that provides a perfect fit to the initial term structure of interest rates and interest rate volatilities that are observed in the market. Unfortunately, the HW process suffers from the same drawback as the Vasicek process, namely that the interest rate can become negative. HW showed that this process leads to closed form solutions for the price of Treasury bonds and for the price of plain vanilla options on such bonds.

Stage 2: Specify the Payoff to the Interest Rate Derivative

Consider a call option on the interest rate with exercise price y and maturity T. The payoff at maturity will be MAX $(r(T) - y, 0)$. This derivative is an example of a non-path dependent derivative. The reason is that the payoff at maturity depends only on the interest rate at maturity and not on the path that the interest rate followed to reach its terminal value at maturity.

Similarly, consider a call option on the price of a zero-coupon Treasury bond (of maturity TB) with exercise price X and maturity T. The payoff at maturity will be MAX $(P(T, TB) - X, 0)$, where $P(T, TB)$ is the bond price at T. This qualifies as an interest rate derivative because the bond price depends on the interest rate. Also, it is a non-path dependent derivative because the payoff at maturity depends only on the interest rate at maturity (which in turn determines the bond price at maturity) and not on the path that the interest rate followed during the option's life.

Let us now give an example of a path dependent derivative. A European lookback put option on a zero-coupon Treasury bond has all the features of a regular European put except that the exercise price equals the maximum bond price during the option's life. In other words, the owner of this lookback option is entitled to sell at the option's maturity the underlying Treasury bond for a price equal to the maximum price at which this bond traded during the option's life. It follows that the payoff to this option at its maturity will be equal to the difference between the maximum bond price during the option's life and the bond price at maturity .

This lookback put is path dependent because the payoff at maturity depends not only on the bond price at maturity (as in the case of a regular put) but also on the path that the bond price followed during the option's life. The reason is that it is this path of bond prices that determines the maximum bond price during the option's life. Of course, the path of bond prices will depend on the path of interest rates during the option's life.

Such a derivative is traded (over the counter) since there is substantial demand for it. The reason is that it enables investors to achieve perfect market timing (i.e., sell at the highest price). This derivative is called "lookback" because at its maturity, its payoff can only be determined by "looking back in time" to determine the maximum bond price during the option's life.

Stage 3: Calculate the Derivative Price as the Discounted Expectation of its Payoff

Harrison and Kreps[4] and Huang[5] show that any interest rate derivative can be priced using a no-arbitrage methodology, given an appropriate assumption about the evolution of the interest rate. Using this methodology, the correct derivative price is equal to the discounted expectation of its payoff under a particular probability measure. This will be analysed further in the sections that follow.

Depending on the derivative we are pricing, it may or may not be possible to derive a closed form formula for its price. To calculate a price we must calculate a discounted expected value of the payoff to the derivative at its maturity. In general, the more complicated this payoff is the less likely it is that we can get a closed form formula. For example, in the case of path dependent derivatives it is usually impossible to get a closed form formula. In such cases, we calculate the discounted expected value of the payoff using Monte Carlo simulation of the interest rate stochastic process.

VALUATION OF A EUROPEAN CALL OPTION ON A ZERO-COUPON TREASURY BOND

We will now apply the three stage methodology to the valuation of two interest rate derivatives. One derivative is a European call option on the price of a zero-coupon Treasury bond and the other a European lookback put option on a zero coupon Treasury bond. We will price both derivatives using the CIR and HW stochastic processes for the interest rate in Stage 1. The Vasicek process is not used because it is a special case of the HW process.

Applying the CIR Model

Recall that CIR assume that the short-term interest rate $r(t)$ follows a square root process i.e.,

$$dr = k(\theta - r)dt + \sigma\sqrt{r}dw$$

k = intensity of mean reversion

θ = long-run mean of interest rate

σ = volatility of r

w = standard Brownian motion under a probability measure P.

Consider any interest rate derivative paying a random payoff $x(\tau)$ at time $\tau >$ 0. To avoid the existence of arbitrage opportunities, its (normalized) price can be cal-

---

[4] Michael Harrison and David Kreps, "Martingales and Arbitrage in Multiperiod Securities Markets," *Journal of Economic Theory*, 1979.

[5] Chi-Fu Huang, "The Term Structure of Interest Rates and the Pricing of Interest Rate Sensitive Securities," working paper, Sloan School, M.I.T., 1991.

culated as the conditional expectation of the (normalized) payoff under an equivalent martingale probability measure. In particular, let

$x(t)$ = price at t of security paying random payoff $x(\tau)$ at $\tau > t$

$B(t)$ = price process for the instantaneously riskless asset that is used as the numeraire i.e.,

$$B(t) = \exp\left(\int_0^t r(s)ds\right)$$

$w^*(t)$ = standard Brownian motion under a measure Q equivalent to P, where

$$w^*(t) = w(t) + \int_0^t \frac{\lambda}{\sigma}\sqrt{r(s)}ds \; ; \lambda \text{ is a scalar.}$$

Substituting for $w(t)$ in the interest rate process we get the risk-adjusted interest rate process

$$dr = (k\theta - (k + \lambda)r)dt + \sigma\sqrt{r}dw^* \tag{1}$$

Then, if E^* denotes expectation under the risk-adjusted interest rate process.

$$\frac{x(t)}{B(t)} = E^*\left[\frac{x(\tau)}{B(\tau)}\right] \tag{2}$$

Since a zero-coupon Treasury bond of maturity TB pays \$1.00 with certainty at TB, its price at t, denoted $P(t, TB)$, is given by

$$\frac{P(t, TB)}{B(t)} = E^*\left[\frac{1}{B(TB)}\right] \Rightarrow P(t, TB) = E^*\left[\exp\left(-\int_t^{TB} r(s)ds\right)\right] \tag{3}$$

CIR show that

$$P(t, TB) = A(t, TB) \exp(-r(t)G(t, TB)) \tag{4}$$

$$A(t, TB) = \left[\frac{2\gamma\exp\left[(b + \gamma)\dfrac{TB - t}{2}\right]}{(\gamma + b)(\exp(\gamma(TB - t)) - 1) + 2\gamma}\right]^{\frac{2c}{\sigma^2}} \tag{5}$$

$$G(t, TB) = \frac{2(\exp(\gamma(TB - t)) - 1)}{(\gamma + b)(\exp(\gamma(TB - t)) - 1) + 2\gamma} \tag{6}$$

$$b = k + \lambda \; ; c = k\theta; \gamma = \sqrt{b^2 + 2\sigma^2}$$

Consider now a European call option on a Treasury bond of maturity TB. The current time is t and the option has maturity T (with $TB > T > t$) and exercise price X. Let $C(t)$ be the option price at time t. Then, using equation (2),

$$\frac{C(t)}{B(t)} = E^*\left[\frac{MAX(P(T, TB) - X, 0)}{B(T)}\right] \tag{7}$$

CIR provide the following closed form formula for $C(t)$:

$$C(t) = P(t, TB)\chi^2\left(2r^*(\varphi + \psi + G(T, TB)), \frac{4c}{\sigma^2}, \frac{2\varphi^2 re^{\gamma(T-t)}}{(\varphi + \psi + G(T, TB))}\right)$$

$$- XP(t, T)\chi^2[2r^*(\varphi + \psi), 4c/\sigma^2, 2\varphi^2 re^{\gamma(T-t)}/(\varphi + \psi)] \tag{8}$$

where

χ^2 = the non-central chi-square distribution function
φ = $2\gamma/(\sigma^2(e^{\gamma(T-t)} - 1))$
ψ = $(b+\gamma)/\sigma^2$
r^* = $\log(A(T, TB)/X)/G(T,TB)$

We now apply this formula to a specific example. To do this we must first specify the parameters of the CIR process. It is assumed that these parameters are those estimated by Chan, Karolyi, Longstaff, and Sanders (henceforth CKLS).[6] These parameter estimates are:

$$\kappa\theta = 0.0189, \ \kappa + \lambda = 0.2339, \ \sigma = 0.0085 \tag{9}$$

Consider a European call on a zero-coupon Treasury with $T = 3$ years and $TB = 6$ years. The bond has a face value of 100, and the exercise price of the option is presumed to be equal to the current bond price. Exhibit 1 gives the option price for different initial interest rates and bond prices.

Applying the HW Model

We now consider the pricing of the identical call option under the HW model and compare the prices obtained with those of Exhibit 1 for the CIR model.

HW assume that the short-term interest rate $r(t)$ follows a process that is described by the stochastic differential equation

$$dr = [\theta(t) + \alpha(t)(b - r)]dt + \sigma(t)dw(t) \tag{10}$$

$\theta(t)$ = time dependent drift
$\alpha(t)$ = time dependent reversion rate
b = long-term level of interest rate
$\sigma(t)$ = time dependent volatility
$w(t)$ = standard Brownian motion under measure P.

---

[6] K. Chan, G. Karolyi, F. Longstaff, and A. Sanders, "An Empirical Comparison of Alternative Models of the Short Term Interest Rate," *Journal of Finance* (1992), pp. 1209-1227.

Exhibit 1: Bond and Call Prices Using the CIR Model

$r(0)$	Bond Price	Call Price
0.20	42.62	16.66
0.19	43.98	16.62
0.18	45.39	16.54
0.17	46.84	16.42
0.16	48.35	16.27
0.15	49.91	16.08
0.14	51.50	15.84
0.13	53.15	15.55
0.12	54.86	15.22
0.11	56.61	14.81
0.10	58.43	14.35
0.09	60.30	13.83
0.08	62.24	13.23
0.07	64.23	12.56
0.06	66.29	11.82
0.05	68.42	10.98
0.04	70.61	10.06
0.03	72.88	9.04
0.02	75.22	7.91
0.01	77.62	6.69

As in the case of the CIR model, the (normalized) price of any security paying a random interest dependent payoff $x(\tau)$ at $\tau > 0$ is calculated as the conditional expectation of the (normalized) payoff under an equivalent martingale measure. Let $x(t)$ and $B(t)$ be defined as in the case of the CIR model, and define:

$w^{**}(t)$ = standard Brownian motion under a measure Q equivalent to P,

where

$$w^{**}(t) = w(t) + \int_0^t \lambda(s)ds \ ; \ \lambda(s) = \text{bounded function of time.}$$

Using the equation for $w^{**}(t)$ to substitute for $w(t)$ in the interest rate process, we get

$$dr = (\phi(t) - \alpha(t)r)dt + \sigma(t)dw^{**}$$

$$\phi(t) = \theta(t) + \alpha(t)b - \lambda(t)\sigma(t) \tag{11}$$

This is the risk-adjusted HW interest rate process. Then,

$$\frac{x(t)}{B(t)} = E^{**}\left[\frac{x(\tau)}{B(\tau)}\right] \tag{12}$$

where E^{**} denotes expectation under the risk adjusted HW interest rate process.

Since a zero-coupon Treasury bond of maturity *TB* pays $1.00 with certainty at *TB*,

$$\frac{P(t, TB)}{B(t)} = E^{**}\left[\frac{1}{B(TB)}\right] \Rightarrow P(t, TB) = E^{**}\left[\exp\left(-\int_t^{TB} r(s)ds\right)\right] \quad (13)$$

HW provide a closed form solution for $P(t, TB)$ of the form

$$P(t, TB) = A(t, TB) \exp[-r(t)G(t, TB)] \quad (14)$$

where $A(t, TB)$ and $G(t, TB)$ are given by

$$G(t, TB) = \frac{G(0, TB) - G(0, t)}{\partial G(0, t)/\partial t}$$

$$F(t, TB) = \log A(t, TB)$$

$$F(t, TB) = F(0, TB) - F(0, t) - G(t, TB)\frac{\partial F(0, t)}{\partial t}$$

$$- \frac{1}{2}\left[G(t, TB)\frac{\partial G(0, t)}{\partial t}\right]^2 \int_0^t \left[\frac{\sigma(\tau)}{\partial G(0, \tau)/\partial \tau}\right]^2 d\tau$$

Furthermore, HW show that $\phi(t)$ and $\alpha(t)$ are related to $A(0, t)$ and $G(0, t)$ through the following equations:

$$\alpha(t) = -\frac{\partial^2 G(0, t)/\partial t^2}{\partial G(0, t)/\partial t} \quad (15)$$

$$\phi(t) = -\alpha(t)\frac{\partial F(0, t)}{\partial t} - \frac{\partial^2 F(0, t)}{\partial t^2} + \left[\frac{\partial G(0, t)}{\partial t}\right]^2 \int_0^t \left[\frac{\sigma(\tau)}{\partial G(0, \tau)/\partial \tau}\right]^2 d\tau \quad (16)$$

Consider now a European call option on a Treasury bond of maturity *TB*. The current time is *t* and the option has maturity *T* (with *TB* > *T* > *t*) and exercise price *X*. Let $C(t)$ be the option price at time *t*. Then, using equation (12),

$$\frac{C(t)}{B(t)} = E^{**}\left[\frac{MAX(P(T, TB) - X, 0)}{B(T)}\right] \quad (17)$$

HW provide the following closed form solution:

$$C(t) = P(t, TB)N(h) - XP(t, T) N(h - \sigma_p) \quad (18)$$

where

$$N(\ ) = \text{the cumulative normal distribution function}$$

$$h = (\sigma_p/2) + (1/\sigma_p) \log[P(t,TB)/(X\,P(t,T))]$$

$$\sigma_p^2 = [G(0, TB) - G(0, T)]^2 \int_t^T \left[\frac{\sigma(\tau)}{\partial G(0, \tau)/\partial \tau}\right]^2 d\tau$$

HW argue that the price of an interest rate derivative is insensitive to the assumption made about the evolution of the interest rate in stage 1 as long as one very important condition is met. This condition states that as long as the parameters of the stochastic process are estimated in such a way that this stochastic process is consistent with the current term structure of bond yields the choice of stochastic process does not affect that much the prices obtained. From now on, we will refer to this condition as the *consistency condition*.

To demonstrate this, HW assume that the correct yield curve is the one given by the CIR process and figure out a way of estimating the parameters of the HW process assuming that the CIR yield curve is the correct one. Thus, they obtain two stochastic processes whose estimated parameters are consistent with the yield curve and therefore satisfy the previously mentioned consistency condition. This is the procedure we will employ here too, in order to compare the prices given by the two stochastic processes. As in the previous section, we assume that the parameters of the CIR process are those estimated by CKLS.

The assumption that the CIR model is correct implies that the $A(0, t)$ and $G(0, t)$ functions that would be estimated for the HW model from market data are given by equations (5) and (6); that is

$$A(0, t) = \left[\frac{2\gamma \exp\left[(b + \gamma)\frac{t}{2}\right]}{(\gamma + b)(\exp(\gamma t) - 1) + 2\gamma}\right]^{\frac{2c}{\sigma^2}} \tag{19}$$

$$G(0, t) = \frac{2(\exp(\gamma t) - 1)}{(\gamma + b)(\exp(\gamma t) - 1) + 2\gamma} \tag{20}$$

$$b = k + \lambda; \; c = k\theta; \; \gamma = \sqrt{b^2 + 2\sigma^2}$$

$k, \theta, \lambda,$ and σ are the parameters of the CIR model. Also, HW set

$$\sigma(t) = \sigma\sqrt{r(0)} \tag{21}$$

to ensure that the initial short-term interest rate volatility in the two models is the same.

$P(t, TB)$, $\phi(t)$, and $\alpha(t)$ can be calculated from equations (14), (15), and (16) using equations (19), (20), and (21).

Consider the same option that we priced under the CIR model: a European call on a zero-coupon Treasury with $T = 3$ years and $TB = 6$ years. The bond has a face value of 100, and the exercise price of the option is presumed to be equal to the current bond price. Exhibit 2 reports the option price for different initial interest rates and bond prices under the HW model using equation (18). For comparison purposes, the CIR prices calculated in the previous section are also given.

Exhibit 2 shows that the prices given by the two models are very similar. This confirms the assertion of HW that the prices of interest rate derivatives are not sensitive to the choice of stochastic process for the interest rate as long as the consistency condition is met.

VALUATION OF A LOOKBACK PUT ON A ZERO-COUPON TREASURY

We now consider whether the CIR model and the HW model will also provide similar prices for exotic options. Specifically, we will value a lockback put option on a zero-coupon Treasury bond using both models.

Exhibit 2: Comparison of Call Prices Using CIR and HW Models (Bond Price the Same)

$r(0)$	Bond Price	Call Price (CIR)	Call Price (HW)
0.20	42.62	16.66	16.65
0.19	43.98	16.62	16.61
0.18	45.39	16.54	16.53
0.17	46.84	16.42	16.42
0.16	48.35	16.27	16.27
0.15	49.91	16.08	16.07
0.14	51.50	15.84	15.84
0.13	53.15	15.55	15.55
0.12	54.86	15.22	15.21
0.11	56.61	14.81	14.81
0.10	58.43	14.35	14.35
0.09	60.30	13.83	13.83
0.08	62.24	13.23	13.24
0.07	64.23	12.56	12.57
0.06	66.29	11.82	11.82
0.05	68.42	10.98	10.98
0.04	70.61	10.06	10.05
0.03	72.88	9.04	9.02
0.02	75.22	7.91	7.88
0.01	77.62	6.69	6.64

Applying the CIR Model

A lookback put option on a zero-coupon Treasury bond, written at time 0 and expiring at time $T > 0$, entitles its owner to receive at T the difference between the maximum bond price in the time interval 0 to T and the bond price at T. It is obvious that a lookback put has all the features of a regular put except that the exercise price is equal to the maximum bond price during the option's life. We define:

0	=	time at which option written
T	=	option maturity at time 0
TB	=	maturity of the bond on which the option is written at time 0
t	=	current time
$P(t, TB)$	=	price at t of a zero coupon Treasury bond paying \$1 at TB
$M(t)$	=	$\max\limits_{0 \le \tau \le t} P(\tau, TB)$

From equation (2) we know that the price of this option at $t = 0$, denoted $PMAX\,(P(0, TB), M(0), 0, T)$, is given by

$$PMAX(P(0, TB), M(0), 0, T) = E^*\left[\frac{M(T) - P(T, TB)}{B(T)}\right] \tag{22}$$

Using equation (3),

$$PMAX(P(0, TB), M(0), 0, T) = E^*\left[\frac{M(T)}{B(T)}\right] - P(0, TB)$$

$$= E^*\left[M(T)\left(\exp\left(-\int_0^T r(s)ds\right)\right)\right] - P(0, TB) \tag{23}$$

Unfortunately, no closed form solution exists to this valuation problem because of the path dependent nature of the option. For this reason, we calculate the price using Monte Carlo simulation.

We first divide the time interval between 0 and T into m subintervals such that

$$0 = t_0 < t_1 < \ldots < t_m = T$$

We simulate the risk-adjusted CIR interest rate process using the stochastic analogue of Euler's integration method; the latter converges uniformly in quadratic mean. In particular, if $\tilde{\varepsilon}$ is standard normal we simulate using the discrete approximation

$$r_{t_i} = r_{t_{i-1}} + (k\theta - (k + \lambda)r_{t_{i-1}})(t_i - t_{i-1}) + \sigma\sqrt{r_{t_{i-1}}}\sqrt{(t_i - t_{i-1})}\tilde{\varepsilon} \tag{24}$$

for $i = 1, \ldots, m$.

We repeat the simulation N times and let $r_n(t_i)$ denote the simulated value of $r(t_i)$ in the nth simulation, $n = 1, 2, \ldots, N$.

Let $P\widehat{MA}X$ $(P(0, TB), M(0), 0, T)$ = estimate of $PMAX$ using this Monte Carlo technique. Then,

$$P\widehat{MA}X(P(0, TB), M(0), 0, T) = \left\{ \frac{1}{N} \sum_{n=1}^{N} M_n(T) \exp\left[-\sum_{i=1}^{m} r_n(t_{i-1})(t_i - t_{i-1}) \right] \right\}$$
$$- P(0, TB) \tag{25}$$

where $M_n(T)$ = simulated value of $M(T)$ in nth simulation.

It can be shown that as m and N increase to infinity, $P\widehat{MA}X$ converges to $PMAX$.

As in the previous section for the regular call option on the bond, we follow the methodology of HW in order to be able to compare the prices given by the two stochastic processes. We assume that the correct Treasury yield curve is the one given by the CIR process with parameters estimated by CKLS. We then estimate the parameters of the HW process on the basis of the assumption that the CIR process is the correct one. In this way, we ensure that the consistency condition is met. We assume that the lookback put has a maturity of 3 years and is written on a bond having a maturity of 6 years. The results for different initial interest rates and bond prices are presented in Exhibit 3.

Exhibit 3: Bond and Lookback Prices for Different Initial Interest Rates Using CIR Model

$r(0)$	Bond Price	Lookback Price (CIR)
0.20	42.62	0.4420
0.19	43.98	0.4595
0.18	45.39	0.4778
0.17	46.84	0.4968
0.16	48.35	0.5166
0.15	49.91	0.5371
0.14	51.50	0.5582
0.13	53.15	0.5800
0.12	54.86	0.6027
0.11	56.61	0.6264
0.10	58.43	0.6511
0.09	60.30	0.6766
0.08	62.24	0.7028
0.07	64.23	0.7300
0.06	66.29	0.7583
0.05	68.42	0.7875
0.04	70.61	0.8173
0.03	72.88	0.8475
0.02	75.22	0.8774
0.01	77.62	0.9056

Applying the HW Model

To compare the prices in Exhibit 3 to those obtained by using the HW model, we begin by describing how the HW model can be used to value the lookback put.

The lookback put is structured as in the case of the CIR model. We define:

0	=	time at which option written
T	=	option maturity at time 0
TB	=	maturity of the bond on which the option is written at time 0
t	=	current time
$P(t, TB)$	=	price at t of a zero coupon Treasury bond paying \$1 at TB
$M(t)$	=	$\max\limits_{0 \le \tau \le t} P(\tau, TB)$

From equation (12) above we know that the price of this option at $t = 0$, denoted $PMAX\,(P(0, TB), M(0), 0, T)$, is given by

$$PMAX(P(0, TB), M(0), 0, T) = E^{**}\left[\frac{M(T) - P(T, TB)}{B(T)}\right] \qquad (26)$$

Using equation (13),

$$PMAX(P(0, TB), M(0), 0, T) = E^{**}\left[\frac{M(T)}{B(T)}\right] - P(0, TB)$$

$$= E^{**}\left[M(T)\left(\exp\left(-\int_0^T r(s)ds\right)\right)\right] - P(0, TB) \qquad (27)$$

As in the case of the CIR model, no closed form solution exists to this valuation problem because of the path dependent nature of the option. For this reason, we calculate the price using Monte Carlo simulation.

The simulation is carried out in exactly the same way as for the CIR process. The only thing that changes is the use of the risk-adjusted interest rate process

$$r_{t_i} = r_{t_{i-1}} + (\phi(t_{i-1}) - \alpha(t_{i-1})r_{t_{i-1}})(t_i - t_{i-1}) + \sigma\sqrt{r(0)}\sqrt{t_i - t_{i-1}}\,\tilde{\varepsilon} \quad (28)$$

The parameters of the HW process are estimated by assuming that the CIR term structure is the correct one with parameters estimated by CKLS. This implies that the consistency condition is satisfied and enables us to compare CIR and HW prices using Exhibit 4.

There are two striking features of Exhibit 4: (1) the magnitude of the differences in the price given by each stochastic process and (2) for some initial interest rates one model gives a higher price whereas for other initial interest rates it is the other model that gives a higher price. For example, note that for an initial interest rate of 0.01 (1%) the price given by the CIR model exceeds the price given by the HW model by a multiple of four. Alternatively, for an initial interest rate of 0.2 (20%) the price given by the HW model exceeds that given by the CIR model by a multiple of approximately two. These results are very different from the results of HW and indicate that even if the consistency condition is met, different stochastic processes can give very different prices for complex interest rate derivatives. We now turn to an explanation of these price differences.

Explanation of Price Differences

The HW model gives higher lookback put prices than the CIR model for interest rates above or very close to the long-run mean of the interest rate process, which was estimated by CKLS to be 0.08. However, for interest rates below 0.07, the HW model gives lower lookback put prices.

To explain these results, consider the benefit and cost of exercising this option at maturity. The benefit is the maximum bond price over the option's life, and the cost is the bond price at maturity. The option will always be in the money at maturity.

Exhibit 4: Comparison of Bond and Lookback Prices for Different Initial Interest Rates Using CIR and HW Models

$r(0)$	Bond Price	Lookback Price(CIR)	Lookback Price (HW)
0.20	42.62	0.4420	0.7493
0.19	43.98	0.4595	0.7651
0.18	45.39	0.4778	0.7803
0.17	46.84	0.4968	0.7946
0.16	48.35	0.5166	0.8077
0.15	49.91	0.5371	0.8194
0.14	51.50	0.5582	0.8291
0.13	53.15	0.5800	0.8364
0.12	54.86	0.6027	0.8409
0.11	56.61	0.6264	0.8419
0.10	58.43	0.6511	0.8385
0.09	60.30	0.6766	0.8293
0.08	62.24	0.7028	0.8131
0.07	64.23	0.7300	0.7877
0.06	66.29	0.7583	0.7504
0.05	68.42	0.7875	0.6974
0.04	70.61	0.8173	0.6236
0.03	72.88	0.8475	0.5217
0.02	75.22	0.8774	0.3821
0.01	77.62	0.9056	0.1971

For comparison purposes, let us take the CIR model as the base case and investigate how the benefit and cost of exercising the option at maturity change under the HW model. Since we are comparing the current (i.e., time 0) prices under the two models, we should examine the present value of the benefit and the present value of the cost of exercising the option at maturity. The present value of the cost of exercising is the same in both models: it is the current price of the bond with maturity $TB = 6$ which is the same in both models. As a result, the differences in the current option prices arise because of differences in the present value of the benefit.

To investigate how the present value of the benefit might differ in the two models, let us examine the nature of the stochastic process for the interest rate in the two models. We begin by considering the drift term. Both the CIR and HW interest rate processes are mean reverting. The long-run mean estimated by CKLS is 0.08. This means that whenever the interest rate is below (above) 0.08, the drift term will tend to increase (decrease) it. Furthermore, the volatility terms in the two models are different. The volatility of the interest rate in CIR at time t is $\sigma\sqrt{r(t-1)}$ whereas the volatility term in HW at all t is $\sigma\sqrt{r(0)}$. The reason for this is that we fit the HW model in such a way that its initial (i.e., time 0) interest rate volatility is the same as in the CIR model. A direct consequence of this is that for a given initial interest rate, the volatility term implies a higher probability of a lower interest rate in the HW model and a higher probability of a higher interest rate in the CIR model.

The key to understanding why the HW model gives higher (lower) look-back put prices when the interest rate is above (below) its long-run mean is to realize that a low interest rate in either the CIR or the HW model is much more useful in establishing a high maximum bond price over the option's life if it occurs late during the option's life. The reason for this is that for a given interest rate, bond prices in both models increase with the passage of time.

Consider the case where $r = 0.01$ (i.e., the interest rate is substantially below its long-run mean of 0.08). Early in the option's life, the HW model will be more likely to give a lower interest rate than the CIR model. However, for the reason given in the previous paragraph, this will not be very useful in establishing a high maximum bond price over the option's life.

Furthermore, note that the drift term will tend to increase the interest rate in both models over time; as a result, by the time the option has been outstanding for, say 80% of its life, the interest rate will be, on average, much higher in both models. The crucial thing to realize is that at that time, the volatility of the interest rate will be much higher in the CIR model — recall that time t volatility in CIR is given by $\sigma\sqrt{r(t-1)}$, whereas, volatility in HW at all t is $\sigma\sqrt{0.01}$. A direct consequence of this is that towards the end of the option's life the higher volatility in CIR will imply a higher probability of a lower interest rate in CIR (compared to HW). As explained in the previous section, a low interest rate will be much more useful in establishing a high maximum bond price over the option's life if it occurs late in the option's life. Since we established that the HW (CIR) model will imply a higher probability of a lower interest rate early (late) in the option's life, the probability of a higher maximum bond price is higher in the CIR model and, therefore, the option's benefit is higher in the CIR model. This explains why the CIR model gives higher lookback put prices for an interest rate of 0.01. Similar considerations apply for interest rates in the 0.02 to 0.06 range (i.e., for interest rates below the long-run mean). The CIR model gives higher lookback put prices in these cases too.

Let us now consider the case where $r = 0.20$. Early in the option's life, the HW model will imply a higher probability of a lower interest rate. As explained above, this will not be very useful in establishing a high maximum bond price over the option's life. The important thing to realize is that, unlike the case where $r = 0.01$, the HW model will also imply a higher probability of a lower interest rate late in the option's life. On average, the interest rate will reach a much lower level by the time the option has been outstanding for, say, 80% of its life. At that time, the volatility of the interest rate will be much higher in the HW model. (Recall that volatility at time t is $\sigma\sqrt{r(t-1)}$ in the CIR model and $\sigma\sqrt{0.2}$ in the HW model.) Hence, towards the end of the option's life, the higher volatility in the HW model will imply a higher probability of a lower interest rate (compared to the CIR model). The HW model will therefore imply a higher probability of a lower interest rate both early and late in the option's life; as a result, the probability of a higher maximum bond price over the option's life and therefore the option's benefit is higher for the HW model. This explains why the HW model gives a higher price for a lookback put option when $r = 0.20$. Similar considerations apply for interest rates in the 0.08 to 0.19 range, i.e., for interest rates above the long-run mean. The HW model gives higher lookback put prices in these cases too.

CONCLUSION

This chapter has presented a methodology that can be used to value any interest rate derivative. This methodology was applied to the valuation of two derivatives, one plain vanilla (a call on the bond price) and the other exotic (a lookback put on the bond price). In the case of the plain vanilla derivative, it was shown that its price is insensitive to the modeler's choice of stochastic process for the short-term interest rate as long as a consistency condition is met. However, in the case of the exotic derivative, the price is very sensitive to the modeler's choice of stochastic process for the short-term interest rate even if the consistency condition is met.

Where does this leave us? The problem is that there is widespread disagreement as to which stochastic process provides a better fit to market data (for example, see CKLS). Part of the problem is that the empirical results are very sensitive to the period from which the market data is drawn and to the choice of econometric methodology. It therefore appears that different researchers will, in general, disagree on the price they obtain for complex interest rate derivatives because each researcher will prefer to use a different stochastic process for the short-term interest rate. One can only hope that advances in econometric methodology will permit the development of a consensus on the correct stochastic process in the not too distant future.

Chapter 6

Recent Advances in Corporate Bond Valuation

Louis L. Gagnon, Ph.D.
Associate Professor of Finance
School of Business
Queen's University

William J. Hurley, Ph.D.
Associate Professor of Business Administration
Royal Military College of Canada

Lewis D. Johnson, Ph.D.
Professor of Finance
School of Business
Queen's University

INTRODUCTION

Fixed-income securities are essential components of any investment portfolio, so the analyst should be keenly aware of whether the price paid for a bond is appropriate for the risk undertaken. The promised cash flows from most bonds are fairly well defined in their amount and timing (as distinct from common stock where neither element of *ex ante* certainty prevails); nonetheless, bonds are far from being risk-free investments. For all bonds, including government bonds, there is the prospect of adverse interest rate movement or unexpected inflation, among other hazards. For corporate and non-federal government bonds, there is also the possibility of promised payments not being made, either through default or through less drastic disruptions in the payment schedule.

Our purpose in this chapter is to detail some recent advances in the valuation of corporate fixed-income securities. To properly value a corporate bond, the analyst must be aware of the likely determinants of value and their quantitative effect on the bond's price. In particular, the determination of the appropriate value of the risk premium is crucial for proper bond pricing. By the risk premium, we mean, as usual, the amount of extra return required, over that of a default-free security. Put another way, we are concerned with the pricing of default risk.

Any competent fixed-income analyst can list the determinants of default risk: the effect of the economic cycle; the shape of the term structure; the level and volatility of interest rates; the term to maturity; the level of the coupon; and the underlying profitability and financial strength of the issuing company. These factors are variously captured with measures such as duration, beta, bond ratings, probability of default, and standard deviation.

In this chapter we examine the formal pricing of default risk. After the fact, it is always easy to see when one has paid too much for a bond (as with so-called junk bonds in the post-euphoric early 1990s). It is also possible to get a sense of whether, before the fact, one might be paying too much for a bond (or indeed whether a particular bond might be a bargain) using empirical methods such as the "yield premium model" of Altman and Bencivenga.[1] We have nobler motives: we want to examine recent developments in the corporate bond pricing literature, so as to not only ascertain the determinants of value but also their quantitative effect on value.

We first review the literature on corporate bond performance and mortality in order to set the scene and to give a sense of the magnitude of the default risk premium. We then examine in detail two recent approaches to corporate bond valuation. In our view, the theory has mostly been developed on two fronts: equilibrium contingent-claims approaches and various non-equilibrium approaches. Consequently, we first examine the contingent-claims approach of Longstaff and Schwartz;[2] in particular we demonstrate the complexity of the calculations underlying their model. Next we examine a computationally simple non-equilibrium approach, the model of Hurley and Johnson.[3] Our purpose with this comparison is to provide to analysts a flavor of the intuition behind and complexities associated with corporate bond valuation models. To conclude the chapter, we discuss the implications of these approaches for the practicing analyst.

CORPORATE BOND MORTALITY AND PERFORMANCE: THE EMPIRICAL EVIDENCE

In this section we review the literature on corporate bond risk and return with particular reference to evidence on experienced defaults. This review is dominated by references to the work of Edward Altman, an expert on empirical bond default studies.

---

[1] E.I. Altman and J.C. Bencivenga, "A Yield Premium Model for the High-Yield Debt Market," *Financial Analysts Journal* (September/October 1995), pp. 49-56.
[2] F.A. Longstaff and E.S. Schwartz, "A Simple Approach for Valuing Risky Fixed and Floating Rate Debt," *Journal of Finance* (1995), pp. 789-819.
[3] W.J. Hurley and L.D. Johnson, "On the Pricing of Bond Default Risk," *Journal of Portfolio Management* (Winter 1996), pp. 66-70.

Default Experience

Altman and Nammacher examine the default rate experience of corporate debt for the period 1970 to 1984.[4] They measure the default rate for a given class of bonds and for a given year by dividing the face value of all defaulting debt issues belonging to that class during the year by the face value of all outstanding bond issues comprising that class during that year. The historical default rate for all public debt outstanding, including convertible debt, ranged between 0.011% in 1979 and 0.743% in 1970 while the average annual default rate of 0.16% of par value for the entire period. For straight debt only, the average default rate during the same period was lower at 0.080%.

Turning to the default experience of high-yield corporate debt for the period 1970 to 1984, where high-yield debt consists of issues having a rating below Baa3 using Moody's or BBB using Standard & Poor's classification, Altman and Nammacher report an average annual default rate of 2.24% of par value of outstanding low-rated straight debt including utilities and 2.54% of par value of outstanding debt excluding utilities. The number of issuers of high-yield debt in the United States had increased from 145 in 1970 to 335 in 1984. While the number of high-yield debt issuers increased during this period, the issuer default rate declined slightly. Altman and Nammacher report that the average price at which defaulting bonds traded at the end of the defaulting month was on average 41% of par.[5] They report that a representative portfolio of straight high-yield bonds held from December 31, 1977 to December 31, 1983 would have earned an annual compound excess return of 580 basis points over a bond portfolio mimicking Shearson Lehman's Long Term Government Bond Index. According to the findings of Altman, there is no relationship between individual bond ratings at issuance and the average price after default.[6]

Altman reports that the average annual default rate on low-rated straight debt including utilities was 2.216% of par value for the period 1970 through 1986.[7] The corresponding default rate for the 1983 to 1986 period was 1.727%. The default rate from 1970 to 1986 was 0.199% in terms of the percentage of the par value of all outstanding issues of straight and convertible debt in the United States.

Default Rate and Bond Age

Altman presents evidence on bond mortality rates, adjusted for redemptions and defaults, for the period 1971 to 1987.[8] He introduces a new measure of bond mortality which eliminates the potential for bias induced by the fact that the original

---

[4] E. I. Altman and S. A. Nammacher, "The Default Rate Experience on High-Yield Corporate Debt," *Financial Analysts Journal* (July/Aug 1985), pp. 24-41.

[5] See E. I. Altman, "Measuring Corporate Bond Mortality and Performance," *Journal of Finance* (1989), pp. 909-922. In that study, he reports an average price of 44.58% of par for the period 1971 to 1987. The average price was 78.67% of par for a small sample of five AAA-rated bonds, 45.90% of par for A-rated issues, 45.30% of par for BBB-rated issues, and 31.18% for nonrated issues.

[6] Altman, "Measuring Corporate Bond Mortality and Performance."

[7] E. I. Altman, "The Anatomy of the High-Yield Bond Market," *Financial Analysts Journal* (July/August 1987), pp. 2-25.

[8] Altman, "Measuring Corporate Bond Mortality and Performance."

population changes over time. The traditional approach to the measurement of default risk consisted of dividing the aggregate par-value of all defaulting bond issues in a given year by the aggregate par-value of all outstanding bond issues belonging to the same class as of the end of the year. Hence, in a rapid growth environment such as the one characterizing the original issue high-yield corporate bond market in the 1980s and where new issues represent an increasingly high proportion of the market,[9] this measure would clearly understate the default rate since new issues exhibit a lower probability of default than older issues.

Altman's evidence shows that five years after issuance, for instance, the cumulative adjusted mortality rate was 0.00% for AAA-rated debt, 2.33% for AA-rated debt, 0.71% for A-rated debt, 0.91% for BBB-rated debt, 1.84% for BB-rated debt, 11.53% for B-rated debt, and 30.22% for CCC-rated debt. These default rates are higher than those reported in previous studies of bond default.

Asquith, Mullins, and Wolff conducted an aging analysis of defaults, exchanges and calls on all public original issue high-yield debt issued by corporations between January 1977 and December 1986.[10] The beginning of their sample period coincides with what is considered to be the beginning of the original issue high-yield debt market, 1977. Prior to 1977, the high-yield market essentially consisted of so-called fallen angels (i.e. investment-grade bonds which experienced a downgrading since their issue date which pushed them below the investment grade category). Asquith, Mullins, and Wolff employ a cohort-based measure of default similar to the one introduced by Altman in an effort to reduce the downward aging bias inherent in default rate calculations of previous studies.

Asquith, Mullins, and Wolff's findings indicate that yearly defaults for high-yield corporate bonds increase over time such that older issues exhibit a higher cumulative probability of default. One year after issue, cumulative defaults range between 1.00% and 2.73% while five years after issue, they range between 3.03% and 20.97%. Their results also show that cumulative default rates for more recent issues are similar to those of bonds issued in the earlier years of this market. Evidence by Blume, Keim, and Patel[11] indicates that changes in economic activity may play an important role in the relation between age and bond default rate observed by Altman and Asquith, Mullins, and Wolff.

Rosengren extends the high-yield corporate bond default literature by examining all original low-grade bonds issued between 1978 and 1988, including convertible and nonrated high-yield issues which had not been examined by previous studies.[12] Using the same approach in the measurement of default rates as the

---

[9] See M. E. Blume, D. B. Keim, and S. A. Patel, "Returns and Volatility of Low-Grade Bonds 1977-1989," *Journal of Finance* (1991), pp. 49-74 for an analysis of the patterns in age composition of the high-yield corporate bond market from 1982 to 1988.

[10] P. Asquith, D. W. Mullins, and E. D. Wolff, "Original Issue High-Yield Bonds: Aging Analyses of Default, Exchanges, and Calls," *Journal of Finance* (1989), pp. 923-952.

[11] Blume, Keim, and Patel, "Returns and Volatility of Low-Grade Bonds 1977-1989."

[12] E. S. Rosengren, "Defaults of Original Issue High-Yield Convertible Bonds," *Journal of Finance* (1993), pp. 345-362.

one adopted by Altman and Asquith, Mullins, and Wolff, Rosengren reports that cumulative default rates for rated convertible high-yield bonds were much smaller than those of rated nonconvertible issues. For instance, as of December 31, 1989, as much as 34% of the rated nonconvertible high-yield debt issued in 1978 had defaulted while only 12.5% of the rated nonconvertible issued during the same year had defaulted. Rosengren argues that the most likely reasons for the difference in default rates between nonconvertible and convertible high-yield debt are (1) the lower coupon rates which are usually associated with convertible debt and which reflect the value of the conversion privilege, and (2) the greater likelihood that the issue will be retired by the issuer if the firm does well. Rosengren also reports that nonrated nonconvertible debt exhibits a lower default rate than rated nonconvertible issues but given the data limitations characterizing this part of the sample (the status of 27% of the nonrated issues could not be verified), this evidence is not conclusive.

Ma, Rao, and Peterson examined the impact of large default events on default probabilities implied from the spread between high-yield and U.S. Treasury securities around the well-publicized LTV bankruptcy in 1986.[13] Their findings reveal that the market's perception of the default probabilities in the high-yield market experienced a significant increase after the LTV bankruptcy but that the impact of this major event only lasted for six months.

Return Performance

Blume and Keim report that, over the 10-year period beginning in 1977 and ending in 1986, the realized return on a broadly diversified portfolio of low-grade bonds exceeded that of a portfolio of high-grade bonds.[14] They show that while the portfolio of low-grade bonds offered higher returns, its risk level was no greater than that of the portfolio of high-grade bonds. For the sample period studied by Blume and Keim, the correlation between the low-grade bond portfolio and the high-grade bond portfolio was equal to 0.79 while that between the former portfolio and the S&P 500 index was 0.5, suggesting that there may be diversification benefits associated with the inclusion of low-grade bonds in a bond or a stock portfolio.[15] Furthermore, the estimate for the systematic risk of the low-grade bond portfolio is equal to 0.34, which is slightly less than 0.36, the systematic risk of the high-grade bond portfolio, although most likely not from a statistical standpoint. Furthermore, Blume and Keim report that the excess-return or alpha associated with their low-grade bond portfolio is positive and that the alpha estimate associated with the high-grade portfolio is negative, but neither estimate appears to be statistically different from zero.

---

[13] C. Ma, R.P. Rao, and R.L. Peterson, "The Resiliency of the High-Yield Bond Market: The LTV Default," *Journal of Finance* (1989), pp. 1085-1097.

[14] M. E. Blume and D. B. Keim, "Lower-Grade Bonds: Their Risks and Returns," *Financial Analysts Journal* (July/August 1987), pp. 26-33.

[15] See also T.L. Bennett, S.F. Esser, and C.R. Roth, "Corporate Credit Risk and Reward," *Journal of Portfolio Management* (Spring 1994), pp. 39-47, for supporting evidence on the diversification benefits associated with the inclusion of investment-grade corporate bonds in asset portfolios.

Altman investigates the net return performance of various risky bond categories relative to default risk-free U.S. Treasury securities.[16] His return calculations provide for the reinvestment of cash flows, at market prevailing interest rates, from coupon payments on the surviving bond population, sinking funds, calls, and the recovery from defaulted bond issues. During the sample period 1971-1987, Altman reports average annual yield spreads over Treasuries of 47 basis points (bp) for AAA-rated debt, 81 bp for AA-rated debt, 108 bp for A-rated debt, 177 bp for BBB-rated debt, 305 bp for BB-rated debt, 409 bp for B-rated debt, and 707 bp for CCC-rated debt.

Blume, Keim, and Patel examine the risks and returns of long-term low-grade bonds for a sample period beginning in 1977 and ending in 1989.[17] During this period, low-grade bonds offered an annually compounded rate of return of 10.2% compared to 9.7% for high-grade bonds, 9.3% for long-term U.S. government bonds, 14.6% for the S&P 500 Index, and 19.1% for a portfolio consisting of the stocks belonging to the smallest size quintile on the NYSE.

Although low-grade bonds posted a strong return performance for the overall sample period studied by Blume, Keim, and Patel, their performance was far from superior during the sub-samples they considered. For instance, between 1982 and 1989, low-grade bonds posted an annual compounded rate of return of 7.5%, which was only superior to small stocks whose return over the same period was equal to 7.0%. All other asset classes posted higher returns than low-grade bonds: high-grade bonds produced an annual compounded return of 17.1% while long-term U.S. government bonds and the S&P 500 Index posted a return of 16.3% and 18.9%, respectively.

In spite of the evidence of a relationship between years from issuance and default rates uncovered by the studies, Altman and Asquith, Mullins, and Wolff's, Blume, Keim, and Patel show that this relationship does not translate into an age profile for bond returns. They test this proposition by stratifying the components of their low-grade bond index into two maturity classes (10 to 15 years and 15 to 20 years) and three age categories (0 to 2 years, 2 to 5 years, and 5 to 10 years) and are essentially unable to uncover any significant differences in returns across sub-indices. Goodman stresses the fact that default enters in the calculations of bond returns like any other negative information through lower end-of-month prices.[18] Hence, the evidence obtained from previous studies focusing on the risk-return performance of bonds is still valid in the presence of the aging bias uncovered by Altman and Asquith, Mullins, and Wolff's.

Volatility

Blume, Keim, and Patel report that the volatility of their low-grade bond index is lower than the volatility of indices of long-term high-grade corporate bonds, long-term U.S. government bonds, the S&P 500 index, and small stocks. They argue that low-grade bonds exhibit lower volatility than high-grade bonds and govern-

---

[16] Altman, "Measuring Corporate Bond Mortality and Performance."

[17] Blume, Keim, and Patel, "Returns and Volatility of Low-Grade Bonds 1977-1989."

[18] L. S. Goodman, "High-Yield Default Rates: Is There Cause for Concern?" *Journal of Portfolio Management* (Winter 1990), pp. 54-59.

ment bonds because they tend to have shorter maturities, they generally offer higher coupons, and they have weaker call protection, than their high-grade corporate or long-term government counterparts. Other things equal, these features contribute to reduce the duration, and hence the volatility, of low-grade-bonds relative to these other classes of bonds. Once these differences are taken into account, Blume, Keim, and Patel show that the relative volatility of low-grade bonds is not lower but indeed larger than the volatility of the other classes of long-term bonds, as one would expect in any well functioning market.

The findings of Blume, Keim, and Patel are corroborated by Cornell and Green who investigate the return performance of low-grade bond mutual funds for the 1960-1989 period.[19] Cornell and Green also report evidence which shows that low-grade bond returns are much more sensitive to changes in stock prices and that high-grade bonds are more sensitive to changes in long-term interest rates. They conclude that the risk of low-grade bonds may be best measured from the perspective of a two-factor model which captures the sensitivity of low-grade bonds to both stock prices and interest rates.

Summary

We have reviewed here much of the evidence on default rate experience, returns by default risk category, and the relative volatility of different types of bonds. The magnitude of the default risk problem is sufficient to warrant a closer examination, which we pursue theoretically in the next two sections.

A CONTINGENT-CLAIMS APPROACH

The contingent claims approach to valuing risky can be traced to the pioneering work of Black-Scholes[20] and Merton.[21] These models fall into two classes: (1) partial equilibrium models such as the models proposed by Geske,[22] Ingersoll,[23] Merton,[24] Smith and Warner,[25] and Longstaff and Schwartz,[26] and (2) yield curve

---

[19] B. Cornell and K. Green, "The Investment Performance of Low-Grade Bond Funds," *Journal of Finance* (1991), pp. 29-48.

[20] F. Black and M. Scholes, "The Pricing of Options and Corporate Liabilities," *Journal of Political Economy* (1973), pp. 637-654.

[21] R.C. Merton, "On the Pricing of Corporate Debt: The Risk Structure of Interest Rates," *Journal of Finance* (1974), pp. 449-470.

[22] R. Geske, "The Valuation of Corporate Liabilities as Compound Options," *Journal of Financial and Quantitative Analysis* (1977), pp. 541-552.

[23] See J.E. Ingersoll, "A Contingent-Claims Valuation of Convertible Securities," *Journal of Financial Economics* (1977), pp. 289-231 and J.E. Ingersoll, "An Examination of Corporate Call Policies on Convertible Securities," *Journal of Finance* (1977), pp. 463-468.

[24] R.C. Merton, "On the Pricing of Contingent Claims and the Modigliani-Miller Theorem," *Journal of Financial Economics* (1977), pp. 2241-250.

[25] C.W. Smith and J.B. Warner, "On Financial Contracting: An Analysis of Bond Covenants," *Journal of Financial Economics* (1979), pp. 117-161.

[26] F.A. Longstaff and E.S. Schwartz, "A Simple Approach for Valuing Risky Fixed and Floating Rate Debt."

based (or arbitrage-free) models such as Hull and White,[27] Jarrow, Lando, and Turnbull,[28] Jarrow and Turnbull,[29] and Das and Tufano.[30] Models belonging to the first group are easier to implement while those in the second are more general in that they can value credit risk for a wide array of interest-rate sensitive claims, including complex derivative securities.

Although contingent-claims based models are often considered to be more appealing from a theoretical perspective, most of them are also quite computationally demanding. We illustrate this point by describing a compelling technology, the Longstaff and Schwartz model (hereafter LS), which has been gaining currency among practitioners in the fixed-income industry. In this section, we give a brief summary of the LS model and discuss some of the challenges associated with its implementation.

Consider a risky discount bond which will pay $1 at time T if it does not default and $1-w$ if it does. w represents the percentage writedown on the security. Alternatively $1-w$ is termed the recovery rate. Let the price of this bond be $P(T)$ and let $D(T)$ be the price of a default free bond which pays $1 at time T. The LS valuation is

$$P(T) = [1 - wQ(T)]\, D(T) \tag{1}$$

where $Q(T)$ is the probability the firm defaults some time before time T. Hence the default free bond price is adjusted downward by a factor $1 - wQ(T)$, where the factor $wQ(T)$ is the expected writedown.

We can use equation (1) to value a risky coupon bond which pays a coupon c, has a face value F and matures in n years:

$$V(c, n) = c \sum_{t=1}^{n} P(t) + F \cdot P(n) \tag{2}$$

Hence to value risky coupon bonds we need only focus on equation (1)

There are two critical exogenous assumptions which lead to equation (1). First, financial distress is assumed to occur when the value of the firm's assets, v, reaches a critical level, K. As it turns out, the ratio of v to K is all that is needed. Hence, defining $X = v/K$, financial distress is assumed to occur when $X = 1$. Second, when the firm enters a period of financial distress, the writedown percentage is exogenously fixed at w. LS deal only briefly with techniques for estimating K and w. They suggest that values for w can be derived from actuarial information such as that avail-

[27] J. Hull, and A. White, "The Impact of Default Risk on the Prices of Options and Other Derivative Securities," *Journal of Banking and Finance* (1995), pp. 299-322.

[28] R.A. Jarrow, D. Lando, and S.M. Turnbull, "A Markov Model for the Term Structure of Credit Risk Spreads," Working Paper, Cornell University, 1994.

[29] R.A. Jarrow, and S.M. Turnbull, "Pricing Derivatives on Financial Securities Subject to Default Risk," *Journal of Finance* (1995), pp. 53-85.

[30] S. R. Das and P. Tufano, "Pricing Credit-Sensitive Debt When Interest Rates, Credit Ratings, and Credit Spreads are Stochastic," Working Paper, Harvard Business School, 1995.

able in Altman as discussed above.[31] According to LS, estimation of X for a firm "can be implied from the market price of the most liquid bond and then used to value the other bonds. This is similar to the familiar technique of solving for the implied variance of an at-the-money option and using it to price the remaining options."

The other assumptions of the model are as follows.

1. The value of the firm's assets follows a standard continuous time random process.
2. The model of short-term interest rate movement is drawn from Vasicek.[32]
3. The value of the firm is independent of the capital structure of the firm.

Given these assumptions, LS show the price of a corporate discount bond to be:

$$P(X, r, T) = [1 - wQ(X, r, T)]D(r, T) \tag{3}$$

where r is the short-term riskless interest rate and $D(r,T)$ is calculated by

$$D(r, T) = e^{(A(T) - B(T)r)}$$

where

$$A(T) = \left(\frac{\eta^2}{2\beta^2} - \frac{\alpha}{\beta}\right)T + \left(\frac{\eta^2}{\beta^3} - \frac{\alpha}{\beta^3}\right)(e^{-\beta T} - 1) - \left(\frac{\eta^2}{4\beta^3}\right)(e^{-2\beta T} - 1) \tag{4}$$

$$B(T) = \frac{1 - e^{-\beta T}}{\beta} \tag{5}$$

and α, β, η are parameters. Note that equation (1) and equation (3) are the same except that equation (3) makes functional dependencies explicit.

To produce values of $P(X, r, T)$, the main computational difficulty lies with the evaluation of $Q(X, r, T)$. LS propose the following approximation for $Q(X, r, T)$

$$Q(X, r, T, n) = \sum_{i=1}^{n} q_i \tag{6}$$

where

$$q_1 = N(a_1), N(\cdot) \text{ is the cum. standard normal density function} \tag{7}$$

$$q_i = N(a_i) - \sum_{j=1}^{i-1} q_j N(b_{ij}) \qquad i = 2, 3, ..., n \tag{8}$$

---

[31] E. I. Altman, "Revisiting the High-Yield Bond Market," *Financial Management* (1992), pp. 78-92.
[32] O. Vasicek, "An Equilibrium Characterization of the Term Structure," *Journal of Financial Economics* (1977), pp. 177-188.

$$a_i = \frac{-\ln(X) - M(iT/n, T)}{\sqrt{S(iT/n)}} \tag{9}$$

$$b_{ij} = \frac{M(jT/n, T) - M(iT/n, T)}{\sqrt{S(iT/n) - S(jT/n)}} \tag{10}$$

and where

$$M(t, T) = \left(\frac{\alpha - \rho\sigma\eta}{\beta} - \frac{\eta^2}{\beta^2} - \frac{\sigma^2}{2} \right) t + \left(\frac{\rho\sigma\eta}{\beta^2} + \frac{\eta^2}{2\beta^3} \right) e^{-\beta T} (e^{\beta T} - 1)$$

$$+ \left(\frac{r}{\beta} - \frac{\alpha}{\beta^2} + \frac{\eta^2}{\beta^3} \right) (1 - e^{-\beta T}) - \frac{\eta^2}{2\beta^3} e^{-\beta T} (1 - e^{-\beta T}) \tag{11}$$

$$S(t) = \left(\frac{\rho\sigma\eta}{\beta} + \frac{\eta^2}{\beta^2} + \sigma^2 \right) t - \left(\frac{\rho\sigma\eta}{\beta^2} + \frac{2\eta^2}{\beta^3} \right) (1 - e^{\beta T}) + \left(\frac{\eta^2}{2\beta^3} \right) (1 - e^{-2\beta T}) \tag{12}$$

and where ρ and σ are additional parameters. LS suggest that a value of $n = 200$ "results in values of $Q(X, r, T)$ and $Q(X, r, T, n)$ that are virtually indistinguishable."

We wish to emphasize that our goal in this discussion is not to explain in detail how to estimate and use this model in practice but to illustrate the computational challenges associated with its use, especially the evaluation of the function $Q(X, r, T, 200)$. The main difficulty lies in the recursion step in equation (8). In theory the complexity is relatively low, $O(n^2)$; however each step in the recursion involves a significant number of function calls including the computation of cumulative normal distribution values. Hence, in practice, computing $Q(X, r, T, 200)$ is a time consuming endeavor. By way of example, we implemented the LS model in the EXCEL spreadsheet environment, writing Visual Basic modules for the functions $D(r,T)$, $M(t,T)$, $S(t)$, and $Q(X, r, T, n)$. Values of $Q(X, r, T, n)$ for $n = 200$ took approximately 16 minutes on a Pentium PC running at a speed of 90 megahertz. Clearly the EXCEL spreadsheet environment is not the appropriate platform for significant numerical computations such as those required for the implementation of the LS model. Nonetheless, this example illustrates the need for very powerful computing resources in order to implement this or similar models in a trading environment.

A SIMPLE APPROACH

Given the numerical complexity associated with the implementation of the LS and similar models, there may be a great deal of merit in exploring more simple alternatives in the context of straight debt. In this section, we present the details of a simple valuation model developed by Hurley and Johnson.[33] This model takes as

---

[33] Hurley and Johnson, "On the Pricing of Bond Default Risk."

input the prices and characteristics (coupon, term to maturity, writedown percentage in the case of default) of a subset of corporate bonds. For each bond in the subset, the model returns an estimate of value and the bond's probability of default. The details are as follows.

For a default-free bond, the traditional valuation formula is

$$V_f = \frac{c}{1 + k_f} + \frac{c}{(1 + k_f)^2} + \dots + \frac{c + F}{(1 + k_f)^n} \tag{13}$$

where c is the dollar coupon, F is face value, n is the term to maturity, and k_f is the promised yield to maturity. One approach for a risky corporate bond is to model the discount rate as an increment to the risk-free rate:

$$V_c = \frac{c}{1 + k_c} + \frac{c}{(1 + k_c)^2} + \dots + \frac{c + F}{(1 + k_c)^n} \tag{14}$$

where $k_c = k_f + \theta$. Generally θ is termed the risk premium. Since this model is consistent with the 1-period Capital Asset Pricing Model (CAPM) under certain assumptions, we call it the CAPM model.[34]

Our approach to the valuation of default risk consists in modeling the bond issuer's survival as a Markov process. Following Jonkhart,[35] Bierman and Hass,[36] Fons, Ma, Rao, and Peterson,[37] and Yawitz,[38] we assume that, between coupon payments, an issuer can default (go bankrupt) with a constant probability p. We assume that p is the probability that the issuer will go bankrupt between coupon payment dates t and $t+1$, given that the issuer has survived to make the t-th coupon payment. Assuming that there are x coupon payments remaining, define $V_M(x)$ to be the bond's value immediately after coupon payment $n - x$. Then, conditioning on whether the issuer will go bankrupt before the next coupon payment, we have the following difference equation:

$$V_M(x) = (1 - p)\left[\frac{c + V_M(x - 1)}{(1 + k)}\right] + p(1 - w)\left[\frac{c + V_M(x - 1)}{(1 + k)}\right] \tag{15}$$

where w is the bond's percentage writedown, and k is a discount rate. That is, with probability $1 - p$, the bond investor gets $c + V_M(x - 1)$, and with probability p, $(1 - w)(c + V_M(x - 1))$.

Equation (15) can be rewritten

---

[34] See M.I. Weinstein, "Bond Systematic Risk and the Option Pricing Model," *Journal of Finance* (1983), pp. 1415-1429.

[35] M. Jonkhart, "On the Term Structure of Interest Rates and the Risk of Default: An Analytical Approach," *Journal of Banking and Finance* (1979), pp. 253-61.

[36] H. Bierman Jr. and J. E. Hass, "An Analytical Model of Bond Risk Differentials," *Journal of Financial and Quantitative Analysis* (1975), pp. 757-773.

[37] C. Ma, R.P. Rao, and R.L. Peterson, "The Resiliency of the High-Yield Bond Market: The LTV Default."

[38] J. B. Yawitz, "An Analytical Model of Interest Rate Differentials and Different Default Recoveries," *Journal of Financial and Quantitative Analysis* (1977), pp. 481-490.

$$V_M(x) = a + bV_M(x-1) \qquad (16)$$

where

$$a = \frac{c(1-wp)}{1+k} \quad \text{and} \quad b = \frac{1-wp}{1+k} \qquad (17)$$

The difference equation given by equation (16) can be easily solved using the method of successive substitution as follows. First substitute $x-1$ for x in equation (16) to obtain

$$V_M(x-1) = a + bV_M(x-2) \qquad (18)$$

Now substitute equation (18) into equation (16) for $V_M(x-1)$ to obtain

$$V_M(x) = a + ab + b^2 V_M(x-2) \qquad (19)$$

Continuing this process, substitute $x-2$ for x in equation (16) to obtain

$$V_M(x-2) = a + bV_M(x-3) \qquad (20)$$

Substituting equation (20) into equation (19) for $V_M(x-2)$ gives

$$V_M(x) = a + ab + ab^2 + b^3 VM(x-3) \qquad (21)$$

Continuing this process of evaluation and substitution, and letting $x = n$, we have

$$V_M(x) = a(1 + b + b^2 + \dots + b^{n-1}) + b^n V_M(0) \qquad (22)$$

Using the boundary condition,

$$V_M(0) = F \qquad (23)$$

substituting for a, and simplifying, we obtain

$$V_M(p) = c\left[\frac{1-(1+R)^{-n}}{R}\right] + \frac{F}{(1+R)^n} \qquad (24)$$

where

$$R = \frac{k+wp}{1-wp} \qquad (25)$$

We term equations (24) and (25) the *Markov Model* to distinguish it from the CAPM approach. Note that equation (24) is the usual expression for the present value of a bond. The expression in square brackets is the present value of an annuity which pays \$1 per period. The last term in equation (24) is just the present value of the bond's face value.

For a risk neutral investor, we can set $k = k_f$, and equation (25) becomes

$$R = \frac{k_f + wp}{1 - wp} \tag{26}$$

For a risk averse investor having a constant certainty equivalent factor $q<1$ per period (the certainty equivalent of an expected cash flow in period t, c_t, is qc_t), equation (25) becomes

$$R_q = \frac{(1 - q + k_f)/(q + k_f + wp)}{1 - wp} \tag{27}$$

Again, we remark that the Markov Model is simply a reparameterization of CAPM. Hence there is a simple relationship between the Markov and CAPM valuations. For a risk neutral investor, the Markov approach gives the same valuation as the CAPM if r is the same as $k_f + \theta$, or if

$$\theta = \theta_N = \frac{wp}{1 - wp}(1 + k_f) \tag{28}$$

For a risk averse investor the expression is

$$\theta_q = \frac{wp}{1 - wp}(1 + (1 - q + k_f)/q) \tag{29}$$

The bond's beta can be expressed in terms of p. For a risk neutral investor,

$$R = \frac{k_f + wp}{1 - wp} = k_f + \beta(k_m - k_f)$$

where k_m is the expected return on the market portfolio. Hence, we have that

$$\beta = \frac{wp}{1 - wp}\frac{1 + k_f}{k_m - k_f} = \frac{\theta_N}{k_m - k_f} \tag{30}$$

Note that beta is monotonically increasing in p.

Finally we can express the bond's standard deviation of return in terms of p. The beta of asset a is defined as

$$\beta_a = \rho_{am}\frac{\sigma_a}{\sigma_m} \tag{31}$$

where ρ_{am} is the correlation between the asset and the market, σ_a is the standard deviation of the asset, and σ_m is the standard deviation of the market. Using equations (30) and (31), we obtain

$$\sigma_a = \frac{wp}{1 - wp}\frac{1}{\rho_{am}}\frac{1 + k_f}{k_m - k_f}\sigma_m$$

Hence the volatility of the asset, as measured by σ_a, depends directly on p and w. Moreover, as p increases, σ_a increases. These results are all intuitive and consistent with the literature on bond default risk.

To estimate p for a particular bond, let P_0 be the price of a corporate bond having coupon, c, term, n, and face, F. Let k_f be the yield of a default-free bond with the same coupon, term and face. Then the issuer's *period risk* is defined to be the value of p which solves

$$P_0 = c\left[\frac{1-(1+R)^{-n}}{R}\right] + \frac{F}{(1+R)^n} \tag{32}$$

where R is defined above. Hence computing p is essentially the problem of computing an internal rate of return, which generally has to be done numerically. On the other hand, if there are yield data available, that is, we have the promised yield on the corporate as well as the equivalent default-free bond, then we can estimate p using equation (27):

$$p = \frac{k_c - k_f}{w(1 + k_c)} \tag{33}$$

One benefit of our model is that it allows us to compute some interesting survival probabilities. For instance: the probability that the issuer makes at least m coupon payments is $(1-p)^m$; the probability that an issuer makes exactly m coupon payments is $p(1-p)^m$, for $m = 0, 1, ..., n-1$; and the probability that the issuer makes all of the promised payments is $(1-p)^n$.

In turn, these probabilities allow us to construct different kinds of capital risk measures. For instance, to compute the probability that δ percent of the invested capital (the price, P_0) is returned, then the issuer must survive m periods where m is the lowest integer satisfying

$$\sum_{t=1}^{m} \frac{c_t}{(1+k_c)^t} \geq \delta P_0 \tag{34}$$

Let this integer be $m(\delta)$. Then the probability that at least δ percent is returned is

$$\phi(\delta) = (1-p)^{m(\delta)} \tag{35}$$

Example 1

Consider a default-free and corporate bond with the characteristics:

$$c = 8\%, n = 10, \text{ and } F = 100 \tag{36}$$

The price of the default-free bond is \$87.71; the price of the corporate is \$77.40. Given these prices, the risk-free yield is 10% and the corporate yield is 12%. Based on equation (33), the period risk is $p = 0.018$. The probability that at least 5 coupon payments are made is $(1-0.018)^5 = 0.914$. The probability that the issuer makes all 10 payments is $(1-0.018)^{10} = 0.835$.

We can now construct a table of the capital risk measure developed in the previous section. Recall that $\phi(\delta)$ is the probability that an investor is returned at least δ percent of the original investment of \$77.40. Exhibit 1 presents values of $\phi(\delta)$ for various values of δ.

We can compare these hypothetical numbers to some empirical evidence provided by Bennett, Esser and Roth.[39] Referring to their Exhibit 15, a default risk premium of 200 basis points (recall that, in our example, the corporate bond yield was 12% and the risk-free rate, 10%) would be consistent with a bond rated Baa(−) to Ba(+). Such a bond would have a 10-year cumulative default rate of about 17% (found through interpolation of columns 1 and 2 in Bennett, Esser and Roth's Exhibit 15). This figure is very close to our model's estimate of 16.5% (which is one minus the probability that the issuer makes all 10 payments, 0.835).

Example 2

Still another approach to the estimation of default probabilities is a joint approach. Consider a subset of corporate bonds where P_{ij} is the price of bond i issued by firm j. Given the rating category of bond ij, we take as exogenous the default writedown w_j. Moreover all bonds of firm j are assumed to have a constant period default probability p_j. Let $V_{ij}(p_j|w_j)$ be the value for bond ij based on equations (24) and (25). Then the default probabilities can be estimated by solving the following least-squares problem:

$$\min_{p_j} \sum_j \sum_i [P_{ij} - V_{ij}(p_j|w_j)]^2 \tag{37}$$

Let p_j^* solve this problem. Then we can compare P_{ij} and $V_{ij}(p_j^*|w_j)$: bonds for which the difference

$$\left| P_{ij} - V_{ij}(p_j^*|w_j) \right|$$

Exhibit 1: The Risk Measure, $\phi(\alpha)$

δ	$\phi(\delta)$
10	0.965
20	0.947
30	0.930
40	0.898
50	0.866
60	0.835
70	0.835
80	0.835
90	0.835

---

[39] Bennett, Esser, and Roth, "Corporate Credit Risk and Reward."

Exhibit 2: Data for Example 2

Bond	Firm	Risk Class	Coupon	Term	Price	True Default Probability	True Yield
1	1	1	10	7	99.4795	0.010	0.1013
2	1	1	12	12	112.6971	0.010	0.1013
3	1	1	15	15	136.1609	0.010	0.1013
4	2	1	12	8	109.1305	0.012	0.1016
5	2	1	14	12	126.2293	0.012	0.1016
6	3	2	12	6	106.8906	0.020	0.1046
7	3	2	15	12	130.7871	0.020	0.1046
8	3	2	16	18	144.8265	0.020	0.1046
9	4	2	10	7	96.8952	0.022	0.1051
10	4	2	16	14	138.4918	0.022	0.1051

Exhibit 3: Comparison of True and Estimated Default Probabilities

Firm	True Default Probability	Estimated Default Probability
1	0.010	0.012
2	0.012	0.013
3	0.020	0.017
4	0.022	0.026

is large are candidates for further consideration. The benefit of this estimation procedure is that it allows the simultaneous estimation of default probabilities across rating categories for any subset of bonds an analyst cares to consider.

Here is an example. Consider the set of bonds in Exhibit 2. The sample comprises 10 bonds taken from 4 firms in 2 rating categories. Firms 1 and 2 are in rating category 1 and have respective default probabilities of 0.01 and 0.012. Firms 3 and 4 are in rating category 2 and have respective default probabilities of 0.02 and 0.022. Assuming that the default-free term structure is flat at 10%, that risk category 1 has a writedown percentage of 0.12 and that risk category 2 has a writedown percentage of 0.21, the true yield of each bond can be calculated by equation (27). For instance, bond 1's true yield is

$$ R_1 = \frac{k_f + wp}{1 - wp} = \frac{0.10 + 0.12(0.01)}{1 - 0.12(0.01)} = 0.1013 $$

The prices in the exhibit are calculated by using the true yield to get a price and then adding a small random error to this price.

The optimization in equation (37) was set up in a spreadsheet. The solution is the third column in Exhibit 3 (Estimated Default Probability). Note that the estimated default probabilities are in the same rank order and close to the true probabilities.

Exhibit 4: A Comparison of Prices and Model Values

Bond	Market Price	Model Value	Absolute Difference
1	99.4795	99.3594	0.2526
2	112.6971	112.6446	0.2549
3	136.1609	136.7475	0.3221
4	109.1305	109.7671	0.5465
5	126.2293	125.9718	0.3853
6	106.8906	106.5999	0.0185
7	130.7871	130.2172	0.0095
8	144.8265	144.0846	0.0004
9	96.8952	97.5556	0.1828
10	138.4918	139.3380	0.931

Besides the estimates of default probabilities, the model returns values which can then be compared to actual prices. The table in Exhibit 4 compares model value with price for each bond. Bonds with high absolute differences are candidates for further consideration.

CONCLUSIONS

The pricing of risky debt is of obvious importance, and we hope that the reader will now have a sense of some of the issues associated with recent developments in the literature. Approaches to the valuation of risky bonds involve the basic trade-off between computational complexity and model accuracy. The more sophisticated modeling approaches such as the Longstaff and Schwartz model require a significant investment in computational resources. We present a simpler alternative which retains many of the desirable features of a risky bond valuation model but which is easier to implement than its more sophisticated counterparts. Empirical comparisons between the many extant models proposed to date in this literature would be highly desirable but, unfortunately, we know of none.

The implications of this review are manifold. We have shown much of the empirical evidence regarding the default experience, and have provided some evidence on the determinants of bond default. The theoretical approaches which have been presented will help the analyst to more systematically assemble the data needed for meaningful analysis, and will assist in organizing and processing these data so as to reach meaningful conclusions.

There are no definitive models of bond pricing, and, of course, the market often goes its own way with little or no reference to underlying fundamental relationships. In the long term, however, an understanding of these fundamental relationships can only help the analyst to make sense of the data and to make better fixed-income investment decisions. In this chapter we have examined many of the important fundamental relationships and have presented two versions of models which attempt to capture these relationships in a formal way. At the least, the analyst should now have a better sense of how these various factors interrelate, and of some of the measurement issues associated with implementing the models.

Chapter 7

An Options Approach to Commercial Mortgages and CMBS Valuation and Risk Analysis

David P. Jacob
Managing Director and
Director of Research & Securitization
Nomura International Securities, Inc.

Ted C.H. Hong
Director
Nomura International Securities, Inc.

Laurence H. Lee
Senior Research Analyst
Nomura International Securities, Inc.

INTRODUCTION

Investment in commercial mortgages and commercial mortgage-backed securities (CMBS) is receiving increasing attention from mainstream fixed-income investors. Yet, much of the quantitative technology that has been developed for analyzing relative value in such areas as residential mortgage-backed securities (MBS) and corporate bonds has not been applied to commercial mortgages. Investors in agency mortgage-backed securities and callable corporate bonds, for example, have used option pricing to determine fair value for securities whose cash flows are uncertain due to the possibility of an early call. Commercial mortgages typically have greater call protection than residential MBS and corporate bonds, although they still have some callability. Most commercial mortgages have lock-out periods followed by a period during which a penalty is applied to premature principal payments, followed in turn by a free period. The technology applied to other fixed-income instruments to value these features could be used for assessing risk and relative value in commercial mortgages and CMBS.

In addition to the risk of early principal payment, commercial mortgages, like corporate bonds, are subject to the risk of losses in a foreclosure following a default. Pricing methodology described in academic journals has been applied to this risk for corporate bonds, but for a variety of reasons it has not proven to be practical.[1] The analysis and valuation of this risk for commercial mortgages using similar quantitative analysis, while discussed in the academic world, has not been applied in the market for commercial mortgages.[2]

The need for improved tools has increased with the introduction of securitization, where the most popular method of credit enhancement is the senior-subordinated structure. Whole loans are aggregated and their cash flows are then allocated to create securities with credit ratings from AAA down to B and unrated. As a result, the risk of loss due to default is leveraged up in the junior classes and leveraged down in the senior classes. The analogy in the residential MBS area is the creation of planned amortization class (PAC) bonds and support tranches where the PAC bond has leveraged down prepayment risk and the support bond has leveraged up prepayment risk. Moreover, the senior subordinated structure requires that recoveries from foreclosures first be used to pay senior bondholders. From the perspective of these bondholders a prepayment event has occurred, even though the unscheduled cash flow came about due to a credit event. Nevertheless, it must be considered in the valuation and risk of these AAA rated securities.

When an investor looks at a CMBS deal it would be useful to know whether or not the AAA class at 90 basis points over Treasuries is a better value than the B class at a +600 basis point spread. How should one compare the risk of a bullet loan with one that amortizes? How does the risk of default affect the value of a security trading at a premium? What is the fair value of an interest-only strip when the loans underlying the deal have percentage penalties versus yield maintenance, versus lockout. This chapter describes a two-factor contingent-claims theoretic framework and applies option pricing methodology to commercial mortgages to answer these questions.

In the next section we outline the elements of valuation and the basic analytic approach to pricing commercial mortgages. Following this, we apply the approach to commercial whole loans and show the effects of each factor on the value of the mortgage. Next, a multi-class senior-subordinated deal is evaluated.

---

[1] The complexity of the capital structure of a corporation and the possibility of a leveraged buyout make the application of the option approach less practical for corporate bonds. For more details on the option approach to pricing default risk in high yield bonds, see Richard Bookstabber and David P. Jacob, "Controlling Interest Rate Risk," Chapter 8 in *The Composite Hedge: Controlling the Credit Risk of High-Yield Bonds* (New York: John Wiley & Sons, 1986).

[2] There has been some work published in this area. See Chapter 12 and Patrick J. Corcoran "Commercial Mortgages: Measuring Risk and Return,"*Journal of Portfolio Management* (Fall 1989);Sheridan Titman and Walter Torous, "Valuing Commercial Mortgages: An Empirical Investigation of the Contingent Claims Approach to Pricing Risky Debt," *Journal of Finance* (June 1989); and, Paul D. Childs, Steven H. Ott, and Timothy J. Riddiough, "The Pricing of Multi-Class Commercial Mortgage-Backed Securities," Working Paper (December 1994).

We then use the model to look at the relative risk of different securities. Finally, we draw some conclusions, discuss practical issues relating to the model, and propose some future applications. In the appendix we show some of the mathematics behind the model.

THE ELEMENTS OF VALUATION

The value of all real estate securities is contingent upon the value of the underlying real estate asset since they each have a claim on this asset. For example, the equity holder has a residual claim on the income stream after the debt holder is paid. If the income from the real estate asset is insufficient to meet the debt obligation and a default results, the debt holder has a claim on the real estate. Usually, the equity holder defaults only when the value of the real estate is less than the value of the loan and in when income is insufficient to pay debt service. The debt holder, in this case, will receive the smaller of the debt payment or the value of the real estate and the equity holder receives nothing.

The analytic approach we use is to view the owner (lender/investor) of a commercial mortgage as having a long position in a credit risk-free, non-callable mortgage, a short call option, and a short put option. The commercial mortgage investor/lender (debt holder) has written an option to the borrower (equity holder) to call (prepay) the debt, and an option to put (default) the real estate to the debt holder. That is,

$$\text{Commercial mortgage} = (\text{Default-free and non-callable mortgage})$$
$$- (\text{Call option}) - (\text{Put option})$$
$$\text{PREPAYMENT} \quad \text{DEFAULT}$$

As compensation for writing these options the debt holder receives a spread over the yield on Treasury bonds usually in the form of a higher coupon. Therefore, in order to value the commercial mortgage, one can value the risk-free cash flows and the associated call (prepayment) and put (default) options. To properly value the options, the default and prepayment options need to be analyzed *simultaneously* since as we will show they are interrelated.

To value the options we need to define what circumstances would cause the property owner to exercise his options.

Prepayment option — triggering conditions: Prepayment is triggered for two reasons:

    a. economic benefit from refinancing which occurs if
        1. the general level of interest rates drop.
    or
        2. the property value increases, thus allowing the borrower to refinance at a tighter spread to Treasuries.

or

b. Owner wants to sell property and the mortgage is not assumable.

For condition *a* to be viable net operating income (NOI) must be sufficiently greater than the scheduled payments required under the new rate, since otherwise the borrower would not qualify for the loan. If the borrower does qualify, he will refinance so long as the present value of the future promised payments minus the value of the options (fair market value of the debt including its embedded options) is greater than the face value of the remaining debt plus refinancing costs such as prepayment penalties. Thus, as interest rates drop (for newly originated fixed-rate mortgages) and as the quality of the property improves the likelihood of refinancing increases since under these circumstances the market value of the debt increases.

In addition, property owners sometimes want to realize the return on their properties particularly as the tax benefits of ownership decline through time. If the mortgage is assumable or a substitution of collateral is permitted, the owner could sell the property with the loan remaining intact. Otherwise the owner would have to prepay the mortgage. Another situation that could occur that would lead to prepayment even in a rising rate environment is if the property appreciates in value, and the owner desires to re-leverage the property. If the mortgage note prohibits additional financing (this almost always the case for CMBS), then the borrower must first repay his loan.

Empirical evidence on commercial mortgage prepayments suggests that when it is economic for commercial property owners to prepay, they do so at an even faster rate then owners of residential properties.[3] Moreover, turnover rates in property ownership indicate that even if refinancing is uneconomic property owners sell their properties to realize profits. For example, Abraham and Theobald found that the cumulative prepayment rate for low coupon mortgages that were outstanding for 10 years was 82.4%. [4]

Default option triggering option conditions: For the property owner to exercise his default option there are two necessary conditions.

(i) Net operating income is less than the current period's scheduled mortgage payment[5]

and

(ii) The market value of the property is less than the market value of the debt.[6]

---

[3] Jesse M. Abraham and E. Scott Theobald, "Commercial Mortgage Prepayments," Chapter 3 in Frank J. Fabozzi and David P. Jacob (eds.), *The Handbook of Commercial Mortgage-Backed Securities* (New Hope, PA: Frank J. Fabozzi Associates, 1996).

[4] This is one reason why interest strips from CMBS deals that have lockout provisions as opposed to simply yield maintenance are far less risky and should trade at tighter spreads.

[5] Net cash flow might be more appropriate, but here we use NOI for simplicity.

[6] The market value of the debt is the present value of the future promised payments plus the current payment that is due minus the value of the options.

For a non-callable mortgage, default will never be necessary for a rational borrower if the NOI is enough to cover debt payment. Default starts to occur when the NOI is insufficient to meet the debt service. When that happens and the property value is also less than the value of the debt, the default option would be exercised. Both conditions are necessary because if the property value is greater than the value of the debt, but the NOI is insufficient to pay the debt service, the property owner would attempt to sell the property and payoff the debt rather than go through foreclosure.

Default as a method of prepayment — triggering conditions: Sometimes the property owner may try to use a default as a method of prepaying so as to avoid the prepayment penalty and/or lock-out feature.[7] In this case, the triggering conditions for default are more complicated. The conditions would be triggered to default as follows:

> (i) The NOI has to be greater than the payments that would be required at the time if the loan were to be refinanced.
> and
> (ii) the present value of the future promised payments minus the value of the options (fair market value of the debt including its embedded options) is greater than the face value of the remaining debt plus foreclosure expenses.

If these two conditions hold the borrower can default, go through foreclosure, pay off the face value of the debt with the proceeds, and then refinance. This situation can arise when interest rates drop and property value and NOI increase, but the loan is either locked-out or there is a stiff prepayment penalty. In this case if the foreclosure expenses are not too onerous, the borrower has an incentive to default. It is unclear, however, how the courts would treat this situation. It is possible that the bankruptcy judge would force the borrower to compensate the lender.

The Combined Default and Prepayment

Since the call and put options are embedded in the mortgage debt, the call option and the put option cannot actually be separated. The incentive to prepay as we have discussed is linked not just to the general level of interest rates, but to the ever changing level of operating income of the property and the resulting available refinancing spread. Thus, the value of the prepayment option is related to factors that affect the value of the default option. Similarly the incentive to default is related to the level of interest rates which in turn affects the value of the prepayment option. Moreover, borrowers who either prepay or default terminate the contract of the mortgage. This results in the termination of both options. Our triggering conditions, thus, do not work independently, but need to be evaluated simultaneously.

---

[7] Experts in bankruptcy law feel that in a true default, prepayment penalties could be construed by the judge as usury and therefore disallowed.

Exhibit 1: Prepayment Option of a Commercial Mortgage

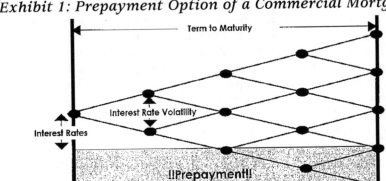

Source: Nomura Securities International, Inc.

To visualize the triggering process for the prepayment option, look at Exhibit 1. The horizontal axis measures time. The vertical axis tracks interest rates which in turn determines the present value of the promised payments. As time passes, interest rates can move up or down. As interest rates drop, the market value of the debt increases above the face value making it economically worthwhile for the borrower to refinance.

A lock-out or penalty reduces the value of the call option since it lessens the likelihood of the option being exercised. In general, the longer the term to maturity and the more volatile the interest rate, the more valuable the prepayment option since the likelihood of exercise increases.

In order to visualize the triggering process for a loan default, we make use of the metaphor of a drunk person walking along the edge of a cliff trying to go from point A to point B. The closer he is to the edge when he begins his walk, the more erratic his walk, and the longer the distance from point A to point B, the more likely he will fall off the cliff before reaching point B. Similarly, in the case of an income generating property, the more volatile the NOI, the greater the initial loan-to-value (LTV), the lower the debt service coverage ratio (DSCR), and the longer the maturity of the debt, the higher probability of default prior to maturity. In Exhibit 2 the horizontal axis measures time to maturity. The vertical axis measures the level of NOI and LTV. As time passes NOI and LTV can move up or down. If NOI/LTV moves down/up sufficiently, the property owner will default and hand the keys of the property to the lender.

Determinants of Option Values

Now that we have defined the conditions that lead to the exercise of the options, we need to identify the determinants of the options' values. The value of the embedded options depends upon many factors. The direct determinants are

1. Current balance of mortgage
2. Term to maturity of mortgage

Exhibit 2: Default Option of a Commercial Mortgage

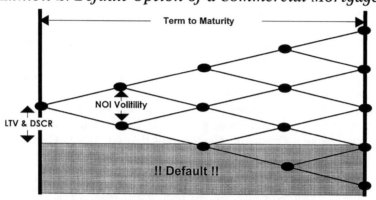

3. Mortgage payments including interest and principal, and the amortization schedule
4. Prepayment terms and penalties
5. Net operating income from the collateral property
6. Volatility of net operating income
7. Terms of default and foreclosure costs
8. Interest rates
9. Volatility of interest rates
10. Correlation between interest rates and net operating income

The first four items specify the information necessary to calculate the promised cash flows of the underlying mortgage. This information in conjunction with current and the potential future interest rates are necessary for calculating the value of the prepayment option. Items 5, 6, and 7 which relate to the property are essential for valuing the default option. The last three items are critical for valuing all assets, including the mortgage, the real estate, and the options.

The Valuation Process

The process of interest rates and net operating income determine the entire valuation procedure of the commercial mortgage and its embedded options. In our framework, we assume that interest rates and NOI are the two underlying building blocks. The property value which is the present value of all future NOI's can be calculated from interest rates and NOI. To solve for the option values, a two-dimensional binomial tree or pyramid is constructed (by combining Exhibit 1 and Exhibit 2) based on the assumptions of the process and volatility governing future NOI and interest rates.[8]

---

[8] When a multi-class commercial mortgage-backed security is evaluated, the path-independent condition for the remaining balances of the bond classes does not necessarily hold. Fortunately, so long as the underlying loans satisfy the path-independent condition, Monte Carlo simulations which randomly select a finite number of paths from a virtually infinite number of paths can be utilized to calculate the option values. Since a huge path selection process is involved, variance reduction techniques turn out to be very important to improve the sampling method.

For every path of interest rates there is a whole set of possible paths of NOI. The tree will specify the future cash flows of the mortgage under the full range of interest rates and NOI scenarios. Once the pyramid is created, the value of the property can be calculated at each node of the pyramid.[9] Similarly other relevant variables such as LTV and DSCR can be calculated as well. At each node, the action taken by the borrower (prepayment, default, or scheduled payment) determines the cash flow that the debt holder receives. The option values and the fair value of the mortgage can then be calculated by discounting the cash flows backward in time through the pyramid. The values are equal to the expected discounted value of the cash flows through the pyramid. The theoretical or fair value of the commercial mortgage can be obtained by combining these terms.

Option-Adjusted Spread Since the market value or market price of a financial security may differ from its fair value, the fixed-income market has developed the concept of *option-adjusted spread* (OAS).

OAS is a spread relative to the Treasury curve, quoted in basis points, which is used for measuring the relative value of securities with a series of uncertain cash flows. The OAS can be obtained by calibrating the theoretical present value to the current market price. The theoretical present value takes all possible cash flow streams discounted by the corresponding discount rates and weighted by assumed probabilities. The OAS, thus, is a constant spread added to the risk-free interest rate and is used as the discount rate for the corresponding cash flows. The procedure involves solving for the spread which equates the price obtained via discounting the cash flows to the market price.

The larger or more positive the OAS, the cheaper the security is relative to its theoretical value. The OAS can be thought of as the risk premium which the investor would earn if he repurchased or hedged, at fair value, the options that he has implicitly shorted by owning the security. The concept of OAS was originally introduced to analyze relative value in residential mortgage-backed securities and callable corporate bonds, where the borrower's prepayment option substantially negatively impacts the value of these securities. If the OAS is positive/negative, then the investor is receiving more/less than he should have for shorting the embedded options.

Parameter Estimation and Practical Considerations Like all option models, a number of parameters need to be estimated and assumptions need to be made regarding the process governing the random variables. In our case, we need to have an estimate for the volatility of NOI for the property, the volatility of interest rates, and the correlation between these. If the loan or a security is backed by a number of properties, then we also need the correlation matrix of NOI of all the properties.

---

[9] In our model we specify a term which indicates the growth rate, if any, in the NOI. We define the property value to be equal to $NOI/(R - R \times G)$ where R equals prevailing interest rates, NOI is net operating income, and $R \times G$ is the growth rate in NOI. $R - R \times G$ equals the traditional cap rate.

Regarding interest rates there is a voluminous body of literature which addresses the interest rate process necessary to properly price fixed-income income options and to satisfy the arbitrage-free condition for the term structure of interest rates.[10] In this chapter, we use the Black, Derman, and Toy model and its binomial tree to calibrate the interest rate lattice to the initial yield curve.

To empirically estimate the NOI volatility, we first used the Russell/NCREIF Property Index (RNPI) despite all of its drawbacks.[11] The RNPI index is the most widely quoted index for real estate property performance. It provides data such as net operating income and appraisal value of commercial buildings by region and by property type on quarterly basis. We also used the RNPI series to estimate the correlation between interest rates and net operating income. The 6% volatility of NOI that was estimated from the large and diversified pool of properties that underlie the RNPI series greatly understates the true NOI volatility of individual properties. Based on our own data we expect the volatility of NOI to range between 9% and 15%. There are differences by property type. As we would expect multi-family properties have lower NOI volatilities and hotels tend to have higher volatilities. In practice one needs to estimate the volatility for the property in question.[12]

One way to calibrate the NOI volatility assumption is to see what pattern and level of defaults is produced using the parameter assumptions. In Exhibit 3 we show the actual average cumulative default rates for investment grade and speculative grade corporate bonds as a function of time as computed by Moody's Investors Service for the years 1970- 1994. One can see that for the high quality debt the marginal default rate starts out low and increases over time. On the other hand, the marginal default rate for the speculative grade debt declines over time. The reason for this is that lower quality debt that survives the early years has a decreasing probability of defaulting. Whereas, high quality debt has an increasing (or at least non-decreasing) chance of defaulting as time passes.

---

[10] Ho and Lee used a binomial tree to create an arbitrage-free interest rate model. See Thomas S.Y. Ho and S.B. Lee, "Term Structure Movements and Pricing of Interest Rate Contingent Claims," *Journal of Finance* (December 1986). Black, Derman, and Toy also constructed a binomial tree model and, furthermore, allowed various volatilities for the entire term structure. See Fischer Black, Emanuel Derman, and William Toy, "A One-Factor Model of Interest Rates and its Application to Treasury Bond Options," *Financial Analysts Journal* (January-February 1990). Hull and White created a trinomial tree and provided a closed form solution for arbitrage-free model in continuous time. See John Hull and Alan White, "One-Factor Interest-Rate Models and the Valuation of Interest-Rate Derivative Securities," *Journal of Financial and Quantitative Analysis*, (June 1993). Both Jamshidian and Chan assumed a variety of interest rate process to calibrate to the term structure. See Farshid Jamshidian, "Forward Induction and Construction of Yield Curve Diffusion Models," *Merrill Lynch Research* (March 1991); and, Y.K. Chan, "Term Structure as a Second Order Dynamical System, and Pricing of Derivative Securities," *Bear Stearns Research*, 1992.

[11] The Russell/NCREIF property index is an appraisal-based index of property returns and values. This index represents data collected from the Voting Members of the National Council of Real Estate Investment Fiduciaries. Many researchers feel that the appraisal process causes the data to significantly understate the price volatility. The volatility of the income component, on the other hand, might be representative for a large pool of assets.

[12] Specific features such as cross-collateralization, which would lower NOI volatility need to be modeled.

Exhibit 3: Average Cumulative Default Rates for Corporate Bonds

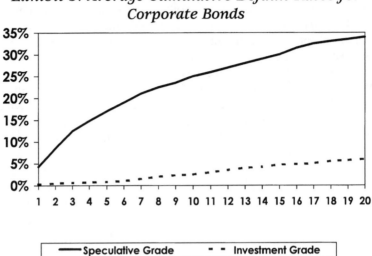

Source: Moody's Investors Service.

In Exhibit 4 we show the marginal default rates for high quality (low LTV) and low quality (high LTV) loans that are implied by our model using an assumption of 15% volatility of NOI. In Exhibit 5 we show the implied cumulative default rates. The pattern is very consistent with the Moody's data and demonstrates the ability of the model to differentiate the default pattern associated with different quality loans. Moreover, the level of defaults, while higher than what Moody's found for corporate bonds, in our view represents a conservative level of defaults.[13]

Aside from parameter estimation, there are some practical considerations when implementing the model that differ from the theory. The theory assumes the following conditions: (1) liquidity, (2) symmetry of market information, (3) optimal exercise, and (4) refinancing ability.

Liquidity refers to how easy it is to buy or sell real estate and commercial mortgages in the secondary market. The theoretical model assumes that transactions costs are low and that the markets are very liquid. Symmetry of market information refers to whether borrowers and investors have the same information. Optimal exercise refers to how efficiently the borrower exercises his options if arbitrage opportunities emerge. Refinancing ability refers to the fact that financing is based solely on the property consideration irrespective of the borrower. Even though many of these conditions do not hold in practice, the model provides value by incorporating in a single framework the primary factors driving the value of the mortgage. As a result it becomes useful as a relative value tool and for comparing risk.

---

[13] The cumulative default level after 10 years implied the by the model for a 70% LTV loan with an initial DSCR of 1.5X using a 15% NOI volatility is about 26%. Moreover, the implied loss severity is about 19%, both of these statistics exceed the levels found with the historical data. We feel that our standard of 15% NOI volatility is conservative.

Exhibit 4: Implied Marginal Default Rates for Commercial Mortgages

50% LTV

90% LTV

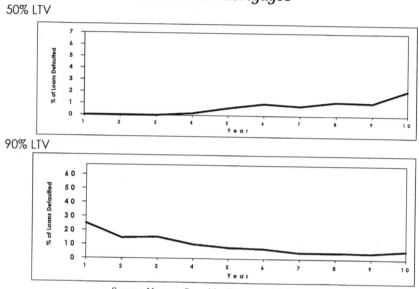

Source: Nomura Securities International, Inc.

Exhibit 5: Implied Cumulative Default Rates for Commercial Mortgages

50% LTV

90% LTV

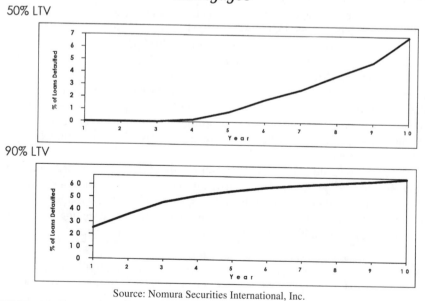

Source: Nomura Securities International, Inc.

COMPARATIVE ANALYSIS

In this section we use OAS as the measure to analyze the factors that affect the value of a commercial mortgage. In the next section, we apply the framework to a multiclass CMBS structure. In order to use the model to analyze the factors affecting the value of a commercial mortgage, we could either keep the spread constant (OAS), and see how the price varies as we change each of the factors. Or, we could keep the price constant and see how the factors affect the OAS as we change each of the factors. We adopt the latter approach since, in general, the market sets the price.

Since the OAS is considered compensation for shorting options, the OAS decreases for a fixed mortgage price as the default or prepayment risks increase. The degree of risk exposure depends upon the characteristics of the mortgage debt, the performance of underlying collateral as well as the economic factors such as interest rates. We analyze default risk with respect to four factors — DSCR, LTV, volatility of NOI, and mortgage maturity date. These factors are the usual measures of risk quoted in real estate markets for analyzing default risk.

In this section we use as an example, a commercial mortgage with a 10 year maturity, 9% coupon, initial DSCR of 1.50x, initial LTV of 70%, initial risk-free interest rate of 7%, and volatility of 11% and 15% for interest rates, and NOI, respectively.[14] Thus, the initial spread of the loan is +200bp. A correlation of 0.2 between interest rates and NOI is used. We assume that the loan follows a 30 year amortization schedule and pays a balloon payment at the end of year 10. *Initially, we assume that the mortgage is noncallable.*

Debt Service Coverage Ratio (DSCR)

The debt service coverage ratio (DSCR) is defined as the annual NOI divided by annual cost of debt service including principal payments. Normally, as DSCR gets larger, the probability of default and a resulting loss decreases. Thus, as DSCR increases the value of the default option decreases. As a result for a fixed-income price the OAS increases. This can be seen in Exhibit 6 for a wide range of DSCR. Moreover, as DSCR gets very large, further increases do not result in a higher OAS.[15] For lower initial values of DSCR, the OAS is lower, indicating that the investor is really getting on average something less than +200 bp implied by his coupon. For example, at a DSCR of 2.50x the OAS is 170bp, or equivalently the default option is worth +30bp.

As one would expect the model shows that the OAS line for a bullet loan always lies below the line for the amortizing loan, since the amortizing loan has a built-in risk reduction mechanism. Even though both loans start with the same LTV, the LTV of the amortizing loan decreases through time, thus reducing its risk. The model computes the value of the amortization to be worth 30-40bp.

---

[14] To reduce the number of calculations we assumed a semi-annual pay mortgage.

[15] Since we kept initial LTV constant at 70%, the OAS does not increase much above 180 bp. Thus, the probability of default does not go to zero. In reality LTV would likely to lower and the OAS would go to +200bp.

Exhibit 6: OAS versus DSCR: Default Option

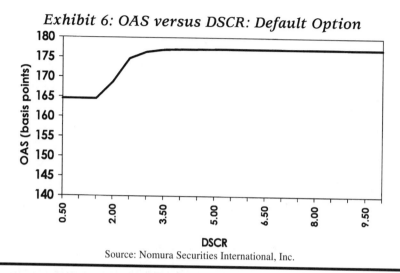

Source: Nomura Securities International, Inc.

Loan-To-Value Ratio (LTV)

The loan-to-value ratio (LTV) is defined as the ratio of loan amount to the value of the collateral property. This ratio is frequently used as a measure of leverage to assess the level of protection from default. A lower LTV loan is considered more credit worthy due to its better default protection. In terms of OAS, the OAS should increase as the initial LTV drops since the probability of a default and a loss decreases. This can be seen in Exhibit 7. When the LTV is sufficiently low, the loan is so default-protected that the OAS will start to level off. Lower initial LTVs do not lead to further increases in OAS. At this point the probability of default is near zero and the OAS equals the nominal spread of +200bp.

The impact on OAS due to change of LTV is more significant for bullet loans than amortizing loans.[16] This is because, as we stated earlier, the amortizing loan has a built-in LTV decreasing mechanism to automatically reduce default risk over time.

Volatility of Net Operating Income

The more volatile a property's income stream, the greater the probability of default. From the model's perspective volatility of NOI affects value because with greater volatility there will be more paths under which income will be insufficient to pay the debt service and under which the value of the property declines below the value of the debt (see Exhibit 2). Thus, given a mortgage price, the corresponding OAS decreases as the volatility increases. Exhibit 8 clearly indicates this result: the greater the volatility of NOI, the lower the OAS. It should be clear from the graph that at a 70% initial LTV, the volatility of NOI has a profound influence on the value of the loan.[17]

---

[16] A bullet loan pays no principal until the maturity and then the entire principal amount is fully paid. The amortizing loan pays principal according to its amortization schedule until the maturity and then the remaining principal amount is fully paid.

[17] Note that for sufficiently high LTV, as NOI volatility increases to a certain level, the OAS levels off.

Exhibit 7: OAS versus LTV: Default Option

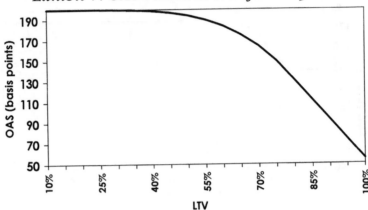

Source: Nomura Securities International, Inc.

Exhibit 8: OAS versus Volatility of NOI: Default Option

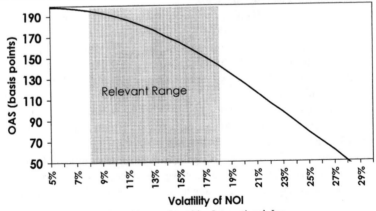

Source: Nomura Securities International, Inc.

This parameter enables investors to estimate the required excess spread for different property types. For example, mortgages on hotels or other property types with relatively high operating margins should offer higher spreads than mortgages on property types such as multi-family which tends to have a more stable income stream, assuming the same initial LTV and NOI. In practice, loans and CMBS backed by hotel or office properties tend to have lower initial LTVs (in the case of CMBS greater subordination which translates into a lower effective LTV) and therefore the difference is not reflected in the spread.

Term to Maturity

As previously shown in Exhibit 2, the longer the term to maturity, the higher default risk is. This is because there is more time for things to go bad. The cumulative probability of default increases as the term to maturity lengthens. As a result, the OAS should decrease as the term to maturity lengthens. Our model shows that OAS decreases as term to maturity increases, particularly for the higher quality loan (see Exhibit 9). On the other hand, when the loan starts out as a lower quality loan, increasing the maturity of the debt can actually lead to increasing OAS indicating increasing value. At first this seems strange, since the probability of default should increase with time. There are two reasons for the odd result. First, even though the cumulative probability of default increases, with a longer term to maturity the time to default is pushed further into the future. [18] Second, when a loan is really at risk of default, additional time gives the property owner some chance of getting the property back on track. An analogy can be made to a sporting event. Suppose a team is down by seven runs. It would far prefer it to be the first inning instead of the ninth, whereas the team that is ahead by seven runs would prefer that it be the bottom of the ninth inning.

Another interesting phenomenon is that even for the higher quality loan, after a certain point the OAS stops declining and even rises a bit until it levels off. This happens because even though the probability of default increases, on a present value basis, this added risk of default does not add much to the expected loss. The result is interesting in that it shows that longer term to maturity does not necessarily mean greater risk.

Valuing the Prepayment Option

Thus far we have assumed that the commercial mortgage was completely non-callable. In reality, while most commercial mortgages are more call-protected than residential mortgages, many have free periods. For example, the borrower in a 10-year balloon mortgage may be locked-out from prepayment for five years, and then is permitted to prepay. In addition, many commercial mortgages do not have lock-out provisions, but instead prepayment penalties which come in a variety of forms. The investor in the mortgage needs an ability to place a value on the lock-out and/or penalties in order to properly compare investment alternatives.

In order to analyze the effects of callability we continue with our example where we assumed a commercial mortgage with a 10-year maturity, 9% coupon, initial DSCR of 1.50x, initial LTV of 70%, initial risk-free interest rate of 7%, interest rate volatility of 11%, and NOI volatility of 15%. We assume that the loan follows a 30-year amortization schedule and has a balloon payment at the end of year 10. In addition, we assume that the loan is fully callable after 5 years without penalty at par.

Naturally, if the loan is also callable, the investment is less attractive. As a result, the OAS is lower as can be seen in Exhibits 9, 10, and 11. For our prototype loan with 70% LTV and 1.5x DSCR, the investor is really only getting +145 bp instead of the stated spread of +200 bp. It is interesting to note that the difference gets larger for lower quality loans. This is because the option to call in lower quality debt is even more valuable.

---

[18] This is similar to the results found in Robert Merton, "On the Pricing of Corporate Debt: The Risk Structure of Interest Rates," *Journal of Finance* (May 1974).

Exhibit 9: OAS versus Term to Maturity: Default Option

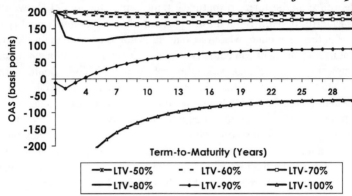

Exhibit 10: OAS versus DSCR: Refinance and Default Options

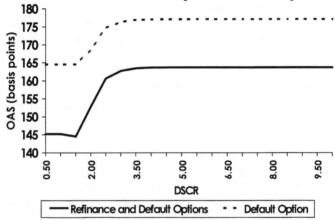

Exhibit 11: OAS versus LTV: Refinance and Default Options

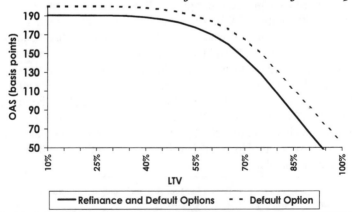

Exhibit 12: OAS versus Volatility of NOI: Refinance and Default Options

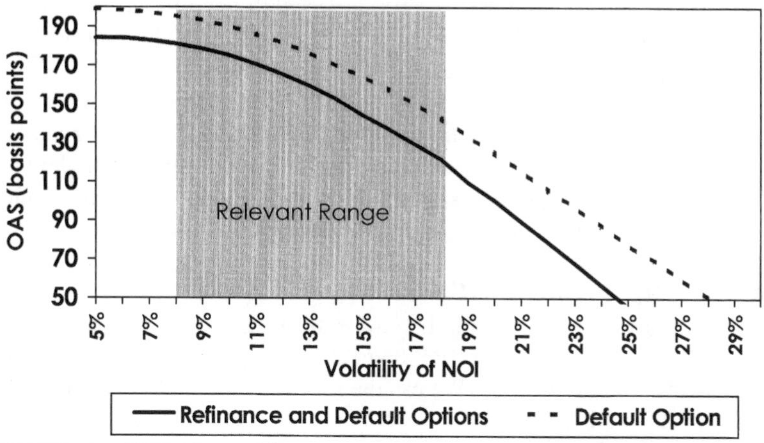

Exhibit 12 shows the OAS versus volatility of NOI. Once again, if the loan is callable, the OAS is lower.

In addition to the issues of callability there are factors which, while not discussed here, have an impact on value and show up in the OAS. These include the particular penalty structure; what happens in a default, extension, and modification provision in a balloon default; the price of the loan (assumed in all of the above analysis to be priced at par[19]); the shape of the yield curve; etc. All of these can be analyzed by the model.

VALUING MULTI-CLASS COMMERCIAL MORTGAGE-BACKED SECURITIES[20]

Thus far, we have applied the model to the valuation of a commercial mortgage. In this section we use the model to analyze multi-class commercial mortgage-backed securities. Securitization is the process of converting financial assets that produce cash flows into securities that trade in the financial markets. The cash flows from the loans are used to pay the certificate holders. Often many loans are pooled together in the securitization. A single class of bondholders can be created or there can be numerous classes. In addition to creating liquidity, the securitization process can be used to alter credit quality through various means of credit enhancements. These credit enhancements can take the form of guarantees, over collateralization, or senior-subordination. Today,

---

[19] If the investor purchased the loan at a deep discount, a default could be a favorable event if the proceeds from the foreclosure are sufficient. Similarly, a loan purchased at a premium will suffer if there is a default even if the foreclosure process only recovers the par amount

[20] Note that there will be some differences in the valuation results since in this section we use Monte Carlo simulation rather than obtaining an exact solution from the binomial tree.

senior-subordination is used almost exclusively. By creating a credit and payment prioritization, credit risk is reallocated among the bond classes. Typically, all principal payments that are made by the borrower(s) are used to pay off the most senior outstanding bond class, whereas losses are allocated to the most junior outstanding class. This process effectively decreases the LTV of the most senior bond class.

Because the losses are mostly absorbed by the junior classes, the senior class has more credit protection than its underlying collateral. By utilizing subordination, one can create securities which have higher credit ratings than the underlying collateral. The rating agencies set the effective LTV and DSCR requirements in each deal in order to achieve the desired bond ratings.

A Simple Sequential CMBS Structure

The question which investors would like to be answered is: Which has better value — the AAA bond at +85bp or the BBB bond at +190 bp? Our model can be used to help answer this type of question. We use the following example to demonstrate the application of the model.

We start with the same type of loan as in the prior section, i.e. a 9% coupon, 10-year balloon loan with a 30-year amortization schedule, Treasury rates at 7%, NOI volatility of 15%, interest rate volatility of 11%, and a correlation of 20% between interest rates and NOI. For analytic purposes we assume that instead of a single $100 million loan, we have a pool of ten $10 million loans with LTVs ranging from 54% to 90% (weighted average 70%) and DSCRs ranging from 1.94x to 1.11x (weighted average 1.5x).

Exhibit 13 depicts a typical CMBS deal.[21] In the deal, the C class is structured as the most junior tranche which provides credit support to the A and B classes while the B classes provides support to the A classes. Since the collateral is priced at par and has a coupon of 9.00%, the senior tranches whose yields are below that of the collateral will have prices above par, and the junior classes will have prices that are at a discount.

As was the case with the unstructured commercial mortgage, when the NOI volatility is low, the OAS is almost equal to the stated yield spread.[22] At higher levels of NOI volatility, the OAS declines. As expected, the largest declines take place in the most junior classes since they are the first to absorb losses caused by defaults. Interestingly, the OAS also declines for the most senior class. This is because the recoveries from defaults are used to pay the most senior classes first. Since, in this example, the senior classes are priced at a premium, the premature receipt of principal at par leads to a degradation in the bond's yield. (In Exhibits 14 and 15 we show the results for a case when the senior bonds are priced at a discount. In that situation the OAS of the senior bonds initially increases as the NOI volatility increases.)

---

[21] In this example, the spreads are reasonably representative of the market as of the fourth quarter of 1995. However, the sizing of the tranches is a bit too conservative. In particular, the unrated class is too large. As a result this deal would not have been done since the arbitrage is negative.

[22] As before this is true for a flat Treasury yield curve. If the Treasury curve were positively sloped the OAS would still be below the stated yield spread due to the dispersion of the cash flows.

Exhibit 13: An Example of a Sequential Structure of CMBS: Default Option (10 Loans)

Class	Size ($MM)	Aver Life	Rating	Price	Yield Spread	OAS 6% Volatility	OAS 10% Volatility	OAS 16% Volatility	OAS 30% Volatility
A-1	65	9.33	AAA	107.08	90 bp	89	82	71	63
A-2	5	10.00	AA	105.39	120 bp	120	120	120	120
A-3	5	10.00	A	103.32	150 bp	150	150	150	150
B-1	5	10.00	BBB	100.00	200 bp	200	200	200	197
B-2	5	10.00	BB	88.05	400 bp	400	400	400	332
B-3	5	10.00	B	77.96	600 bp	600	600	590	245
C	10	10.00	N/R	38.63	2000 bp	1963	1868	1610	563
Loan	100	9.56	N/A	100.00	200 bp	195	186	163	72

Note: Each tranche is priced at spread over its benchmark Treasury.

Exhibit 14: OAS versus Volatility of NOI for Senior Tranches: Discount Bonds Default Option

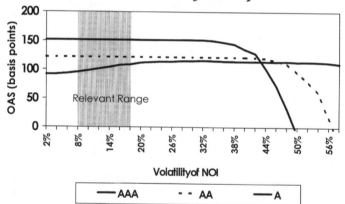

Exhibit 15: OAS versus Volatility of NOI for Senior Tranches: Discount Bonds Refinance and Default Options

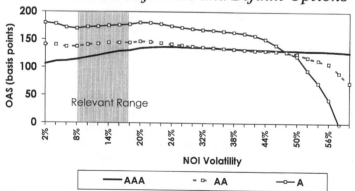

Exhibit 16: An Example of a Sequential Structure of CMBS: Refinance and Default Options (10 Loans)

Class	Size ($MM)	Average Life	Rating	Price	Yield Spread	OAS 6% Volatility	OAS 10% Volatility	OAS 16% Volatility	OAS 30% Volatility
A-1	65	9.33	AAA	107.08	90 bp	34	30	22	15
A-2	5	10.00	AA	105.39	120 bp	77	76	77	86
A-3	5	10.00	A	103.32	150 bp	117	119	122	128
B-1	5	10.00	BBB	100.00	200 bp	180	182	186	192
B-2	5	10.00	BB	88.05	400 bp	421	419	418	393
B-3	5	10.00	B	77.96	600 bp	655	649	632	373
C	10	10.00	N/R	38.63	2000 bp	2170	1977	1645	262
Loan	100	9.56	N/A	100.00	200 bp	177	167	140	32

Note: Each tranche is priced at spread over its benchmark Treasury.

There are several other points worth noting. First, the most protected classes are the AA, A, and BBB. Their OAS changes the least as a function of NOI volatility since they are not the first to absorb losses or recoveries. Second, the BBB CMBS at NOI volatilities above 9% appears to be a better value than the underlying loan if the two are offered at the same stated spread. Finally, the lowest rated classes appear to be the cheapest unless NOI volatilities substantially above observed levels are assumed.

In Exhibit 16, we allow the loans to be callable after 5 years without penalty. This substantially hurts the value of the most senior classes, particularly because they are priced at a premium. This is why a complete prepayment lockout on these classes is so important and valuable. The subordinate classes can actually benefit as shown by the improvement in their OAS because they are priced at a discount.

Exhibits 17 and 18 show that only at substantially higher levels of NOI volatility does the A rated bond have a lower OAS than the AA and AAA rated bonds. The conclusion is that the market is paying up too much for the higher rated classes.

Subordinate Bonds

The subordinate bond classes (B-pieces) in a CMBS deal are usually priced at a discount. Our analysis shows that the OAS of the B-pieces remains wide compared to the senior tranches even when a volatility as high as 18% is assumed for the NOI. This indicates the market view on the B-pieces is very conservative.

Interest-Only Strips

As we noted earlier, since senior bonds are priced with lower yields than the collateral, they would have prices substantially above par if they had the same coupon. Since many investors do not want to purchase premium bonds, interest is stripped off and interest-only (IO) classes are created.[23] Interest is usually stripped in order to price the senior class close to par or at low premium in the CMBS deal. It is in

---

[23] This can be done either at the loan level or the bond class level.

the interest of the issuer to create the strip class if the proceeds from the strip class and the par bond is greater than the proceeds from a premium bond. Since the price of an IO strip is more sensitive than its principal bond with the same credit rating, it is traded at a much wider spread. Exhibit 21 takes the deal that we have considered and strips three IOs from three A-classes in order to create discount bonds. Notice how the OAS on the AAA class increases as NOI volatility increases, as shown in Exhibits 14 and 15. This is because the bond is priced at a discount and any early payments from recoveries in a default are paid at par.

Exhibit 17: OAS versus Volatility of NOI for Senior Tranches: Premium Bonds with Default Option

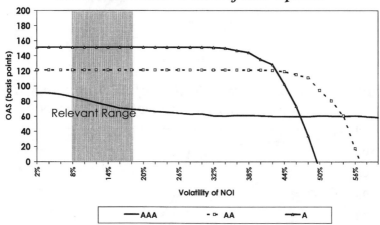

Exhibit 18: OAS versus Volatility of NOI for Senior Tranches: Premium Bonds with Refinance and Default Options

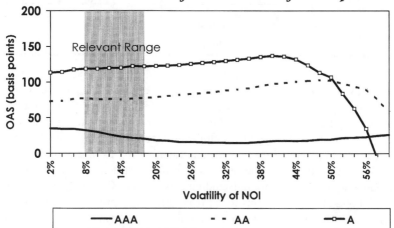

Exhibit 19: OAS versus Volatility of NOI for Subordinate Tranches: Default Options

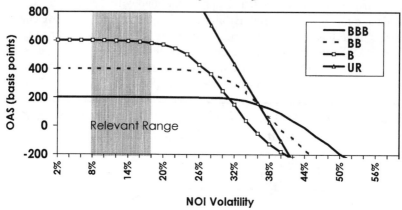

Exhibit 20: OAS versus Volatility of NOI for Subordinate Tranches: Refinance and Default Options

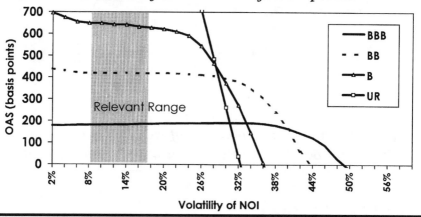

IO strip classes have special characteristics, which make the use of an OAS model in their valuation extremely useful. Since interest is paid only when the notional principal is outstanding, when the notional principal upon which the IOs payments are based is reduced, the amount of interest paid to the IO holder declines. There are two ways in which the erosion of notional principal can occur. The reduction in principal takes place due to either losses or due to principal payments. In the case of a loss, the senior-subordinated structure requires that the loss be allocated to the most junior outstanding class. Thus, IOs which are stripped from the AAA bond are relatively insulated from erosion of principal due to the allocation of losses. On the other hand, erosion of principal also occurs due to principal payments. The senior-subordinated structure requires that the most senior outstanding class receive principal payments. Thus, even a minor amount of prepayments leads to the erosion of principal associated with the IO stripped from the AAA bond. Principal payments can be either voluntary or involuntary. Voluntary prepayments are related to refinancing or the selling of the property. The IO holder, thus, derives considerable protection from prepayment protection features.[24]

Involuntary principal payment is a slightly more subtle concept. It arises from recoveries from foreclosure proceedings. These recoveries also must go to the most senior outstanding class. Thus, high defaults with a high rate of recovery also can erode the principal of the IO stripped from the most senior bond. The senior IO holder is in the odd position in the case of a default of hoping for zero recovery.

As can be seen in Exhibit 21 the IO stripped from the AAA bond is more sensitive to the volatility of NOI. At a high levels of volatility the OAS can become negative. While we do not show it here, adding the call feature would also negatively impact the IO class.

Investors should be willing to pay up substantially for IO's that are backed by well call protected loans. Note that while we assumed immediate foreclosure, the foreclosure process on average takes about a year. This would substantially improve the value of the IO classes.

Exhibit 21: An Example of a Sequential Structure of CMBS: Default Option

Class	Size ($MM)	Aver Life	Rating	Price	Yield Spread	OAS 6% Volatility	OAS 10% Volatility	OAS 16% Volatility	OAS 30% Volatility
A-1	65	9.33	AAA	94.21	90 bp	93	98	108	115
A-2	5	10.00	AA	91.92	120 bp	121	121	121	121
A-3	5	10.00	A	90.03	150 bp	151	151	151	151
B-1	5	10.00	BBB	100.00	200 bp	201	201	201	197
B-2	5	10.00	BB	88.05	400 bp	401	401	401	332
B-3	5	10.00	B	77.96	600 bp	601	600	590	245
C	10	10.00	N/R	38.63	2000 bp	1963	1868	1610	563
AAA IO	65*	5.11	AAA	12.71	220 bps	174	37	−185	−339
AA IO	5*	5.25	AA	12.36	320 bps	321	321	321	321
A IO	5*	5.25	A	12.20	350 bps	351	351	351	351
Loan	100	9.56	N/A	100.00	200 bp	195	186	163	72

* Notional amount

Note: Each tranche is priced at spread over its benchmark Treasury.

[24] Lockout, however, provides better protection than yield maintenance for two reasons. First, while yield maintenance serves as a disincentive, in the event of prepayment the IO holder may not be allocated his fair share. More importantly, as we mentioned earlier property owners may want to prepay even when interest rates rise. In this in instance there is no yield maintenance to distribute.

Exhibit 22: OAS versus Volatility of NOI for Interest-Only Strips: Default Option

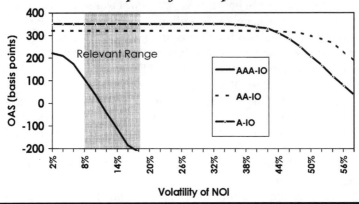

Exhibits 21 and 22 confirm our view that interest strips from bonds that are neither the first nor the last in the sequential structure are the least risky. This is because (1) they are protected from erosion of principal due to losses, (2) there are bond classes below them, and (3) they are protected from principal payments by bond classes that are in front of them. Interestingly, the market does not price them that way. The AAA strip is typically priced at a tighter spread than the AA strip, which in turn is priced at a tighter spread than the A strip. For example, in Exhibit 22, the OAS of the IO stripped from the most senior class declines rapidly as the volatility of NOI and the ensuing default rate rises. The IO strips from the AA and A rated bond classes are actually less risky in a more volatile market. This suggests that less senior IO strips should be traded at a tighter spread.

DISPERSION OF LOAN QUALITY

Investors need to give serious consideration to the diversity of the loans backing the bond classes in a CMBS deal. In the prior CMBS examples, we assumed there were ten loans with a range of LTVs and DSCRs. While the average LTV was 70% and the average DSCR was 1.5x, the dispersion in quality generally has a negative impact on the bond classes. In Exhibits 23 and 24 we compare the OAS versus NOI volatility for the AAA bond and the unrated class assuming a ten loan portfolio and a single loan portfolio. In general, one can see that the dispersion lowers the OAS. For the unrated class this is obvious. As the most junior class, it suffers the downside of the lower quality loans without an equal benefit from the higher quality loans. The AAA bond on the other hand gets hurt if it is priced at a premium, since the lower quality loans will increase the likelihood of defaults leading to recoveries which get paid to the AAA class. At higher levels of NOI volatility, the AAA benefits from the dispersion because the lower quality loans default, and the remaining pool consists of much higher quality loans.

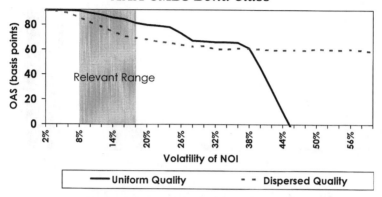

Exhibit 23: Effect of Loan Quality Dispersion:
AAA CMBS Bond Class

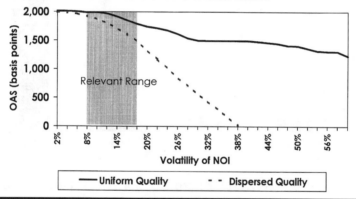

Exhibit 24: Effect of Loan Quality Dispersion:
Unrated CMBS Bond Class

RELATIVE RISK OF CMBS BOND CLASSES

Up to this point we have used OAS model mostly as a tool for pricing and assessing relative value. The model, because it is based on the evaluation of the securities in the probability space, can also be used to determine relative risk. We use the prices that are obtained from the price distribution. One would expect that the price variation for the less risky securities be smaller (as a percent of the security's price) than for the more risky securities. This is generally the case. In Exhibits 25, 26, and 27 we show the price distribution resulting from the model assuming NOI volatility of 15%. To focus on the credit risk we held interest rates constant. Notice how much tighter the price range is for the AAA bond than for the collateral; look how wide the range is for the unrated class.

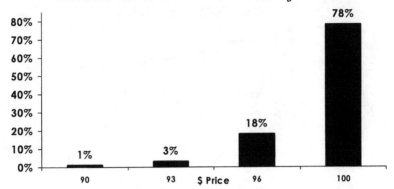

Exhibit 25: Price Distribution of Loan

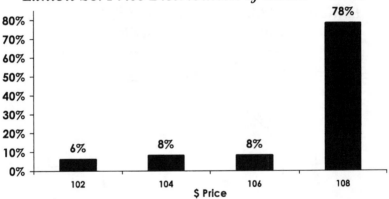

Exhibit 26: Price Distribution of CMBS — AAA

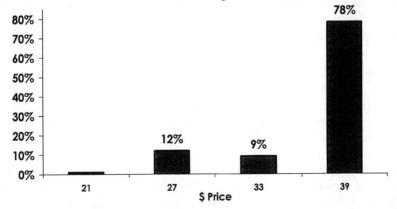

Exhibit 27: Price Distribution of CMBS — Unrated Class

Exhibit 28: CMBS Summary Statistics

	Mean*	OAS	Standard Deviation	Coefficient of Variation	Range
AAA	106.41	71	1.45	1.37%	4.65
AA	104.86	120	1.13	1.07%	3.61
A	103.00	150	0.69	0.67%	2.21
BBB	100.00	200	0.00	0.00%	0
BB	89.03	400	2.52	2.86%	17.82
B	77.95	590	8.43	10.81%	59.34
UR	36.38	1610	4.36	13.24%	14.69
Loan	98.63	163	2.64	2.69%	10.46

* The data are for the single loan case. The standard deviations will be significantly lower for the ten loan case.

Exhibit 29: OAS versus Coefficient of Variation — CMBS Bond Classes and Loan

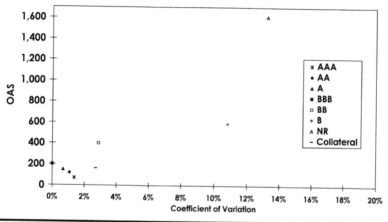

In Exhibit 28 we summarize the statistics of the distributions for each of the bond classes. In general, the lower rated classes have the highest risk as measured by the coefficient of variation.[25] However, since the recoveries from default negatively impact the senior bonds which are priced at a premium, the standard deviation for the AAA is higher than the AA, and similarly for the A. The BBB shows a standard deviation of nearly zero, which indicates from a default perspective it is well protected and it is also not impacted by recoveries from foreclosures.

If we use the coefficient of variation as our risk measure, and OAS as our measure of relative value, we can construct the "efficient frontier" for investment analysis. In Exhibit 29, we plot OAS versus the coefficient of variation for each of the bond classes. One can see how clearly the BBB bonds and the unrated class lie on the boundary of the efficient frontier. This suggests that portfolios consisting of BBB and

---

[25] The coefficient of variation normalizes the risk by looking at the ratio of standard deviation to the mean.

unrated class bonds can be formed to outperform combinations of the other bonds. Perhaps investors should take the ratio of OAS to the coefficient of variation as the measure of relative value, much like the Sharpe ratio in stock analysis.[26]

CONCLUSION

In this chapter we introduced a model which uses the borrower's behavior to construct a decision payoff matrix for exercising default and prepayment options and utilizes option theory to value these options. The model employs interest rates and the net operating income of the mortgaged property as the two underlying factors. Based upon the model, the option values can be assessed. We then derived an option-adjusted spread (OAS) to measure the relative value of commercial mortgages and commercial mortgage-backed securities. Given a market price, the OAS decreases as the risk exposure increases. The model serves as a unifying framework, bringing real estate valuation, fixed-income pricing, and option theory together. Factors affecting the real estate, mortgages, and structure are evaluated simultaneously across a wide range of scenarios. This sort of analysis helps reveal hidden weaknesses in the structure and enables the analyst to compare deals.

APPENDIX: MODEL SPECIFICATION

The embedded options of commercial mortgages are American options which can be exercised at any time prior to expiration. Given state variables — interest rate and net operating income — we denote the rest of the variables as follows:

r = default-free one-period spot rate
N = net operating income
S = the expected present value of the future promised payments
C = the value of the prepayment option
D = the value of the default option
H = the total embedded option value which is equal to C plus D
G = the expected present value of the next period H
W = the market value of the underlying loan which is equal to S minus G
B = the market value of the collateral property
M = the scheduled mortgage payment
M^* = the potential refinancing scheduled mortgage payment
U = the face amount of mortgage remaining balance
Δ_d = foreclosure expense
Δ_c = prepayment penalty

---

[26] William F. Sharpe, "Mutual Fund Performance," *Journal of Business* (January 1966).

We assume the process of r and N in discrete time as follows:

$$\log r_t = \alpha_t + \log r_{t-1} + \varepsilon_t$$

$$\log N_t = a_t + \log N_{t-1} + \zeta_t$$

where t is time index and, for any given t, ε, and ζ have constant variances, σ^2 and s^2 respectively, and is correlated with correlation coefficient ρ.

To satisfy the above conditions, instead of generating ε and ζ directly, we generate ε and ζ and assume a relationship between ζ, ε, and ξ as follows:

$$E\left[\varepsilon^2\right] = \sigma^2$$

$$E\left[\xi^2\right] = (1-\rho)s^2$$

$$\zeta = b\varepsilon + \xi$$

where

$$E[\xi] = E[\varepsilon\xi] = 0,$$

$$b = (\rho s)/\sigma$$

Then we have

$$E[\varepsilon] = E[\zeta] = 0$$

$$E[\varepsilon\zeta] = \rho s\sigma$$

$$E\left[\zeta^2\right] = s^2$$

To obtain property value B, we assume $B = N/(r-rg)$ where g is a content along time. The property value B can be interpreted as the present value of an infinite series of prevailing net operating income with a growth rate r multiplied by g and discounted by the prevailing interest rate r. Since r, B, and N are known initially, g can be obtained through the equation. The value of $(r-rg)$, in essence, is the capitalization rate of the property.

Triggering Conditions

The prepayment triggering conditions:

(i) $N > M^*$
(ii) $G + \Delta_c < S - U$

The default triggering conditions:

(i) $N < M$

(ii) $G < S + M - B$

The default-as-a-method-of-prepayment triggering conditions:

(i) $N > M^*$

(ii) $G + \Delta_d < S - U$

Exhibit 30 provides an arbitrage table for decision support.

Exhibit 30: Arbitrage Table for Decision Support

Triggering Condition				Action Code	H value	
I	II	III	IV		$t < T$	T
$B-M = \text{Min}[B-M, U+\Delta_d, U+\Delta_c] < S-G$	$N<M$			1	$S+M-B$	$U+M-B$
	$N>M$	$U+\Delta_d = \text{Min}[U+\Delta_d, U+\Delta_c] < S-G$	$N>M^*$	2	$S-U-\Delta_d$	0
			$N<M^*$	0	G	0
		$U+\Delta_c = \text{Min}[U+\Delta_d, U+\Delta_c] < S-G$	$N>M^*$	3	$S-U-\Delta_c$	0
			$N<M^*$	0	G	0
$U+\Delta_d = \text{Min}[B-M, U+\Delta_d, U+\Delta_c] < S-G$	$N>M^*$			2	$S-U-\Delta_d$	0
	$N<M^*$	$B>S+M-G$		0	G	0
		$B< S+M-G$	$N>M$	0	G	0
			$N<M$	1	$S+M-B$	$U+M-B$
$U+\Delta_c = \text{Min}[B-M, U+\Delta_d, U+\Delta_c] < S-G$	$N>M^*$			3	$S-U-\Delta_c$	0
	$N<M^*$	$B> S+M-G$		0	G	0
		$B< S+M-G$	$N>M$	0	G	0
			$N<M$	1	$S+M-B$	$U+M-B$
$\text{Min}[B-M, U+\Delta_d, U+\Delta_c] \geq S-G$				0	G	0

Note: numbers 0, 1, 2, and 3 in Action column denote to "no action," "default," "default-as-a-method-of-prepayment," and "prepay" respectively.

Implementation of the Options Calculation

Based on the stochastic processes of N and r, as well as generic mortgage debt information, we are able to generate r, N, B, M, M^*, U and S to span the whole solid binomial pyramid.

Starting from the maturity date of the mortgage debt, the option value G can be calculated backward in time.

At maturity date of period T:
Given r, N, B, M, and $S = U$, based on the default and prepayment trigger condition:

$$H = \begin{cases} U + M - B \text{ (default)} \\ 0 \text{ (otherwise) and } G = 0 \end{cases}$$

At time t where $t < T$:
Given r, N, B, M, M^*, U and S, based on the default and prepayment trigger condition:

$$H = \begin{cases} S + M - B \text{ (default)} \\ S - U - \Delta_d \text{ (default as involuntary prepayment)} \\ S - U - \Delta_c \text{ (prepay)} \\ G \text{ (otherwise)} \end{cases}$$

and then G can be calculated from next-step H by discounting the interest rates with weighted probabilities.

Chapter 8

A Two-Factor Model for the Valuation of the T-Bond Futures Contract's Embedded Options

Soren S. Nielsen, Ph.D.
Assistant Professor of Management Science
University of Texas at Austin

Ehud I. Ronn, Ph.D.
Professor of Finance
University of Texas at Austin

INTRODUCTION

The U.S. Treasury bond futures contracts and its associated options rank among the most liquid contracts on interest rate-sensitive securities in the world, second only to the LIBOR-based Eurodollar futures contracts. The specifications of the futures contract traded on the Chicago Board of Trade (CBOT) give the short side the right to take advantage of several embedded options. The purpose of this chapter is to present a consistent, arbitrage-free model for the stochastic behavior of interest rates that will simultaneously explain the movements of the underlying Treasury bonds as well as the valuation of the options embedded within the T-bond futures contract. Naturally, the derivation of such valuation results for the embedded options also permits their hedging by market participants.

Traditional modeling approaches for the valuation of the embedded options in the T-bond futures contract have relied on bond-futures adaptations of option pricing models originally developed for stocks, and in which the stochastic process for the underlying asset in the risk-neutral economy follows a geometric

The authors would like to thank Merrill Lynch & Co. for providing data in support of this project.

Brownian motion. While these models are simple and easy to use, they are subject to criticism when applied to the entire array of interest rate-dependent securities.

Specifically, there are theoretical deficiencies to employing price-based option pricing models to interest rate contingent claims. The Black-Scholes model and its Black[1] and Barone-Adesi/Whaley[2] successors assume that: (1) the risk-neutral stock price is lognormally distributed; (2) the stock's volatility is constant; and (3) the rate of interest is constant. Thus, there are several well-known criticisms of the application of such equity-based option models to the interest rate arena:

1. Absent default, the bond matures at par.[3] Therefore, the asset price cannot follow a geometric Brownian motion.
2. Lognormally-distributed bond prices may result in negative future interest rates, i.e., zero-coupon bonds may in the future be priced above par.
3. The Black-Scholes model posits a constant rate of interest, which in turn implies that bond prices are non-random: that is, bond prices at any future dates are known with certainty. Thus, there is a fundamental inconsistency in the model: interest rates cannot simultaneously be constant as well as stochastic.

The financial-economics literature contains numerous models which explicitly address these concerns. These papers model the time-series process of the short-term rate of interest or, alternatively, the set of forward rates of interest, as following some specific stochastic process; further, several of these models can be "calibrated" to match the term structure of interest rates and the term structure of volatilities.[4]

---

[1] Fischer Black, "The Pricing of Commodity Contracts," *Journal of Financial Economics*, 3 (1976), pp. 167-179.
[2] Giovanni Barone-Adesi and Robert Whaley, "Efficient Analytical Approximations of American Option Values," *Journal of Finance*, 42 (June 1987), pp. 301-320.
[3] In the absence of default, the phenomenon of "pull-to-par" refers to bond prices converging towards par as their maturity date approaches.
[4] Broadly, these models can be divided into three types:

1. *One-factor short-term interest rate models:* John C. Cox, Jonathan E. Ingersoll, Jr., and Stephen A. Ross, "A Theory of the Term Structure of Interest Rates," *Econometrica*, 53:2 (March 1985), pp. 385-407; Oldrich Vasicek, "An Equilibrium Characterization of the Term Structure," *Journal of Financial Economics*, 5 (1977), pp. 177-188; L. Uri Dothan, "On the Term Structure of Interest Rates," *Journal of Financial Economics*, 6 (1978), pp. 59-69; G. Courtadon, "The Pricing of Options on Default-Free Bonds," *Journal of Financial and Quantitative Analysis*, 17 (March 1982), pp. 75-100.
2. *One-factor models that match the term structure of interest rates:* Thomas S. Y. Ho and Sang-Bin Lee, "Term Structure Movements and Pricing Interest Rate Contingent Claims," *Journal of Finance*, 41 (December 1986), pp. 1011-1029; Fischer Black, Emanuel Derman, and William Toy, "A One-Factor Model of Interest Rates and Its Application to Treasury Bond Options," *Financial Analysts Journal*, 46 (January/February 1990), pp. 33-39; Fischer Black and Piotr Karasinski, "Bond and Option Pricing when Short Rates are Lognormal," *Financial Analysts Journal* (July/August 1991), pp. 52-59; John Hull and Alan White, "Pricing Interest-Rate-Derivative Securities," *Review of Financial Studies*, 4 (1990), pp. 573-592.
3. *One- and multi-factor models of the term structure of forward rates of interest:* David Heath, Robert Jarrow and Andrew Morton, "Bond Pricing and the Term Structure of Interest Rates: A Discrete Time Approach," *Journal of Financial and Quantitative Analysis*, 25 (December 1990), pp. 419-440; David Heath, Robert Jarrow, and Andrew Morton, "Bond Pricing and the Term Structure of Interest Rates: A New Method for Contingent Claims Valuation," *Econometrica*, 60 (January 1992), pp. 77-105.

In the modeling of the T-bond futures' embedded options, we must take cognizance of the result that timing/quality options have an inherently switching nature: they include the right to switch either time or bond in the delivery process. Such options will only recognize their full potential in a more-than-one-factor model, and indeed we choose a two-factor model of the term structure. A multi-factor modeling of interest rates is entirely consistent with observed behavior of the term structure. The work of Litterman and Scheinkman considerered three factors, *"level, steepness* and *curvature* [Emphasis in original],"[5] and note that these "explain — at a minimum — 96% of the variability of excess returns of any zero" coupon bond.[6] While a three-factor model might be desirable, it would be numerically intensive. Moreover, Ronn demonstrates the well-known result that a *two*-factor model explains 92.8% of the variability in the movements of the term structure of interest rates,[7] well within striking distance of the three-factor's 96%.

Several authors have attempted to evaluate the "switching" option in the timing and deliverability of bonds against the futures contract.[8] Their modeling of the stochastic process did not attempt a simultaneous, consistent, arbitrage-free modeling of: the interest-rate process; term-structure estimation; and valuation of Treasury bonds, futures contract, and embedded options. Ronn and Bliss did make such an earlier attempt,[9] but their non-stationarity assumption coupled with the non-recombining nature of that lattice implementation did not permit an accurate estimate of the futures contract's embedded options.

The objective of this chapter, then, is to model the movements of interest rates in such a manner that *all* interest rate-contingent securities — the T-bonds, the

---

[5] Robert Litterman and José Scheinkman, "Common Factors Affecting Bond Returns," *Journal of Portfolio Management* (June 1991), pp. 54-61.

[6] Several *two*-factor models are reported in the literature: (1) Michael J. Brennan and Eduardo S. Schwartz, "An Equilibrium Model of Bond Pricing and a Test of Market Efficiency," *Journal of Financial and Quantitative Analysis*, 17 (September 1982), pp. 301-329, who allowed for a non-perfect correlation between the long- and short-term rates of interest; (2) Francis A. Longstaff and Eduardo S. Schwartz, "Interest-Rate Volatility and the Term Structure: A Two-Factor General Equilibrium Model," *Journal of Finance*, 47 (September 1992), pp. 1259-1282 and H. Gifford Fong and Oldrich A. Vasicek, "Interest Rate Volatility as a Stochastic Factor," Working Paper, Gifford Fong Associates, February 1991. These two papers considered two-factor models in which interest rates and interest rate volatility are both stochastically changing through time; and, (3) the previously-cited Heath-Jarrow-Morton papers, "Bond Pricing and the Term Structure of Interest Rates: A Discrete Time Approach" and "Bond Pricing and the Term Structure of Interest Rates: A New Method for Contingent Claims Valuation," provided a rigorous theoretical framework for one- and two-factor no-arbitrage interest rate models. These latter papers implicitly permitted a non-perfect correlation between the long- and short-term rates of interest.

[7] See Ehud I. Ronn, "The Impact of Large Changes in Asset Prices on Intra-Market Correlations in the Stock and Bond Markets," Working Paper, University of Texas at Austin, November 1995.

[8] See, for example, A. Kane and A. J. Marcus, "Conversion Factor Risk and Hedging in the Treasury-Bond Futures Market," *Journal of Futures Markets*, 4 (1984), pp. 55-64; Phelim Boyle, "The Quality Option and the Timing Option in Futures Contracts," *Journal of Finance*, 44 (1989), pp. 101-113; and, Hemler, M.L, "The Quality Delivery Option in Treasury Bond Futures Contracts," *Journal of Finance*, 45 (December 1990), pp. 1565-1586.

[9] See Ehud I. Ronn and Robert R. Bliss, "A Nonstationary Trinomial Model for the Valuation of Treasury Bond Futures Contracts," *Journal of Futures Markets*, 14 (1994), pp. 597-617.

T-bond futures contract, and the option written on the contract — all move in an accurate, consistent and arbitrage-free manner. Furthermore, the interest rate model developed below accommodates the option features embedded within the futures contract: the quality option, the end-of-month option, and the timing option.[10]

THE VALUATION MODEL

The Interest-Rate Model

We posit the following two-factor model for the (risk-neutral) evolution of interest rates:

$$dr/r = \mu_{rt}dt + \sigma_r dz_r$$

$$dl/l = \mu_{lt}dt + \sigma_l dz_l \tag{1}$$

where

r	= the short-term (3-month) rate of interest
l	= the 20-year zero-coupon rate of interest
μ_{rt}	= the drift in the 3-month rate of interest; μ_{rt} is chosen so that the risk-neutral expected value of the 3-month rate of interest equals its original, time 0 forward rate
μ_{lt}	= the drift in the 20-year zero-coupon rate of interest; μ_{lt} is chosen so that the risk-neutral expected value of the 20-year rate equals its time 0 forward rate
σ_r	= the proportional volatility of the 3-month rate of interest
σ_l	= the proportional volatility of the 20-year zero-coupon rate of interest

dz_r and dz_l are increments of standard Brownian processes
Corr $(dr/r,\ dl/l) \equiv \rho$, the correlation coefficient between the 3-month and 20-year rates of interest

The above model has the following attributes:

1. It is a two-factor interest-rate model, wherein the two factors are the 3-month and 20-year zero-coupon rates.
2. The two factors are imperfectly correlated
3. In the spirit of the Ho-Lee and Black-Karasinski models, the drift terms μ_{rt} and μ_{lt} are chosen to match the original term structure. This is accomplished by centering the distribution of future values of r and l about their current forward rates. The intuition for this assumption follows from the recognition that under the "risk-neutral" probability measure dictated by

---

[10] In principle, the model can also accommodate the so-called "wild card" option, but that requires a numerical implementation beyond the scope of this chapter. We discuss the "wild card" option at greater length later.

no-arbitrage valuation, the expected value of the security is its forward price. (It is, of course, definitionally *equal* to its forward price under zero uncertainty.) As is well-known, setting the expected value of the interest rate equal to its forward rate is an approximation, since we know from the works of Ho-Lee and Heath, Jarrow and Morton, among others, that the risk-neutral expectations contains a so-called "convexity drift," which separates the expected value of the interest rate from its forward rate. Fortunately, this term is of second-order for short-term maturities such as the 1-to-4 months ranges considered here.[11]

Estimation of the Term Structure of Interest Rates

We require an estimate of the prevailing term structure of interest rates. For that, we use the reported prices of C-STRIPS, "Coupon-Separate Trading of Interest and Principal," the stripped zero-coupon bonds representing payment of interest on U.S. Treasury notes and bonds. This provides us with an estimate of the discount function, DF_t, through the 30-year maturity horizon. In order to obtain discount factors for *all* maturities t, we have interpolated using the assumption of constant forward rates through adjacent C-STRIPS prices.

The simultaneous availability of prices for coupon-paying Treasury bonds and the zero-coupon C-STRIPS confronts us with the discrepancy between the "fair market value" of the C-STRIPS-determined present value of cash flows on the one hand, and the market prices of Treasury bonds on the other:

$$P_{i0} \equiv CF_{i0} + \varepsilon_{i0} \tag{2}$$

where

P_{i0} = full bid price of bond i at time 0, including quoted bid price plus accrued interest

CF_{i0} = present value of bond i's cash flows at time 0, using C-STRIPS prices for the DF_t: $CF_{i0} \equiv \Sigma_t a_{it} DF_t$ for a_{it} constituting coupon and/or principal payments to bond i at time t

As is stated in Chapter 13 of this book, the small but non-zero value of the ε_{it}'s is attributable to potential non-simultaneous or erroneous price quotes; liquidity effects of "on-the-run"/"off-the-run" bonds; tax clientele/market segmentation in bond markets; and tax timing option effects.

There exist two sets of bonds with special economic reasons for discrepancies between market prices and discounted present values of cash flows. The first are the callable bonds; although these are no longer *currently* deliverable (as of September 1996), they did qualify for the delivery set in the past. The second is the set of "flower"

---

[11] The no-arbitrage features of the model could probably be improved if the drift in the long rate were adjusted to equal the (path-by-path) short-term rate of interest $\bar{r}$. For the relatively short 3-month span of the futures contract dealt with in this chapter, such modification would add computational complexity without significantly contributing to the valuation model.

bonds containing special estate-tax provisions which increase their market price above their discounted "fair value." Proper valuation of the callable bonds would require the specification of the interest-rate model through their maturity date, thereby requiring the specification of the term structure of volatility, as well as rendering the program far more computationally intensive. Consequently, the callable bonds were valued either to the first call date or maturity, whichever produced the lower value.

Any bond-valuation procedure must accommodate or ignore the presence of these pricing errors. That is, valuation requires an assumption regarding the future existence or absence of these pricing discrepancies. In our model, we choose to assume that, irrespective of their source, these discrepancies will persist and the market will not immediately revert to full fair-value pricing. Hence for any future state s,

$$P_{is} \equiv CF_{is} + \varepsilon_{is}$$

and

$$\frac{P_{is}}{P_{i0}} = \frac{CF_{is}}{CF_{i0}} \tag{3}$$

The assumption embodied in equation (3) posits that the proportional, state-contingent return embodied in the bond's fair value, CF_{is}/CF_{i0}, will be reflected in the state-contingent market return P_{is}/P_{i0}. From equation (3), this results in the state-contingent market price P_{is} being given by the scale factor-adjusted expression $(P_{i0}/CF_{i0})CF_{is}$. This adjustment for price discrepancy was also applied to the set of callable and flower bonds.[12]

The Trinomial Interest-Rate Lattice

The two-factor model equation (1) requires, at minimum, a trinomial interest rate "tree" for implementation. We use the following discretization:

$$\begin{bmatrix} r(t+\Delta) \\ l(t+\Delta) \end{bmatrix} = \begin{cases} \begin{bmatrix} r(t)\exp\{\mu_r(t)\Delta + a_1\sqrt{\Delta}\} \\ l(t)\exp\{\mu_l(t)\Delta + a_2\sqrt{\Delta}\} \end{bmatrix} & \text{with Prob. } = p \\[2ex] \begin{bmatrix} r(t)\exp\{\mu_r(t)\Delta + b_1\sqrt{\Delta}\} \\ l(t)\exp\{\mu_l(t)\Delta + b_2\sqrt{\Delta}\} \end{bmatrix} & \text{with Prob. } = q \\[2ex] \begin{bmatrix} r(t)\exp\{\mu_r(t)\Delta + c_1\sqrt{\Delta}\} \\ l(t)\exp\{\mu_l(t)\Delta + c_2\sqrt{\Delta}\} \end{bmatrix} & \text{with Prob. } = 1-p-q \end{cases} \tag{4}$$

---

[12] The empirical results we report cover the time period September 30 to December 30, 1993, for which time the callable bonds were in the set of bonds deliverable against the T-bond futures contract. As of the writing of this document in September 1996, all callable bonds have fallen below the 15-years-to-first-call-date threshold, hence are no longer deliverable against the T-Bond futures contract. Since the remaining bonds are all "bullet" bonds, which depend only on the term structure of interest rates and are independent of *volatility* changes in the marketplace, the adjustment factor implicit in equation (3) is currently even more appropriate.

The system of equations given by (4) results in an efficient, recombining tree (see the appendix for details).

The parameter set $\{a_i, b_i, c_i, p, q; i = 1, 2\}$ is chosen to satisfy the mean, variance, and covariance conditions implied in equation (1). Specifically, we require that, under the risk-neutral probability measure,

$$E\begin{bmatrix} dr/r \\ dl/l \end{bmatrix} = \begin{bmatrix} \mu_{rt} \\ \mu_{lt} \end{bmatrix} dt \tag{5}$$

$$\text{Var}\begin{bmatrix} dr/r \\ dl/l \end{bmatrix} = \begin{bmatrix} \sigma_r^2 \\ \sigma_l^2 \end{bmatrix} dt \tag{6}$$

$$\text{Cov}\left(\frac{dr}{r}, \frac{dl}{l}\right) = \sigma_{rl} dt \tag{7}$$

The appendix demonstrates that the system of equations (5), (6) and (7) gives rise to five equations in eight unknowns and is therefore underidentified. The appendix also demonstrates that the trinomial tree can be constructed with the following special values $c_1 = 0$ and $p = q = \frac{1}{3}$.

The system of equations (4) certainly provides for the values of r and l at all future states and times. However, recall that for T-bond valuation purposes, we require the entire term structure, and not solely two points on the curve. Thus, based on the *realized* values of $\tilde{r}_t$ and $\tilde{l}_t$ at time t, we flesh out the remainder of the time t term structure of interest rates. Consider the following notation:

$\tilde{r}_{Tt}$ = the random zero-coupon rate for maturity T realized at time t

f_{Tt} ≡ $(DF_t / DF_T)^{1/(T-t)} - 1$, the current, time 0 forward rate for maturity T at time t

then,

$$\tilde{r}_{Tt} = \begin{cases} f_{Tt}\left[\left(\dfrac{T-1/4}{20-1/4}\right)\dfrac{\tilde{l}_t}{f_{lt}} + \left(1 - \dfrac{T-1/4}{20-1/4}\right)\dfrac{\tilde{r}_t}{f_{rt}}\right] & \text{for } 1/4 < T < 20 \text{ years} \\[4mm] f_{Tt}\left(\dfrac{\tilde{l}_t}{f_{lt}}\right) & \text{for } T > 20 \text{ years} \end{cases} \tag{8}$$

The interpretation of equation (8) is as follows. Consider an arbitrary maturity T at time t: conditional on the realized values of the 3-month rate $\tilde{r}$ and the 20-year rate $\tilde{l}$, the maturity T realized value is its forward rate scaled up by a weighted ratio of the realized values of $\tilde{r}$ and $\tilde{l}$ relative to their respective forwards, where the weights $\{(T - \frac{1}{4})(20 - \frac{1}{4}), 1 - (T - \frac{1}{4})(20 - \frac{1}{4})\}$ are the proximity of T to the 3-month maturity of r and the 20-year maturity of l. For maturities T

in excess of 20 years, the realized $\tilde{r}_{Tt}$ are obtained from their realized forwards using only the *20-year* rate's proportional deviation l_t / f_{lt}.

Valuation of Futures Contract

Exhibit 1 details the sequence of events in the valuation of a T-bond futures contract at the beginning of the delivery month, and two months prior to the delivery month:
     Consider now the valuation alternative of the T-bond futures at three alternate dates: one day before first delivery (t_0), one month before first delivery (t_{-1}), and two months before first delivery (t_{-2}).

Step 1: Proceeding via the method of stochastic dynamic programming, consider the value of the futures contract if delivery takes place at time t_1. Let the state-dependent term structure be denoted $\tilde{DF}_t(t_1)$, where "~" is used to denote random, state-contingent realization. It is possible to compute the state-dependent cheapest-to-deliver (CTD) bond. For each bond j in the deliverable set at t_1, first calculate the fitted $\tilde{CF}_j(t_1)$, and then "forecast" its market price as

$$\tilde{P}_j(t_1) = (P_{j0} / CF_{j0}) CF_j(t_1)$$

Let $I_j(t_1)$ represent the accrued interest on bond j at time t_1, and C_j the conversion factor of the bond for purposes of delivery against a Treasury bond futures contract.[13]

Exhibit 1: Sequence of Events for T-bond Futures Contract

Date	Example	Time Index	Event
Two months prior to first delivery	September 30,1993	t_{-2}	
One month prior to first delivery	October 31, 1993	t_{-1}	
One day prior to delivery	November 30, 1993	t_0	
Throughout month	December 1993	$t_{i\Delta}$, $i= 0,1,2,...,1/\Delta-1$	Timing and delivery options*
End of delivery month	December 30, 1993	t_1	Last day for delivery

* Delivery times are modeled as discrete, rather than continuous, to reflect the lattice implementation of the futures contract's embedded, American-style options reflecting the timing and delivery of Treasury bonds against the contract.

---

[13] As is well-known, the conversion factor for a given issue with coupon rate c_j and maturity date m_j is the price per dollar of face value of a bond yielding 8% compounded semi-annually with coupon rate c_j and maturity date m_j. Formally, the conversion factor for a given issue with coupon rate c_j is given by:

$$C_j(t) = 1.04^{-X/6} \left[\frac{c_j}{2} + \frac{c_j}{0.08}(1 - 1.04^{-2N}) + 1.04^{-2N} \right] - \frac{c_j(6 - X)}{12}$$

where N is the whole number of years to call if callable or to maturity if not, and X is the number of months that time to maturity or first call exceeds N, rounded down to the nearest quarter. Note that if $X = 9$, set $2N$ = $2N+1$ and $X = 3$ before using the above formula. The conversion factor is dependent on time through the remaining time to maturity or call. For a given futures contract in the delivery month, the conversion factor is fixed.

Then the random value of the futures contract at time t_1, $\tilde{F}(t_1)$, is given by

$$\tilde{F}(t_1) = \min_j \frac{\tilde{P}_j(t_1) - I_j(t_1)}{C_j(t_1)} \tag{9}$$

Step 2: Now consider the valuation of the futures contract at all dates $t_{i\Delta}$, $i = 0, 1, 2,$ ..., $1/\Delta - 1$:

$$\tilde{F}(t_{i\Delta}) = \min\left\{ \min_j \frac{\tilde{P}_j(t_{i\Delta}) - I_j(t_{i\Delta})}{C_j(t_{i\Delta})}, \tilde{E}_{i\Delta}[\tilde{F}(t_{(i+1)\Delta})] \right\} \tag{10}$$

$$\text{for } i = 0, 1, 2, ..., 1/\Delta - 1$$

where $\tilde{P}_j(t_{i\Delta}) = (P_{j0}/CF_{j0})\tilde{CF}_j(t_{i\Delta})$ and $\tilde{E}_{i\Delta}(\bullet)$ is the state-dependent (hence random) time-$i\Delta$ risk-neutral expectations of

$$\tilde{F}(t_{(i+1)\Delta})$$

using the postulated process in equation (1). In particular, this yields $F(t_0)$, a non-random quantity as of t_0.

Step 3: The calculation of $F(t_0)$ permits the computation of $F(t_{-1})$ and $F(t_{-2})$. These values,

$$F(t_{-1}) = E_{-1}[\tilde{F}(t_0)]$$

$$F(t_{-2}) = E_{-2}[\tilde{F}(t_{-1})] \tag{11}$$

are obtained by backward induction along the interest-rate tree back towards times t_{-1} and t_{-2}. Of course, the sole difference between equations (10) and (11) is that the former permits immediate delivery during the delivery month, hence chooses the lesser of: immediate delivery, $\min_j [\tilde{P}_j(t_{i\Delta}) - I_j(t_{i\Delta})]/C_j(t_{i\Delta})$; or expected value of future delivery, $\tilde{E}_{i\Delta}[\tilde{F}(t_{(i+1)\Delta})]$. In contrast, the computation of the values of the futures contract at times t_{-1} and t_{-2} recognizes that these times lie outside the delivery month. Finally, note that in the computation of futures contract values, we take expectations of future values but do not discount, since futures contracts are zero-cost-at-initiation positions.

Valuation of the Embedded "End-of-Month" and "Wild Card" Options

The futures contract also includes two other options. The first, the "end-of-month" option, permits the short to deliver at any time during the last seven business days of the delivery month at the invoice price based on the last futures settlement price — determined seven business days before the end of the delivery month, at which point the futures stops trading. The *sole* reason this option has any value is the absence of marking-to-market on the futures contract for the last week of the delivery month. Empirically, researchers have found that the differences between futures and forward contracts, although occasionally statistically significant, are typically economically marginal. Moreover, such mark-to-market effects are unlikely to be significant over the relatively short span of one week. In any case, since we have abstracted from marking-to-market effects in this chapter, we do not assign any positive value to this option.[14]

The wild card option refers to the option the short has to decide whether or not to deliver against the futures contract by 8 p.m. Central time at the futures delivery price fixed at 2 p.m. Central time any day within the delivery month. Since bond markets remain open after 2 p.m., we could in principle value this option by creating additional tree branches between 2 and 8 p.m. Unless annualized volatilities were unreasonably high, however, this short time interval would not result in significant valuation under the maintained assumption of diffusion processes for the two interest-rate factors. We believe it would be theoretically more appropriate to value this option using a jump-diffusion process, with the jump component potentially occurring between 2 and 8 p.m. and essentially determining this option's value. Such a valuation is, however, beyond the scope of this chapter.

DATA

The data for the empirical work reported in this chapter comprises the following items:

1. Deliverable bonds are those U.S. Treasury bonds, maturing at least 15 years from delivery date of the futures contract if not callable, and, if callable, not so for at least 15 years from delivery date. The CRSP Government Bonds File was scanned for the set of all bonds satisfying this requirement at date t_0, November 30, 1993.
2. The sets of C-STRIPS prices for the estimates of the discount functions on dates t_{-2} (September 30, 1993), t_{-1} (October 31, 1993) and t_0 were provided by Merrill Lynch & Co.
3. Prices of the futures contract for the dates t_{-2}, t_{-1} and t_0 were obtained from the appropriate editions of *The Wall Street Journal*.
4. Estimates of the volatilities and covariance for the 3-month and 20-year zero-coupon rates were obtained from the Bloomberg data retrieval system. Using comparable-maturity C-STRIPS, estimates of $\hat{\sigma}_r$ and $\hat{\sigma}_l$ were given by the (annualized) 50-day volatilities of $\ln r_t / r_{t-1}$ and $\ln l_t / l_{t-1}$ on December 30, 1993. The correlation coefficient was obtained from $\text{Corr}(\ln r_t / r_{t-1}, \ln l_t / l_{t-1})$ over the first six months of 1996.

---

[14] To see the impact of non-tradability in another case, consider the valuation of a call option in a Black-Scholes world. If trading in a call option were for some reason precluded, that would not preclude us from dynamically reproducing its Black-Scholes value by trading in the underlying stock and the riskless asset.

Exhibit 2: Time-Series Volatiltites and Correlations, 12/30/93

$\hat{\sigma}_r$	11.69%
$\hat{\sigma}_l$	10.70%
Corr($\ln r_t/r_{t-1}$, $\ln l_t/l_{t-1}$)	0.589

In the subsequent empirical work, we made two additional assumptions. The estimation of very short-term rates is problematical due to their cash-equivalent special status. Hence, we assumed that the term structure is flat out to three months. Second, in the implementation of the trinomial lattice and the Step 2 calculation of futures values, we set $\Delta = 1$ week, or $1/52$ of a year.

EMPIRICAL RESULTS

In this section, we report on the empirical values of the two embedded options of interest — the timing option and the quality option — for the December 1993 T-bond futures contract evaluated at the three dates in 1993: September 30th, October 31st, and November 30th.

The joint presence of the quality and timing options requires that we define the value of each option. First, compute the fair value of the T-bond futures contract with all its attendant embedded options. Then, revalue the futures under the assumption that you must precommit to the identity of the bond you intend to deliver — although you do not commit yourself to the *date* at which such delivery will take place. (This requires that you calculate the value of the futures contract assuming that each of the deliverable bonds is the sole one in existence, and then take the min across all bonds.) The difference between these two magnitudes is the value of the quality option.

Similarly, consider the value of the futures contract under the proviso that you must precommit to a specific delivery date — though now you do *not* commit to which bond you will delivery. (This will, in turn, require that we check each date in the delivery month as the sole deliverable date, and then select the minimum across all dates.) The difference between this value and the unconstrained futures value is the value of the timing option.

As noted above, the time-series volatilities for the respective processes in 1993 were calculated as reported in Exhibit 2. These statistics now permit the valuation of the T-bond futures contract and its embedded options, as reported in Exhibit 3. Several conclusions may be drawn from Exhibit 3:

1. As expected, the values of the quality and timing options are monotonically increasing functions of volatility and time to maturity. Of course, for the zero volatility case, all option values are zero as expected; they are included in the exhibit for verification purposes only.

Exhibit 3: Valuation of T-Bond Futures Contract

	Date: September 30, 1993 Futures market price = 118.531			Date: October 31, 1993 Futures market price = 118.75			Date: November 30, 1993 Futures market price = 115.5		
	Zero Vols	Historical Vols	Adjusted Historical Vols	Zero Vols	Historical Vols	Adjusted Historical Vols	Zero Vols	Historical Vols	Adjusted Historical Vols
$\left(\dfrac{\sigma_r}{\sigma_l}\right)' \left(\dfrac{\hat{\sigma}_r}{\hat{\sigma}_l}\right)'$	0	1	1.847	0	1	2.605	0	1	3.563
$\rho / \hat{\rho}$	—	1	1	—	1	1	—	1	1
(1) Futures value, all options	119.27	118.994	118.531	119.465	119.361	118.75	116.164	116.14	115.5
(2) $\min_j\{$Must deliver Bond $j\}$	119.27	119.236	119.156	119.465	119.441	119.305	116.164	116.153	116.033
(3) $\min_i\{$Must deliver on date $t_{i\Delta}\}$	119.27	118.994	118.532	119.465	119.361	118.751	116.164	116.14	115.5
(2)-(1) Quality option	0	0.252	0.625	0	0.08	0.555	0	0.013	0.533
(3)-(1) Timing option	0	0	0.001	0	0	0.001	0	0	0

Notes:
1. The historical vols are $[\hat{\sigma}_r, \hat{\sigma}_l]' = [11.69\%, 10.70\%]'$ and correlation is $\mathrm{Corr}(\ln r_t/r_{t-1}, \ln l_t/l_{t-1}) = 0.589$.
2. The "Adjusted" vols are (time-dependent) multiplicative constants of the historical vols, chosen so that the futures values at times t_i, $i = -2, -1, 0$ equal their respective market prices, while keeping the correlation coefficient at its historical value.
3. In the row denoted "(3)," dates $t_{i\Delta}$ include all dates within the delivery month $(t_0, t_\Delta, t_{2\Delta}, \cdots t_{1-\Delta}, t_1)$.

2. Consistent with the findings of other researchers, the CTD prior to delivery generally differs from the CTD at time of delivery.

3. For the December 1993 contract, the quality option on September 30th, *two* months prior to the first delivery date, has value between 24.2 and 62.5 cents (per $100 face value). In comparing these figures with those of previous researchers, our findings are consistent with the results reported by Hemler for the time period 1977 to 1986;[15] under his twin assumptions that delivery takes place at either end of the delivery month and no more than three optimally-chosen T-bonds are considered for delivery, he reports a mean value of the quality option *three* months prior to delivery of $1.243. In contrast, it should be noted that Kane and Marcus reported significantly higher figures for their highervolatility 1978 to 1982 reporting period.[16]

4. The value of the timing option is negligible. Consider equation (9). The positive difference between the coupon rates of the deliverable bonds and the prevailing interest rate implied that the invoice price of the bonds was accumulating value faster than the interest foregone on the cash that would otherwise be received for a delivered bond, consequently inducing the short to defer optimal delivery to the last possible moment.

5. The "adjusted historical vols" refer to historical volatilities scaled up so that the fair value of the futures contract equals its market price. In that sense, they are implied volatilities, and we find that these implied vols exceed historical vols. This is not surprising: just as forward rates may exceed expected spot rates (under the liquidity preference or Cox-Ingersoll-Ross hypotheses) markets may well require compensation for allowing participants to "lock in" a volatility level. While the multiplicative constants of 1.847, 2.605, and 3.563 may appear large, recall that the time period remaining to first delivery is relatively small, consisting of two months, one month, and one day in the respective cases. In this light, any conclusions regarding the substantial $0.533 value of the quality option using the significantly-high implied vols on November 30th should be confirmed in subsequent tests on alternate futures contracts.

It is instructive to examine the number of bonds which may be optimally-deliverable on at least one node of the interest-rate lattice. Exhibit 4 presents this number by quote date and interest-rate volatility parameters. From Exhibit 4, we find that:

1. In each case, strictly more bonds are "in play" as vols increase, but not necessarily more the earlier the quote date.

2. Although not evident from this exhibit, no bond is optimally-deliverable in only one node of the interest rate lattice.

---

[15] Hemel, "The Quality Delivery Option in Treasury Bond Futures Contracts."

[16] Kane and Marcus, "Conversion Factor Risk and Hedging in the Treasury Bond Futures Market."

Exhibit 4: Number of Potentially-Optimal Deliverable Bonds

Total Size of Deliverable Set: 26 Bonds

	Date: September 30, 1993			Date: October 31, 1993			Date: November 30, 1993		
	Zero Vols	Historical Vols	Adjusted Historical Vols	Zero Vols	Historical Vols	Adjusted Historical Vols	Zero Vols	Historical Vols	Adjusted Historical Vols
$\begin{pmatrix}\sigma_r\\ \sigma_l\end{pmatrix} / \begin{pmatrix}\hat{\sigma}_r\\ \hat{\sigma}_l\end{pmatrix}$	0	1	1.847	0	1	2.605	0	1	3.563
$\rho/\hat{\rho}$	—	1	1	—	1	1	—	1	1
Number of Optimally-Deliverable Bonds	1	5	7	1	4	9	1	3	4

Notes:
The "Number of Optimally-Deliverable Bonds" refers to the *ex-ante* number of bonds which are optimally deliverable against the futures contact on at least one node of the interest-rate lattice constructed on the given quote date using a specific set of volatility parameters.

3. The point made in Exhibit 4 is that, of the 26 bonds which qualify for delivery, far more than two or three bonds can come into play. Previous researchers, such as Hemler, have explicitly assumed that two or at most three bonds are optimally deliverable. In contrasting our analysis with that of Hemler, we should qualify the impact of our empirical results: while it is true that we demonstrate the presence of multiple optimally-deliverable bonds, our model nevertheless remains by assumption a *two*-factor model, and hence the full potential of multiple-bond delivery has not necessarily been captured herein; nor is it true that our model necessarily dominates Hemler's three-asset case in terms of the magnitude of the multiple-bond effect on the valuation of the futures contract.

Exhibit 5 now presents a perspective on the value of the timing option by showing the cumulative *ex-ante* probability, viewed as of the quote date using alternate measures of volatility, of delivery at any of the five points within the delivery month. The calculation of these probabilities was performed by calculating the *un*discounted value of an Arrow-Debreu security paying $1 if delivery took place at or before a given time period within the delivery month. Such calculations result in the cumulative probability of early delivery under the risk-neutral probability and using the different assumed magnitudes of volatilities.

From Exhibit 5 we conclude that:

1. For the given deliverable couon rates and interest rates prevailing in the last quarter of 1993, optimal delivery nearly always takes place at the end of the delivery month.
2. Increasing volatility does tend to disperse the optimal delivery within the delivery month. However, even for two- or three-fold multiples of historical volatilities one or two months before the beginning of the delivery month, only about 5% to 6% of the cases call for delivery before the end of the delivery month.
3. As of November 30, 1993, one day before first possible delivery, all optimal deliveries are forecasted to take place at the end of the month.

SUMMARY

In contrast to previous valuation approaches, in this chapter we present a consistent and arbitrage-free two-factor model for the valuation of the interest rate-dependent securities whose values impinge on the Treasury bond futures contract. This methodology has permitted the combined valuation of two important options embedded in that futures contract: the quality and timing options. This objective has been accomplished by assuming the two factors to be the short, 3-month, and long, 20-year, zero-coupon rates of interest, with a (risk-neutral) lognormal distribution centered about their respective forward rates of interest. We used Treasury C-STRIPS

Exhibit 5: Cumulative Risk-Neutral Probability of Optimal Timing Delivery

	Date: September 30, 1993			Date: October 31, 1993			Date: November 30, 1993		
	Zero Vols	Historical Vols	Adjusted Historical Vols	Zero Vols	Historical Vols	Adjusted Historical Vols	Zero Vols	Historical Vols	Adjusted Historical Vols
$\left(\dfrac{\sigma_r}{\sigma_l}\right)\Big/\left(\dfrac{\hat\sigma_r}{\hat\sigma_l}\right)$	0	1	1.847	0	1	2.605	0	1	3.563
$\rho/\hat\rho$	—	1	1	—	1	1	—	1	1
Cumulative Probability of delivery by									
$i = 0$	0	0	0.67%	0	0	0	0	0	0
$i = \Delta$	0	0.005%	1.89%	0	0	0	0	0	0
$i = 2\Delta$	0	0.020%	4.24%	0	0	0.137%	0	0	0
$i = 3\Delta$	0	0.144%	5.76%	0	0	5.170%	0	0	0
$i = 4\Delta$	100%	100%	100%	100%	100%	100%	100%	100%	100%

Notes:

1. The exhibit reports the *ex-ante* probability (using the alternate measures of volatility) viewed as of the three quote dates, of optimal delivery within the delivery month.

2. Since $\Delta = 1$ week, optimal delivery can take place at one of five times — $i = 0$, $i = \Delta$, $i = 2\Delta$, $i = 3\Delta$, $i = 4\Delta$ — within the delivery month.

3. Thus, viewed from September 30, 1993 using the adjusted historical vols, there was 5.76% probability that the short would deliver the bond at or before the third week of the delivery month.

prices to estimate the discount function, and inferred the state-specific realization of all other interest rates from the specific realization of the 3-month and 20-year zero-coupon rates. The approach explicitly recognizes the market-induced price-deviation of Treasury bonds from their fair values. For the valuation of the futures contract's embedded options, we used backward induction, or stochastic dynamic programming, in a lattice implementation to generate state-specific prices for all deliverable bonds, and hence for the value of the Treasury bond futures contract. This approach yielded the valuation of the T-bond futures contract at three dates: one day before first delivery, and one and two months prior to the first delivery date. For the December 1993 futures contract, we found the quality option two months prior to the first delivery date to have value in the region of 24.2 to 62.5 cents per $100 face value, whereas the value of the timing option at that point did not exceed the 1-penny mark.

We believe future work in this area has several clear directions. First, attention should be given to the magnitude of the state-dependent switching across bonds and delivery times. Second, the analysis should be extended beyond the December 1993 date, to see the impact under different levels and slopes of the term structure. Third, the two-factor model proposed herein should be tested for its hedging implications and effectiveness. Finally, this work should encompass another clearly identified set of interest-rate derivative securities, specifically, exchange-traded options on T-bond futures contracts. Such an extension would permit the clear inference of implied volatilities and their term structure, as well as an explicit contrast between implied volatilities and correlations on the one hand, and historical, time series-based statistics on the other.

APPENDIX: CONSTRUCTION OF THE TRINOMIAL TREE

Equation (4) in the text specifies the trinomial lattice to be used for valuation of the T-bond futures contract. This appendix demonstrates the numerical validity of that specification in fulfilling the first and second moment requirements of the joint process equation (1).

Consider initially the first-moment conditions given by equation (5). For $i = 1, 2$, we require that

$$pa_i + qb_i + (1 - p - q)c_i = 0 \qquad (12)$$

For $i = 1, 2$ and $\sigma_1 \equiv \sigma_r$, $\sigma_2 \equiv \sigma_l$, the variance condition given by equation (6) is

$$pa_i^2 + qb_i^2 + (1 - p - q)c_i^2 = \sigma_i^2$$

Finally, with $\sigma_{12} \equiv \sigma_{rl}$, the covariance condition given by equation (7) is

$$pa_1a_2 + qb_1b_2 + (1 - p - q)c_1c_2 = \sigma_{12}$$

We now demonstrate the tree can be constructed to satisfy all requirements under the special case when $c_1 = 0$ and $p = q = \frac{1}{3}$. We obtain the following five equations in five unknowns:

$$a_1 + b_1 = 0 \tag{13}$$

$$a_1^2 + b_1^2 = 3\sigma_1^2 \tag{14}$$

$$a_2 + b_2 + c_2 = 0 \tag{15}$$

$$a_2^2 + b_2^2 + c_2^2 = 3\sigma_2^2 \tag{16}$$

$$a_1 a_2 + b_1 b_2 = 3\sigma_{12} \tag{17}$$

The solution to this system can be seen by inspection as follows. Equations (13) and (14) yield values for a_1 and b_1. The three equations (15), (16), and (17) are then jointly solved for a_2, b_2 and c_2. The quadratic nature of the problem gives rise to two alternate set of equally acceptable parameters. Without loss of generality, and with $\rho \equiv \sigma_{12}/(\sigma_1 \sigma_2)$, one solution to the system is given by:

$$a_1 = \sqrt{3/2}\,\sigma_1$$

$$b_1 = -\sqrt{3/2}\,\sigma_1$$

$$a_2 = \sigma_2[\sqrt{3/2}\,\rho + \sqrt{(1-\rho^2)/2}]$$

$$b_2 = \sigma_2[-\sqrt{3/2}\,\rho + \sqrt{(1-\rho^2)/2}]$$

$$c_2 = -\sigma_2\sqrt{2(1-\rho^2)}$$

The tree's computational efficiency may be observed as follows. At time $t + n\,\Delta$,

$$r(t+n\Delta) = r(t)\exp\left\{\sum_{i=1}^{n} \mu_r(t+i\Delta)\Delta + (n_1 a_1 + n_2 b_1 + n_3 c_1)\sqrt{\Delta}\right\}$$

$$l(t+n\Delta) = l(t)\exp\left\{\sum_{i=1}^{n} \mu_l(t+i\Delta) + (n_1 a_2 + n_2 b_2 + n_3 c_2)\sqrt{\Delta}\right\}$$

The computational efficiency follows from the fact that the expressions for both $r(t + n\Delta)$ and $l(t + n\Delta)$ depend only on n_1, n_2, and $n_3 = n - n_1 - n_2$. Thus, the relevant nodes on the tree are fully identified by the triplet (n, n_1, n_2), and the number of nodes at time step n, $n = 1, 2, \ldots$ is given by $(n + 1)(n + 2)/2$.

Chapter 9

Pricing and Hedging Interest Rate Risks with the Multi-Factor Cox-Ingersoll-Ross Model

Ren-Raw Chen, Ph.D.
Assistant Professor of Finance
School of Business
Rutgers University

Louis O. Scott, Ph.D.
Associate Professor of Finance
School of Business
University of Georgia

INTRODUCTION

Interest rate fluctuation is an important financial risk. There are several competing models that are used to price this risk and, in turn, provide hedging strategies. In this chapter, we examine the Cox-Ingersoll-Ross (CIR) model of the term structure, with multiple factors.

Equilibrium term structure models with hedging implications can be traced back to Vasicek[1] and Cox-Ingersoll-Ross[2] (CIR), who developed one factor, fixed parameter term structure models. Since the development of the these models, there have been numerous extensions and variations. A good term structure model should accomplish two goals: (1) it should reflect historical experience and actual volatility, and (2) it should explain market prices. Unfortunately, neither the Vasicek nor the CIR model can accomplish these goals. Empirical evidence has demonstrated that one fac-

---

[1] O. Vasicek, "An Equilibrium Characterization of The Term Structure," *Journal of Financial Economics* (1977), pp. 177-188.

[2] J. Cox, J. Ingersoll, and S. Ross, "A Theory of The Term Structure of Interest Rates," *Econometrica* (March 1985), pp. 385-407.

tor, fixed parameter models do not capture the historical variability of interest rates, and these models do not fit observed yield curves. The motivation for more recent models has been to resolve some of these problems.

One approach is to add more factors to the model. In doing so, the model becomes more flexible. The other approach is to make parameters of the one-factor model time dependent. In doing so, the prices calculated by the model are flexible across all maturities, and the model can fit any observed yield curve. The multi-factor approach preserves the simplicity of the Vasicek/CIR models, but it does not necessarily fit all of points along an observed yield curve. On the other hand, the time dependent parameter models can fit any yield curve, but there exist no econometric methods to estimate the parameters, and these models have not been tested against actual data. As the yield curve changes, one must continually revise the deterministic functions used to model the parameter drift.

In this chapter, we develop a multi-factor version of the CIR model, and we demonstrate how it can be used to provide hedging strategies.

MULTI-FACTOR MODELS IN THE PAST

In their original work, CIR solved a term structure model with a single factor. In their model, the economy is characterized by only one state variable and the short-term interest rate is determined endogenously within the model. They further show that the short-term interest rate will follow the same stochastic process as the state variable. Later on, CIR demonstrate how to incorporate more factors into the model. They show that with a particular structure for the state variables, the short rate is a linear function of the factors. This method is then used in two different ways. The direct method, which is carried out by Chen and Scott, is to decompose the short-term interest rate into independent random factors.[3] The other method is to transform the factors into meaningful financial variables as in Longstaff and Schwartz, who transform the factors into the short rate and short-rate volatility.[4]

Independent of the work extending the CIR model, there are a number of other multi-factor models. Similar to CIR, Langetieg proposed a multivariate model for the term structure in which the short rate is a linear combination of state variables.[5] The Langetieg model differs from the CIR model in that each state variable follows a normal process instead of the square root process. Observing that the yield curve often has non-parallel shifts, Brennan and Schwartz proposed a two-factor model that captures the movements of the short rate and the long rate.[6] In their model,

---

[3] R. Chen and L. Scott, "Pricing Interest Rate Options in a Two-Factor Cox-Ingersoll-Ross Model of the Term Structure," *Review of Financial Studies* (1992), pp. 613-636.

[4] F. Longstaff and E. Schwartz, "Interest Rate Volatility and the Term Structure: A Two Factor General Equilibrium Model," *Journal of Finance* (September 1992), pp. 1259-82.

[5] T. Langetieg, "A Multivariate Model of the Term Structure," *Journal of Finance* (March 1980), pp. 71-97.

[6] M. Brennan and E. Schwartz, "A Continuous Time Approach to the Pricing of Bonds," *Journal of Banking and Finance* (1978), pp. 133-155.

the short rate converges to the long rate while the long rate follows a positive random process. Using the Fisher equation, Richard proposed a two-factor model for interest rates which he derived under interest rate uncertainty.[7] He modeled both the inflation rate and the real interest rate with the square root processes. To obtain a solution, he had to assume that these two variables are independent.

THE ONE-FACTOR CIR MODEL

The Fundamental Valuation Technique — Risk Neutral Measure and Forward Measure

In the CIR model, if the state variable that determines the investment opportunity set follows a square root process and the representative agent has a log utility function, then the instantaneous interest rate will follow a process of the same form and the risk premium will be proportional to the level of the state variable. The interest rate process used by CIR is:

$$dr = \kappa(\theta - r)dt + \sigma\sqrt{r}dW \tag{1}$$

where κ and θ are fixed constants representing the speed of mean reversion and the mean reverting level. The other fixed parameter σ with the square root of the interest rate, determines the instantaneous volatility of the interest rate. This process is called "mean-reverting" because the interest rate is expected to increase when it is below θ and decrease when it is above θ. The process is pulled back to the mean reverting level. With this process, the short rate is distributed as a noncentral chi-squared.[8]

Subtracting the risk premium from the original process, we can write the risk neutralized for the short rate as:

$$dr = (\kappa\theta - \kappa r - \lambda r)dt + \sigma\sqrt{r}d\hat{W} \tag{2}$$

where λ is a constant. After some rearrangement of the drift term, this risk neutralized process is identical to the original process except that the speed and level parameters are adjusted as follows:

$$dr = (\kappa + \lambda)\left(\frac{\kappa\theta}{\kappa + \lambda} - r\right)dt + \sigma\sqrt{r}d\hat{W} = \hat{\kappa}(\hat{\theta} - r) + \sigma\sqrt{r}d\hat{W} \tag{3}$$

The risk neutralized process also has a noncentral chi-squared distribution, but the parameters of the distribution have been adjusted. Note that $\hat{\kappa}\hat{\theta} = \kappa\theta$, and the only change is the replacement of κ with $\kappa + \lambda$.

---

[7] S. Richard, "An Arbitrage Model of the Term Structure of Interest Rates," *Journal of Financial Economics* (1978), pp. 33-57.

[8] See W. Feller, "Two Singular Diffusion Problems," *Annals of Mathematics* (July 1951), and Cox, Ingersoll, and Ross, "A Theory of The Term Structure of Interest Rates."

When the discount rate and the payoff of a contingent claim are stochastic, the risk-neutralized expectation can be difficult to evaluate because the expectation involves the joint distribution of the discount factor and the payoff. Jamshidian demonstrates that with a change of measure, the calculation can be simplified.[9] The separation theorem says,

$$\hat{E}_t\left[e^{-\int_t^T r(u)du} g(r(T))\right] = \hat{E}_t\left[e^{-\int_t^T r(u)du}\right]\hat{E}_t\left[\frac{e^{-\int_t^T r(u)du} g(r(T))}{\hat{E}_t\left[e^{-\int_t^T r(u)du}\right]}\right] \tag{4}$$

$$= \hat{E}_t\left[e^{-\int_t^T r(u)du}\right]\bar{E}_t[g(r(T))]$$

where $\bar{E}[\cdot]$ is the expectation defined under the following process:

$$dr = [\hat{\kappa}(\hat{\theta}-r) - \sigma^2 rB(t, T)]dt + \sigma\sqrt{r}d\overline{W} \tag{5}$$

The interest rate in this process also has a noncentral chi-squared distribution with additional adjustments on the parameters of the distribution. This process is called the *forward adjusted* process because the expected value of a future discount bond price, under this process, is equal to the forward price:

$$F(t, T_F, T) = \bar{E}_t[P(T_F, T)] = \frac{P(t, T)}{P(t, T_F)} \tag{6}$$

where $F(t, T_F, T)$ is the forward price observed at time t for the delivery of T-maturity discount bond at time T_F, and $P(t, T)$ is the pure discount bond price at time t for the delivery of $1 at time T.

The Basic Zero-Coupon Bond Formula

With the model as just described, one can derive formulas for bond prices, futures prices, and European-style options prices. The most important formula that serves as the base of all other formulas is the pricing formula for a pure discount bond. A T-maturity discount bond price, with a par value of $1, is the risk-neutralized expectation of:

$$P(t, T) = \hat{E}_t\left[\exp\left(-\int_t^T r(u)du\right)\right] \tag{7}$$

This bond price has a closed form solution derived by CIR as follows:

$$P(t, T) = A(t, T)e^{-r(t)B(t, T)} \tag{8}$$

[9] F. Jamshidian, "Pricing Contingent Claims in the One Factor Term Structure Model," working paper, Merrill Lynch Capital Markets (1987).

where

$$A(t, T) = \left[\frac{2\gamma e^{(\kappa + \lambda + \gamma)(T-t)/2}}{(\kappa + \lambda + \gamma)(e^{\gamma(T-t)} - 1) + 2\gamma} \right]^{2\kappa\theta/\sigma^2}$$

$$B(t, T) = \frac{2(e^{\gamma(T-t)} - 1)}{(\kappa + \lambda + \gamma)(e^{\gamma(T-t)} - 1) + 2\gamma}$$

$$\gamma = \sqrt{(\kappa + \lambda)^2 + 2\sigma^2}$$

From this model, one can derive a yield curve by using the following relationship between continuously compounded yields and bond prices:

$$R(t, T) = -\frac{\ln P(t, T)}{T - t} \tag{9}$$

It should be noted that for a set of values for the fixed parameters and the interest rate, this theoretical yield curve may not match the observed yield curve in the market.

The pure discount bond price can also be used as a discount factor under stochastic interest rates. A coupon bond price can be valued as a portfolio of discount bonds as follows:

$$Q(t) = \sum_{i=1}^{N} c(T_i) P(t, T_i) \tag{10}$$

where $c(s)$ is the cash flow received at time s. This valuation formula does not depend on the specific assumptions of an interest rate model. It can be obtained by a simple arbitrage argument. If the observed market coupon bond price is greater than Q, then we can sell short the coupon bond and use only part of the proceed to buy a series of pure discount bonds with maturities equal to coupon arrival dates. The cash flows from the maturing discount bonds can be used to cover all of the coupons and par value on the short position in the coupon bond. Thus, the coupon bond price cannot exceed Q. Reversing the arbitrage will prevent the coupon bond price from being less than Q. Because this valuation formula does not depend on a specific model, it works for any model, including one with multiple factors.

Zero-Coupon Bond Option

Zero-coupon bond options are not common in the marketplace. However, the pricing formula is important because it serves as the basic valuation equation for more complex option pricing formulas such as Eurodollar futures options, coupon bond futures options, swaps, and over-the-counter caps and floors. The payoff at maturity for a European style call option on a zero-coupon bond is:

$$C(t, T_C, T) = \max\{P(T_C, T) - K, 0\} \tag{11}$$

The option value today is the risk-neutralized expectation of the payoff at maturity. For the call option, we calculate the following expectation:

$$C(t, T_C, T) = \hat{E}_t\left[\exp\left(-\int_t^{T_C} r(u)du\right)\max\{P(T_C, T) - K, 0\}\right]$$ (12)

This expectation can be evaluated by using the noncentral chi-squared distribution. From equation (4), we know that the expectation can be evaluated by separating the two parts as follows:

$$\hat{E}_t\left[\exp\left(-\int_t^{T_C} r(u)du\right)\right]\bar{E}_t[\max\{P(T_C, T) - K, 0\}]$$ (13)

and

$$\bar{E}_t[\max\{P(T_C, T) - K, 0\}] = \bar{E}_t[P(T_C, T)1_{(P > K)}] - K\bar{E}_t[1_{(P > K)}]$$

$$= \bar{E}_t[P(T_C, T)]\tilde{E}_t[1_{(P > K)}] - K\bar{E}_t[1_{(P > K)}]$$ (14)

where $1_{\{.\}}$ is an indicator function. The expectation of the indicator function produces a probability function. The second expectation is the probability under the forward measure. $\tilde{E}_t[1_{\{P > K\}}]$ is a probability function in which an additional adjustment is made to the distribution under the forward measure. Following the result that any asset under the expectation of $\bar{E}[\cdot]$ always gives its forward price, i.e.,

$$\bar{E}_t[P(T_C, T)] = \frac{P(t, T)}{P(t, T_C)}$$ (15)

By applying a simple arbitrage argument, the ratio of two bond prices produces the forward price. Substituting this into equation (4), we obtain the CIR option pricing formula:

$$C(t, T_C, T) = P(t, T)\chi^2\left(2r^*(\phi + \psi + B(T_C, T)), \frac{4\kappa\theta}{\sigma^2}, \frac{2\phi^2 re^{\gamma(T_C - t)}}{\phi + \psi + B(T_C, T)}\right)$$

$$- KP(t, T_C)\chi^2\left(2r^*(\phi + \psi), \frac{4\kappa\theta}{\sigma^2}, \frac{2\phi^2 re^{\gamma(T_C - t)}}{\phi + \psi}\right)$$ (16)

where

$$\gamma = \sqrt{\kappa + \lambda^2 + 2\sigma^2}$$

$$\phi = \frac{2\gamma}{\sigma^2\left(e^{\gamma(T_C - t)} - 1\right)}$$

$$\psi = (\kappa + \lambda + \gamma)/\sigma^2$$

$$r^* = [\ln A(T_C, C) - \ln K]/B(T_C, T)$$

Fast numerical algorithms for computing the noncentral chi-squared distribution function are available in many software packages.[10]

Zero-Coupon Bond Futures and Futures Options

The futures price is the risk neutralized expectation of the bond price at the settlement date or maturity of the futures contract, and the solution is,

$$F(t, T_F, T) = \hat{E}_t[P(T_F, T)] = \hat{E}_t\left[A(T_F, T)e^{-r(T_F)B(T_F, T)}\right] \tag{17}$$

In this case the futures price is obtained from the moment generating function for the interest rate:

$$F(t, T_F, T) = A(T_F, T)\hat{E}_t\left[e^{-r(T_F)B(T_F, T)}\right] = X(t, T_F, T)e^{-r(t)Y(T_F, T)} \tag{18}$$

where

$$X(t, T_F, T) = A(T_F, T)\left[\frac{x(t, T_F)}{x(t, T_F) + B(T_F, T)}\right]^{2\kappa\theta/\sigma^2}$$

$$Y(t, T_F, T) = B(T_F, T)\left[\frac{x(t, T_F)e^{(\kappa + \lambda)(T_F - t)}}{x(t, T_F) + B(T_F, T)}\right]$$

$$x(t, T_F) = \frac{2(\kappa + \lambda)}{\sigma^2\left(1 - e^{(\kappa + \lambda)(T_F - t)}\right)}$$

This solution is an application of the analysis in a 1981 paper by CIR.[11]

The price for a futures option on a discount bond can be derived in a similar manner. We use the risk neutralized expectation and the separation of the discount factor. The option pays the difference between the futures price and the strike price, or 0 whichever larger.

$$C = P(t, T_C)\bar{E}_t[\max\{F(T_C, T_F, T) - K, 0\}] \tag{19}$$

This result has been derived by Feldman[12] and Jamshidian,[13] and the solution is

---

[10] Examples include the International Mathematical & Statistical Library (IMSL) and Mathematica. For a discussion of the properties of the noncentral chi-squared distribution, see N. Johnson and S. Kotz, *Distributions in Statistics: Continuous Univariate Distributions – 2* (Boston: Houghton Mifflin Company, 1970).

[11] J. Cox, J. Ingersoll, and S. Ross, "The Relation between Forward Prices and Futures Prices," *Journal of Financial Economics* (1981), pp. 321-346.

[12] D. Feldman, "European Options on Bond Futures: A Closed Form Solution," *Journal of Futures Markets* (1993), pp. 325-333.

[13] Jamshidian, "Pricing Contingent Claims in the One Factor Term Structure Model."

$$C(t,T_C,T) = H(t,T)\chi^2\left(2r^*[\phi + \psi + \chi(T_C, T_F, T)], \frac{4\kappa\theta}{\sigma^2}, \frac{2\phi^2 re^{\gamma(T_C-t)}}{\phi + \psi + D(T_C, T_F, T)}\right)$$

$$- K P(t, T_C)\chi^2\left(2r^*(\phi + \psi), \frac{4\kappa\theta}{\sigma^2}, \frac{2\phi^2 re^{\gamma(T_C-t)}}{\phi + \psi}\right) \tag{20}$$

where

$$H(t) = P(t,T_C)X(T_C,T_F,T) \, \exp\left(\frac{-2(\phi+\psi)B(T_C,T)\Lambda}{1+4(\phi+\psi)B(T_C,T)}\right)$$

$$\times [1+4(\phi+\psi)B(T_C,T)]^{(-2\kappa\theta)/\sigma^2}$$

$$\Lambda = \phi^2 e^{\gamma(T_C-t)}\sigma^2 B(t, T_C)r(t)$$

A Brief Digression on Gaussian Models

Similar solutions have been derived for the Vasicek model. Jamshidian[14] derived the bond option pricing formula and Chen derived pricing formulas for futures and futures option.[15] In the Vasicek model, the interest rate and the integral of the interest rate have normal distributions and the solutions are easy to derive using the properties of the normal distribution.

THE EQUILIBRIUM CIR MULTI-FACTOR MODEL

Toward the end of their paper, CIR show how to develop a term structure model when there are multiple factors in the economy. The model for the short-term rate has the following form:

$$r(t) = \sum_{j=1}^{J} y_j(t) \tag{21}$$

where each factor (or state variable) follows a stochastic process. This approach has been applied in a number of papers.[16]

The resulting solution for the price of a discount bond is

$$P(t, T) = \prod_{j=1}^{J} P_j(t, T) \tag{22}$$

---

[14] F. Jamshidian,"An Exact Bond Option Formula," *Journal of Finance* (March 1989).

[15] R. Chen, "Exact Solutions for Futures and European Futures Options on Pure Discount Bonds," *Journal of Financial and Quantitative Analysis* (March 1992), pp. 97-107.

where each bond price is given by equation (8). Option prices can be obtained by solving the following expectation:

$$C(t, T_C, T) = \hat{E}_t\left[\exp\left(-\int_t^{T_C} r(u)du\right)\max\{P(T_C, T) - K, 0\}\right]$$

$$= \hat{E}_t\left[\exp\left(-\int_t^{T_C} r(u)du\right)\right]\bar{E}_t[\max\{P(T_C, T) - K, 0\}] \qquad (23)$$

Chen and Scott provide the solution for a two-factor model and they show how to reduce the solution to a univariate numerical integration.[17] A more general solution for the model with multiple factors can be written as follows:[18]

$$C(t, T_C, T) = \int_0^\infty \cdots \int_0^\infty e^{-\int_t^{T_C} r(u)du} \max\{P(T_C, T) - K, 0\} \prod_{j=1}^J \hat{f}(z_j; v_j, \xi_j)dz_j$$

$$= P(t, T_C)\int_0^\infty \cdots \int_0^\infty \max\{P(T_C, T) - K, 0\} \prod_{j=1}^J \bar{f}(z_j; v_j, \xi_j)dz_j \qquad (24)$$

where $\hat{f}(\cdot)$ is the risk-neutralized density function and $\bar{f}(\cdot)$ is the forward-adjusted density function.

In a more recent paper, Chen and Scott have shown that the multi-factor model can be solved by using Fourier inversion methods.[19] Every distribution has a characteristic function defined as follows:

$$\Phi(u) = \int_{-\infty}^\infty e^{iux}dF(x) \qquad (25)$$

where $F(x)$ is the cumulative distribution function and

$$F(x) = \int_{-\infty}^x f(z)dz$$

---

[16] See Langetieg, "A Multivariate Model of the Term Structure"; G. Chaplin, "A Formula for Bond Option Values under an Ornstein-Uhlenbeck Model for the Spot," working paper, University of Waterloo, (1987); R. Chen, "A Two Factor, Preference Free Model for Interest Rate Sensitive Claims," *Journal of Futures Markets* (May 1995), pp. 345-372; J. Hull and A. White, "Pricing Interest Rate Derivative Securities," *Review of Financial Studies* (1990), pp. 573-592; S. Turnbull and F. Milne, "A Simple Approach to Interest Rate Option Pricing," *Review of Financial Studies* (1991), pp. 87-120; Chen and Scott, "Pricing Interest Rate Options in a Two-Factor Cox-Ingersoll-Ross Model of the Term Structure"; N. Pearson and T. Sun, "Exploiting the Conditional Density in Estimating the Term Structure: An Application to the Cox, Ingersoll, and Ross Model," *Journal of Finance* (September 1994), pp. 1279-1304; and F. Longstaff and E. Schwartz, "Interest Rate Volatility and the Term Structure: A Two Factor General Equilibrium Model," *Journal of Finance* (September 1992).

[17] Chen and Scott, "Pricing Interest Rate Options in a Two-Factor Cox-Ingersoll-Ross Model of the Term Structure."

[18] See R. Chen and L. Scott, "Interest Rate Options in Multi-Factor CIR Models of the Term Structure," *Journal of Derivatives* (Winter 1995), pp. 53-72.

[19] Chen and Scott, "Interest Rate Options in Multi-Factor CIR Models of the Term Structure,"

if the density function exists. In these cases, an inverse Fourier transform of the characteristic function produces the density function:

$$f(x) = \frac{1}{2\pi} \int_{-\infty}^{\infty} \Phi(u)e^{-iux}du \qquad (26)$$

Since:

$$e^{iux} = \cos(ux) + i\sin(ux) \qquad (27)$$

one can separate the integration into a sin transform and a cosine transform. One can also use Fourier inversion of the characteristic function to get the probability function. In this model with nonnegative random variables, the following Fourier inversion formula can be used:

$$Pr(X \le x) = \frac{1}{\pi}\int_{-\infty}^{\infty} \frac{\sin ux}{u}\Phi(u)du \qquad (28)$$

In the multi-factor CIR model, we need probability functions for linear combinations of the state variables, and the characteristic function is useful in the analysis of linear combinations of independent random variables. Let

$$X = \sum_{j=1}^{J} B_j(t, T)y_i \qquad (29)$$

The characteristic function of X is

$$\Phi(u) = \int \int \cdots \int e^{iuX} f_1(y_1)f_2(y_2)\cdots f_J(y_j)dy_1 dy_2 \cdots dy_J$$

$$= \prod_{j=1}^{J} \Phi(uB_j(t, T)) \qquad (30)$$

The resulting solution for this option pricing function is

$$C(t;T_C,T) = P(t, T)\Pr\left\{ \sum_{j=1}^{J} B_j(T_C, T)y_j^*(T_C) \le Z; v, \delta^* \right\}$$

$$- P(t, T_C)K\Pr\left\{ \sum_{j=1}^{J} B_j(T_C, T)y_j(T_C) \le Z; v, \delta \right\} \qquad (31)$$

where

$$Z = -\ln K + \sum_{j=1}^{J} \ln A_j(T_C, T)$$

and v, δ, and δ^* are vectors containing the elements

$$v_j = \frac{4\kappa_j\theta_j}{\sigma_j^2}$$

$$\delta_j = \frac{2\phi_j^2 y_j(t)\,\exp\{\gamma_j(T-t)\}}{\phi_j+\varphi_j}$$

$$\delta_j^* = \frac{2\phi_j^2 y_j(t)\,\exp\{\gamma_j(T-t)\}}{\phi_j+\varphi_j+B_j(T,s)}$$

The characteristic functions for the two probability functions are

$$\Phi^*(u) = \prod_{j=1}^{J}\left(1-\frac{B_j(T_C,T)iu}{\phi_j+\varphi_j+B_j(T_C,T)}\right)^{(-1/2)v_j} \tag{32}$$

$$\exp\frac{\frac{1}{2}B_j(T_C,T)\delta_j^* iu}{\phi_j+\varphi_j+B_j(T_C,T)(1-iu)}$$

and

$$\Phi(u) = \prod_{j=1}^{J}\left(1-\frac{B_j(T_C,T)iu}{\phi_j+\varphi_j}\right)^{(-1/2)v_j}\exp\frac{\frac{1}{2}B_j(T_C,T)\delta_j iu}{\phi_j+\varphi_j+B_j(T_C,T)iu} \tag{33}$$

HEDGING

With these closed form solutions, hedging is simplified. To form a delta-neutral hedge, we form a portfolio as follows:

$$V = C + \sum_{j=1}^{J} h_j A_j \tag{34}$$

A dynamically hedged position is one in which $dV=0$. The dynamics in matrix form are:

$$dV = \begin{bmatrix}\dfrac{\partial C}{\partial y_1}\\[2mm]\dfrac{\partial C}{\partial y_2}\\[1mm]\vdots\\[1mm]\dfrac{\partial C}{\partial y_J}\end{bmatrix} + \begin{bmatrix}\dfrac{\partial A_1}{\partial y_1} & \dfrac{\partial A_1}{\partial y_2} & \cdots & \dfrac{\partial A_1}{\partial y_J}\\[2mm]\dfrac{\partial A_2}{\partial y_1} & \dfrac{\partial A_2}{\partial y_2} & \cdots & \dfrac{\partial A_2}{\partial y_J}\\[1mm]\vdots & \vdots & \ddots & \vdots\\[1mm]\dfrac{\partial A_J}{\partial y_1} & \dfrac{\partial A_J}{\partial y_2} & \cdots & \dfrac{\partial A_J}{\partial y_J}\end{bmatrix}\begin{bmatrix}h_1\\[2mm]h_2\\[1mm]\vdots\\[1mm]h_J\end{bmatrix} = 0 \tag{35}$$

In matrix notation, we write:

$$dV = \mathbf{C} + \mathbf{A} \times \mathbf{H} = 0$$

These partial derivatives can be obtained analytically with the closed form solutions derived in the previous section. As long as the matrix $\mathbf{A}$ is not singular, one can solve for all hedge ratios:

$$\mathbf{H} = \mathbf{A}^{-1}\mathbf{C} \tag{36}$$

Of course, one must carefully choose the hedging securities, which should include the underlying security.

PARAMETER ESTIMATION

To implement the multi-factor CIR model, one must have values for the fixed parameters and the random state variables. Given a set of values for the fixed parameters, one can set the state variables to fit the yield curve at any point in time. The fixed parameter values control the mean reversion and the volatility of interest rates, and it is important to use reliable estimates for these parameter values. At a minimum, these parameter values should be set to capture the potential variability of the term structure.

Several econometric techniques have been used to estimate these parameter values from historical data. These include maximum likelihood estimation (MLE), the generalized method of moments (GMM), and estimation of a state space model with a Kalman filter. Examples of MLE and GMM estimation can be found in several papers.[20] There is a complete specification of the joint distribution for interest rates in the multi-factor CIR model, so that it would appear that MLE is more efficient than GMM. The GMM estimators are easier to implement, but the standard errors for some of the estimates tend to be large. There is, however, a potential specification error in the applications of MLE because one must specify arbitrary structures for the measurement errors in order to generate tractable estimators.

An alternative to MLE is the state space model with a Kalman filter used to estimate the state variables. With this econometric model, one can allow for measurement errors on all of the bond rates. The continuously compounded yields are linear functions of the state variables:

---

[20] For MLE, see R. Chen and L. Scott, "Maximum Likelihood Estimation of a Multi-Factor Equilibrium Model of the Term Structure of Interest Rates," *Journal of Fixed Income* (December 1993), pp. 14-32, and N. Pearson and T. Sun, "Exploiting the Conditional Density in Estimating the Term Structure: An Application to the Cox, Ingersoll, and Ross Model." For GMM see R. M. Gibbons and K. Ramaswamy, "A Test of the Cox, Ingersoll, and Ross Model of the Term Structure," *Review of Financial Studies* (1993) and Longstaff and Schwartz, "Interest Rate Volatility and the Term Structure: A Two Factor General Equilibrium Model."

$$R(t, T_m) = -\sum_{j=1}^{J} \frac{\ln A_j(t, T_m)}{T_m - t} + \sum_{j=1}^{J} \frac{B_j(t, T_m)}{T_m - t} y_j(t) \tag{37}$$

for $m = 1, ..., M$.

The conditional mean and variance for each state variable can be derived from the non-central chi-square distribution (see CIR(1985)):

$$E(y_j(t)|y_j(t-1)) = \theta_j\left(1 - e^{-\kappa_j \Delta t}\right) + e^{-\kappa_j \Delta t} y_j(t-1) \tag{38}$$

$$Var(y_j(t)|y_j(t-1)) = \sigma_j^2 \left[\frac{1 - e^{-\kappa_j \Delta t}}{\kappa_j}\right]$$

$$\left[\frac{\theta_j\left(1 - e^{-\kappa_j \Delta t}\right)}{2} + e^{-\kappa_j \Delta t} y_j(t-1)\right] \tag{39}$$

where Δt is the size of the time interval between the discrete observations. Combining these two and adding measurement errors to the equations for $R(t, T_m)$, we have a linear model that fits into the state space framework:

$$y_j(t) = a_j + b_j y_j(t-1) + \eta_j(t)$$

$$R(t, T_m) = -\sum_{j=1}^{J} \frac{\ln A_j(t, T_m)}{T_m - t} + \sum_{j=1}^{J} \frac{B_j(t, T_m)}{T_m - t} y_j(t) + \varepsilon_m(t) \tag{40}$$

Parameter estimates for equation (40) are reported in Exhibit 1 and represent estimates from four bond rates over the period 1980 to 1988.[21] On selected days, the errors between the actual bond rates and rates computed from the one-, two-, and three-factor models for all of the bonds traded in the U.S. Treasury market were examined. Some of the graphs are reproduced here in Exhibits 2 through 5.

MODEL CALIBRATION

One must also determine values for the random state variables to implement a multi-factor CIR model. A natural way to proceed is to set the values for the state variables, given a set of values for the fixed parameters, so that the model matches as closely as possible the current yield curve. With a three-factor model, one could set the three state variables so that the model matches three current bond

[21] R. Chen, and L. Scott, "Multi-Factor Cox-Ingersoll-Ross Models of the Term Structure: Estimates and Tests from a Kalman Filter Model," working paper, Rutgers University and University of Georgia (1995).

rates; an example would be to match the rates on 6-month Treasury bills, 5-year bonds, and 10-year bonds. An alternative strategy would be to set the state variables so that the sum of the squared errors between the model rates and the actual rates is minimized for a set of bonds.

The empirical evidence on multi-factor models suggests that this last strategy would provide a good fit for the current term structure, but it would not produce an exact match for all of the bond rates across the term structure. At this point, one could adjust some of the fixed parameter values to bend the yield curve so that it matches all, or most, of the observed points along the yield curve. The disadvantage of this type of calibration is that it also changes the mean reversion characteristics and the volatility of the model. Another approach to calibration is to make some of the fixed parameters deterministic functions of time. This extra flexibility makes it possible to match every point in an initial term structure, but many of the analytic solutions described in the previous sections are lost. An alternative suggested by Scott is to add a deterministic function directly to the interest rate equation.[22]

Exhibit 1: Estimates from Weekly Data, 1980-1988

	One Factor Model	Two Factor Model		Three Factor Model		
κ	0.13974	0.7298	0.021185	1.4298	0.01694	0.03510
	(0.03408)	(0.3013)	(0.004139)	(0.2761)	(0.11319)	(0.02776)
θ	0.08480	0.04013	0.022543	0.04374	0.00253	0.03209
	(0.02050)	(0.01660)	(0.003616)	(0.00838)	(0.016991)	(0.002543)
σ	0.10001	0.06885	0.054415	0.16049	0.1054	0.04960
	(0.003846)	(0.01015)	(0.002786)	(0.01047)	(0.00679)	(0.0003148)
λ	-0.07132	-0.01730	-0.044041	-0.2468	0.03411	-0.1569
	(0.03475)	(0.30105)	(0.005692)	(0.2635)	(0.11281)	(0.03077)
lnL	8505.09	10008.65		10424.24		

Note: This exhibit contains the ML estimates of the parameters for the state space model with 1, 2, and 3 factors. Four bond rates have been used for R. The maturities are 3 months, 6 months, 5 years, and the longest maturity available. The bond rates are continuously compounded yields that have been computed from bond prices sampled every Thursday. All of the sample sizes are $T = 470$. The numbers in parentheses are asymptomatic standard errors.

Source: R. Chen, and L. Scott, "Multi-Factor Cox-Ingersoll-Ross Models of the Term Structure: Estimates and Tests from a Kalman Filter Model," working paper, Rutgers University and University of Georgia (1995).

[22] L. Scott, "The Valuation of Interest Rate Derivatives in a Multi-Factor Term Structure Model with Deterministic Components," University of Georgia, paper presented at the Chicago Board of Trade Academic Seminar (May 1996).

Exhibit 2: Yield Curve: December 4, 1980

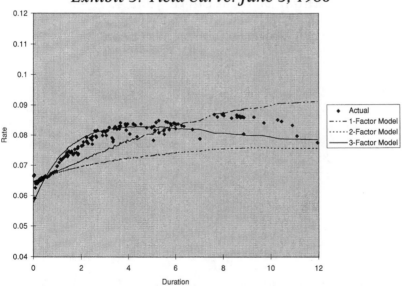

Source: R. Chen, and L. Scott, "Multi-Factor Cox-Ingersoll-Ross Models of the Term Structure: Estimates and Tests from a Kalman Filter Model," working paper, Rutgers University and University of Georgia (1995).

Exhibit 3: Yield Curve: June 5, 1986

Source: R. Chen, and L. Scott, "Multi-Factor Cox-Ingersoll-Ross Models of the Term Structure: Estimates and Tests from a Kalman Filter Model," working paper, Rutgers University and University of Georgia (1995).

Exhibit 4: Yield Curve: June 2, 1988

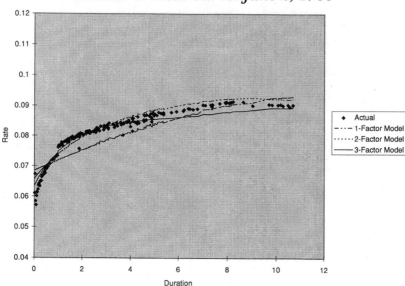

Source: R. Chen, and L. Scott, "Multi-Factor Cox-Ingersoll-Ross Models of the Term Structure: Estimates and Tests from a Kalman Filter Model," working paper, Rutgers University and University of Georgia (1995).

Exhibit 5: Yield Curve: June 4, 1992

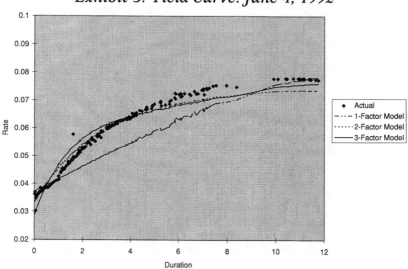

Source: R. Chen, and L. Scott, "Multi-Factor Cox-Ingersoll-Ross Models of the Term Structure: Estimates and Tests from a Kalman Filter Model," working paper, Rutgers University and University of Georgia (1995).

$$r(t) = \hat{\theta}(t) + \sum_{j=1}^{J} y_j(t) \qquad (41)$$

The deterministic function of time, $\hat{\theta}(t)$, provides the extra flexibility to match every point in the term structure, and the model retains all of its analytical tractability. The strategy behind a model of this form is to capture most of the variability with the random state variables and to use the deterministic function of time to fine tune the model so that it matches an initial term structure.

One should always remember that the econometric estimates provide a description of past variability of the term structure. In many situations, one may need to adjust some of the volatility parameters. One possibility is to calibrate the model with the historical estimates for the fixed parameters and then adjust the volatility parameters in the model so that it matches the prices for some actively traded interest rate options. Along these lines, one might try a time dependent volatility factor, as suggested by Chen and Yang.[23]

CONCLUSION

In this chapter, we have discussed methods for using the multi-factor CIR model to price interest rate derivatives and to hedge interest rate risk. The model produces closed form solutions that are easy to use. Adjustments can be made to the model so that it can be calibrated to match an initial term structure and match selected volatilities. Term structure variability can occur in different forms. There can be a general shift up or down for the entire yield curve, but the slope and the curvature of the yield curve may also change. The multiple factors, or state variables, allow one to capture these different types of variability that are observed over time.

---

[23] R. Chen and T. Yang, "An Integrated Model for the Term and Volatility Structures of Interest Rates," working paper, Rutgers University (1996).

Chapter 10

Valuation and Analysis of ARMs

Satish M. Mansukhani

Associate Director
Financial Analytics and Structured Transactions Group
Bear, Stearns, & Co.

INTRODUCTION

An adjustable-rate mortgage (ARM) has a coupon rate that tracks interest rate movements. In general, an ARM floats off a benchmark index plus a margin, bound on each reset date by periodic and lifetime caps. A homeowner choosing fixed-rate financing locks in his borrowing costs, whereas he faces the uncertainty of fluctuating interest rates when choosing adjustable-rate financing. This basic characteristic attracts a specific type of homeowner, leading to inherently different risks of investing in ARMs than fixed-rate mortgages (FRMs).

Since the introduction of ARMs in the 1980s, banks and thrifts have been the largest investors. The short-duration of ARMs make these a good asset/liability management tool to match the floating liabilities of depository institutions. Moreover, over the last few years, ARMs have appealed to a variety of new investors, ranging from money managers to international financial institutions. As investor understanding and analytical techniques have improved, so too has demand. Even traditional mortgage investors, who had previously invested only in FRM passthroughs and collateralized mortgage obligations, have turned to ARMs as a short duration alternative.

In this chapter, we explain the structural characteristics of ARMs, and how these characteristics affect the value and risk profile of ARMs. Further, we discuss a variety of methods to discern relative value.

THE ARM MARKET

ARM securities constitute about 13.6% of the total amount of mortgage securities currently outstanding. The greater affordability permitted by adjustable-rate financ-

171

ing (either due to lower rates on ARMs versus FRMs or the added appeal of below market teaser rates) make ARMs an attractive choice, particularly among first-time home buyers. The interest rate environment has a large bearing on a homeowner's choice. In periods of low fixed mortgage rates, homeowners typically opt for a fixed-rate mortgage, seizing an opportunity for low-cost financing that may not recur in the foreseeable future. When interest rates are high (and especially if the yield curve is positively sloped), homeowners are inclined towards ARMs since they are priced off the front end of the curve.

Prior to 1991, when rates on FRMs were relatively high, ARM originations tracked the spread between fixed- versus adjustable-rate financing. However, when fixed mortgage rates have been unusually low this relationship has not held despite ARMs offering a rate incentive over FRMs. Notably, during 1993 homeowners could not turn down the opportunity of a 7% fixed rate mortgage. Thus, *both* the absolute level of interest rates and the shape of the yield curve interactively impact ARM market share. Further, alternative mortgage products, such as 5- and 7-year balloons, have wooed homeowners away from adjustable-rate financing. When the yield curve was flat in 1995, an interesting innovation was "hybrid" ARMs. These offer the safety of a fixed mortgage rate for an initial period of 3, 5, 7, or 10 years, floating annually thereafter.

The three mortgage agencies — Government National Mortgage Association (GNMA), Federal National Mortgage Association (FNMA) and Federal Home Loan Mortgage Corporation (FHLMC) — dominate ARM issuance. Twenty-four percent of the overall ARM market consists of non-agency securities. The three agencies issue ARMs under different guidelines. All GNMA ARMs are issued under the GNMA II program. GNMA ARM pools are comprised of mortgages insured by the Federal Housing Administration. (Prior to September 1995, GNMA ARMs also included loans guaranteed by the Department of Veterans Affairs.) Additionally, GNMA ARMs are Multiple Issuer pools, in that separate issuers can contribute loans to one single pool. FHLMC ARMs are originated under either the Cash or Guarantor programs. Under the Cash program, FHLMC buys mortgages outright for cash. The guidelines of this program make it better suited for the pooling of new-production loans. In the Guarantor program, lenders swap mortgages in return for the Participation Certificate (security) created from these very mortgages. A Guarantor ARM can be either a Margin or a WAC ARM. Mortgages underlying the Margin program are homogeneous, in terms of reset and convertibility dates. On the other hand, a WAC ARM contains mortgages that may have different characteristics (reset, conversion dates, life caps, etc.), but float off a common index. The characteristics of the resulting PC security are weighted averages of the underlying loans. Also, FHLMC has a GIANT program, which pools together existing FHLMC PC's into larger, more diversified and liquid securities. Correspondingly, FNMA offers the Flex and Mega programs.

From a trading perspective, the ARM market can be segregated into TBA (To-Be-Announced) and specified-pool sectors. Since new-production GNMA ARMs are the most homogeneous they trade on a TBA basis enabling investors to finance them in the dollar roll market. Older GNMA ARMs, however, trade on a pool-specific basis. Similarly, most FNMA and FHLMC ARMs trade on a pool-specific basis, due to the heterogeneity of conventional securities. The one exception is COFI-indexed ARMs, which trade as TBAs. Generally, TBA instruments consist of recently originated (2-3 years old) loans. However, the Public Securities Association does not place any origination date restrictions on the underlying loans for TBA-eligible COFI ARMs. As a result thrifts sporadically securitize large portions of their COFI loan portfolio causing large monthly swings in TBA COFI origination.

Among fixed-rate mortgages, relative-value opinions are primarily based on differences in homeowner profile, seasoning, coupon, etc. ARMs have the added intricacy of different indices, net margins, caps and floors, reset frequencies, look-backs, payment caps, negative amortization, and convertibility features. These are discussed in detail in a later section.

DURATION OF FLOATING-RATE SECURITIES

Before immersing ourselves into the intricacies of ARM valuation, we would like to briefly re-introduce the concept of duration. Duration measures the interest-rate sensitivity of a bond, and is calculated as the percentage price change for a parallel 100 basis-point rate shift.

We can illustrate the duration of a capped floating-rate instrument, such as an ARM, by starting with a pure floater. The coupon rate of a pure floater perfectly tracks changes in interest rates. Thus, as shown in Exhibit 1 below, a pure floater has a duration of zero, i.e., no interest-rate risk. The price of a pure floater remains constant since it will always pay the prevailing market rate. An investor in a pure floater, however, faces credit risk of its issuer. With incremental constraints, like caps and floors, the duration of a security extends (see Exhibit 1). The following section introduces various contractual features, and highlights their impact on ARM security valuation.

ARM STRUCTURAL CHARACTERISTICS

Index
The ARM coupon resets off a given benchmark index. Banks and thrifts favor ARM securities pegged off an index which most closely matches their funding costs. Some common indices are reviewed below.

Weekly Average Yield of Constant Maturity 1-Year Treasuries U.S. government securities dealers report daily closing prices of the most actively traded bills, notes, and bonds to the Federal Reserve Bank of New York. Yields are then computed by the Treasury Department. The Federal Reserve publishes this index, which is the weekly average yield of the actively traded securities with a constant maturity of one year, in its weekly statistical H.15 release. This report is available at the start of the week, for the previous Monday-Friday period (accessible on Telerate page 7052). The index is not the yield of the 1-year Treasury bill; however, the two will be closely related.

11th District Cost of Funds Index (COFI) The Federal Home Loan Bank of San Francisco calculates this monthly index, reflecting the actual interest expenses of all savings institutions headquartered in Arizona, California, and Nevada. These three states make up the 11th District of the Federal Home Loan Bank System. The COFI index is *not* a market interest rate. Savings institutions rely on medium- and long-term maturity fixed-rate deposits as primary funding. Since these deposit rates are not affected by changing market interest rates until the deposit matures, the total interest expense paid by savings institutions in a particular month largely reflect interest rates that were prevalent in previous months or years. This creates a natural 6- to 9-month lag in the index, since longer deposits must mature before they are rolled into new deposits. This causes the index to register smaller and delayed moves relative to other short-term rates. The updated COFI index for the prior monthly period is obtained by calling (415) 616-2600, after 6 p.m. Eastern time on the last business day of every month. Historical and updated values of the index are available on Telerate page 7058.

Exhibit 1: Interest Rate Sensitivity Analysis of Pure, Capped, and Capped/Floored Floaters

		Reference Rate								
		−300	−225	−150	−75	Flat	75	150	225	300
Pure Floater	Price	100:00	100:00	100:00	100:00	100:00	100:00	100:00	100:00	100:00
	ROR	0.80	1.562	2.216	3.070	3.839	4.610	5.385	6.162	6.941
	Duration	NA	0.00	0.00	0.00	0.00	0.00	0.00	0.00	NA
9% Capped Floater	Price	99:29	99:21+	99:6+	98:14+	97:12	95:31+	94:7+	92:5	89:26
	ROR	3.426	3.986	4.304	4.357	4.117	3.503	2.474	1.092	−0.600
	Duration	NA	0.48	0.82	1.23	1.69	2.19	2.71	3.18	NA
9% Cap/ 3% Floor Floater	Price	103:17	101:19+	99:31+	98:18+	97:12	95:31+	94:7+	92:5	89:26
	ROR	6.952	5.867	5.041	4.446	4.117	3.503	2.474	1.092	−0.600
	Duration	NA	2.33	2.02	1.76	1.78	2.19	2.71	3.18	NA
Effective Fixed Rate	Price	123:20+	117:5+	111:1+	105:10+	99:29+	94:28	90:3	85:19+	81:12
	ROR	23.411	18.309	13.341	8.532	3.898	−0.560	−4.892	−9.078	−13.13
	Duration	NA	7.17	7.12	7.05	6.97	6.90	6.89	6.78	NA

Reference Treasury Curve	1–year	2–year	3–year	5–year	7–year	10–year	30–year
	3.44	4.11	4.60	5.52	6.06	6.56	7.38

National Monthly Median Cost of Funds Index SAIF-insured depository institutions report monthly cost of funds data to their regulator, the Office of Thrift Supervision. After ranking all the institutions by cost of funds, the OTS reports the statistical median which is the value of the index. Though similar to the 11th District Cost of Funds Index, the primary difference between the two is that the Monthly Median calculation uses the *current* months' liabilities as the base while the 11th District COFI calculation uses the *average* liabilities of the current and prior month. Further, the 11th District COFI is a weighted average measure, while the National Median COFI is a median. The updated value of this index can be obtained by calling the Office of Thrift Supervision at (202) 906-6988, or by referring to Telerate page 7058.

6-Month LIBOR The London Interbank Offer Rate is the rate at which major international banks offer to place deposits with one another for maturities ranging from overnight up to five years. Six-month LIBOR, which is commonly used for ARMs, is the rate offered for 6-month U.S. dollar denominated deposits. Updated values are available daily in *The Wall Street Journal* and on Telerate page 7050.

6-Month CD This rate is calculated by the Federal Reserve Bank of New York. It reflects the average of the dealer offering rates on nationally traded certificates of deposit with a maturity of six months. The Federal Reserve publishes this index in its weekly statistical H.15 release (accessible on Telerate page 7052).

Exhibit 2 illustrates historical levels of the most commonly-used indices. Movements in the 1-year CMT, 6-month LIBOR, and 6-month CD are closely correlated, while the 11th District COFI and National Median COFI lag interest rates. Exhibit 3 provides a breakdown of the ARM market by index.

The index of an ARM will affect its duration. The more an index lags market interest rates, the more a security will behave like a fixed-rate security rather than a pure floater. Thus the duration of COFI-indexed ARMs is largely derived from the lagging nature of the index.

Exhibit 2: Historical Levels of Commonly Used Arm Indices

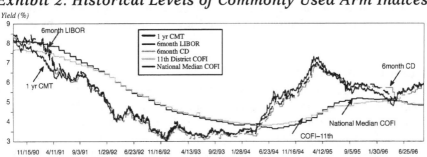

Exhibit 3: ARM Agency and Non-Agency Issuance Market Share by Index

Index	Market Share (%)
1-year CMT	58.39
COFI	24.04
6-month LIBOR	8.46
1-month LIBOR	2.09
3-year Treasury	1.62
6-month CD	1.06
Other	4.34

Net Margin

The *net margin* is the spread above the index that an ARM coupon adjusts to. Almost all GNMA ARMs have a 150 basis point net margin. However, conventional ARMs carry a wider range of net margins depending on loan underwriting guidelines. Let us consider a sample 6.5% ARM with a net margin of 150 basis points (security A1). At an index level of 7%, the coupon rate resets to a fully-indexed rate of 8.5% (see Exhibit 4).

Gross Margin

The *gross margin* is the net margin plus servicing and guarantee fees. Therefore the coupon of the ARM security plus the gross margin equals the actual loan rate charged to the homeowner. If the servicing and guarantee fees on the sample ARM introduced above are 75 basis points then the gross mortgage rate will be 9.25% (see Exhibit 4).

Loans underlying GNMA ARMs tend to have more homogeneous features than FNMA and FHLMC ARMs. However, the gross borrowing rate may vary from loan to loan within a given GNMA ARM security. With inadequate loan level data on GNMA ARMs, market convention has assumed a gross margin of 225 basis points on GNMA ARMs (GNMA is scheduled to release security specific gross margins on ARMs by the end of 1996). In actuality a particular loan may have a different gross margin since mortgage bankers may incorporate different excess servicing when underwriting these loans. For example, in environments when business volume is low mortgage bankers have been known to generate revenues by originating loans with higher gross margins.

Periodic Cap and Floor

Periodic caps/floors limit how much the ARM rate can reset *relative to the current coupon rate*. An important feature of periodic caps and floors is that they are path dependent. They do not represent absolute but rather are relative constraints. Since the periodic cap/floor is relative to the current coupon rate, the strike level of the periodic caps and floors change from reset to reset. The periodic cap protects the homeowner from facing "payment shock" (a large jump in his monthly payment).

Exhibit 4: Net and Gross Margins

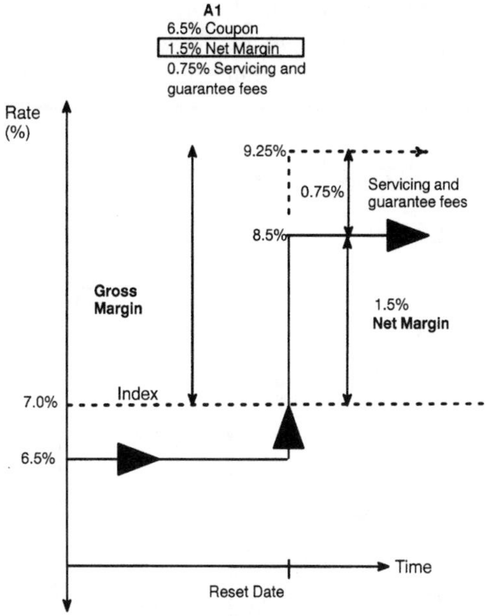

Exhibit 5 examines the reset mechanism with periodic caps. Note the two example ARMs, A1 and A2, with a 1% and 2% periodic cap/floor, respectively. Like A1, A2 also has a 6.5% coupon rate but a 225 basis point net margin. The 1% cap on A1 limits its adjustment to a 7.5% coupon, bringing the cap 100 basis points "in-the-money," whereas an uncapped security would reset to a fully-indexed rate of 8.5%. Likewise, the 2% periodic cap on A2 is 75 basis points "in-the-money." The net margin determines the extent to which a cap is "in- or out-of-the-money." In general for a given periodic cap, the higher the Net Margin, the *greater* the likelihood of the cap being "in-the-money."

Exhibit 6 illustrates rate adjustments on the sample ARMs when the index drops to 3%. The fully-indexed rate on these securities will be 4.5% and 5.25%, respectively. However, the 1% floor on A1 limits its downward adjustment to 5.5% bringing the floor 100 basis points "in-the-money." Correspondingly, the 2% floor on A2 is "at-the-money" as its coupon adjusts to the fully-indexed rate. In contrast to the interaction between net margin and periodic caps, the larger the net margin, the *lesser* the likelihood of a floor being "in-the-money."

Investors commonly ignore periodic floors while focusing solely on the caps. All else being equal, periodic caps hinder the performance of ARMs when rates rise, and periodic floors enhance their performance when rates fall. Periodic caps and floors raise the duration of an ARM, by preventing the coupon rate from keeping pace with market rate movements, making the security behave more like a fixed-rate bond. Generally, the lower the caps and the higher the floors, the greater the duration extension. GNMA ARMs have an annual cap/floor of 1% movements relative to their prior coupon rate. On the other hand conventional ARMs have either 1% *semiannual* caps and floors or 2% *annual* caps and floors. Thus, 1% capped GNMA ARMs have longer durations than 2% capped conventional ARMs.

Exhibit 5: Periodic Caps

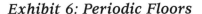

Exhibit 6: Periodic Floors

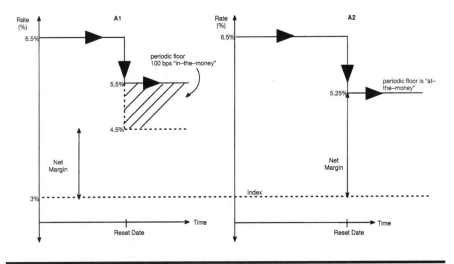

Exhibit 7: Effect of Lifetime Caps

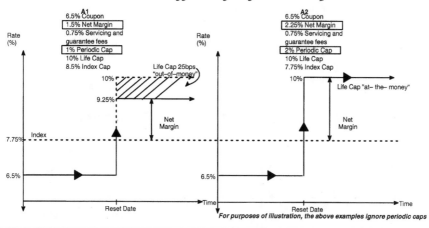

For purposes of illustration, the above examples ignore periodic caps

Lifetime Cap

The lifetime cap sets the maximum coupon rate over the life of a loan. Unlike the periodic cap, which is path dependent and relative, the lifetime cap is an absolute level and therefore supersedes the periodic caps. Once market rates surpass a given level, the ARM becomes "capped" out and behaves like a fixed-rate security unless rates subsequently decline. Securities with similar lifetime caps but different net margins will "cap" out at different levels of the index. Let's consider securities A1 and A2 again, both with a life cap of 10%. Since A1 has a net margin of 150 basis points, the coupon will "cap" when the index hits 8.5% (10% - 1.5%) whereas, the coupon on A2 will "cap" at an index level of 7.75% (see Exhibit 7).

The lifetime cap increases the duration of an ARM. The lower the index cap the longer the duration of the ARM. All GNMA ARM securities have lifetime caps 5% points above the original coupon rate. Correspondingly, most conventional ARMs have lifetime caps pegged about 5 to 6% above the original coupon.

Reset Date and Frequency

The reset date is when the ARM coupon rate adjusts to market rates. The reset frequency is the number of times a year the ARM coupon rate adjusts. Most ARMs offer a semiannual or an annual reset. Some exceptions are monthly-resetting COFI and 1-month LIBOR ARMs.

GNMA ARMs are issued on a quarterly rolling schedule which determines the specific reset date of the security. For example, all GNMA ARM securities issued during the first quarter of a year reset on April 1 of the following year, those issued in the second quarter reset on July 1 of the following year, and so on (see Exhibit 8 — GNMA ARM production schedule). Since the security has a single reset date, it is called a bullet reset. Conventional ARMs, on the other hand, generally offer stratified resets because the underlying loan reset dates are distributed through the year.

Exhibit 8: GNMA ARM Production Schedule

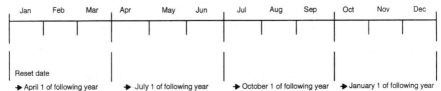

Exhibit 9: GNMA ARM Rate Adjustment

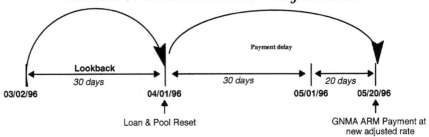

Exhibit 10: FHLMC WAC PC ARM Rate Adjustment

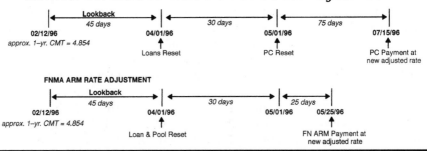

The farther out the reset dates are the longer is the duration; the closer the reset dates, the shorter the duration. The more delayed the reset dates, the longer is the lag before an ARM fully adjusts to market rates, making the ARM behave more like a fixed-rate instrument.

Index Lookback

The lookback period is the time between the index determination date and the reset date. ARMs issued by different issuers vary considerably in terms of their lookback features. We present the coupon reset adjustment process for GNMA, FNMA, and FHLMC ARMs in Exhibits 9 and 10).

Exhibit 9 illustrates a sample GNMA ARM pool with an April 1, 1996 reset date. The lookback period of 30 calendar days refers to the index rate as of Saturday, March 2, 1996. The index value is obtained from the most recently available H.15 release as of that date or the prior business day.

Exhibit 10 compares the lookback and reset procedures for FNMA and FHLMC WAC PC ARM securities. The primary difference between the two are:

- In the case of FNMA ARMs both the underlying loans and security reset simultaneously. In the case of FHLMC WAC ARM PC's the security coupon adjusts 30 days after the loan coupon adjustment (compare Loans versus PC/Pool reset for FHLMC/FNMA ARM in Exhibit 10).
- The payment delay after the security adjusts is 55 days for FNMA and 75 days for the PC issues.

The lookback features are crucial in a highly volatile rate environment. For example, between February and May 1996, the 1-year CMT rate rose by 65 basis points. Ignoring the lookback period could result in a 65 basis point error in estimating the coupon reset, leading to misstating the yield by 10-15 basis points. Further, investors typically disregard the reset lag between coupon adjustments on the underlying loans versus the overlying security.

Because of the lookback and payment delays FNMA ARM securities take 100 days (over three months) and FHLMC WAC PC ARM securities take over 150 days (6 months) for interest payments to reflect market rates. Thus, shorter lookbacks translate into shorter durations. Conversely, longer lookbacks translate into longer durations.

Payment Adjustment Cap/Floor and Reset Frequency

The payment cap/floor limits the percentage change of the borrower's monthly payment. This is a common feature in COFI-indexed ARMs. TBA-eligible COFI ARMs have an *annual* payment cap/floor of 7.5%. This implies that, on an annual basis, the monthly payment cannot increase nor decrease by more than 7.5%. Payment caps/floors are similar to periodic caps/floors since both shield the borrower from payment shock.

Negative Amortization

Negative amortization is the capitalization of interest payments, accrued to principal. This is a common feature in COFI-indexed ARMs. Mortgages originated in the United States are typically level-paying mortgages. Upon origination a level monthly-paying amortization schedule is specified, a portion of which is applied towards principal write down and the remainder towards interest due. Initially, most of the payment is applied towards interest due, and as the principal balance keeps declining, an increasing portion of the payment goes towards principal amortization.

Negative amortization arises due to two reasons: a mismatch between payment and rate adjustment frequencies and the imposition of payment caps. For example, in a rapidly rising interest rate environment, frequent rate adjustments increase the interest portion of the monthly payment without a corresponding increase in the monthly payment amount. If the interest due surpasses the amount of the monthly payment the unpaid interest will be added to the principal outstanding leading to negative amortization. As a general rule of thumb, a 200 basis point instantaneous upward move in the COFI index causes immediate negative amortization.

However, there are contractual limits on negative amortization. In general, the maximum negative amortization on COFI-indexed ARMs is limited to 110-125% of the original outstanding principal balance. Once this limit is reached, any payment caps are waived and the borrower's monthly payment is increased.

Payment Recast and Recast Frequency

Payment recast forces the full amortization of a mortgage. In a negatively amortizing mortgage, a cutoff point is necessary to force the eventual pay down of the balance to zero. The payment recast overrides any payment caps and establishes a new amortization schedule. The payment recast frequency is generally five years.

Convertibility

ARM borrowers may choose between convertible or non-convertible adjustable-rate mortgage loans. Convertibility allows the homeowner to change from adjustable-rate into fixed-rate financing. This option is typically exercisable during the first five years after origination. However, the option does have a cost, in the form of higher up front fees. Upon exercising the conversion option, the loan will carry a coupon equal to the then prevailing fixed rate plus a premium (0.25% to 0.75%). Typically, the conversion rate is based on the FNMA or FHLMC 30- or 60-day mandatory delivery rate. Despite the premium, it is generally assumed to be cheaper to convert an adjustable-rate loan rather than refinancing it. The exercise of the conversion option represents a prepayment for the security holder. As one would expect, a convertible ARM would tend to have a more rate sensitive prepayment profile than a non-convertible ARM.

Exhibit 11 summarizes generic ARM characteristics and presents PSA guidelines on TBA-eligible GNMA and FNMA COFI ARMs.

RELATIVE VALUE TOOLS FOR ADJUSTABLE-RATE MORTGAGES

ARMs can be viewed as hybrids, sometimes performing like an uncapped floater, and sometimes like a fixed-rate security. The tighter the caps and floors, the more the ARM will mimic a fixed-rate security. In fact, one can think of a fixed-rate security as a limiting case of an ARM, with caps and floors that equal the MBS coupon rate. A fixed-rate mortgage security is generally viewed as:

Fixed-Rate MBS = Long non-callable bond + Short prepayment option.

Likewise an ARM is generally viewed as:

Adjustable-Rate MBS = Long pure floater + Long Floors + Short Caps
+ Short prepayment option

Exhibit 11: Summary of Generic ARM Characteristics

	Conventional			GNMA	Impact on Duration (holding all else equal)
Index	1-yr. CMT	6-mo. LIBOR	11th District COFI	1-yr. CMT	
Periodic Cap	2% annual	1% semi-annual	NA on monthly 1% on semiannual 2% on annual	1% annual	Decreases with larger caps/floors
Lifetime Cap	6% over original coupon	5-6% over original coupon	Greater than 12%	5% over original coupon	Decreases with higher index caps
Reset Frequency	12 months	6 months	Monthly Semi-annual Annual	12 months	Decreases with shorter resets
Lookback	45 days	45 days	45 days	30 days	Decreases with shorter lookbacks
Payment Cap & Freq.	NA	NA	7.5% Annually	NA	Decreases with larger caps
Negative Amortization	NA	NA	110 - 125%	NA	
Payment Recast Freq.	NA	NA	5 years	NA	
Net Margin	150-250 bp	150-250 bp	Generally 125 bp	150 bp	
Gross Margin	215 to 315 bp	215 to 315 bp	Generally 200 bp	Assumed to be 225 bp	
Convertible	Allowed	Allowed	Allowed	Not allowed	

Specifications of TBA eligible FNMA 11th District COFI ARMs:

1. 12% and higher original life cap.
2. 125 basis points margin or higher.
3. Fully indexed.
4. 25- to 40-year maturities.
5. 2-3-4 month lag is allowable within each million-dollar lot.
6. Adjustable monthly, +/−7.5% payment cap.

Specifications of TBA eligible GNMA ARMs:

1. All pools must be multiple-issuer pools.
2. 150 basis points margin or higher.
3. Reset off the one year CMT index annually.
4. Coupons should be the same on all pools.
5. 1% annual cap.
6. All pools should have a lifetime cap equal to 500 basis-point above the original coupon.
7. The settlement date implies the reset date that must apply to all pools.

The *best* relative value measure is one that correctly values each component of the security — caps, floors and prepayment options.

Net Effective Margin

The *net effective margin* (NEM) measures the difference between the yield of the ARM security (at an assumed constant prepayment speed and current index) and the current value of the index over which the ARM security resets. It helps indicate the income spread if the investor were funding liabilities resetting over the same index. Hence, NEM is a popular gauge amongst banks and thrifts.

The NEM is similar to the *discount margin* (DM) measure used to value floating-rate securities like CMO floaters. However, there is one key difference between the two measures. While NEM assumes semiannual compounding, DM uses monthly compounding.

NEM has limited usage being a static measure. If interest rates and prepayments indeed turn out to be static, the NEM would be an appropriate relative value measure. However, the world is rarely static. Let us consider the sample securities, A1 and A2, to illustrate. The two bonds are similar except that one has a 1% periodic cap and the other has a 2% periodic cap. The coupon rate adjustment for the two securities is shown in Exhibit 12. The two securities are assumed to prepay at the same constant prepayment rate. NEM is calculated using these projected cash flows.

Exhibit 12: Calculating Yield/NEM on ARMs

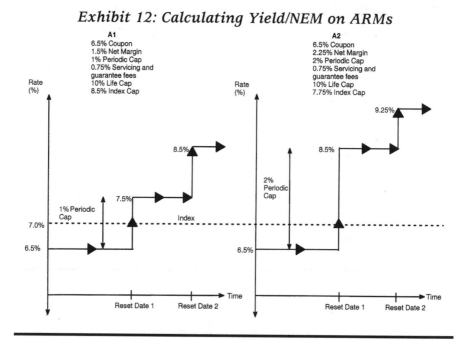

The drawback of the NEM calculation is that it ignores the *full* impact of the caps and floors and the prepayment option. Even the value of the periodic caps that are currently "in-the-money" is measured only with respect to the current value of the index. Further, NEM is only useful as a relative value measure within a specific universe of ARM securities using the same index. It falls short when comparing ARMs with different indices and against other mortgage/fixed-income instruments.

Despite its problems, the simplicity of the calculation, easy replication, and long standing prevalence continues to support its use as an initial valuation screen.

Curve-Adjusted Yield/NEM

Although NEM and yield are static measures they can still be useful. As investor understanding and analytical techniques constantly improve, the markets do price in the various embedded options, reflected in the widening/tightening of these static spreads.

Let us consider an investor trying to ascertain relative value between FRM and ARM passthroughs. Curve shape should exert a larger impact on the valuation of ARMs than FRMs. Given a steeper curve and higher implied forward rates, periodic and lifetime caps are more likely to go "in-the-money." Hence, the spread represented by the NEM/yield is less likely translated into realized total return. In an attempt to net out the impact of curve shape on the spread valuation of ARMs, we analyze daily yield spreads between par-priced 30-year FNMA FRMs and par-priced GNMA ARMs, plotting them against the $\frac{1}{10}$-year spread. We restrict the analysis to par-priced securities in order to screen out the prepayment characteristics generally associated with discount and premium securities. Since the duration of par-priced FRMs is higher than that of par-priced GNMA ARMs, swapping from the former and into the latter entails a yield give up. According to the scatter plot (see Exhibit 13), a steeper curve implies a greater yield give up while a flatter curve reduces the yield give up. Notably, observations outside the 95% confidence intervals indicate relative cheapness/richness. The plot identifies two historical points when GNMA ARMs proved to be cheap (1/03/95) and rich (5/31/95) versus FRMs. The time series graphs plot the daily actual spreads versus the predicted, and the 95% confidence bands.

This analysis serves only as an initial screen on relative value since the yields are calculated under static prepayment assumptions. Our scatter plot assumes a lifetime prepayment assumption of 8% CPR on the GNMA ARMs. Yields on FRM's are generated using the Bear Stearns' prepayment models. Additionally, the analysis uses history as a benchmark. Relative cheapness/richness is determined by comparing current versus prior spreads for similar curve shape.

Similar analysis is replicated by examining the NEM of GNMA ARMs and netting out the influence of curve shape. In this case we use the $\frac{1}{2}$ year and $\frac{1}{10}$ year spread as the independent variables. The dependent variables are the difference between the NEM and the $\frac{1}{2}$ year, and $\frac{1}{10}$ year spread, respectively (see Exhibits 14 and 15). This helps measure the income that will most likely be earned. The analysis helps identify risk/reward with any outliers indicating relative cheapness/richness.

Exhibit 13: (Par-Priced FNMA FRM Yield – Par-Priced GNMA ARM Yield) Versus 1-10 Year Spread

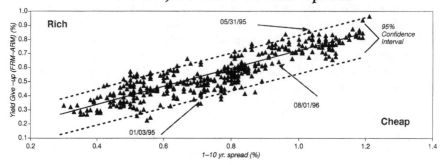

Time Series of FRM/ARM Spread Model

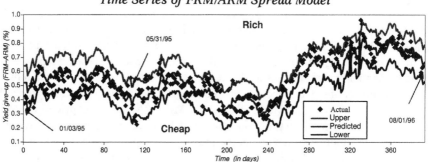

Exhibit 14: (Par-Priced GNMA ARM NEM – 1-2 Year) Versus 1-2 Year Spread

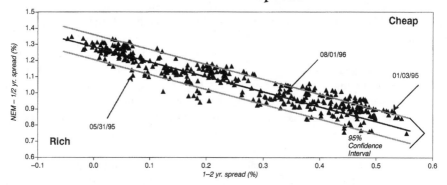

Exhibit 14: (Continued)
Time Series of 1-2 year Spread Model

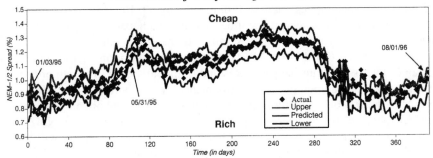

Exhibit 15: (Par-Priced GNMA ARM NEM – 1-10 Year Spread)
Versus 1-10 Year Spread

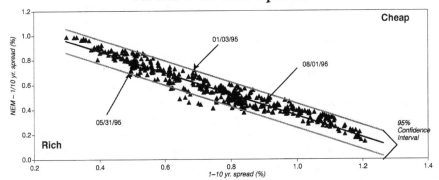

Time Series of 1-10 year Spread Model

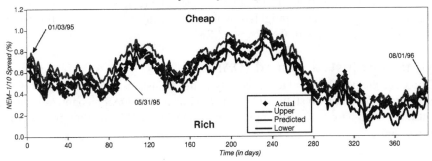

Market Implied Returns

This is a simple tool used to examine inter-coupon relationships. The analysis assumes that when interest rates shift in parallel by 50, 100, 150 basis points, then the terminal price of a security will be that of the adjacent coupon 50, 100, 150 basis points higher/lower, as the case may be, than the security being examined. Thus in studying GNMA 6% ARMs, the base case horizon period returns are obtained by assuming unchanged prices and historical speeds (3-month or 6-month averages depending upon the rate environment) over the horizon period. In a down 50 scenario the projected returns are obtained by assuming a horizon price and historical speeds of the adjacent coupon 50 basis points higher, i.e., GNMA 6.5% ARMs. The analysis is simplistic in that it assumes that a security will behave exactly like the adjacent coupon when rates move. Reinvestment rates are adjusted in up/down scenarios from a base case reinvestment rate equal to the fed funds rate.

The drawback of the analysis is that it can only be used to value homogeneous securities. Given the diversity of ARM securities, the analysis is limited to examining inter-coupon relationships between TBA GNMA ARMs. TBA GNMA ARMs are issued with coupons, lifetime caps, periodic caps, etc., that change in increments of 50 basis points, making the technique easily applicable. Further, they are issued with the same reset date, eliminating any complications arising from varying reset dates on valuations.

The advantage of the analysis is that it incorporates factual information available in the market. However, actual price changes, even if the curve experienced parallel 50, 100, or 150 basis point moves, may not be exactly the same as implied by the adjacent coupons. For example, technical supply/demand forces may have an unforeseeable impact on actual pricing (particularly in the case of the GNMA ARM sector where monthly supply influences market pricing).

Despite the disadvantages, the model has had good predictive value in examining the inter-coupon relationships in the past. Exhibit 16 illustrates the results as of July 25, 1996. The analysis reflects the relative cheapness of GNMA 5.5 and 6.5% ARMs, as highlighted by their projected returns across all scenarios, and the relative richness of GNMA 6% ARMs.

Option Adjusted Spread (OAS)

The OAS methodology values a security under thousands of possible interest rate scenarios. Compared to static yield and NEM measures, OAS recognizes scenarios other than the base case. The application of OAS to ARM valuation involves four basic steps:

1. A large sample of potential risk-free rate paths are generated, using a probabilistic model that is consistent with the current term structure and assumed level of volatility;
2. For each path of risk-free rates, a corresponding path for the ARM index is generated;

Exhibit 16: Adjacent Coupon Analysis of GNMA ARMs

Using 3-Month Speeds, 3:00 pm Closing Prices as of 07/25/96				
	Rate Movement	-50	0	+50
	Reinvestment Rate	4.75	5.25	5.75
GNMA	Coupon	5.5	5.0	4.5
5.0	3-month Speed (CPR)	3.7	1.9	0.1
	Terminal Price	97:12+	95:25	94:17
	Proj. 12mo ROR	6.99	5.39	4.08
GNMA	Coupon	6	5.5	5.0
5.5	3-month Speed (CPR)	6.1	3.7	1.9
	Terminal Price	98:28+	97:12+	95:25
	Proj. 12mo ROR	7.19	5.79	4.21
GNMA	Coupon	6.5	6.0	5.5
6.0	3-month Speed (CPR)	11.9	6.1	3.7
	Terminal Price	100:01	98:28+	97:12+
	Proj. 12mo ROR	7.08	6.13	4.74
GNMA	Coupon	7.0	6.5	6.0
	3-month Speed (CPR)	14.8	11.9	6.1
	Terminal Price	101:4	100:01	98:28+
	Proj. 12mo ROR	7.21	6.40	5.46
12-Month ROR Pickups (in basis points)				
	5.5 over 5	20.5	39.7	13.2
	6 over 5.5	(11.4)	33.8	52.8
	6.5 over 6	13.4	27.3	72.0

3. For each rate scenario, cash flows are generated that reflect prepayment variability, and all contractual features affecting cash flows, such as the periodic and lifetime caps and floors, reset frequency, teaser rates, etc.

4. A value of the security is found for each scenario by discounting the cash flows at the projected risk-free rates plus a spread; this generates a distribution of values for the security; for a given price, the OAS is the spread such that the average of the distribution of values equals that price.

Valuing ARMs using OAS is superior to making relative value comparisons based on static measures. OAS captures the effect of yield curve shape on the valuation of the embedded options — caps, floors and prepayments. Further, OAS is a dynamic measure which investors can use as a yardstick to compare ARMs against other fixed-income securities.

There are some drawbacks of relying solely on OAS as a relative value tool. The output generated by an OAS model is contingent upon the inputs; namely the quality of the prepayment model, and the ability to accurately value the caps and floors. OAS calculations depend significantly on the robustness and predictive power of the underlying prepayment model. Further, volatility assumptions have an impact on the valuation of the embedded caps and floors. Most OAS models use a single volatility assumption as opposed to utilizing volatility curves, as is the practice in the derivatives market. The sensitivity of OAS values to the interactive effects of any errors in prepayment projections and cap valuations make it crucial to question these inputs prior to making relative value judgements based on OAS.

Finally, market participants generally assume that higher yielding OAS securities are more valuable. In practice, however, different securities trade within their respective OAS trading range. Thus, GNMA ARMs, for example, trade within a different range than GNMA FRM's. Further, under technical supply/demand conditions, a security's high OAS valuation could reflect the oncome of further widening as opposed to a prudent investment opportunity. Though an advancement over static measures, OAS should not be employed blindly.

Swap Spreads to a Benchmark Index

All the analytical measures discussed above help gauge relative value of ARMs. However, apart from OAS, all the tools either do not fully value the various embedded options or require homogeneity amongst the securities to identify relative value. The heterogeneity amongst ARM securities make it difficult to answer realistic questions such as: should an investor buy TBA GNMA ARMs or specified GNMA ARMs? GNMA ARMs or conventional ARMs? While OAS aims to answer these questions, it falls short due to the various reasons already discussed. Further, it fails to isolate where the arbitrage opportunity lies, i.e., is the high OAS due to undervaluing the prepayment option and/or the caps and floors?

Generally, investors in floating-rate securities aim to take limited risk and capture a spread to their cost of funding. Hence, the cheapest security would be the one that, net of all the underlying options, prepayment and caps, translates to the highest spread over a benchmark index. The technology to swap ARM interest cash flows into an uncapped interest cash flow has been in place since 1994. For GNMA ARMs, swap dealers offer to swap the underlying ARM interest cash flows with coupon adjustment constraints into uncapped cash flows indexed to 1-month LIBOR. Investors have the choice to remove both periodic and lifetime caps or simply remove the periodic caps and lift the lifetime caps. Exhibit 17 illustrates the working of a swap using GNMA ARMs. Swaps on GNMA ARMs are generally structured with a stated maturity of ten years.

Swap spreads on TBA GNMA ARMs help ascertain relative value between ARMs and other floating-rate sectors. For instance, Exhibit 18 presents spreads over 1-month LIBOR on par-priced TBA GNMA ARMs. This is commonly used to compare ARMs against other floating-rate securities such as asset-backed floaters. Since the swap is generally structured such that at the end of ten years the investor retains the remainder of the ARM with the caps and floors, investors need to consider the impact of this "tail" risk. It is becoming increasingly common for swap dealers to sell the "tail" to a third party, thus increasing the attractiveness of the swap to traditional buyers of floating-rate instruments.

Exhibit 17: ARM Asset Swaps: Example Trade

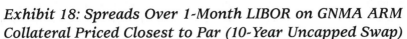

Exhibit 18: Spreads Over 1-Month LIBOR on GNMA ARM Collateral Priced Closest to Par (10-Year Uncapped Swap)

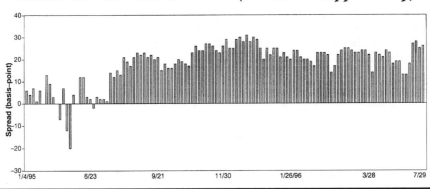

Swap spreads also assist in studying inter-coupon relationships. Typically, lower dollar priced securities swap to higher spreads because of the call risk associated with higher dollar priced securities, which the swap dealer assumes. Exhibit 19 plots the historical difference between swap spreads on GNMA 6s over GNMA 6.5s. A negative spread, i.e., when GNMA 6.5s swap to *higher* spreads than GNMA 6s, generally indicates a buying opportunity for the higher dollar priced securities.

Technology from the derivatives market can be used to value caps and floors, and indicate swap levels on most conventional ARMs. This makes the universe of ARM securities — teasers versus fully-indexed, low versus high caps, GNMAs versus conventionals, TBA versus specified, etc. — easily comparable against each other and helps identify investment opportunities.

In summary, comparing swap spreads on ARM securities provides an objective measure, netting out the interactive effect of various ARM characteristics on investment performance.

Exhibit 19: Inter-Coupon Swap Spreads: GNMA 6 - GNMA 6.5

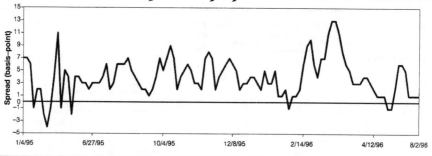

CONCLUSION

This chapter serves as an introduction to the market and issues that investors should consider when trying to ascertain relative value of ARM securities. Continued technological advancements in valuing ARM securities will lead to the increasing appeal of this sector to a variety of institutional investors. The development of state-of-the-art tools that help encapsulate differences between the structural characteristics of the variety of ARM securities will help identify relative value opportunities in a transparent yet comprehensive manner.

Chapter 11

Valuation and Portfolio Risk Management with Mortgage-Backed Securities

Stavros A. Zenios, Ph.D.

Professor of Management Science
University of Cyprus

INTRODUCTION

Mortgage-backed securities (MBS) are complex and difficult to value because they embody features of both bonds and options. The homeowner's ability to *prepay* outstanding principal represents a call option on the underlying mortgage. For any specific mortgage within a pool, it is uncertain whether this call option will be exercised and, if so, when. Many factors outside the charactestics of the pool can also affect the option's value. These include the level, structure and history of interest rates, the market's perception of future interest rates, and total and disposable consumer income. Adding to the complexity has been the constant stream of innovative new derivative securities based on MBS, the risk and return characteristics of which may bear little resemblance to the original security.

Valuation of a MBS involves relating possible future paths of interest rates to the cash flows generated by the security. The valuation should take into account both principal and interest payments, as well as the possibility of prepayment of the mortgage (i.e., exercise of the underlying call option). The analysis is carried out using simulations, which generate paths of interest rates, usually in monthly intervals for a period of 30 years until maturity of the underlying mortgage loans.

The general framework of the valuation analysis has three phases.

Phase I. Generate arbitrage free interest rate scenarios consistent with the prevailing term structure of interest rates.

Phase II. Generate cash flows for each interest rate scenario. This requires a model that can project the prepayment activity of homeowners under a host of economic conditions.

Phase III. Use the cash flows and the short-term interest rates along each path to compute expected net present value of the cash flows (i.e., the *price*), and the usual derivatives (i.e., *duration* and *convexity*) or to compute an *option-adjusted premium* over the Treasury yield curve.

Phase III can be easily extended to calculate *holding-period returns*. This analysis projects the return of the MBS under a range of economic scenarios for a target holding period. Armed with the wealth of information about the pool's behavior generated in Phase III we can then address issues of portfolio management for large protfolios of MBS.

In this chapter we discuss both valuation and portfolio risk management techniques. We assume throughout that readers are familiar with the calculations required to estimate the principal and interest payment of an MBS. Cash flow calculations for a given prepayment are also assumed known.

VALUATION TECHNIQUES

Pricing

A fair price for a fixed-income security can be obtained as the expected discounted value of its cash flows, with discounting done at the risk-free rate.[1] The pricing model is based on Monte Carlo simulation of the term-structure which is used to generate paths of risk-free rates.[2] The security cash flows for each path are then generated and the present value of these discounted cash flows can be computed and averaged, thus estimating the fair market value of the projected cash flow streams. This is, in turn, the fair price for the security.

To make this idea precise we need to hypothesize first a model of the term structure of interest rates. We use here a binomial lattice model[3] such as the one illustrated in Exhibit 1. The lattice discretizes the time horizon from 0 to T into, say, monthly steps and it assumes that the short-term rates at each step can move to one of two possible states (UP or DOWN). All possible states of the binomial lattice can be described using a series of *base* rates $\{r_{0t}, t=0,1,..., T\}$, and *volatilities* $\{k_t, t=0,1, ..., T\}$. The short-term rate at any state σ of the binomial lattice at some point t is then given by

$$r_t^{\sigma} = r_t^0 (k_t)^{\sigma}$$

---

[1] See John C. Cox, Jr. Jonathan E. Ingersoll, and Stephen A. Ross, "A Theory of the Term Structure of Interest Rates," *Econometrica* (March 1985), pp. 385-407.

[2] The use of Monte Carlo simulations for options pricing was pioneered by P. Boyle, "Options: A Monte Carlo Approach," *Journal of Financial Economics* (May 1977), pp. 323-338. See J.M. Hutchinson and S.A. Zenios, "Financial Simulations on a Massively Parallel Connection Machine," *International Journal of Supercomputer Applications* (1991), Vol. 5, pp. 27-45, for its application to the pricing of mortgage securities.

[3] See F. Black, E. Derman, and W. Toy, "A One-Factor Model of Interest Rates and its Application to Treasury Bond Options," *Financial Analysts Journal* (Jan./Feb. 1990), pp. 33-39.

Exhibit 1: A Binomial Lattice of Interest Rates

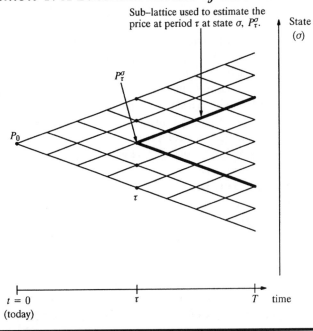

Sub–lattice used to estimate the
price at period τ at state σ, P_τ^σ.

State (σ)

P_τ^σ

P_0

τ

$t = 0$ (today) τ T time

The base rate and volatility parameters of the model are calibrated using market data. In particular, for the model we have assumed (i.e., Black-Derman-Toy) we need as input the term structure of interest rates ($\{r_t\}$, $t=1,2,..., T$) and the term structure of interest rate volatilities.

Let S_0 denote a set of interest rate scenarios that emanate from the current, zero, state of the binomial lattice. Let also r_t^s be the short-term discount rate at time period t associated with scenario $s \in S_0$, and C_{jt}^s be the cash flow generated by security j at period t, under the given scenario. A fair price for the security is given by

$$P_{j0} = \frac{1}{|S_0|} \sum_{s=1}^{|S_0|} \sum_{t=1}^{T} \frac{C_{jt}^s}{\displaystyle\prod_{i=1}^{t}(1 + r_i^s)} \tag{1}$$

This is the fundamental pricing equation that provides the basis for more advanced valuation tools developed later. We point out that this equation can be easily extended to price the security at some future time period τ, conditioned on the state of the lattice at that period. (See equation (3) below and the discussion that follows.)

It is also worth noting the computational complexity of this equation. The number of paths emanating from the origin of a binomial lattice is 2^T, which is an extremely large number even for moderate time horizons T. While for simple securities, such as straight bonds, we can simply compute discounted cash flows at the vertices of the lattice (and there are only $T^2/2$ vertices), for MBS we need to examine paths of interest rates. This is so because the cash flows generated by a MBS depend not only on the current level of interest rates but also on the path that interest rates followed from the origination of the MBS until the present. This *path-dependence* is a result of the prepayment activity of the MBS. Hence, we cannot avoid working with paths of interest rates obtained from the binomial lattice. We hasten to add, however, that it is possible to work only with a small sample of paths using techniques from statistical sampling. The use of high-performance computers and networks of workstations also speeds up substantially the computations[4] and such pricing calculations are now performed routinely by institutions dealing with MBS.

Option-Adjusted Premia

Most fixed-income securities cannot be priced using the riskless discount rates implied by the Treasury yield curve, as we did in equation (1). In particular, the price of the security has to reflect the credit, liquidity, default, and prepayment risks associated with this instrument. In order to value the risks associated with a fixed-income instrument we compute an *option-adjusted premium* (OAP).[5] The OAP analysis estimates the multiplicative adjustment factor for the Treasury rates that will equate today's (observed) market price with the "fair" price obtained by computing the expected present value of the cash flows. The discrepancy between the market price and the theoretical price is due to the various risks that are present in most fixed-income securities, but are not present in the Treasury market. Hence, this analysis will price the risks.

The OAP for a given security, denoted by ρ_j, is estimated based on the current market price, P_{j0}. In particular, it is the solution of the following nonlinear equation in ρ_j

$$P_{j0} = \frac{1}{|S_0|} \sum_{s=1}^{|S_0|} \sum_{t=1}^{T} \frac{C_{jt}^s}{\prod_{i=1}^{t}(1+\rho_j r_i^s)} \tag{2}$$

Now, however, we have what appears at first glance to be a gap in our analysis: in order to price the security we need the option-adjusted premium, while the option-adjusted premium is calculated using the market price of the security. Indeed, it is impossible to price a security unless we know the risks associated with it. However, for securities as complex as MBS we need to resort to market information to deter-

---

[4] See L.D. Cagan, N.S. Carriero, and S.A. Zenios, "Computer Network Approach to Pricing Mortgage-Backed Securities," *Financial Analysts Journal* (March/April 1993), pp. 55-62.

[5] See D.F. Babbel and S.A. Zenios, "Pitfalls in the Analysis of Option-Adjusted Spreads," *Financial Analysts Journal* (July/August 1992), pp. 65-69, or Y. Ben-Dov, L. Hayre, and V. Pica, "Mortgage Valuation Models at Prudential Securities," *Interfaces*, 22 (1992), pp. 55-71.

mine the appropriate risk premium. The typical remedy in completing the gap of our analysis is to use market prices for actively traded MBS to determine the OAP for a broad family of similar MBS, and then use this premium to price new securities, or securities with similar risk characteristics. Furthermore, differences in the OAP values of similar securities are used as indicators for identifying mispriced securities.

Once we have priced the various risks associated with the security we can proceed to price the security at some future time period, τ, conditional on the state σ of the lattice. Assuming a set S_σ of interest rate scenarios emanating from the state σ at period τ, the option-adjusted price of the security, $P_{j\tau}^\sigma$, can be calculated using a simple modification of equation (2) as:

$$P_{j\tau}^\sigma = \frac{1}{|S_0|} \sum_{s=1}^{|S_0|} \sum_{t=1}^{T} \frac{C_{jt}^s}{\prod_{i=\tau}^{t} (1 + \rho_j r_i^s)} \tag{3}$$

We point out that the price $P_{j\tau}^\sigma$ does not depend only on the state σ but also on the history of interest rates from $t = 0$ to $t = \tau$ that pass through this state.[6] We could now sample paths from $t = 0$ that pass through state σ at $t = \tau$. Let $S_{0,\sigma}$ denote the set of such paths, and let $P_{j\tau}^{s(\sigma)}$, $s(\sigma) \in S_{0,\sigma}$, be the price of the security at state σ obtained by applying equation (3), conditioned on the fact that interest rate scenarios s in S_σ originate from scenarios $s(\sigma)$ in $S_{0,\sigma}$. Then the expected price of the security at σ is given by

$$P_{j\tau}^\sigma = \frac{1}{|S_{0,\sigma}|} \sum_{s(\sigma) \in S_{0,\sigma}} P_{j\tau}^{s(\sigma)} \tag{4}$$

However, as we will see later, the path-dependent prices $P_{j\tau}^{s(\sigma)}$ provide useful information in the calculation of scenarios of holding period returns. The price computed using equation (4) is of little use in practice.

Duration and Convexity
The next step in the valuation analysis is to estimate the sensitivity of the computed prices to changes in the term structure. *Duration* and *convexity* are commonly used to measure the first and second derivative of the price of a security with respect to changes of the term structure of interest rates.

In order to capture the complex dependency of the cash flows of a fixed-income security to changes in the term structure we resort to the Monte Carlo simula-

---

[6] In particular, the cash flows generated by a MBS at periods after τ will depend on the economic environment experienced prior to τ. For example, if the security has experienced periods of high prepayments then subsequent changes of interest rates will have less impact on the generated cash flows. Although the short-term rates prior to τ do not appear explicitly in the pricing equations, the economic activity prior to τ is used in the estimation of the cash flows C_{jt}^s for $t \geq \tau$

tion procedure described next. Using Monte Carlo simulations to calculate option-adjusted duration and convexity involves the following steps:

Step 0: Initialize the stochastic process of interest rates, based on the current term structure, and use it to compute the option-adjusted premium ρ_j implied by the current market prices P_{j0} (equation (2)).

Step 1: Shift the term structure by -50 basis points, and recalibrate the stochastic process of interest rates.

Step 2: Sample interest rate paths $\{r_t^{-s}\}$ from the stochastic process calibrated in Step 1, and use the security cash flow projection model to compute option-adjusted prices:

$$P_j^- = \frac{1}{|S_0|} \sum_{s=1}^{|S_0|} \sum_{t=1}^{T} \frac{C_{jt}^s}{\prod_{i=1}^{t} (1 + \rho_j r_i^{-s})} \tag{5}$$

Step 3: Shift the term structure by $+50$ basis points, and recalibrate the stochastic process of interest rates.

Step 4: Sample interest rate paths $\{r_t^{+s}\}$ from the stochastic process calibrated in Step 3, and use the security cash flow projection model to compute option-adjusted prices:

$$P_j^+ = \frac{1}{|S_0|} \sum_{s=1}^{|S_0|} \sum_{t=1}^{T} \frac{C_{jt}^s}{\prod_{i=1}^{t} (1 + \rho_j r_i^{+s})} \tag{6}$$

Step 5: The *option-adjusted duration* of the security is given by

$$\Delta_j = \frac{P_j^+ - P_j^-}{100} \tag{7}$$

and the *option-adjusted convexity* by

$$\Gamma_j = \frac{P_j^+ - 2P_{j0} + P_j^-}{50^2} \tag{8}$$

Holding Period Returns

We now extend the valuation tools further, and estimate scenarios of returns of the MBS during a target holding period. These scenarios are, once more, generated using Monte Carlo simulation and they incorporate all available information about prepayment activity, option-adjusted premia, and interest rates.

The rate of return of a security j during the holding period τ is determined by the price of the security at the end of the holding period and the accrued value of any cash flows generated by the security. For a MBS we need to estimate the accrued value of principal, interest, and prepayments during the holding period, and price the unpaid balance of the security at the end of the holding period. To this end we rely again on a procedure for generating scenarios of the term structure, and on the model that predicts the prepayment activity for each scenario. For a given interest rate scenario s, the rate of return of security j is given by

$$R^s_{j\tau} = \frac{F^s_{j\tau} + V^s_{j\tau}}{P_{j0}} \qquad (9)$$

where

$F^s_{j\tau}$ is the accrued value of the cash flows generated by the security, reinvested at the short-term rates under scenario s.

$V^s_{j\tau}$ is the value of unpaid balance at the end of the holding period, conditioned on scenario s. This is given by

$$V^s_{j\tau} = B^s_{j\tau} P^s_{j\tau}$$

where $B^s_{j\tau}$ is the unpaid balance of the mortgage security and $P^s_{j\tau}$ is the price, per unit face value, of the security. Both quantities are computed at the end of the holding period, and are conditioned on the scenario s. The estimation of security prices at the end of a holding period, given a scenario s, has been discussed above, see equation (3) and the discussion that follows.

P_{j0} denotes the current market price of the security.

Exhibit 2 illustrates the distribution of prices of a typical MBS during different time horizons. Note that for shorter time horizons the distribution is highly asymmetric, a result of the embedded prepayment option. As the holding period approaches the maturity of the security then the prepayment option is, for all practical purposes, worthless and the prices are symmetric. Furthermore, the average price of the security converges to par, as it should towards its maturity.

PORTFOLIO RISK MANAGEMENT TECHNIQUES

Having mastered the techniques for the valuation of MBS we can now address the problem of managing the risk of a portfolio of such securities. We will see how the valuation models developed in the previous section (i.e., the models for estimating duration, convexity, option-adjusted premia, and holding period returns) can be incorporated in a hierarchy of portfolio risk management models. These models capture increasingly more complex aspects of the portfolio manager's problem.

Exhibit 2: Distribution of the Estimated Prices of a MBS at Different Points in Time Obtained Using Monte Carlo Simulations

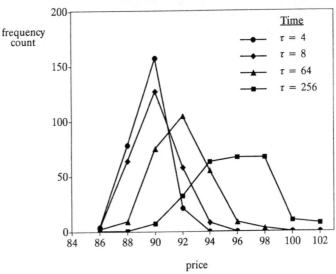

We loosely define the portfolio manager's problem as follows:

Construct a portfolio of mortgage securities whose performance measures will remain invariant under a wide range of uncertain scenarios.

For now we leave unspecified what we mean by *performance measures* and the precise nature of uncertainty. The key idea is to decide what goals we want our portfolio to achieve, specify measures that indicate that the goals are achieved, and make sure that these goals are still met when the economic environment changes. The three models we introduce in the next section allow the portfolio managers to specify increasingly more complex goals, and ensure that these goals are met for a broad set of scenarios.

Example Applications

The precise goals of the portfolio manager depend on the underlying application. We describe here three practical applications where one needs to deal with MBS and their inherent uncertainties:

> *Indexation:* Passive portfolio managers would like to build a portfolio of fixed-income securities that will track a prespecified index. For example, Lehman Brothers and Salomon Brothers publish a monthly mort-

gage index that is (presumably) indicative of the overall state of this segment of fixed-income markets. Investors who wish to invest in mortgages may be satisfied if their portfolio closely tracks the index. The performance measure of such a portfolio is the difference in return between the portfolio and the index. This difference has to be very small for all changes in the index caused by interest rate movements and by variations in prepayment activity.

Liability Payback: Insurance and pension fund companies are typically heavily exposed to MBS. These instruments are considered as an investment for paying back a variety of the liabilities of these institutions. The goal of the portfolio manager is to construct a portfolio of MBS that will pay the future stream of liabilities. Uncertainty here appears once more in the form of interest rate changes and changes in the timing of payments from the MBS. Furthermore, the timing of the liability stream may also be subject to uncertain variations: For example, the timing of payments to holders of single premium deferred annuities may change as annuitants exercise the option to lapse.

Debt Issuance: Government agencies, like Fannie Mae and Freddie Mac, fund the purchase of fixed-income assets (typically mortgages) by issuing debt. The problem of a portfolio manager is to decide which type of debt — maturity, yield, call-option — to issue in order to fund the purchase of a specific set of assets. Of course, there is no reason to assume that the assets have been pre-specified: the model may choose an appropriate asset mix from a large universe of available MBS or other fixed-income securities. The timings of both assets and liabilities may be uncertain in this application. The goal of the portfolio manager is to ensure that the payments against the issued debt will be met from the available assets, irrespectively of the timing of cash flows and fluctuations in interest rates.

Classification of Portfolio Management Models

We first start with a general classification of portfolio management models. We assume that a portfolio of MBS (the *assets*) are bought in order to fund some future obligation (the *liability*). Hence, the portfolio problem we are dealing with is the classical asset/liability management model, with MBS as assets.

The asset/liability management models we develop in the next section can be classified as: (1) static, (2) single-period, stochastic, and (3) multiperiod, dynamic, and stochastic. It is important to understand how the models address increasingly more complex aspects of the asset/liability management problem. Only then can the portfolio manager decide which model may be more appropriate for the application at hand. Of course, this decision has to be weighted against the increasing complexity — both conceptual and computational — of the models.

Static models hedge against small changes from the current state of the world. For example, a term structure is input to the model which matches assets and liabilities under this structure. Conditions are then imposed to guarantee that if the term structure deviates somewhat from the assumed value, the assets and liabilities will move in the same direction and by equal amounts. This is the fundamental principle behind *portfolio immunization.*[7]

Single-period, stochastic models do not permit the specification of a stochastic process that describes changes of the economic environment from its current status. However, modern finance abounds with theories that describe interest rates, and other volatile factors, using stochastic processes. Stochastic differential calculus is often used to price interest-rate contingencies. For complex instruments analysts resort to Monte Carlo simulations as we have seen in previous sections. A stochastic asset/liability model describes the *distribution* of returns of both assets and liabilities in the volatile environment, and ensures that movements of both sides of the balance sheet are highly correlated. This idea is not new: Markowitz pioneered the notion of risk management for equities via the use of correlations in his seminal paper.[8] However, for the fixed-income world this approach has only recently received attention.[9] The implementation of this strategy requires the generation of scenarios of holding period returns, as explained earlier.

The single-period stochastic model outlined above is *myopic*. That is, it builds a portfolio that will have a well behaved distribution of error (error = asset return − liability return) under the specified stochastic process. However, it does not account for the fact that the portfolio manager is likely to rebalance the portfolio once some surplus is realized. Furthermore, as the stochastic process evolves across time different portfolios may be more appropriate for capturing the correlations of assets and liabilities. The single-period model may recommend a conservative strategy, while a more aggressive approach would be justified once we explicitly recognize the manager's ability to rebalance the portfolio.

What is needed is a model that explicitly captures both the stochastic nature of the problem, but also the fact that the portfolio is managed in a dynamic, multi-period context. Mathematical models under the general term of *stochastic programming with recourse* provide the framework for dealing with this broad problem. Stochastic programming has a history almost as long as *linear programming.*[10] However, it was not until the early 1970s[11] that its significance for portfolio management was

---

[7] See P.E. Christensen and F.J. Fabozzi, "Bond Immunization: An Asset Liability Optimization Strategy," in F.J. Fabozzi and I.M. Pollack (editors) *The Handbook of Fixed Income Securities* (Dow Jones Irwin, 1987), for a discussion of the finance-theoretic principles behind immunization. See H. Dahl, A. Meeraus, and S.A. Zenios, "Some Financial Optimization Models: I. Risk Management," Chapter 1 in S.A. Zenios (ed.), *Financial Optimization* (Cambridge University Press, 1993), for operational models.

[8] H. Markowitz, "Portfolio Selection," *Journal of Finance,* 7 (1952), pp. 77-91.

[9] The framework for the diversification of fixed-income portfolios was developed by J.M. Mulvey and S.A. Zenios, "Capturing the Correlations of Fixed-Income Instruments," *Management Science,* 40 (1994), pp. 1329-1342. For an application to MBS by Fannie Mae see M.R. Holmer, "The Asset/Liability Management System at Fannie Mae," *Interfaces,* 24 (1994), pp. 3-21.

realized. With the recent advances in high-performance computing this approach has been receiving renewed interest from the academic literature.[12] We are also aware of work in several industrial settings for the deployment of such models in practice.

We continue now with a mathematical description of a model from each class. The formulations are general since our goal is to describe the key components of the models. In order to operationalize each model for the applications mentioned earlier additional specifications are needed. We do not completely specify the details, as those will only distract from the general principles we want to convey.

The following notation is generic to all models. Additional information will be defined as needed later. The universe of MBS is indexed by a set J and the market price of each security $j \in J$ is denoted by P_{j0}. The stream of liabilities is denoted by L_t, where $t = 0,1,...,T$, denotes a time index. Given is also a term structure, specified by a set of forward rates $\{r_t\}$, $t = 1,2,..., T$. The problem of the portfolio manager is to decide the holdings of each security x_j in a portfolio that will match the assets with the target liability stream.

For the stochastic models we also need to specify a set of scenarios S. The scenarios can be very general: they can represent a series of term structures drawn from some stochastic process of interest rates, or they can represent levels of prepayment activity for the mortgage securities, or they can represent levels of the liability stream, and so on. Whenever a model parameter is super-scripted by an index $s \in S$ it is understood that the value of the parameter is scenario dependent. In this respect, we will use C_{jt}^s to denote the cash flow generated by security $j \in J$ (per unit face value), and r_t^s to denote the discount rate at period $t = 1,..., T$, under scenario $s \in S$.

A Static Model: Duration Matching

Given the term structure, a stream of projected cash flows for the fixed-income security, and a stream of liabilities we can build a *dedicated* portfolio. That is, a portfolio of least cost — or maximum yield — of MBS that will match the stream of liabilities. Let C_{jt} denote the cash flow generated by security j at period t. This stream is projected conditional on the current term structure. Consider now the following optimization model:

---

[10] See G. B. Dantzig, "Linear Programming under Uncertainty," *Management Science*, 1 (1955), pp. 197-206, and R. J. B. Wets, "Stochastic Programs with Fixed Resources: the Equivalent Deterministic Problem," *SIAM Review*, 16 (1974), pp. 309-339.

[11] S.P. Bradley and D.B. Crane, "A Dynamic Model for Bond Portfolio Management," *Management Science* (October 1972), pp. 139-151.

[12] B. Golub, M. Holmer, R. McKendall, L. Pohlman, and S.A. Zenios, "Stochastic Programming Models for Money Management," *European Journal of Operational Research*, 85 (1995), pp. 282-296; R.S. Hiller and J. Eckstein, "Stochastic Dedication: Designing Fixed Income Portfolios Using Massively Parallel Benders Decomposition," *Management Science*, 39 (1994), pp. 1422-1438; J.M. Mulvey and H. Vladimirou, "Stochastic Network Optimization Models for Investment Planning," *Annals of Operations Research*, 20 (1989), pp. 187-217; and, S.A. Zenios, "Massively Parallel Computations for Financial Modeling under Uncertainty," in J. Mesirov (ed.) *Very Large Scale Computing in the 21st Century* (Philadelphia, PA, 1991), pp. 273-294.

$$\text{Minimize}_{x} \sum_{j \in J} P_{j0} x_j \tag{10}$$

$$\text{s.t.} \sum_{j \in J} \left(\sum_{t=1}^{T} \frac{C_{jt}}{\prod_{\tau=1}^{t}(1+r_{\tau})} \right) x_j \geq \sum_{t=1}^{T} \frac{L_t}{\prod_{\tau=1}^{t}(1+r_{\tau})} \tag{11}$$

$$x_j \geq 0 \tag{12}$$

This model will choose the least-cost portfolio, with the property that the present value of the portfolio cash flows will be at least equal to the present value of the liabilities. If the timing and magnitude of assets and liabilities does not change, and neither do the discount factors, then it is easy to see that the portfolio will ensure timely payments against the liabilities. (It is assumed in this model that unlimited borrowing is allowed, at all time periods, at the prevailing discount rate r_{τ}. The model can be modified to eliminate borrowing, or permit limited borrowing at a spread over the rate r_{τ}.)

To account for the stochasticity of the security's cash flow, and the changes of the term structure, the model can be extended to match the sensitivities of both assets and liabilities to such stochasticity. As discussed earlier, the duration of a security measures the sensitivity of its price to small parallel shifts to the term structure. Hence, we extend the model to develop an *immunized* portfolio which will match both present values and durations of assets and liabilities. If Δ_l is the liability duration we can obtain an immunized portfolio by solving the following linear program:

$$\text{Minimize}_{x} \sum_{j \in J} P_{j0} x_j \tag{13}$$

$$\text{s.t.} \sum_{j \in J} \left(\sum_{t=1}^{T} \frac{C_{jt}}{\prod_{\tau=1}^{t}(1+r_{\tau})} \right) x_j \geq \sum_{t=1}^{T} \frac{L_t}{\prod_{\tau=1}^{t}(1+r_{\tau})} \tag{14}$$

$$\sum_{j \in J} \Delta_j x_j = \Delta_l \tag{15}$$

$$x_j \geq 0 \tag{16}$$

The model could be extended further to match the convexities of assets and liabilities. Matching higher derivatives is also possible. At the limit the derivative matched portfolio will be identical to a cash flow matched portfolio.

A Stochastic Model: Capturing Correlations

Portfolios of fixed-income securities have traditionally been managed using the simple concepts of duration and convexity matching of the previous section. With the increased volatility of the term structure, following monetary deregulation in the late 1970s, this approach became overly simplistic. The difficulty is further exacerbated with the constant stream of innovations in this market. In this respect the tradition of models based on diversification, that started with Markowitz's seminal work, has much to offer to the managers of fixed-income portfolios.[13]

In this section we introduce a stochastic model for managing portfolios of MBS. The model explicitly recognizes the volatility of MBS prices, and the correlation of prices in a portfolio, and develops the tradeoffs between return and volatility. The optimization model we adopt is based on the *mean-absolute deviation* (MAD) framework.[14] A MAD model is suitable for the fixed-income securities with embedded options since they exhibit highly asymmetric distributions of return.

One of the challenges in applying the MAD model — or any other risk-return model for that matter — to fixed-income securities is that instruments with a fixed term to maturity are vanishing. Furthermore, the payout function of several kinds of fixed-income securities is path-dependent. Hence, at any point in time we have only one observation of price variations. Therefore, we cannot resort to the statistical analysis of historical data in order to capture the volatility and correlation of returns. Hence, we need to resort to Monte Carlo simulation of the short-term risk-free rates in order to obtain holding period returns of the fixed-income security during the target holding period. Such a Monte Carlo simulation procedure was developed in previous sections (see, for example, equation (9)) and the discussion that follows. For now we assume that a random vector of holding period returns has been generated for each security.

Let $(R_j)_{j \in J}$ denote this vector random variable and let $\overline{R}_j = E(R_j)$ denote its expected value. (For simplicity we have dropped the subscript τ that denotes the dependence of the return on the holding period τ.) Let also $x = (x_j)_{j \in J}$ denote the composition of the portfolio that contains a liability with return ρ. The return of the portfolio is $R = \sum_{j \in J} R_j x_j + \rho$. The mean-absolute deviation of return of this portfolio is defined by:

$$w(R) = E\{|R - E(R)|\} \tag{17}$$

where $E(.)$ denotes expectation.

Assume now that a sample of the random variables R_j is available. That is, R_j takes the value R_j^s for some scenario $s \in S$, and we assume for simplicity that all scenarios in S are equiprobable. Then, an unbiased estimate for the mean-absolute deviation of return of the portfolio is:

---

[13] See Mulvey and Zenios, "Capturing the Correlations of Fixed-Income Instruments."

[14] See H. Konno and H. Yamazaki, "Mean-Absolute Deviation Portfolio Optimization Model and its Applications to Tokyo Stock Market," *Management Science*, 37 (1991), pp. 519-531.

$$w(R) = E\{|R - E(R)|\} \tag{18}$$

$$= E\left\{\left|\sum_{j \in J}(R_j - \bar{R}_j)x_j\right|\right\} \tag{19}$$

$$= \frac{1}{|S| + |J|}\sum_{s \in S}\left|\sum_{j \in J}(R_j^s - \bar{R}_j)x_j\right| \tag{20}$$

The MAD model is written as:

Minimize $w(R)$ $\tag{21}$

s.t. $\displaystyle\sum_{j \in J}\bar{R}_j x_j \geq \rho$ $\tag{22}$

$\displaystyle\sum_{j \in J} x_j = 1$ $\tag{23}$

$0 \leq x_j \leq u_j, \quad \text{for all } j \in J \tag{24}$

This model can be reformulated into a linear programming problem. (We use the standard reformulation for minimizing absolute values. The minimand |x| is replaced by y, where y is constrained as $y \geq x$ and $y \geq -x$.) In doing so it is also possible to differentially penalize the upside from the downside deviation of the portfolio return from its mean. Let μ_d and μ_u denote penalty parameters for the downside and upside errors respectively. Then the MAD model can be written as the following linear program:

Minimize $\displaystyle\frac{1}{|S| + |J|}\sum_{s \in S} y^s$ $\tag{25}$

s.t. $\displaystyle y^s + \mu_d\sum_{j \in J}(R_j^s - \bar{R}_j)x_j \geq 0, \quad \text{for all } s \in S \tag{26}$

$\displaystyle y^s + \mu_u\sum_{j \in J}(R_j^s - \bar{R}_j)x_j \geq 0, \quad \text{for all } s \in S \tag{27}$

$\displaystyle\sum_{j \in J}\bar{R}_j x_j \geq \rho$ $\tag{28}$

$\displaystyle\sum_{j \in J} x_j \geq 1$ $\tag{29}$

$0 \leq x_j \leq u_j, \quad \text{for all } j \in J \tag{30}$

A Multiperiod, Dynamic Model: Stochastic Optimization

We extend now the stochastic model of the previous section to a setting with multiple time priods. The multiperiod, stochastic model captures the dynamics of the following situation:

A portfolio manager must make investment decisions facing an uncertain future. After these *first-stage* decisions are made, a realization of the uncertain future is observed, and the manager determines an optimal *second-stage* (or, recourse) decision. The objective is to maximize the expected utility of final wealth.

The first-stage decision deals with the purchase of a portfolio of fixed-income securities. Uncertainty in this decision making framework is reflected in the level of interest rates, and the cash flows that will be obtained from the portfolio. The second-stage decision deals with borrowing (lending) decisions when the fixed-income cash flows lag (lead) the target liabilities. Decisions to rebalance the portfolio at some future time period(s), by purchasing or selling securities, are also included in the second stage.

This model is substantially more flexible than the previous two models in that it explicitly allows for portfolio rebalancing at future time periods, as more information about the uncertain scenarios becomes available. Transaction costs can, therefore, also be incorporated. Furthermore, by explicitly representing the scenarios in the constraints we can include scenarios not only of interest rates but also of prepayments, spreads, risk premia and the like. The detailed mathematical program for the multiperiod stochastic programming model is defined in the appendix.

PORTFOLIO RISK MANAGEMENT APPLICATIONS

We now illustrate the application of the models developed in this chapter to two specific real-world settings. We first show how MBS can be included in an immunized portfolio to fund a liability stream. Furthermore, we use this application to illustrate that stochastic models, even single-period ones, have superior performance than static models, such as immunization. The second application summarizes results from a successful implementation of the stochastic portfolio management ideas to track the Salomon Brothers index of MBS.

Immunization of an Insurance Liability Stream
We apply the MAD model for funding a liability stream obtained from a major insurance corporation. Using the term structure of April 26, 1991, we calculated the following descriptors of the liability:

Term	100 months
Present value	$166,163,900.00
Modified duration	4.1792 years

Using the portfolio immunization models we built a portfolio that was duration and convexity matched against the liabilities. The portfolio was built from a universe of both MBS and U.S. Treasury securities. Different levels of exposure to the mortgage market were imposed on an ad hoc basis. We list below the percentage savings realized when the liability is funded using a portfolio of MBS and Treasuries, over the cost of funding the liabilities using only the risk-free rate.

Cost of portfolio using Treasuries only	$166,163,861.00
(Savings)	0.00%
Cost of portfolio using up to 25% MBS	$152,993,690.00
(Savings)	7.92%
Cost of portfolio using up to 50% MBS	$142,529,529.00
(Savings)	16.58%
Cost of portfolio using up to 100% MBS	$137,489,656.00
(Savings)	21.07%
Cost of mixed U.S.Treasury-MBS portfolio	$136,124,130.00
(Savings)	22.07%

While it is clear from this example that using MBS in an integrated asset/liability management system produces substantial gains, the savings summarized above will not be necessarily realized in practice. They will be realized only if the term structure shifts in parallel and in small levels from that of April 26, 1991.

To assess the return of the portfolio under different economic conditions we conducted a Monte Carlo simulation of the returns of the immunized portfolio over the holding period. The results are reported in Exhibit 3. The 100% MBS portfolio produced expected returns of 10.469% with a standard deviation of these returns 0.406. The mixed portfolio of U.S. Treasuries and MBS has a slightly reduced expected return of 10.448%, but substantially reduced standard deviation of 0.293.

We also developed a MAD portfolio for funding the insurance liability. The efficient frontier is shown in Exhibit 4. On the same figure we show the results of the simulation of the immunized portfolio. First, we observe from this figure that substantial rates of return can be realized with relatively little risk. Second, we observe that the portfolio obtained using standard immunization techniques lies below the efficient frontier. These results illustrate the superiority of the MAD model in managing portfolios of complex instruments, like MBS, as opposed to traditional fixed-income management tools. Exhibit 3 summarizes the expected return and standard deviation of both immunized and MAD portfolios.

Exhibit 3: Performance of Immunized and MAD Portfolios

Model	100% MBS portfolio		Mixed Portfolio	
	Exp. return	Std. dev.	Exp. return	Std. dev.
Immunized	10.469	0.406	10.448	0.293
MAD (equal risk)	10.783	0.405	10.692	0.293
MAD (equal return)	10.469	0.234	10.448	0.206

Exhibit 4: Efficient Frontier of the Mean Absolute Deviation Portfolio of MBS and the Return-Variance Profile of the Immunized Portfolio

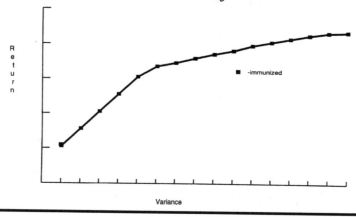

Tracking a Mortgage Index

One of the first successful applications of stochastic portfolio optimization models for fixed-income securities was to the management of the MBS portfolio of a major insurance corporation.[15] A MAD model was developed to track the Salomon Index of mortgage-backed securities. The index consists of a representative of all traded fixed-rate, passthrough securities, issued by FNMA, GNMA and FHLMC. The index is a sanitized image of the mortgage market: for example, cash flows generated by the mortgage pools are assumed to be reinvested in the index itself. There are also holdings in very small pools, and actual investments in such pools may be impossible due to liquidity difficulties. Finally, the composition of the index is changing from month to month without incurring any transaction costs. Since the MBS compromise approximately one-third of broad-based bond indexes, creating a *tradeable* portfolio that closely tracks the index is of great interest to investors.

The model estimates holding period returns of all securities in the index, and builds a portfolio that minimizes the mean-absolute deviation of the returns of the portfolio from the expected return of the index. Upside and downside risks are penalized differentially, with no penalty on upside risk and infinite penalty on downside risk. (Downside risk is realized when the portfolio underperforms the index by an amount that exceeds a small acceptable margin, set to be −5bp in monthly returns.)

The indexation model was tested over the period January 1989 to December 1991. During this period the index realized an annual return of 13.96%. In back-testing the model we used the following methodology: at the beginning of each month a binomial lattice was calibrated based on the term structure of that day. The lattice was used to estimate holding period returns, and the MAD model was used to select a

[15] See K.J. Worzel, C.Vassiadou-Zeniou, and S.A. Zenios, "Integrated Simulation and Optimization Models for Tracking Fixed-Income Indices," *Operations Research*, 42 (1994), pp. 223-233.

portfolio. The performance of the portfolio was recorded at the end of the month, based on observed market prices, and the process was repeated. Transaction costs of ²⁄₃₂bp were charged, and cash flows from the mortgage pools were reinvested at the 1-month Treasury rate. The initial portfolio (January 1989) was selected using the method outlined above, but no transaction costs were paid.

During the testing period the portfolio realized an annual return of 14.18%, +22bp over the index return. The portfolio never underperformed the index by more than −3.6bp in monthly return, while the outperformance was more substantial (Exhibit 5). The standard deviation of the index return over the test period was 0.155, while the portfolio return had a standard deviation of 0.158. The portfolio would typically consist of approximately 25 securities, none of which accounted for more than 12% of the total portfolio.

Exhibit 5: Return of a $100M Investment in the Salomon Brothers Mortgage Index and Tracking Error of the Indexed Portfolio (January 1989 - December 1991)

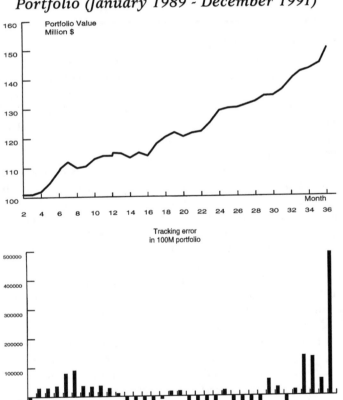

APPENDIX: STOCHASTIC PROGRAMMING
PORTFOLIO FORMULATION

We give in this appendix a detailed mathematical formulation of the stochastic programming model for multiperiod, dynamic portfolio management as introduced in previous sections. We will be using the following notation. The parameters of the model are:

T   = discretization of the planning horizon, $T = \{1, 2, 3, ..., \overline{T}\}$, and T_0 = $\{0, 1, 2, 3, ..., \overline{T}\}$. $\overline{T}$ denotes the end of the planning horizon.

b_j = initial holdings (in face value) of instrument $j \in J$, and b_0 initial holdings in a risk-free asset (e.g., cash).

r_t^s = 1-year forward interest rate at time period $t \in T_0$ under scenario s $\in S$.

spr   = spread between the lending and borrowing rates.

pf_{jt}^s = cash flow generated from instrument $j \in J$ at time period $t \in T$ under scenario $s \in S$, expressed as a percentage of face value. It includes principal and interest payments of the fixed-income security, as well as cash flows generated due to defaults, prepayments, lapse, exercise of the embedded call option, etc.

ξ_{jt}^s = price per unit of face value of security $j \in J$ sold at period t under scenario s. The cost of the transaction is subtracted from the actual price to obtain this coefficient. The price at $t = 0$ is independent of the scenario and denoted by ξ_{j0}.

ζ_{jt}^s = price per unit of face value of security $j \in J$ purchased at period t under scenario s. The cost of the transaction is added to the actual price to obtain this coefficient. The price at $t = 0$ in independent of the scenario, and is denoted by ζ_{j0}.

L_t = liability due at time period $t \in T$. It is assumed here to be independent of the realized scenario, although this assumption can be easily relaxed.

The model variables are:

x_j = first stage variable, denoting the face value of instrument $j \in J$ purchased at the beginning of the planning horizon (i.e., at $t = 0$).

x_{jt}^s = second stage variable, denoting the face value of instrument j $\in J$ purchased at time period t under scenario s.

y_j = first stage variable, denoting the face value of instrument $j \in J$ sold at the beginning of the planning horizon, (i.e., at $t = 0$).

y_{jt}^s = second stage variable, denoting the face value of instrument $j \in$ J sold at time period t under scenario s (i.e., at $t = 0$).

z_{jt}^{s} = second stage variable denoting the face value of instrument $j \in J$ in the portfolio at time period $t \in T$, under scenario s. z_{j0} denotes the starting composition of the portfolio, after first-stage decisions have been made, and is independent of the scenarios.

w_{jt}^{s} = second stage accounting variable indicating the cash flow generated by security j at time period t under scenario s.

y_{t}^{-s} = second stage recourse variable indicating the amount owed at time period $t+1$ due to borrowing decisions made at period t under scenario s.

y_{t}^{+s} = second stage recourse variable indicating the surplus invested in the risk asset at time period t.

$U(WT^{s})$ = the utility of terminal wealth realized under scenario s. Appropriate choices of utility functions are, for example, the isoelastic utility $1/\gamma(WT^{s})^{\gamma}$.

The model can now be formulated as follows:

Maximize $\dfrac{1}{|S|}\displaystyle\sum_{s \in S} U(WT^{s})$

s.t. $z_{j0} + y_{j} - \dfrac{x_{j}}{\zeta_{j0}} = b_{j}, \quad j \in J$

$$y_{0}^{+s} + \sum_{j \in J} x_{j} - \sum_{j \in J}(1 - \xi_{j})y_{j} - \frac{1}{(1 + r_{0}^{s} + spr)}y_{0}^{-s} = b_{0}, \quad s \in S$$

$$z_{jt-1}^{s} + x_{jt}^{s} - w_{jt}^{s} - z_{jt}^{s} - y_{jt}^{s} = 0, \quad t \in T, \ j \in J, \ s \in S$$

$$w_{jt}^{s} - pf_{jt}^{s}z_{jt-1}^{s} = 0, \quad t \in T, \ j \in J, \ s \in S$$

$$\xi_{jt}^{s}y_{jt}^{s} + \sum_{j \in J} w_{jt}^{s} - \frac{x_{jt}^{s}}{\zeta_{jt}^{s}} + (1 + r_{t-1}^{s})y_{t-1}^{+s} - y_{t-1}^{-s}$$

$$+ \frac{1}{(1 + r_{t}^{s} + spr)}y_{t}^{-s} - y_{t}^{+s} = L_{t}, \quad t \in T, \ s \in S$$

$$WT^{s} = \sum_{j \in J} z_{j\bar{T}}^{s}\zeta_{j\bar{T}}^{s} - y_{\bar{T}-1}^{-s}$$

The first constraint of this mathematical program reflects first stage decisions, and is deterministic. Subsequent constraints depend on the realized scenario, as well as the first stage decisions. The terminal wealth WT^{s} is computed by accumulating the total surplus net any outstanding debt at the end of the planning horizon and liquidating any securities that remain in the portfolio.

Chapter 12

An Integrated Framework for Valuation and Risk Analysis of International Bonds

Roveen Bhansali
Associate Director
Global Fixed Income Services
BARRA, Inc.

Lisa Goldberg, Ph.D.
Senior Consultant
Fixed Income Research
BARRA, Inc.

INTRODUCTION

International bonds now represent more than half of the market value of the world's fixed-income markets. In 1985 they comprised less than a third. The years 1993-1995 have seen a tremendous growth in the international fixed-income markets and a corresponding growth in international bonds under management for U.S.-based mutual fund families and institutional investors. There are now over 200 mutual funds devoted to international bonds, more than double the number available just three years ago.

Part of this increased interest in international bonds stems from the more than 390 basis points of out-performance of international bonds as a group over the U.S. bond market over the last decade. Exhibit 1 displays the year by year performance comparison of the J.P. Morgan Government Bond Index ex-U.S. with the J.P. Morgan U.S. Government Bond Index. Another reason is the case made for diversification benefits that international bonds can offer in any fixed-income portfolio.

213

Exhibit 1: Comparison of Bond Returns

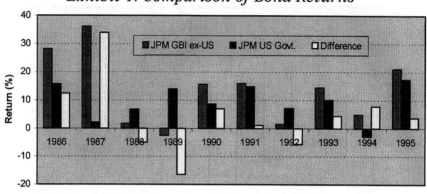

Investing in international bond presents substantial challenges for global investors. There exist idiosyncrasies within individual markets that result in widely differing market structures and trading patterns. When managing an international bond portfolio, one needs to understand not only the diverse types of assets within a market, but also to develop a complete understanding of the institutions that regulate the market. In addition, investors need to be cognizant of the dynamics between markets in order to identify global trends and trading opportunities.

Bond values are driven by macroeconomic variables such as real interest rates, inflation expectations, GDP growth rates, employment outlook, budget deficit and monetary policy. Within each market, these variables determine the relative supply and demand for government securities, which in turn drives the prices. In addition, bond values also depend on the structural features and institutional characteristics within markets, such as liquidity, tax considerations, default risk, cash flow structures, and intra-market spreads. Any asset or market feature that changes investors' willingness to pay for a bond should be considered. We will elaborate on some of these below.

Although most government bond markets are fairly liquid, there clearly are differences across markets. Executing a $500 million trade in the U.S. is very different from executing that trade in Norway. Additionally, different markets exhibit varying levels of liquidity along the yield curve. As an example, consider the Portuguese bond market. Even though the government bond issuance is well balanced across the long end of the curve (5-10 year maturity range).[1] In Japan, lack of an active repo market combined with high demand for KGBs for end-of-March year-end balance sheet purposes has historically resulted in the cash JGBs being relatively illiquid.

Differences in tax treatment across markets should be taken into account as that determines the net real returns to the international investor. Typically, bonds are

---

[1] As of 1995, 33.8% of outstanding amount of government debt was in the 1-3 year range, whereas 27.3% was in the 5-10 year range.

not taxed when held by international investors, but this may not always be the case. For example, Italy has a 12.5% withholding tax on bonds issued after August 31, 1987[2] and a withholding tax levied at maturity on the difference between the face value and issue price. The withholding tax in principle is refundable for international investors. However, due to procedural issues and delays involved in this process, an investor in Italian government bonds may treat the yields on a non-refundable basis. Similarly, tax issues in Japan may make investing in the Euro-yen market preferable to the international investor over the JGB market.

Investors also need to understand default risk of international bond issuers. Even two industrialized sovereign issuers of similarly rated local currency debt, may trade at differential spread in the Eurobond market. This would indicate default risk premium attached to the credit worthiness of one sovereign issuer relative to the other. The magnitude of the default risk premia becomes a more important element of a bond's value when analyzing emerging market debt or for Eurobonds issued by non-investment grade, non-sovereign issuers.

International investors also need to discern between the distinguishing attributes of different bond types. One such feature that needs to be analyzed is an embedded option. For example, in the Italian market the CTOs are putable — so they should trade at a lower yield than the equivalent BTPs.[3] In the U.S. market, some of the long maturity Treasuries have embedded call options — so their yields should be adjusted higher compared to equivalent straight bonds. The UK gilt market has bonds with special features, e.g., perpetuals.[4]

There are other subtleties within markets that merit consideration. Historically, callable bonds in the domestic Japanese market have never been called ñ therefore they trade as straight bonds. Some markets such as the UK gilt market and Danish government bond market use a "tap" issuance system where the issuer adjusts the offering price of the bond to regulate the amount of sales. Hence, there is more issuance when market prices go up than when prices drop.

Market knowledge is also essential in understanding the intricacies of intra-market dynamics. Consider the Pfandbriefe sector in the German market which accounts for over 30% of the domestic market value. Despite this large market share, the Pfandbriefe spread over the sovereign curve has historically been wide due to lack of liquidity in the secondary market. However, the recent establishment of standard indexes in the Pfanbriefe market together with the issuance of "Jumbo Pfand-briefes" targeted to the global investors has increased its appeal overseas. As a result, this market is more liquid and the intra-market spread has tightened.

---

[2] Bonds issued before August 31, 1987, mostly floating-rate *Certificati di Credito del Tesoro* (CCTs), are either tax-exempt or taxed at a 6.25% withholding rate.

[3] *Certificati del Tesoro con Opzione* (CTOs) are fixed-rate notes with a put option at par after three years. *Buoni del Tesoro Poliennali* (BTPs) are fixed-coupon bullet maturity bonds with recent issuances of maturity of 3-, 5-, 10-, and 30-years. For the bulk of CTOs though the option is now expired, hence they are identical to BTPs.

[4] Perpetuals, also called Undated or Irredeemable gilts are low-coupon bonds that have no final maturity date.

Exhibit 2: Currency Risk as a Percentage of Total Portfolio Risk for the Major Global Bond Indexes (February 29, 1996)

Numeraire	JPM GBI* (%)	SAL WGI** (%)
U.S. dollar	63.3	65.7
ECU	65.3	65.8
French franc	70.9	70.5
German deutschemarks	71.8	71.9
British pound	70.8	73.1
Canadian dollar	75.7	76.9
Japanese yen	82.8	81.9
Australian dollar	87.7	87.9
Italian lira	86.3	88.3
Mexican peso	92.9	93.5
South African rand	97.7	96.1

* J.P. Morgan Government Bond Index.
** Salomon Brothers World Government Index.
Source: The BARRA Cosmos™ Model

Clearly, bond valuation has a market-specific component that requires substantial knowledge about each individual market. Before devising a global investment strategy, one must understand the elements that define the value of assets traded in each market. Although there exist differences between bond markets, it is nonetheless important to create a consistent and integrated framework from which to analyze international bonds.

The various factors that contribute to a bond's value also provide insight into its risk. The volatile bond markets, particularly in 1994, exposed the shortcomings of traditional measures of bond risk, namely duration and convexity. Within a single market, duration as a risk measure proved inadequate in predicting the interest rate risk due to non-parallel movements of the yield curve. Additionally, duration — which represents sensitivity to small parallel movement in the yield curve within a particular market — loses its meaning when aggregated across markets. For example, the meaning of a 4.2-year duration for a portfolio consisting of U.S. Treasuries, JGBs, and German Bunds is dubious. Duration would only be a meaningful measure in the context of this portfolio if we were to assume that the all the markets in the portfolio would undergo identical parallel interest rate changes *simultaneously.*

Another major source of volatility in a portfolio that contains international bonds is currency movement. The higher return earned on an international bond can be neutralized if that bond's currency loses value. Typically, in an unhedged international fixed-income portfolio, currency movements can account for almost two thirds of the return and risk. Exhibit 2 shows the percentage of total portfolio risk[5] explained by currency movements in the major global risk indexes for various

---

[5] Portfolio risk is defined as variance of excess return.

numeraire perspectives. Additionally, correlations between local market interest rate movements and foreign currency movements can also contribute to currency risk. A currency hedging strategy is required to take an interest rate view in a particular local market without incurring incidental currency exposure. In developing a strategy for investing in international bonds, managers must assess carefully the currency aspects of their portfolio.

The purpose of this chapter is to describe, in the context of today's marketplace, approaches for constructing valuation models for international fixed income securities. These valuation models will assist investors in making trading decisions, marking portfolios to market, identifying relative value in securities, etc.

After developing a framework for accurate valuation of fixed-income securities, we address the issues pertaining to forecasting the risk of a portfolio of these securities. A successful global fixed-income strategy involves making the right bond and currency choices and managing the risk inherent in those choices. We identify the risk factors, namely interest rate risk and credit risk, that describe risk within an individual market. Using these factors, we develop a local market risk model for each individual market, that is applicable to all the securities in that market. In addition, we develop a security-specific risk model that explains the risk not explained by the market-wide factors. We then add to the risk model the dimension inherent in international portfolios, namely, currency risk. We then describe a model that accounts for correlations existing across local markets and currencies.

This multi-factor risk modeling approach lends itself to identifying the exposures of each security in an international portfolio to the various risk factors and quantifying the volatility and correlations of the different markets within the portfolio. This enables calculation of aggregate portfolio risk measures such as value-at-risk (VAR) and tracking error. At the same time, this approach allows a portfolio manager to decompose and better understand the various sources of risk. Local market interest rate strategies can be separated from currency strategies, facilitating formulation and analysis of alternative investment strategies.

VALUATION ANALYSIS

Technically speaking, a bond is a collection of promised future cash flows subject to a set of terms and conditions. The simplest and most familiar bonds are *straight bonds* for which the cash flow dates and amounts are fixed at the time of issue. As we will see below, bond characteristics can be quite complicated. In particular, they may cause the cash flow stream to be uncertain.

As mentioned in the introduction, a bond's value is affected by the credibility of the "promise" of its cash flows. In other words, the value of a bond is influenced by the likelihood that the issuer may default. Generally, sovereign bonds are considered to be default free while corporate bonds are somewhat riskier.[6] Hence,

---

[6] There are exceptions such as Italy where sovereign bonds are considered riskier than corporate bonds.

the price of a corporate bond typically should be less than the price of an otherwise identical sovereign bond.

The considerations above indicate that any model used to value bonds in a given market must have at least three components. The first is a term structure of interest rates which determines the time value of money. The second is a spread model which captures default risk. The final component is a stochastic interest rate model which describe how interest rates evolve. This is used to value bonds whose future stream of cash flows is uncertain. These components are discussed below in more detail.

Our strategy is to devise a uniform implementation of these three components for each market covered by our model. Then the components are enhanced to reflect the individual characteristics of the market. One of the challenges in designing a model of this type is to strike a balance between tailoring the components to the different markets and having consistency across markets.

Term Structure Model

The *term structure* is a curve that specifies a discount rate for every future time to maturity. For a straight sovereign bond, this is all that is needed to come up with the present value of a bond

$$PM(t) = \sum_{T} cf(T)e^{-s(t,\,T)(T-t)} + \varepsilon(t) = PF(t) + \varepsilon(t) \tag{1}$$

$PM(t)$ = Bond market price at time t
$cf(T)$ = Time T expected ash flow
$s(t,T)$ = Time t (continuously compounded) spot interest rate at maturity T
$Pf(t)$ = Bond model or fitted price at time t
$\varepsilon(t)$ = Time t pricing error

The term structure is a theoretical construct which is inferred from bond prices and other economic factors. One possible estimation procedure is as follows. First, determine the horizon of the market from the time to maturity of the longest bond. Divide the horizon into intervals that reflect the natural maturity sectors in the market. The forward rates can be assumed constant across these intervals. Finally, choose the rates which most closely match market prices, possibly subject to constraints.

The term structure is not uniquely determined. Rather, it depends on its inputs: the choice of bond universe and relative weightings of the bonds, economic factors used, variable constraints, and the precise form of the objective function. The number of parameters in the model depends on the quantity and reliability of the data as well as the way in which bonds are distributed across the maturity spectrum.

Once a term structure is determined, it can be used to compute fair value of bonds not in the estimation universe. Fair value of a bond can be used for the purposes of identifying trading opportunities, performing rich/cheap analysis by comparing fair value against the market price, or for marking portfolios of untraded assets to market.

Of course, the results have to be interpreted with caution. The parameters estimated for each of the market are only as good as the data used in estimating them. Ideally, all the prices used should reflect trades occurring at approximately the same time. In practice, this is rarely the case. The source of a price is often a trader's assessment of a fair market value rather than a report of an actual traded price.

Yield Spread Model

Equation (1) can be enhanced to value straight non-sovereign bonds with the addition of a *yield spread model*. To construct a simple spread model, divide the universe of bonds into sectors based on industry, rating, liquidity, tax features, or other factors relating to the bond issuer or to the bond itself. Each sector is assigned a value or *spread* which affects a bond's model value according to a normalized quantity called an exposure. In some models, an exposure is either 0 or 1. For example, a financial bond has exposure 0 to the industrial spread, while an industrial bond has exposure 1. The total spread of a bond is calculated by multiplying the bond's exposure to each sector spread by the sector spread and summing over sectors:

$$\kappa(t) = \sum_i x_i(t) s_i(t) \tag{2}$$

$\kappa(t)$ = Bond spread at time t
$x_i(t)$ = Bond exposure to i-th sector spread at time t
$s_i(t)$ = i-th sector spread at time t

As we will see in the next section, the spread captures the level of credit risk associated with the rating and sector of the bond.

The bond is valued as in equation (1) with the term structure adjusted by the total spread. In mathematical terms, this is

$$PM(t) = \sum_T cf(T) e^{-[s(t, T) + \kappa(t)](T - t)} + \varepsilon(t)$$

$$= (PF(t) + \varepsilon(t)) \tag{3}$$

Stochastic Interest Rate Model

The third ingredient needed for bond valuation is a *stochastic interest rate model*. This is a probabilistic view of how the term structure will evolve in the future and it is used to value bonds with uncertain future cash flows. A taxonomy of interest models is found elsewhere in this book. There are many standard interest rate models in the literature and the choice of model may have a large impact on the model value of a bond.

Customizing the Model

As mentioned previously, it is important to customize each of the model components to the institutional characteristics of the specific market. Features such as trading conventions vary from market to market. For example, the buyer of a German bund or a U.S. Treasury bond begins to accrue interest as of settlement date. However, a buyer of a French OAT accrues interest as of the trade date and the buyer of an Italian BTP for domestic settlement accrues interest as of the trade date plus three market days plus one calendar day. Similarly, the custody of the coupon goes to the buyer as of settlement date for a Japanese JGB, but as of trade date for a Swiss SGB.[7] Further, the settlement rules differ between markets and bond types. An Australian CGS settles at trade date plus three market days. In the United States, Treasury bonds settle at trade date plus one market day while corporate bonds settle at trade date plus three market days. Details such as these need to be handled in the local implementations of valuation formulas.

Markets differ in obvious ways such as size, distribution of bonds across the maturity spectrum, and investor willingness to substitute bonds of different maturities for one another. These considerations may render it necessary to vary the number of rates calculated. In the same spirit, it may be important to incorporate liquidity properties into the valuation model, since benchmark bonds generally trade at a premium and illiquid bonds generally trade at a discount. In markets where this is a nontrivial effect, extra parameters in the form of "valuation spreads" can be added to the term structure objective function. However, this may have undesirable consequences since adding parameters may over-determine the model in some markets.

Exhibit 3 lists the G7 countries together with the time to maturity of the longest bond, and the total number of traded, actively traded and benchmark bonds as defined by J.P. Morgan as of March 1996. Notice that Japan is an extreme example in that there is a single benchmark bond which typically accounts for over 50% of the total trading volume. This fact alone may have a subtle but important impact on model design. Suppose a benchmark spread is included in the objective function for the Japanese term structure. The benchmark bond will then be priced exactly by the model, but it will have no impact on the estimated forward rates.

Valuation equations (1) and (3) must be modified to account for complicated bond characteristics such as embedded call and put options, optional extensions of maturity date, coupons which float according to an index, and sinking funds. In fact, the category of sinking funds incorporates many variants. In some cases the principal of individual bonds are repaid (sunk) according to a predetermined schedule. In other cases, a certain fraction of the total issue is sunk according to schedule; bonds to be sunk are selected by lottery. Sinking funds can have purchase options, which means that the issuer can redeem bonds by open market purchases, or they can have acceleration factors, where the fraction of the issue to be sunk can be increased by the issuer. Particular types of bonds are characteristic of certain markets during certain periods of time, and they contribute to the "personality" of their markets. As an example, there are many sovereign sinking funds in Denmark and Netherlands but none in Sweden. Historically, U.S. Treasury bonds are never sinkable but U.S corporate bonds frequently are.

---

[7] In particular, a Swiss SGB can have accrued interest that exceeds a coupon.

Exhibit 3: Horizon and Liquidity Breakdown of Estimation Universe (March 1, 1996)

Market	Maturity of the Longest Bond (Years)	Traded	Active	Benchmark
Canada	29.25	11	16	5
France	29.65	6	18	4
Germany	27.84	14	52	5
Italy	27.67	11	14	4
Japan	19.56	43	17	3
United Kingdom	25.27	8	21	4
United States	29.96	139	10	5

Source: JP Morgan

Assessing the Proposed Valuation Model

We will now describe an approach to assess the proposed valuation model. A natural measure is the root mean square of the pricing errors of the bonds.

$$RMSE(t) = \left[\frac{1}{nbonds} \sum_i (PM_i(t) - PF_i(t))^2 \right]^{1/2} \tag{4}$$

$RMSE(t)$ = Root mean square error at time t

$nbonds$ = Number of bonds in the universe at time t

$PM_i(t)$ = Market price of bond i at time t

$PF_i(t)$ = Model or fitted price of bond i at time t

However, equation (4) has to be used with care. The model will price all bonds perfectly if the number of rates is at least equal to the number of bonds. On the other hand, if there are fewer rates than bonds, a single data error might cause the root mean square error to be very large when in fact, most bonds are being priced very well. More seriously, a large data error can have significant impact on rates and skew the entire model. One way to handle this is to rerun the term structure estimation repeatedly, discarding outliers between iterations, until no outliers above a certain threshold remain. Then the model is reasonable if typically, the root mean square pricing error is small, the fraction of bonds discarded is small, and the number of bonds is much higher than the number of rates. Exhibit 4 shows these values for the G7 countries for term structures estimated by BARRA for March 1, 1996.

RISK ANALYSIS

As mentioned in the introduction, the dominant source of the total risk to a portfolio of international bonds is currency risk.[8] Other substantial risks come from within individual markets. These include fluctuations in the term structure of interest rates and credit risk. In precise terms, the *risk* or *volatility* of a portfolio can be defined as the standard deviation of excess returns to the portfolio. Here, *excess return* means the return over and above the return on a riskless investment.

An important related concept is the *active risk* or *tracking error* of a portfolio with respect to a benchmark. This is the standard deviation of the difference between the return to the benchmark and the return to the portfolio. Here, large sources of risk such as currency risk and risk due to parallel shift are typically hedged away. What dominates are higher order sources of local market risk and idiosyncratic or *specific risk*. These concepts will be discussed in more detail below.

Implicit in these definitions is a time horizon over which the return is calculated. In the discussion below, the horizon is taken to be one month. Note that, under the hypothesis that returns over any horizon are independent, the risk of a portfolio scales with the square root of the time horizon. Consequently, a 1-month horizon model can be scaled to give risk estimates over different horizons.

This section outlines the construction of a multi-factor global risk model. The model expresses excess portfolio return as a linear combination of basic variables whose covariance matrix is estimated within the model.

$$EPR = \sum_i x_i(EPR) \cdot r_i + \varepsilon \qquad (5)$$

$$
\begin{aligned}
EPR &= \text{excess portfolio return} \\
x_i(EPR) &= \text{exposure of excess portfolio return to } i\text{-th factor} \\
r_i &= \text{return to } i\text{-th factor} \\
\varepsilon &= \text{error}
\end{aligned}
$$

Hence, the total risk of a portfolio is given by:

$$\sigma_p = sd(EPR) = (h^T[X^T FX + D]h)^{1/2} \qquad (6)$$

Exhibit 4: Term Structure Estimation Diagnostics (March 1, 1996)

	RMSE	Fraction of Bonds Discarded	Number of Bonds	Number of Rates
Canada	0.11	0	32	8
France	0.24	0	28	8
Germany	0.22	0	71	8
Italy	0.22	0	29	8
Japan	0.32	$\frac{1}{64}$	63	7
United Kingdom	0.25	0	33	8
United States	0.33	0	154	8

Source: BARRA

---

[8] This statement applies to a portfolio of sovereign and investment-grade corporate bonds. If "junk" bonds are part of the portfolio, credit risk may become the dominant source of risk.

σ_p = portfolio risk
h = portfolio holdings
X = bond exposures to factors
F = covariance matrix of factor returns
D = diagonal matrix of bond specific variances

The active risk of a portfolio with respect to a benchmark is obtained by replacing the portfolio holdings h with the difference $h_P - h_B$ between the portfolio holdings and the benchmark holdings in equation (6).

Also, given the above calculation for risk, a portfolio's value-at-risk (VAR) can be computed.

$$VAR = s_p \cdot \text{portfolio value} \tag{7}$$

Assuming normal distributions, the probability of losing VAR is 16%.

The strategy for estimating the global risk model is to construct a consistent family of local market risk models as well as a currency risk model. These components are pieced together into a global covariance matrix that accounts for linkages existing across markets and currencies. This covariance matrix is used as in equation (6) to forecast portfolio risk.

Local Market Risk: Variation in Term Structure

In any given market, changes in the term structure of interest rates account for most of the risk of sovereign and highly rated corporate bonds. In fact, in the U.S. bond market, interest rate fluctuations account for approximately 90% of the total portfolio risk. The remaining 10% is attributable to risks due to sector membership, quality rating, relative coupon, liquidity, and covariance factors. Exhibit 5 shows the decomposition of variance of return for a portfolio consisting of all U.S. corporate bonds with a minimum maturity of one year as of March 1, 1996. This exhibit illustrates the fact that interest rate factor is the dominant element of risk *within* a market.

Exhibit 5: Decomposition of Variance of Return
(BARRA All Corporate Index, March 1, 1996)

Source of Risk	Variance (%)
Interest rate effects	45.36
Quality and sector factors	7.23
Liquidity and maturity-dependent factors	2.80
Covariance terms	−5.36
Issue specific	0.01
Total	50.04

Source: BARRA

Exhibit 6: Monthly Standard Deviation/Correlation Matrix for the Japanese Market (January 1, 1988 - March 1, 1996)

	1 year	2 years	3 years	4 years	5 years	7 years	10 years	20 years
1 year	**0.003053**	0.706883	0.774184	0.740236	0.710354	0.605757	0.635143	0.550866
2 years		**0.003098**	0.963059	0.937033	0.900919	0.808655	0.77927	0.683171
3 years			**0.003159**	0.973894	0.943082	0.844661	0.842492	0.711944
4 years				**0.003107**	0.969274	0.895337	0.877645	0.724096
5 years					**0.003129**	0.895042	0.875251	0.753634
7 years						**0.002743**	0.914243	0.757892
10 years							**0.002425**	0.796097
20 years								**0.00224**

Source: BARRA

Theoretically, the term structure is a 1-dimensional curve specifying a discount rate for each time to maturity. To describe the change in term structure, it is convenient to use the discrete approximation outlined in the previous section of this chapter. Hence, for the purposes of this discussion, a term structure is given by a set of distinguished vertices and a discount or spot rate at each of the vertices. Discount rates between vertices are obtained by interpolation. Earlier in this chapter, interpolation based on the assumption of constant forward rates between vertices was mentioned. Other schemes such as piecewise linear interpolation or cubic splines could be used.

An intuitively appealing local market risk model is based on changes in interest rates at the vertices. A local market covariance matrix can be estimated from a time series over a particular data history. The dimension of the matrix is given by the number of vertices used to determine the term structure. Of course, the estimate obtained depends on the time window used, and whether or not the data are weighted to give more importance to recent observations. Assume for the purpose of discussion that these finer points of model structure have been settled.

Exhibit 6 shows a standard deviation/correlation matrix[9] for changes in spot rates for the Japanese market during the period January 1, 1988 through March 1, 1996. Eight vertices at times to maturity 1, 2, 3, 4, 5, 7, 10, and 20 years are used. A glance at the matrix diagonal illustrates the well known assertion that short rates are more volatile than long rates. It is also immediate from this exhibit that there is more to risk than a parallel shift. For if interest rates moved in parallel, the diagonal elements would have the same value and the off-diagonal elements would be equal to 1. This illustrates a point emphasized in the introduction. Duration, the sensitivity of returns to parallel shifts in the yield curve, is an inadequate measure of risk.

Further inspection of Exhibit 6 shows that while interest rates may not move in parallel, changes in interest rates at different times to maturity are highly correlated. This suggests that there may be a more concise way to capture the information held in an 8×8 covariance matrix of interest rate changes.

---

[9] This is an upper triangular matrix with standard deviations on the diagonal and correlations in the upper triangle. This matrix determines and is determined by the corresponding covariance matrix.

Exhibit 7: Percentage of Variance Explained by Principal Components in the Japanese Market

Number of Principal Components	Percentage of Variance Explained
1	84.98
2	91.48
3	95.40
4	97.58
5	98.62
6	99.44
7	99.78
8	100.00

Source: BARRA

Exhibit 8: Percentage of Variance Explained by Three Principal Components in the G7 Countries

Country	Percentage of variance explained by three principal components (%)
Canada	95.65
France	97.10
Germany	96.05
Italy	94.15
Japan	95.40
United Kingdom	97.21
United States	98.60

Source: BARRA

One way to pursue this is to convert from changes in interest rates to distinguished linear combinations of changes in interest rates. This can be done by a *principal components analysis*[10] which captures the largest percentage of variance possible. Exhibit 7 shows the cumulative percentage of variance explained by the 8 principal components of the Japanese covariance matrix. Evidently, by taking the first three principal components, in excess of 95% of the variance can be captured. This phenomenon is not isolated to the Japanese market. Exhibit 8 shows the percentage of variance captured by 3 principal components in each of the G7 countries.

It is an empirical fact, related to the high correlations among changes in interest rates, that the first principal component of a covariance matrix of changes in

---

[10] A principal components analysis decomposes NxN covariance matrix (or more generally, any symmetric matrix) into a sum of N rank 1 matrices generated by the normalized eigenvectors of the original matrix. See Richard A. Johnson and Dean W. Wichern, *Applied Multivariate Statistical Analysis* (Prentice Hall, 1992), pp. 356-395 for more details.

term structures looks roughly, though not exactly, like a parallel shift. This movement is termed *shift* and is viewed as the generalized movement whereby all rates move in the same direction. The shift factor shape for most markets is observed to be downward sloping with maturity, supporting the empirical evidence that short rates are more volatile than long rates. The shift factor has the highest explanatory power of all principal components for each market.

The second factor is a *twist* in the term structure. The twist shape reflects the short and long ends of the curve moving in opposite directions and gives rise to a steepening or flattening of the yield curve. The third factor is called a *butterfly*. The butterfly shape corresponds to the short and long ends moving in the opposite direction from intermediate rates.

The first three principal components of the German, Japanese, and U.S. markets are depicted in Exhibit 9. These principal components are similar in shape across all markets, but vary only in magnitude and the pivot points.

It is interesting to contrast the three factor model with the more traditional risk models given by duration or duration and convexity. A duration model is a one factor model with the single factor given by a parallel shift of the term structure. This is directly comparable to a one factor model given by a shift. But a shift is optimized to capture the maximum variance possible by a single factor and hence accounts for more risk than duration. That is, the shift factor can be viewed as a more generalized form of duration, hence it is expected to explain more local market risk than duration.

Exhibit 10 illustrates the difference in fraction of variance captured by the traditional duration and duration/convexity models along with the shift/twist/butterfly model.

The consistency of the shapes of the first three principal components along with the high fraction of variance they explain in each market support the premise that a reasonable way to build a global risk model is to use three empirical principal components as risk factors in each market. This approach has the added advantage of lowering the dimension of the global covariance matrix. This is important insofar as the data histories of some markets are not long enough to support a global matrix with 8 or 9 factors per country.

Once the factors are determined, the change in term structure over each period is approximated as closely as possible by a linear combination of the factors. The coefficients of the factors are the factor returns, and the history of these returns form the data series on which the 3×3 local market covariance matrix is based.

Local Market Risk: Credit

Unlike sovereign bonds, corporate bonds are exposed to default risk. Within our framework, this can be handled with the addition of one or more risk factors to each local market. Only corporate bonds will have a nonzero exposure to this factor.

Exhibit 9: First Three Principal Components:
U.S.A., Germany, and Japan

U.S.A.

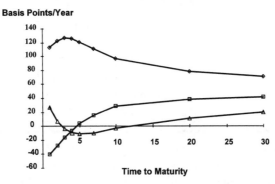

Germany

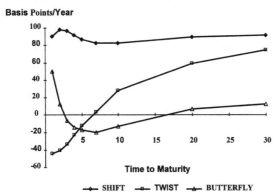

Japan

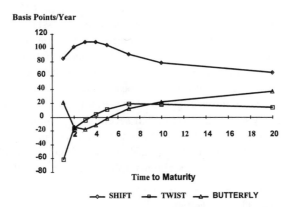

Exhibit 10: Comparison of Percentage of variance Captured by Duration, Duration/Convexity, and Shift/Twist/Butterfly

Country	STB	DC	D
Canada	95.6	88.9	76.7
France	97.1	90.1	81.4
Germany	96.0	90.9	76.7
Italy	94.1	81.7	72.7
Japan	95.4	88.2	79.9
United Kingdom	97.2	88.7	72.9
United States	98.6	94.8	87.8

A natural way to proceed within each market is to segregate the bonds into sectors based on rating, estimate a constant spread for each sector, and add the history of changes in spread to the collection of data series used to generate the covariance matrix. Unsurprisingly, this intuitive approach presents difficulties. The first is that there are many sectors in each market so the size of the matrix will be vastly increased, possibly beyond the natural bounds imposed by the length of the data history. The second issue is one of robustness. The size of a sector can be quite variable over time and at certain times, the spread may be determined by little data. This introduces excessive noise into the estimation.

An alternative is to add a single factor per market, given by the change in spread of the swap curve (approximately a double A rating curve) over the sovereign curve. The change in spread is a robust quantity which captures credit risk.

Currency Risk

In an unhedged portfolio, fluctuations in currency exchange rates are the dominant source of risk. At the same time, they are also the most challenging to model. Currency return series are highly non-stationary. In other words, it is not possible to postulate a single distribution with constant variance to which all the observations in a given time series of currency returns belong. For example, many European currencies were linked together until 1993 when internal economic pressures in many countries caused the ERM[11] crisis. During this period, currencies became unlinked and a period of high volatility followed. Another example is the dramatic fall of the Mexican peso in December 1994 when it lost over 50% of its value with respect to the U.S. dollar. This led to a period of high volatility for the peso-dollar exchange rate.

The discussion above suggests three principles which may be useful in forecasting currency risk. The first is that recent data should be weighted much more heavily than older data. The second is an inertia type principle that exchange rates which are volatile tend to stay volatile while exchange rates that are stable tend to stay stable. Finally, the model must account for external shocks. An econo-

---

[11] ERM stands for European Rate Mechanism.

metric strategy to handle this type of behavior is a GARCH (Generalized Auto Regressive Conditional Heteroskedasticity) model.

A typical[12] GARCH model is specified by the following set of equations.

$$r_t = \text{realized return from time } t \text{ to } t+1 = u + \varepsilon_t \tag{8}$$

$$u = \text{expected return}$$

$$\varepsilon_t = \sqrt{h_t} \cdot Z_t$$

$$Z_t \sim N(0,1)$$

$$h_t = \text{variance forecast at time } t \text{ for period } t \text{ to } t+1$$

$$= c + ah_{t-1}(Z_{t-1}^2 - 1) + b(h_{t-1} - c)$$

$$= c + a(\varepsilon_{t-1}^2 - h_{t-1}) + b(h_{t-1} - c)$$

As can be seen in equation (8), the parameters a, b, and c represent the shock[13] effect, the persistence,[14] and the long-term average respectively. GARCH models are especially suited to currency risk forecasts since they take shocks or regime shifts into consideration.

Exhibit 11 shows a graph of GARCH volatility forecasts along with the $/ Yen exchange rate. The GARCH volatility forecast stays close to its long-term predicted average during periods of stable exchange rates. But during periods of large fluctuations in the $/Yen exchange rates, the model quickly adapts as is evident from the increased volatility.

Integrating the Model

As explained at the beginning of this section, the risk model takes the form of a covariance matrix of factor returns. The discussion above describes local market factors, namely term structure and credit risk, and currency factors that facilitate the analysis of an international bond portfolio from the perspective of a single numeraire or base currency.

The two types of factor returns have rather different statistical properties. While the currency returns are highly non-stationary, empirical studies carried out at BARRA show that the local market returns tend to be roughly normal. As a consequence, it is plausible to estimate the local market block using a maximum likelihood estimate based on a normal distribution. As described in the section above, GARCH models are used to estimate the currency block.

---

[12] The formula here is a GARCH (1,1) model. There are many types of GARCH models, a general reference is Tim Bollerslev, "Generalized Autoregressive Conditional Heteroskedasticity," *Journal of Economics*, 31 (1986), pp. 307-327.

[13] The shock is determined by the impact of a two sigma event on a GARCH model at its long term average.

[14] The persistence determines the number of periods it takes to get halfway back to the log term average.

Exhibit 11: GARCH Model Volatility, U.S.$/Yen Exchange Rate, 1/94-6/96

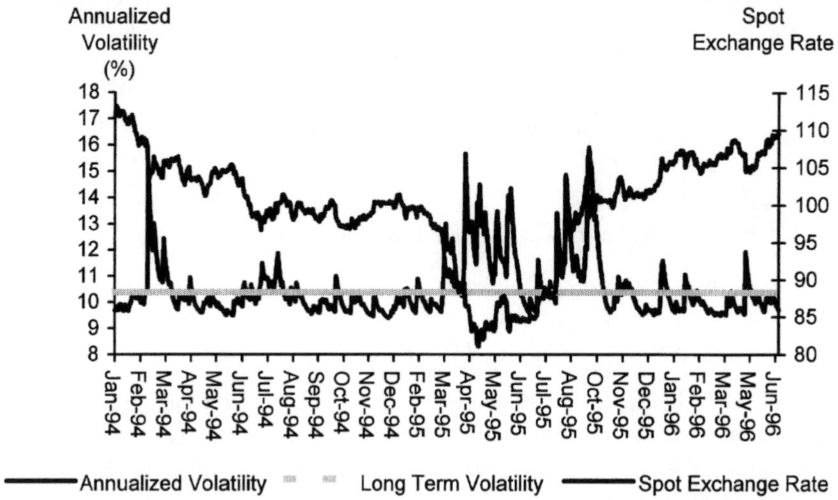

Finally, historical estimates are used to estimate covariances between local market factors and currency factors.

The final covariance matrix supports risk analysis. Additionally, it can provide return forecasts for countries outside the model by making use of correlations between markets.

Factor Exposures

To complete the analysis of equation (6), it remains to explain how to compute exposures. The *exposure* or *sensitivity* of portfolio return to a risk factor is simply the change in portfolio return with respect to a small, or infinitesimal change in the factor return.

Consider first the case of a single bond. Its exposure to a currency risk factor is 1 or 0 depending on whether or not the bond is denominated in the currency associated to the factor. Similarly, the bond's exposure to a local market factor will be 0 if the bond does not belong the local market. For a bond's exposure to the local factors in its own market, simple formulas can be used to compute the exposure. For example, the exposure of a straight German bond to the German shift is given by

$$x = \frac{1}{P}\frac{\Delta P}{\Delta shift} = \frac{1}{P}\sum_{j} cf_j T_j e^{-s_j T_j} \cdot shift_j$$

x = exposure of German bond to German shift
P = price of German bond
cf_j = j-th cash flow

$$T_j \quad = \quad \text{time to maturity of } j\text{-th cash of flow}$$
$$s_j \quad = \quad \text{spot rate at time to maturity } T_j$$
$$shift_j \quad = \quad \text{weight of shift factor at time to maturity } T$$

Note that if the shift were parallel, the shift weights ($shift_j$) would all be 1. In this case, the shift exposure is simply the duration.

Once the bond exposures are known, portfolio exposures are simply weighted averages of bond exposures. To be precise, the exposure of a portfolio to a factor is given by

$$x(P) = h \cdot X = \sum_i h_i x(B_i)$$

$$x(P) \quad = \quad \text{portfolio exposure}$$
$$B_i \quad = \quad i\text{-th bond}$$
$$h_i \quad = \quad \text{portfolio market weight of } B_i$$
$$x(B_i) \quad = \quad \text{exposure of } i\text{-th bond}$$
$$h \quad = \quad \text{vector of portfolio holdings}$$
$$X \quad = \quad \text{matrix of bond exposures}$$

With this calculation complete, it is possible to derive portfolio risk estimates using equation (6).

The factor exposure as explained above measures the sensitivity of a bond to the underlying factor. For example, a shift exposure will measure the sensitivity of the bond to a shift event. That is, the shift exposure would be the return on the bond if the underlying term structure were to move by the shift movement in that market. This approach allows a manager to compare various bonds in the portfolio based on their sensitivities and target their portfolio exposure profile according to their risk/return expectations. This is a similar, yet richer, approach to adjusting the duration of the portfolio to a certain target. It encompasses the major factors that contribute to the variability of portfolio returns. Portfolios that are more highly exposed to these factors than the benchmark, even if duration-matched, can exhibit substantially different returns from the benchmark.

SUMMARY

This chapter has presented a framework for constructing valuation models for international fixed income securities. The valuation approach presented is based on the estimation of interest rates (or term structures) and spreads in each market. Interest rates are the primary determinant in computing the value of a security. The valuation model is further refined by taking into account the market specific factors that distinguish assets from one another.

A multi-factor risk model is developed that quantifies various sources of risk. It takes into account factors, namely, interest rates, currencies and spreads, that contribute to risk in a multi-currency fixed income portfolio. A covariance matrix that embodies the volatilities and correlations of the various factors is constructed using observed returns to these factors. Portfolio risk is calculated by measuring the exposure of each of the asset in the portfolio to these risk factors and mapping the factor exposures into the covariance matrix.

These factors provide more explanatory power than a simple duration based model or a duration and convexity based model. These factors provide further intuition into interest rate risk due to non-parallel term structure movements, such as steepening and flattening or reshaping. Particular emphasis is placed on outlining a currency model since currency risk is the major source of risk in an international bond portfolio.

This approach enables portfolio managers to formulate their strategies by separating out the local market or bond decisions from currency decisions. At the same time it also enables calculation of aggregate portfolio statistics like value-at-risk and identifying, monitoring, and controlling the bets in a portfolio.

Chapter 13

Tax Effects in U.S. Government Bond Markets

Ehud I. Ronn, Ph.D.
Professor of Finance
University of Texas at Austin

Yongjai Shin
Debt Markets Group
Merrill Lynch & Co.

INTRODUCTION

The pricing of non-callable U.S. government bonds and notes is simplified by the deterministic nature of the cash flows: this is, in essence, a present value calculation, using the "term structure of interest rates." Several researchers have found that the pricing errors on such valuation exercises frequently differ from zero.[1] There are a number of factors which have been proposed to explain these price discrepancies: (1) non-simultaneous or erroneous price quotes; (2) liquidity effects of "on-the-run"/"off-the-run" bonds;[2] (3) tax clientele/market segmenta-

---

[1] See J. Huston McCulloch, "Measuring the Term Structure of Interest Rates," *Journal of Business* (1971), pp. 19-31; and J. Huston McCulloch, "The Tax-Adjusted Yield Curve," *Journal of Finance* (1975), pp. 811-830.

[2] See Avraham Kamara, "Liquidity and Short-Term Treasury Yields," Working Paper, University of Washington, 1990; Yakov Amihud and Haim Mendelson, "Liquidity, Maturity and the Yields on U.S. Treasury Securities," *Journal of Finance* (September 1991), pp. 1411-1425; and Arthur Warga, "Bond Returns, Liquidity and Missing Data," Working Paper, Columbia University, 1991. A particularly elegant test of liquidity may be found in the Amihud and Mendelson results. They contrast the yields on Treasury Bonds/Notes with those of Treasury Bills of matched maturities of less than six months and find that the less liquid Notes have higher yields than those of the comparable Bills. Kamara has independently obtained similar results.

The authors acknowledge the helpful comments and suggestions of Michael Berry, Rob Bliss, Gia He, Dilip Madan, Frank Milne, Karlyn Mitchell, and the participants at finance seminars at the University of Pennsylvania, New York University and the University of Maryland. The views expressed in this chapter are solely those of the authors', and not those of Merrill Lynch & Co.

tion in bond markets;[3] and, (4) tax timing option effects.[4] The multiple and potentially confounding influences of these alternative effects have complicated attempts to address these issues. In this chapter, we follow the approach taken by Litzenberger and Rolfo and use triplets of premium or discount bonds with identical maturity dates, a procedure that obviates the need for the estimation of the term structure of interest rates.[5]

Two primary reasons give rise to a worthwhile effort at reexamining the issues visited in the study by Litzenberger and Rolfo. First, the substantial increase in the national debt has provided a significantly larger number of triplets, both premium and discount. Second, the Tax Reform Acts of 1984 and 1986 altered the tax treatment of subsequently issued discount and premium bonds, respectively, thus providing an additional opportunity to examine the effects of taxation on the pricing of U.S. government bonds and notes.

Specifically, the Tax Reform Act of 1986 altered the tax treatment of the amortization of bond premiums. Previously, for taxable investors, any premium paid for a bond in excess of the amount payable at maturity could be amortized over the bond's life by any method regularly employed by the taxpayer, so long as it was "reasonable." The linear amortization rule is the most widely used method for these bonds. The 1986 act still permits these method(s) for bonds issued before September 28, 1985. However, for bonds issued after September 27, 1985, premiums must be amortized by the so-called "constant yield method," which is less favorable to taxable investors in present value terms as it reduces the amount of amortization in the early years in favor of greater amortization in the later years. For this change to have significant price impact, there must exist sufficient investable wealth in the tax-paying category.

The Tax Reform Act of 1984 altered the tax treatment of discount bonds. Previously, if a discount bond were held to maturity, the discount was recognized as a capital gains on the maturity date. The 1984 act grandfathered this capital-gains appreciation to par in all bonds issued prior to July 18, 1984, forcing later-issued

---

[3] See Stephen M. Schaefer, "Tax Induced Clientele Effects in the Market for British Government Securities," *Journal of Financial Economics* (July 1982), pp. 121-159; and Ehud I. Ronn, "A New Linear Programming Approach to Bond Portfolio Management," *Journal of Financial and Quantitative Analysis* (December 1987), pp. 439-466. The tax clientele effect first proposed by Schaefer posits that investors specialize in their holdings of coupon bonds in accordance with the bonds' after-tax cash flows. If investable wealth in bond markets is sufficiently diffused through the different tax brackets and/or specific issues have relatively small amounts outstanding, only the subset of "rationally held" bonds will be fairly priced to any specific tax bracket investor.

[4] See George M. Constantinides and Jonathan E. Ingersoll, Jr., "Optimal Bond Trading with Personal Taxes," *Journal of Financial Economics* (September 1984), pp. 299-335. Constantinides and Ingersoll were the first to examine in detail the impact of a tax-timing option on bond prices. They noted that bondholders have an option to realize short term losses and defer gains for tax purposes, and showed that this tax consideration may represent a significant factor in the pricing of bonds.

[5] Robert H. Litzenberger and Jacques Rolfo, "Arbitrage Pricing, Transaction Costs and Taxation of Capital Gains, A Study of Government Bonds with the Same Maturity Date," *Journal of Financial Economics* (1984), pp. 337-351.

bonds to recognize that (fully predictable) appreciation as ordinary income. For the 1984 change to have significant price impact, there must exist sufficiently numerous investors for whom the difference between the ordinary income and capital gains rate is substantial. Prior to January 1, 1991,[6] with the Tax Reform Act of 1986 in effect, this applied only to the investors in the so-called "bubble," i.e., investors whose marginal tax rates temporarily climb above 28% (to 33%) as their deductions are phased out. In contrast, for the premium-bond effect of 1986 to result in a price impact requires only that there exist (sufficiently wealthy) *taxable* investors. We thus devote more attention to the premium bond taxation issue than to its discount counterpart.

These changes of tax code provide an excellent opportunity for studying the impact of taxation on bond values. By definition, tax-exempt investors will be indifferent to the amortization properties of premium bonds or the appreciation treatment of bonds selling at a discount. In this chapter, we examine the pricing of the tax code-induced distinction between "grandfathered" and new (non-grandfathered) bonds and examine the pricing discrepancies between them while accounting for the simultaneous presence of tax clientele, tax timing and liquidity effects. We find that the bond market does indeed price these tax-code related properties, thus leading to the conclusion that no single tax bracket (including the tax-exempt bracket) is the sole price-determining investor class in U.S. government bond markets.

THE PRICE-COUPON RELATIONSHIP

Market Segmentation and Tax-Timing Option Effects

Following the analysis of Litzenberger and Rolfo, we analyze Treasury bond triplets with identical maturity dates and different coupons. Consider the relationship between the prices of coupon bonds with the same maturity date and all selling at a premium or discount:[7]

$$P = C \, AN_T + 100 DF_T \tag{1}$$

where

$$
\begin{aligned}
P &= \text{Price} \\
C &= \text{Coupon} \\
AN_T &= \text{Annuity factor for maturity T} \\
DF_T &= \text{Discount factor for maturity T}
\end{aligned}
$$

Let P_i, $i = 1, 2, 3$ be the prices of bonds i, all maturing on the same date and selling at a premium, and let c_i be their corresponding coupon rates. We assume, without loss of generality, $c_1 < c_2 < c_3$ and $P_1 < P_2 < P_3$.[8] In an economy where

---

[6] Effective January 1, 1991, the top marginal tax rate was increased to 31%. A 39.6% tax bracket became the highest effective tax rate on January 1, 1993.

[7] Due to the asymmetric tax treatment of premium and discount bonds, we examine each type separately.

prices are determined by *tax-exempt* investors, an equilibrium would be reached where the relationship between the bonds in each triplet is linear. For such investors, the cash flow of the intermediate bond can be replicated by an appropriate combination of the other two. Thus, assuming no bid-ask spread, no constraints on short-selling and/or the absence of the segmentation of bond holdings, the following no-arbitrage relationship should hold:

$$P_2 = xP_1 + (1 - x)P_3 \tag{2}$$

where $x = (c_3 - c_2)/(c_3 - c_1)$. Without taxes, or with a single implicit marginal tax rate determining the prices of all coupon bonds — and *linear* amortization rules for the bond premium or discount — the price-coupon relationship is linear, with the (possibly after-tax) annuity factor AN_T constituting the slope of P on C in equation (1).

Without a single implicit tax rate, the price-coupon relationship will be non-linear. Absent grandfathering provisions based on bonds' issue dates, we argue that relationship will be *convex*.

Consider first the tax-clientele/market segmentation hypothesis, where short sales are precluded or prohibitively costly. Taxable investors, who value the right to amortize the bond premium to maturity, will tend to bid up the prices of high premium bonds. Further, if a discount bond's appreciation to par is treated as a capital gain, taxable investors whose ordinary income tax rate exceeded their capital gains rate would bid up the prices of deep discount bonds.

Investors' desire to consider the after-tax status of their bond investments, and the consequent tendency towards bond holdings specialization, is clear. However, whether such tax-clientele inclinations result in an *observable* price impact hinges on (1) the distribution of investable wealth across tax-exempt and taxable economic agents, and (2) the size of outstanding issues: if investable wealth is sufficiently diffused across tax brackets, and/or specific issues have relatively small amounts outstanding, then market prices will indeed reflect such clientele effects. These effects, if manifested in market prices, will result in a convex price-coupon relationship.

Turning now to the tax-timing option,[9] rational bondholders will optimize the realization of capital gains and losses over time — usually by realizing short-term losses and deferring gains — to minimize taxation. Litzenberger and Rolfo noted the potential price impact of the tax-timing option for bond triplets: the intermediate bond should be less valuable than an (appropriately-weighted) combination of two extreme bonds, since the "value of a portfolio of tax options is higher than a single tax option on the portfolio of underlying securities." Hence, if it does have an observable market-price effect, tax-timing will also give rise to a convex relationship between P and C.

Equivalently, since an *x*-weighted portfolio of bonds 1 and 3 offers cash flows identical to bond 2, but the additional tax timing option opportunities of selling

---

[8] Any violation of $P_1 < P_2 < P_3$ given $c_1 < c_2 < c_3$ is discarded as a data error.
[9] Constantinides and Ingersoll, "Optimal Bond Trading with Personal Taxes."

only one bond or the other, the market segmentation or tax timing hypotheses will both tend to produce bond prices which are convex in their coupon rates:

$$P_2 < xP_1 + (1 - x)P_3 \tag{3}$$

The short-sale of government bonds for long periods of time is not possible due to the absence of an active term "repo" market. When there exist violations of the linearity condition, we can infer a tax impact on bond prices. Thus, statistically significant violations would imply either segmentation of holdings across tax clienteles, an economically observable value to the tax-timing option and/or severe institutional impediments to short-selling. If we recognize the complicating factors of the bid/ask spread, transactions costs, nonsynchroneity, no centralized market for bond trading, and potential data errors, empirical analysis will be required to test whether the bond prices are bounded reasonably within a linear pricing relationship, or whether the tax timing and tax clientele effects are manifested in the bonds' market prices.

The Tax Reform Act of 1986

The tax effect induced by the change in premium amortization distinguishes bonds issued before and after September 27, 1985.

To see the impact of this grandfathering provision, let CF_t^{τ} be the after-tax cash flow from a coupon bond at some future time t, where the coupon bond's face value equals unity, and τ is the investor's marginal ordinary income tax rate. Then the after-tax cash flows to a τ-tax bracket investor of a coupon bond issued before September 28, 1985, and currently selling at a premium, is given by

$$CF_t^{\tau} = c(1 - \tau) + \tau \frac{P^a - 1}{T} \qquad t = 1,...,T-1$$

$$CF_t^{\tau} = c(1 - \tau) + \tau \frac{P^a - 1}{T} + 1$$

where

$$
\begin{aligned}
c &= \text{coupon rate} \\
P^a &= \text{current asked price of the bond} \\
t &= \text{a coupon date, } t = 1,..., T \\
T &= \text{maturity date} \\
\text{Par value} &= 1
\end{aligned}
$$

and the premium $P^a - 1$ is amortized linearly

Under the constant yield method, the amortizable bond premium each period is computed on the basis of the bond's before-tax yield to maturity, using the taxpayer's basis for the bond, and compounding at the close of each accrual period. This method implies that for bonds issued after September 27, 1985, the after-tax cash flows are:

$$\text{CF}_t^\tau = c(1 - \tau) + \tau(c - y)\frac{1}{(1 + y)^{T-t+1}} \qquad t = 1,...,T - 1$$

$$\text{CF}_t^\tau = c(1 - \tau) + \tau(c - y)\frac{1}{1 + y} + 1$$

where y = (tax-exempt) yield-to-maturity on the bond, i.e., y such that

$$P^a = c\sum_{t = 1}^{T}\frac{1}{(1 + y)^t} + \frac{1}{(1 + y)^T} = \frac{c}{y}\left[1 - \frac{1}{(1 + y)^T}\right] + \frac{1}{(1 + y)^T}$$

The above cash flow relationships result from applying the tax code provision which calls for the investor's hypothetical rate of return to equal the bond's yield-to-maturity. The proof for this cash flow relationship is provided in the appendix to this chapter.

Note that the present value of premium amortization by the constant yield method will be less than that of its linear amortization counterpart, as the cash flows are more heavily weighted to the latter part of the time to maturity. Mathematically, *if* both the "old" and "new" bonds are fairly priced to the τ-ordinary income tax bracket investor, then the incremental value of the "old" bond versus an identical-maturity and -coupon "new" bond is given by

$$\tau\sum_{t = 1}^{T}\left(\frac{P^a - 1}{T} - \frac{c - y}{(1 + y)^{T-t+1}}\right)\text{PV}(t, \tau)$$

where $\text{PV}(t,\tau)$ is the time t after-tax present value factor to tax bracket τ. However, note that this is not the end of the story, for the yield to maturity has now increased from y to that implied by the lower bond price. The process continues until convergence, at which point the *total* price differential is

$$\Delta(\tau, T, c, y_N) = \tau\sum_{t = 1}^{T}\left[\frac{P^a - 1}{T} - \frac{c - y_N}{(1 + y_N)^{T-t+1}}\right]\text{PV}(t, \tau) > 0 \qquad (4)$$

where y_N is the yield-to-maturity in the final iteration. The positivity of Δ in inequality (4) follows from the time value of money: given the same total premium $P^a - 1$ to be amortized, investors find it desirable to obtain more of the premium in the early years than the later ones.

For $T \le 1$, the total premium is amortized over the current year. Since the amortization does not therefore depend on the method, or the issue date of the bond, the price advantage induced by the 1986 Act must vanish: $\Delta = 0$ for $T \le 1$. It is crucial to recognize that actual market price differentials may differ from the $\Delta(\cdot)$ computed in equation (4) due to the confounding effects of tax timing, tax clientele and/or liquidity effects.

With this in mind, let P_2 and P_3 be the prices of bonds issued before the cut-off date and P_1 the price of the bond issued after the cutoff date.[10] If the disadvantages to the new bond caused by the grandfathering provision of the 1986 Tax Act dominates the tax timing and tax clientele effects, the prices of bonds will be a *concave* function of their coupons:

$$P_1 < x'P_2 + (1 - x')P_3 \tag{5}$$

where $x' = (c_3 - c_1)/(c_3 - c_2)$.

The Tax Reform Act of 1984

The only differential after-tax cash flows to U.S. government bondholders induced by the 1984 tax act occur with respect to the principal payment at maturity. Using the above notation, the "grandfathered" bonds give rise to after-tax payments, inclusive of coupon, of

$$\left[(1 - \tau_O)c - \tau_G\left(1 - P^a\right) + 1\right]\mathrm{PV}(T, \tau_0)$$

where τ_0 (τ_G) is the ordinary (capital gains) tax rate and $\mathrm{PV}(T,\tau_0)$ is as defined above. Conversely, the new bonds give rise to an after-tax cash flow of

$$\left[(1 - \tau_O)c - \tau_0\left(1 - P^a\right) + 1\right]\mathrm{PV}(T, \tau_0)$$

resulting in an after-tax price advantage Δ

$$\Delta(\tau_O, \tau_G, T) = (\tau_0 - \tau_G)(1 - P^a)\mathrm{PV}(T, \tau_0)$$

whenever $\tau_O > \tau_G$.

Considering the discount triplets available in the data for the period following the July 18, 1984 cutoff date, let P_1 and P_2 be the prices of bonds issued before the cutoff date and P_3 the price of the bond issued after the cut-off date, where P_3 is greater than P_1 and P_2. This is the only case observable in the data. Then if the disadvantages to the new bond caused by the grandfathering provision of the 1984 Tax Act dominates the tax timing and tax clientele effects, the prices of bonds will again be a concave function of their coupons:

$$P_3 < x''P_1 + (1 - x'')P_2 \tag{6}$$

where $x'' = (c_1 - c_3)/(c_2 - c_3)$

---

[10] In this case, P_2 and P_3 are larger than P_1. This case constitutes the vast majority of the actual cases in the data, even though there can in principle exist other combinations in which the new bond's price either resides between those of the two older issues, or is greater than the two older bonds.

Exhibit 1: Percentage Holdings of Private Investor Classes in U.S. Government Bonds, 1981 - 1989

	1981	1983	1985	1987	1989
Commercial Banks	18.7%	21.8%	16.2%	13.9%	10.8%
Money Market Funds	3.6%	2.6%	2.1%	1.0%	0.9%
Insurance Companies	4.9%	6.5%	7.9%	7.3%	6.4%
Other Companies	3.0%	4.6%	5.0%	5.9%	5.6%
Individuals	18.6%	15.4%	13.1%	11.9%	12.6%
Foreign and Inter.	23.0%	19.2%	18.1%	20.7%	23.5%
Other misc.	28.2%	30.0%	37.6%	39.3%	40.2%

Exhibit 2: Marginal Tax Rates, 1980 - 1988

	1980		1981 - 1986		1987	1988 - 1992
	τ_O	τ_G	τ_O	τ_G	τ_O/τ_G	τ_O/τ_G
Domestic Banks	46%	46%	46%	46%	34%	34%
Insurance Companies	46%	28%	46%	28%	34%	34%
Individuals	≤ 70%		≤ 50%	40% of τ_O	38.5%	28%
Non-financial Corp.	46%	28%	46%	28%	34%	34%
Foreigners	46%	28%	46%	28%	34%	34%

Notes:
τ_O: Tax rate on ordinary income
τ_G: Tax rate on capital gains

DATA

Taxable Investor Categories

Exhibit 1 reports the percentage holdings across different private investor classes of U.S. government bonds over the decade of the 1980s. Exhibit 2 reports the marginal tax rates for these investor classes for the comparable period. Together, these exhibits demonstrate that investable wealth in U.S. Government Bond markets is indeed diffused across both taxable and tax-exempt investors.

Data Description

Our sample of premium bond triplets consists of 281 sets of price observations contained in the CRSP Government Bond Files. For the definition of a premium bond, the flat ask price is used. As Jordan and Jordan pointed out, this definition is the correct one for tax purposes:[11] according to IRS rules, the basis of the bond is the purchase price plus cost of purchase, but it should not include the accrued interest. As the

---

[11] Bradford D. Jordan and Susan D. Jordan, "Tax Options and the Pricing of Treasury Bond Triplets: Theory and Evidence," *Journal of Financial Economics* (November 1991), pp. 135-164.

accrued interest may be deducted from current-year ordinary income, this rule prevents double-counting of the accrued interest. While the ask price was used in the determination of whether the bond is premium or discount, the mid-point of the bid-ask quote *plus* accrued interest was used as a proxy for the bonds' prices in the concavity/convexity analysis.[12] Callable bonds, flower bonds, tax-exempt issues and original issue discount bonds are excluded.

Among the 776 observations (41 distinct triplets), 243 observations contain prices of bonds all issued before September 1985. An additional 533 triplets consisted of observations in which at least one bond was issued after September 1985 ("new"). For comparative purposes, the period of January 1980 through August 1985 was scanned and 62 observations were retrieved. Exhibit 3 contains a detailed description of the triplets.

Exhibit 3: Description of Premium Bond Triplets
Data Period: September 1985 - December 1990

Data Type	Maturity	Coupons (%)			No. of Observations
Type A	5/15/86	7.875	9.375	13.750	8
	11/15/86	6.125	11.000	13.875	8
	11/15/86	11.000	13.875	16.125	14
	11/15/86	6.125	11.000	16.125	8
	11/15/86	6.125	13.875	16.125	9
	2/15/87	9.000	10.875	12.750	17
	5/15/87	12.000	12.500	14.000	20
	11/15/87	7.625	11.000	12.625	21
	5/15/88	8.250	9.875	10.000	28
	2/15/93	6.750	7.875	10.875	22
	5/15/95	10.375	11.250	12.625	88
Total Number of Observations					243
Type B1	2/15/93	7.875	8.250	10.875	6
	2/15/93	7.875	8.250	10.875	17
	2/15/93	7.875	8.375	10.875	17
	2/15/93	6.750	8.250	10.875	9
	2/15/93	6.750	8.375	10.875	9
	8/15/93	8.625	8.750	11.875	34
	11/15/93	8.625	9.000	11.750	42
Total Number of Observations					134

---

[12] In the study, we were concerned that the ask price might be considered a mechanical "add-on" to the bid price and not representative of true ask prices. A repetition of the analysis using *bid* prices plus interest to proxy for bond prices yielded virtually identical results.

Exhibit 3 (Continued)

Data Type	Maturity	Coupons (%)			No. of Observations
Type B2	11/15/88	8.625	8.750	11.750	24
	5/15/89	6.875	9.250	11.750	10
	11/15/89	6.375	10.750	12.750	1
	5/15/90	7.875	8.250	11.375	5
	8/15/90	7.875	9.875	10.750	5
	2/15/93	6.750	7.875	8.250	9
	2/15/93	6.750	7.875	8.375	9
	8/15/93	8.000	8.625	8.750	20
	8/15/93	8.000	8.625	11.875	23
	11/15/93	7.750	8.625	9.000	25
	11/15/93	7.750	8.625	11.750	25
	8/15/94	6.875	8.750	12.625	17
	8/15/94	8.625	8.750	12.625	35
	11/15/94	6.000	10.125	11.625	14
	11/15/94	8.250	10.125	11.625	31
	2/15/95	5.500	10.500	11.250	7
	2/15/95	7.750	10.500	11.250	25
	5/15/95	5.875	10.375	11.250	8
	5/15/95	5.875	10.375	12.625	8
	5/15/95	5.875	11.250	12.625	8
	5/15/95	8.500	10.375	11.250	30
	5/15/95	8.500	10.375	12.625	30
	5/15/95	8.500	11.250	12.625	30
Total Number of Observations					399

Notes:
1. Type A contains triplets of three "old" bonds.
2. Type B1 contains triplets of two "old" and one "new" bonds. The "new" bond is in the middle.
3. Type B2 contains triplets of "old" and "new" bonds, where the "new" bonds are the highest and/or lowest coupon bond.
4. Both Types A and B triplets exclude those with maturity $\leq$ 1 year.

Descriptive Statistics

We use three statistics to measure the impact of the tax timing option/tax clientele/Tax Reform Acts effects.

Sign Test: The most important statistic repeats the Litzenberger-Rolfo non-parametric test of enumerating the number of convex and concave cases in the data.

Slopes: R denotes the ratio of two slopes for each triplet which is sorted by the magnitude of coupon:

$$R = \frac{\text{slope (2,3)}}{\text{slope (1,2)}} = \frac{(P_3 - P_2)/(c_3 - c_2)}{(P_2 - P_1)/(c_2 - c_1)}$$

This statistic, displayed in Exhibit 4, as well as the price deviation measure described in Exhibit 5, augments the previous non-parametric test by providing a quantitative measure of the effects we are measuring.

Exhibit 4: Definition of R

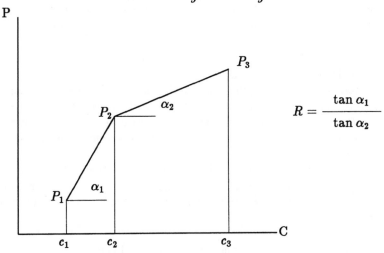

$$R = \frac{\tan \alpha_1}{\tan \alpha_2}$$

Exhibit 5: Definition of Δ

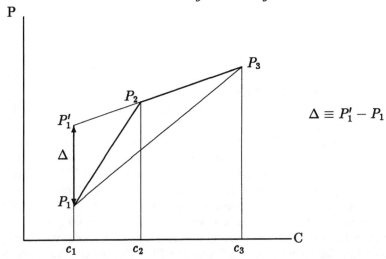

$$\Delta \equiv P_1' - P_1$$

As each triplet is arranged in ascending order to produce positive slopes, $R >$ 1 implies concavity, and $R < 1$ convexity. We calculated the monotonic transformation $\log(R)$ with the objective of making the statistic symmetric and normal with a null hypothesis mean of zero.

For R, the testable implications are as follows. For "old" triplets (Type A) as well as "new" (Type B), the tax-timing option/market segmentation hypotheses imply the convex relationship $R < 1$.

The effect of the Tax Reform Act of 1986 will be to cause a concave result only when the "new" bonds are at the extremes, for their prices will be below otherwise comparable grandfathered bonds. Thus, for "new" triplets of Type B2 only, the effect of the Tax Act of Reform Act of 1986 implies the concave result, $R > 1$.

Price Deviation: Δ denotes the price deviation of one bond from that of the replicating combination of the other two (Exhibit 5).

Across the different types of bond triplets, the definition of Δ is adjusted so that a positive (negative) Δ is associated with concavity (convexity). Note that in contrast to Δ, R is a relative measure of convexity and concavity, because for the same R, the absolute deviation Δ from the linear line will differ depending on the magnitude of the coupon rates.

These two measure will both be taken into consideration for purposes of determining the existence of tax effects. For example, if two of three bonds are quite close in price and coupon, the result can be a fairly large Δ and $\log(R)$ close to 0, or vice versa.

Finally, the null hypothesis for the absence of any tax effects is:

$$H_0: \quad \log (R) = 0$$
$$\Delta = 0$$

RESULTS

Tax Reform Act of 1986

Exhibit 6 presents the results for premium bond triplets by examining the linearity condition $P_2 = xP_1 + (1 - x) P_3$.

For the pre-1982 data, Litzenberger and Rolfo used two alternative data bases to test for linearity. Their results for premium bonds were inconclusive: from the Data Resources, Inc. data base, it was significant (30 out of 34), but not for the CRSP data (34 out of 72) reported in Exhibit 6. Jordan and Jordan corrected the Litzenberger-Rolfo definition of premium bonds by using only the flat price to determine premium bond status, yet the number of violations remains approximately 50% of the cases (14 out of 29). We perform identical tests for the two subperiods period January 1980–September 1985 and September 1985–December 1990. Using triplets of exclusively "old" bonds, we find statistically significant evidence of convexity in both subperiods. Surprisingly, the number of violations of the linearity condition (3) is significantly larger in the second subperiod — 142 convex observations out of 183.

Bond triplets containing two "old"s and one "new" are the sample that we use to test the 1986 Tax Reform Act effect. For this sample, the tax timing option/tax clientele effects and the 1986 Tax Act effect induced by the change in the premium amortization rules mitigate against each other. As the coupons of "new" bonds are always the smallest in this sample, we expect concavity for bond triplets with maturities exceeding 1 year if the 1986 Tax Reform effect prevails.

Turning to the results of these "Type B" triplets in the last column, we find 52 violations of condition (5) out of 73 (71.2%). Thus, we reject linearity in favor of *concavity*. Note that if there were a significant value to liquidity, that effect would augment the value of the "new" bond and would mitigate against concavity. The concavity results we observe are therefore able to overcome whatever value liquidity may have. We conclude that for these triplets, the present value of tax savings induced by the grandfathered linear amortization schedule swamps the convexity result induced by the presence of tax timing/tax clientele/liquidity effects.

Exhibit 7 considers a specific analysis of whether the $T = 1$ year cutoff date does indeed distinguish between concavity and convexity for the Type B triplets. Recall that the theoretical $\Delta = 0$ for $T \le 1$, hence the Tax Reform Act of 1986 should only be observable for those triplets with maturities exceeding one (tax) year.

Exhibit 6: Analysis of Premium Bond Triplets

	Jan. 1926 - Dec. 1982		Jan. 1980 - Aug. 1985		Sept. 1985 - Dec. 1990					
	Litzenberger and Rolfo		Jordan and Jordan		Bond Triplets with Three "old"s — Type A				Triplets with at Least One "New"	
									Type B1	Type B2
	N	n	N	n	N	n	N	n	N | n	N | n
$P_2 \ge P_x$	72	34	29	14	62	49*	243	204*	134 | 115*	— | —
$P_x \ge P_2$	—	—	—	—	—	—	—	—	— | —	399 | 181*
Percent Convex	47.2%		48.3		79.0		84.0		85.8	45.4

Notes:
1. a — Jordan and Jordan correct Litzenberger and Rolfo test for the latter's premium calculation error.
2. b — P_2 and P_3 are "old;" P_1 is "new." For these two columns, results reported are for $T > 1$ Yr. only.
3. N — Number of Observations; n — Number of Violations
4. "old" — Bonds issued before Sept. 28, 1985; "new" — Bonds issued after Sept. 27, 1985.
5. * — indicates significant violations at the 1% level.
6. $P_x = xP_1 + (1 - x) P_3$. Prices are defined as the mid-point of the bid and ask quoted, $c_1 < c_2 < c_3$ and $x = (c_3 - c_2)/(c_3 - c_1)$.
7. $P_2 \ge P_x$: the price of the middle bond should not be less than the appropriate linear combination of the prices of the two extreme bonds.

Exhibit 7: Maturity-Dependent Analysis of Concavity/ Convexity for Two "Old," One "New" Triplets
Data Period: September 1985 - 1990

Maturity ≤ 1 year			Maturity > 1 year		
Concave	Convex	Total	Concave	Convex	Total
8	15	23	52	21	73
(8)	(15)		(47)	(26)	

Note: Numbers in parentheses constitute analysis of bid prices rather than mid-point prices.

Exhibit 8: Delta for 8.625%, 8.75%, 11.75% Triplet

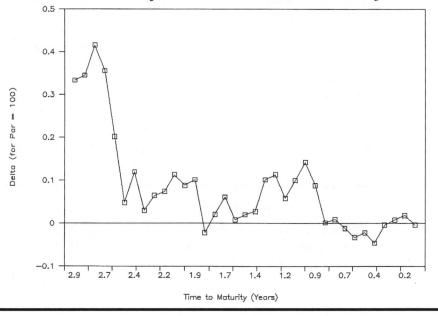

Time to Maturity (Years)

The contrast between $T \leq 1$ and $T > 1$ is striking: whereas the predominant case for $T > 1$ is one of concavity, the convex situation predominates for $T \leq 1$, consistent with the Tax Reform Act of 1986-conjecture.

Exhibit 8 examines the same issue from the perspective of the $\Delta = P_1' - P_1$ defined implicitly in Exhibit 5 (i.e., the computed price deviation from the linear extrapolation of P_2 and P_3 less the observable market price of the "new" P_1). Exhibit 8 presents that Δ for the specific triplet 8.625%, 8.75%, and 11.75% which matured on 11/15/88. Note that the (positive) value of Δ declines as the triplets approach maturity, essentially reaching zero at or about the 1-year-to-maturity mark.

Exhibit 9 examines the non-parametric test of convexity/concavity for Types A and B on a year-by-year basis. This exhibit demonstrates the persistence of the results across the various sub-periods. The Type A bonds are consistently convex, with the Type B bonds demonstrating a stable concave pattern.

Exhibit 9: Analysis of Convex and Concave Triplets
Data Period: September 1985 - 1990

Year	Two "old," one "new"			Three "old"		
	Concave	Convex	Annual Total	Concave	Convex	Annual Total
September 1985 - 1986	18	2	20	24	75	99
1987	12	2	14	13	35	48
1988	11	8	19	3	15	18
1989	4	4	8	0	12	12
1990	7	5	12	1	5	6

Note: Two "old," One "new" analysis excludes triplets with maturity ≤ 1 year.

Exhibit 10: Triplet-by-Triplet Comparison of Type B Bonds
Sample Period: September 1985 - 1990

Maturity	Concavity	Convexity	No. of Obs.
11/15/88	22	1	23
05/15/89	9	1	10
11/15/89	0	1	1
05/15/90	5	0	5
08/15/90	1	4	5
11/15/90	0	7	7
02/15/93	1	0	1
08/15/93	4	0	4
11/15/93	2	0	2
08/15/94	6	1	7
11/15/94	1	6	7
02/15/95	1	0	1

Note: Triplets exclude maturities ≤ 1 year.

Exhibit 10 examines each Type B triplet for within-triplet consistency across time, subject to the condition $T > 1$. This exhibit demonstrates that the Type B bonds are, for the most part, consistently concave prior to entering the $T = 1$ year-to-maturity time period.

Finally, Exhibit 11 focuses on the descriptive statistics $\log(R)$ and Δ defined implicitly in Exhibits 5 and 8. The global means, across all bond triplets and time periods, for $\mu(\log R)$ and $\mu(\Delta)$ have been calculated and denoted $\hat{\mu}(\log R)$ and $\hat{\mu}(\Delta)$. Caution should be employed in the interpretation of these numbers, especially with respect to the t-statistics for $\hat{\mu}(\Delta)$. While it is true that, under the null hypothesis, $\mu(\Delta) = 0$, the variance of Δ presumably varies with the parameters $\{\tau, T, c, y_N\}$, a fact not explicitly accounted for in the t-tests reported in Exhibit 11 below. The calculation of a sample mean for $\log(R)$ and Δ constitutes a first-pass analysis of the quantitative features displayed by the bond premium triplets, and these parametric tests should be cautiously and narrowly interpreted as augmenting the non-parametric results reported above.

With this caveat in mind, note that Exhibit 11 also reports the results for the subsample of triplets that fall into the range of $|\Delta| > 0.25$. The rationale behind this is the belief that even though the violations of the conditions (2) through (5) are statistically significant, only large deviation may be economically meaningful. To be conservative, a bid-ask spread of $\frac{1}{4}$ point is used instead of the more common $\frac{1}{8}$.

The results from Exhibit 11 for bond triplets with three "old" bonds are quite similar for the two subperiods spanning the enactment date of the 1986 Tax Reform Act. The magnitudes of the sample means $\hat{\mu}(\log R)$ and $\hat{\mu}(\Delta)$ for both periods are very small when compared to bid-ask spread, even though they are significantly negative.

In the case of bonds for which the 1986 Tax Reform Act has effect, those with bond triplets with two "old"s and one "new," $\hat{\mu}(\log R)$ and $\hat{\mu}(\Delta)$ are much larger in absolute value and of opposite sign to the corresponding magnitudes of the three "old"s, indicating that the Tax Reform Act effect swamps the tax timing option/ tax clientele effect in magnitude. For the subset of data where $|\Delta| > 0.25$, the magnitude is substantial.

Finally, we are not surprised to see that the magnitudes of Δ are economically small, though statistically significant. Given that we are dealing with the present value *savings* of equation (4), we should not expect these values to be "large." One should also recall the confounding simultaneous effects of tax timing, market segmentation and liquidity.

Exhibit 11: Analysis of Descriptive Statistics log(R) and Δ for Premium Bond Triplets

| | January 1980 - August 1985 | | September 1985 - December 1990 | | | |
| | Bond Triplets with Three "Olds" | | Bond Triplets with Three "Olds" | | Bond Triplets with Two "Olds" and One "New" | |
Sample	$\hat{\mu}(\log R)$	$\hat{\mu}(\Delta)$	$\hat{\mu}(\log R)$	$\hat{\mu}(\Delta)$	$\hat{\mu}(\log R)$	$\hat{\mu}(\Delta)$
Entire	-0.068	-0.083	-0.061	-0.069	0.241	0.384
Sample	(-2.13*)	(-4.64*)	(-7.26*)	(-1.23)	(4.85*)	($3.42*)
N	69		183		73	
Subsample with $|\Delta| > 0.25$	-0.239	-0.392	-0.106	-0.126	0.640	1.12
	(-3.64*)	(-8.64*)	(-5.27*)	(-0.56)	(4.44*)	(3.89*)
N	8		46		24	

Notes: * indicates significance at the 0.01 level.
   $\hat{\mu}$ denotes sample mean.
   Numbers in parentheses are *t*-statistics.
   The number for Δ are for a par bond of *$100*.
   N is the number of observations.

Exhibit 12: Results for Discount Bond Triplets
Data Period: January 1980 - December 1990

Three "old"		Two "old," one "new"	
Concave	Convex	Concave	Convex
22	77	17	9

Notes: "Old" — bonds issued before July 18, 1984
"New" — bonds issued after July 17, 1984
For the "Two 'old,' One 'new'," triplets, the "New" coupons are the *largest*, and have post-December 1987 issue dates. "Old" bonds were issued between 1973 and 1978.

Tax Reform Act of 1984

Analogous to Exhibit 6, Exhibit 12 presents the non-parametric test results for discount bonds. Although the number of observations is small relative to that in Exhibit 6, the results of Exhibit 12 indicate that, for discount bonds as well as their premium counterparts, the grandfathering provisions of the tax treatment appear to have value. The concave results of the two "old," one "new" case indicate that the tax treatment overcomes both tax-timing/market segmentation as well as whatever value there may be to the liquidity of the more recently-issued bond.

CONCLUSION

The empirical results cited above suggest several important conclusions. First, a convexity in the price-coupon relationship for bonds with identical tax treatment (i.e., the "old" bonds) are supportive of *either* a tax-timing option effect or a tax clientele/market segmentation effect. Because both of these tax effects lead to a convex relationship between price and coupon, we cannot empirically distinguish between the two causes of the observable convexity.

Second, the 1986 Tax Reform Act grandfathered the linear premium amortization feature of bonds issued prior to September 1985. We find a significant empirical price impact to this change, in that grandfathered bonds are more valuable than "new" bonds. Qualitatively, we can therefore conclude that the tax-exempt clientele cannot be the dominating price-determining marginal tax bracket. In conjunction with the previous result, we infer that this 1986 Tax Reform Act-effect dominates the tax-timing/tax clientele effect. The 1984 Tax Reform Act grandfathered the capital-gains treatment on the price appreciation to par of discount bonds. We find some evidence of a price impact to this effect as well.

Finally, the foregoing analysis is indicative of a significant tax impact in the U.S. government bond market. We conclude that *taxes matter: the tax-exempt clientele cannot be the dominating price-determining tax bracket in the market for government bonds.*

APPENDIX: DERIVATION OF BOND PREMIUM AMORTIZATION UNDER "CONSTANT YIELD METHOD"

It can easily be shown that if the investor is assumed to earn the bond's yield to maturity, then the yield to maturity on the hypothetical price at the end of the year equals the current yield. Then, of course, the amortized premium is the difference between the bond price at the beginning of the year and the hypothetical bond price at year's end.

Let $P(T)$ be the price of a premium bond T years from maturity. By definition,

$$P(T) = \frac{c}{y}\left(1 - \frac{1}{(1+y)^T}\right) + \frac{1}{(1+y)^T} \tag{7}$$

where y is the yield to maturity. Now, for tax purposes, the assumed one-year holding-period rate of return is given by

$$\frac{P(T-1)+c}{P(T)} - 1$$

where y is also the yield on the bond's price next period, $P(T-1)$. We must show that if $P(T-1)$ has yield to maturity y, then $[P(T-1)+c]/P(T) - 1 = y$.

Expanding the rate of return in terms of equation (7), we have

$$\frac{P(T-1)+c}{P(T)} - 1 = \frac{(c/y)[1-1/(1+y)^T]+1/(1+y)^T+c}{(c/y)[1-1/(1+y)^{T-1}]+1/(1+y)^{T-1}} - 1$$

where the RHS can be shown to simplify to y.

Using the definition of $P(T)$ in equation (7), the amount amortized is given by

$$P(T) - P(T-1)$$

$$= \frac{c}{y}\left[1 - \frac{1}{(1+y)^T}\right] + \frac{1}{(1+y)^T} - \frac{c}{y}\left[1 - \frac{1}{(1+y)^{T-1}}\right] + \frac{1}{(1+y)^{T-1}}$$

$$= \frac{c-y}{(1+y)^T}$$

More generally, for arbitrary year t, $t = 1,..., T$, the amortized premium is

$$\frac{c-y}{(1+y)^{T-t+1}}$$

Since this amount can be deducted from ordinary income, the tax *savings* are given by

$$\tau(c-y)/(1+y)^{T-t+1}$$

in each period $t = 1,..., T$.

Chapter 14

Fixed-Income Risk

Ronald N. Kahn, Ph.D.
Director of Research
BARRA, Inc.

INTRODUCTION

Risk analysis has been central to investing since at least the 1950's, when Harry Markowitz showed mathematically exactly how diversification reduced risk.[1] Since then, risk analysis has developed into a very powerful tool relied upon by institutional investors. If expected return is the protagonist in the drama of fixed income portfolio management, then risk is the antagonist.

This chapter will discuss definitions of risk, describe some key characteristics of risk, present approaches to modeling risk, and discuss risk model uses. The important lessons are:

- The standard deviation of return is the best overall definition of risk.
- Risks don't add.
- Duration measures exposure to risk, rather than risk.
- Institutional investors care more about active than total risk.
- Risk models identify the important sources of risk: interest rates, spreads, prepayment factors, volatility, and currencies.
- Risk model uses include current portfolio risk analysis, portfolio construction and rebalancing, and past portfolio performance analysis.

We start with our definition of risk.

DEFINING RISK

All definitions of risk arise fundamentally from the probability distribution of possible returns. This distribution describes the probability that the return will be between 1% and 1.01%, the probability of returns between 1.01% and 1.02%, etc.

---

[1] H.M. Markowitz, "Portfolio Selection: Efficient Diversification of Investment," *Cowles Foundation Monograph 16* (New Haven CT: Yale University Press, 1959).

The return in question can describe a bond or a portfolio, a total return or return relative to a benchmark.

The distribution of returns describes probabilities of all possible outcomes. As such, it is complicated and full of detail. It can answer all questions about returns and probabilities. It can be a forecast, or a summary of realized returns.

Unfortunately the distribution of returns is too complicated and detailed in its entirety. Hence all definitions of risk attempt to capture in a single number the essentials of risk more fully described in the complete distribution. Each definition of risk will have at least some shortcomings, due to this simplification. Different definitions may also have shortcomings based on difficulties of accurate forecasting. Let's discuss some possible risk definitions in turn.

The *standard deviation* measures the spread of the distribution about its mean. Investors commonly refer to the standard deviation as the *volatility*. The *variance* is the square of the standard deviation. If returns are normally distributed, then two-thirds of them fall within one standard deviation of the mean. As the standard deviation decreases, the band within which most returns will fall narrows. The standard deviation measures the uncertainty of the returns.

Standard deviation was Harry Markowitz' definition of risk, and it has been the standard in the institutional investment community ever since. It will be our definition of risk. Standard deviation is a very well understood and unambiguous statistic. It is particularly applicable to existing tools for building portfolios. Standard deviations tend to be relatively stable over time (especially compared to mean returns and other moments of the distribution), and econometricians have developed very powerful tools for accurately forecasting standard deviations.

Critics of the standard deviation point out that it measures the possibility of returns both above and below the mean. Most investors would define risk based on small or negative returns (though short sellers have the opposite view). This has generated an alternative risk measure: *semivariance*, or *downside risk*.

Semivariance is defined in analogy to variance, based on deviations from the mean, but using only returns below the mean. If the returns are symmetric, i.e. the return is equally likely to be *x* percent above or *x* percent below the mean, then the semivariance is just exactly one-half the variance. Analysts differ in defining *downside risk*. One approach defines downside risk as the square root of the semivariance, in analogy to the relation between standard deviation and variance.

Downside risk clearly answers the critics of standard deviation, by focusing entirely on the undesirable returns. However, there are several problems with downside risk. First, its definition is not as unambiguous as standard deviation or variance, nor are its statistical properties as well known, so it isn't an ideal choice for a universal risk definition. We need a definition which managers, plan sponsors, and beneficiaries can all use. Second, it is computationally challenging for large portfolio construction problems.

Third, to the extent that investment returns are reasonably symmetric, most definitions of downside risk are simply proportional to standard deviation or variance and so contain no additional information. To the extent that investment returns may not be symmetric, there are problems forecasting downside risk. Return asymmetries are not stable over time, and so are very difficult to forecast. Realized downside risk may not be a good forecast of future downside risk. Moreover, we estimate downside risk with only half of the data, losing statistical accuracy.

Shortfall probability is another risk definition, and perhaps one closely related to intuition for what risk is. The shortfall probability is the probability that the return will lie below some target amount. Shortfall probability has the advantage of closely corresponding to an intuitive definition of risk. However, it faces the same problems as downside risk: ambiguity, poor statistical understanding, difficulty of forecasting, and dependence on individual investor preferences.

Forecasting is a particularly thorny problem, and it's accentuated the lower the shortfall target. At the extreme, probability forecasts for very large shortfalls are influenced by perhaps only 1 or 2 observations.

Value at risk is similar to shortfall probability. Where shortfall probability takes a target return and calculates the probability of returns falling below that, value at risk takes a target probability, e.g. the 1% or 5% lowest returns, and converts that probability to an associated return. Value at risk is closely related to shortfall probability, and shares the same advantages and disadvantages.

Where does the normal distribution fit into this discussion of risk statistics? The normal distribution is a standard assumption in academic investment research and is a standard distribution throughout statistics. It is completely defined by its mean and standard deviation. Much research has shown that investment returns do not exactly follow normal distributions, but instead have wider distributions, i.e. the probability of extreme events is larger for real investments than a normal distribution would imply.

The above five risk definitions all attempt to capture the risk inherent in the "true" return distribution. An alternative approach could assume that returns are normally distributed. Then the mean and standard deviation immediately fix the other statistics: downside risk, semivariance, shortfall probability, and value at risk. Such an approach might robustly forecast quantities of most interest to individual investors, using the most accurate calculations and a few reasonable assumptions. Many currently popular estimates of value at risk use exactly this approach.

Faced with these possibilities, we choose the standard deviation as our definition of risk. It is well understood, unambiguous, and accurately forecastable. And, by assuming normal distributions, we can translate standard deviation into value at risk numbers, for example.

DURATION IS NOT RISK

What about duration, the traditional measure of fixed-income risk? There are two problems using duration as risk. First, duration isn't directly connected to the distribution of returns. Duration measures exposure to risk, rather than risk. Second, duration measures only one source of risk: parallel interest rate moves.

For a bond of price P, the duration D measures the return per unit parallel interest rate move Δs:

$$D = -\frac{1}{P} \cdot \frac{\Delta P}{\Delta s}. \tag{1}$$

So duration relates bond returns to parallel interest rate moves:

$$r = \frac{\Delta P}{P} = -D \cdot \Delta s. \tag{2}$$

Assuming stable duration, bond risk relates to interest rate risk as:

$$STD\{r\} = D \cdot STD\{\Delta s\}. \tag{3}$$

If interest rate moves have an annual volatility of 1%, then a 5-year duration bond should exhibit an annual volatility of 5%, based on interest rate risk. Duration measures a bond's exposure to interest rate (parallel shift) volatility.

BASIC RISK MATH

The standard deviation has some interesting and important characteristics. Representing means as μ, standard deviations as σ, and portfolio holdings as h, we know that:

$$\mu\{h_1 \cdot r_1 + h_2 \cdot r_2\} = h_1 \cdot \mu_1 + h_2 \cdot \mu_2. \tag{4}$$

We call this the *portfolio property*. According to equation (4), the portfolio's mean return is the weighted average of the mean returns of its constituents.

The standard deviation does not have the portfolio property. In particular:

$$\sigma^2\{h_1 \cdot r_1 + h_2 \cdot r_2\} = h_1^2 \cdot \sigma_1^2 + h_2^2 \cdot \sigma_2^2 + 2 \cdot h_1 \cdot h_2 \cdot \sigma_1 \cdot \sigma_2 \cdot \rho_{12}, \tag{5}$$

where ρ_{12} is the correlation between r_1 and r_2, and $\sigma_{12} = \sigma_1 \cdot \sigma_2 \cdot \rho_{12}$ is the covariance between r_1 and r_2. Then, because correlations must range between -1 and 1:

$$\sigma\{h_1 \cdot r_1 + h_2 \cdot r_2\} \leq h_1 \cdot \sigma_1 + h_2 \cdot \sigma_2, \tag{6}$$

with the equality above holding only if the two returns are perfectly correlated ($\rho_{12}=1$). For risk, the whole is less than the sum of its parts. This is the key to portfolio diversification.

For further insight into this, the risk of an equal weighted portfolio of N bonds, where every bond has risk σ and all bonds have pairwise correlation ρ, is:

$$\sigma_P = \sigma \cdot \sqrt{\frac{1 + \rho \cdot (N-1)}{N}} . \tag{7}$$

As the correlation drops to zero this becomes:

$$\sigma_P = \frac{\sigma}{\sqrt{N}}, \tag{8}$$

the key to lowering risk is holding many bonds. In the limit that the portfolio contains a very large number of correlated bonds, this becomes:

$$\sigma_P \Rightarrow \sigma \cdot \sqrt{\rho} . \tag{9}$$

This provides a lower bound on risk, even for portfolios containing many bonds.

The Covariance Matrix

In the general case, portfolios contain many bonds of differing volatilities and correlations. Equation (5) then generalizes to:

$$\sigma^2 \{ h_1 \cdot r_1 + h_2 \cdot r_2 + \ldots + h_N \cdot r_N \}$$
$$= h_1^2 \cdot \sigma_1^2 + h_2^2 \cdot \sigma_2^2 + \ldots + h_N^2 \cdot \sigma_N^2 + 2 \cdot h_1 \cdot h_2 \cdot \sigma_1 \cdot \sigma_2 \cdot \rho_{12} + \ldots \tag{10}$$

For large portfolios, this calculation involves quite a number of terms. We can simplify this notationally by introducing the covariance matrix $\mathbf{V}$ which contains all the variances and covariances:

$$\mathbf{V} = \begin{bmatrix} \sigma_1^2 & \sigma_{12} & \cdots & \\ \vdots & \sigma_2^2 & & \\ & & \ddots & \\ & & & \sigma_N^2 \end{bmatrix} \tag{11}$$

and then

$$\sigma_P^2 = \mathbf{h}_P^T \cdot \mathbf{V} \cdot \mathbf{h}_P, \tag{12}$$

where $\mathbf{h}_P$ is an N-vector containing all the portfolio holdings. Equation (12) has the advantage of notational simplicity, though understanding portfolio risk still involves the calculation in equation (10).

Annualizing Risk

We can use equation (10) to annualize risk. The annual return to a bond is the sum of 12 monthly bond returns:

$$r_A = r_J + r_F + \ldots + r_D \tag{13}$$

$$\sigma_A^2 = \sigma_J^2 + \sigma_F^2 + \ldots + \sigma_D^2 + \text{covariance terms} \tag{14}$$

Now we will make two generally valid assumptions. First, we will assume stationarity. The return variance is the same each month. Second we will assume that returns are uncorrelated across time, i.e. all the covariance terms in equation (14) are zero. These assumptions mean that:

$$\sigma_A^2 = 12 \cdot \sigma_{monthly}^2, \tag{15}$$

and more generally variance grows with the length of the return horizon. This allows us to measure risk over different horizons, but report it in consistent units.

Active Risk

Investment managers care about relative risk even more than total risk. If an investment manager is being compared to a performance benchmark then the difference in return between his portfolio's return r_P and the benchmark's return r_B is of crucial importance. The difference is called the *active return*, r_A. The *active risk*, ψ_A, is defined as the standard deviation of active return;

$$\psi_P = \text{STD}\{r_A\} = \text{STD}\{r_P - r_B\}. \tag{16}$$

We sometimes call this active risk the "tracking error" of the portfolio, since it describes how well the portfolio can track the benchmark.

HISTORICAL RISK

The key ingredient for calculating portfolio risk is the covariance matrix. A risk model's job is estimating that covariance matrix. The most obvious approach is to use historical variances and covariances. This procedure is neither robust nor reasonable.

Data from T periods is used to estimate the N by N covariance matrix. But the N by N covariance matrix contains $N(N+1)/2$ independent numbers (all the variances and covariances). Each of the T observations includes N numbers (the set of N returns that period), and each variance and covariance requires at least 2 numbers for estimation. Unless $NT \geq 2N(N+1)/2$, or unless $T > N$, there will be active positions that will appear riskless.

So the historical approach requires $T > N$. For a monthly historical covariance matrix of just 500 bonds, this would require over 40 years of data, a severe problem since most bond maturities are less than 40 years. And, even when T is greater than N, this historical procedure still has several problems:

- Historical risk cannot deal with the changing maturity of bonds. Over the course of a year, each bond's risk will change as its maturity shortens.

- Circumventing the $T > N$ restriction requires short time periods, one day or one week, while the forecast horizon of the manager is generally one quarter or one year.
- Sample bias will lead to some gross misestimates of covariance. A 500 asset covariance matrix contains 125,250 independent numbers. If 5% of these are poor estimates, we have 6,262 poor estimates.

The reader will note limited enthusiasm for historical models of risk. We now turn to more structured models of risk.

STRUCTURAL RISK MODELS

In the previous section, we considered historical risk and found it wanting. In this section we look at structural multifactor risk models and trumpet their virtues.[2]

The multiple factor risk model is based on the notion that the return of a bond can be explained by a collection of common factors plus an idiosyncratic element that pertains to that particular bond. We can think of the common factors as forces that affect a group of bonds, for example interest rate or corporate spread movements. Below, we discuss possible types of factors in detail.

By identifying important factors we can reduce the size of the problem. Instead of dealing with 6,000 bonds (and 18,003,000 independent variances and covariances), we deal with approximately 50 factors. The bonds change, the factors do not. The situation is much simpler when we focus on the smaller number of factors and allow the bonds to change their exposures to those factors.

A structural risk model begins by analyzing returns according to a simple linear structure comprised of four components: the bond's exposures to the factors, the excess returns, the attributed factor returns, and the specific returns. The structure is

$$r_n = \sum_k X_{n,k}(t) \cdot f(t) + u_n(t), \tag{17}$$

where:

$X_{n,k}(t)$ is the *exposure* of asset n to factor k. This exposure is known at time t. Exposures are frequently called *factor loadings*.

$r_n(t)$ is the *excess return* (return above the risk free return) on bond n during the period from time t to time $t + 1$.

---

[2] For references see Richard C. Grinold and Ronald N. Kahn, *Active Portfolio Management* (Chicago: Probus Publishing, 1995, Chapter 3); Richard C. Grinold and Ronald N. Kahn, "Multiple Factor Models for Portfolio Risk," in John W. Peavy III, (ed), *A Practitioner's Guide to Factor Models* (Charlottesville, VA: AIMR, 1994); Ronald N. Kahn, "Fixed Income Risk Modeling," Chapter 34 in Frank J. Fabozzi, (ed), *The Handbook of Fixed Income Securities*, Fourth Edition (Homewood IL: Business One Irwin, 1995); Ronald N. Kahn, "Fixed Income Risk Modeling in the 1990's," *Journal of Portfolio Management* (Fall, 1995), pp. 94-101; and Andrew Rudd and Henry K. Clasing, Jr. *Modern Portfolio Theory*, (Orinda, CA: Andrew Rudd, 1988), Chapters 2 and 3.

$f_k(t)$ is the *factor return* to factor k during the period from time t to time $t + 1$.

$u_n(t)$ is bond n's *specific return* during the period from time t to time $t + 1$. This is the return that cannot be explained by the factors. It is sometimes called the *idiosyncratic return*, the return not explained by the model. However, the risk model will account for specific risk. Thus our risk predictions will explicitly consider the risk of u_n.

We have been very careful to define the time structure in the model. The exposures are known at time t: the beginning of the period. The asset returns, factor returns, and specific returns span the period from time t to time $t + 1$. In the rest of this chapter, we will suppress the explicit time variables.

We do not require causality in this model structure. The factors may or may not be the basic driving forces for security returns. They are, however, dimensions along which to analyze risk.

We will now assume that the specific returns are not correlated with the factor returns, and are not correlated with each other. With these assumptions and the return structure of equation (17), the risk structure is:

$$V_{n,m} = \sum_{k1,k2} X_{n,k1} \cdot F_{k1,k1} \cdot X_{m,k2} + \Delta_{n,m}, \tag{18}$$

where:

$V_{n,m}$ is the covariance of asset n with asset m. If $n = m$, this gives the variance of asset n.

$X_{n,k1}$ is the exposure of asset n to factor $k1$, as defined above.

$F_{k1,k2}$ is the covariance of factor $k1$ with factor $k2$. If $k1 = k2$, this gives the variance of factor $k1$.

$\Delta_{n,m}$ is the specific covariance of asset n with asset m. We assume that all specific risk correlations are zero, so this term is zero unless $n = m$. In that case, this gives the specific variance of asset n.

FIXED-INCOME FACTORS

So much for the framework, what are the important factors? In researching this question, we must keep in mind the diversity of fixed-income instruments: from Treasury bonds to corporate bonds to mortgages and CMOs; and from fixed coupons to floating-rate notes.

The important factors in the market include interest rates, yield spreads, prepayments, volatilities, and currencies for global bonds.

We have extensively analyzed interest rate risk movements and identified the three most important factors as interest rate shift, twist, and butterfly movements. The most important spread movements include movements in sector spreads and movements in quality spreads. These sources of fixed-income risk are well known and fairly well understood.

Prepayment risk concerns the risk of unexpected prepayments. This is a type of model risk and is not well understood. Most models include forecasts of prepayments along interest rate paths. Models then price mortgage-dependent cash flows based on these forecasts. But adjusting mortgage cash flows based on a prepayment model helps to estimate interest rate risk, not prepayment risk. *As defined here, prepayment risk is the risk that the prepayment model is wrong.*

Actually, prepayment risk is somewhat more general than this. A model which correctly predicts prepayments may not match market expectations. And it is market expectations which drive mortgage prices. The prepayment model defines the dimensions of the problem. The volatility along each dimension arises both from forecasting errors and changes in market expectations.

What are these dimensions of the prepayment model? To begin with, the models do not fit all observed prepayments exactly. And so for any particular generic passthrough we expect its prepayments to deviate randomly from the model forecasts. Fortunately these deviations should have mean zero, and so will average out over time and over the different passthroughs in the portfolio.

More critical and systematic sources of prepayment risk involve unexpected changes in model parameters governing baseline (discount mortgage) prepayments, rate dependent prepayments, and burnout. All of these can be significant sources of prepayment risk.

Volatility risk is the risk of unexpected changes in volatility. We use option models to analyze fixed-income instruments, and input estimated term structures of volatility. But the option analysis usually extends only to estimating interest rate risk; that is, option-adjusted durations. But what if short- or long-rate volatility is unexpectedly high? How will that affect the portfolio? This is analogous to an option trader's vega risk.

Exposures

The straightforward way to calculate the exposures $X_{n,j}$ in equations (17) and (18), given a model of instrument pricing, is to "shock" the model successively along each dimension of risk and re-value the instruments. For interest rate factors this corresponds to shocking the term structure, re-valuing, and calculating the returns generated by that shock. For unexpected prepayments, this corresponds to shocking the prepayment model, re-valuing the instruments, and calculating the returns generated.

To mitigate problems of instability, we should define our shocks based on realistic expectations of their possible size. For interest rate risk, this approach to estimating exposures is very different from the traditional duration approach. It is not only more meaningful, it is more flexible: it handles negative duration IOs as easily as Treasury bonds.

Exhibit 1: Term Structure Exposure Examples
Sample Instruments

			Price	Duration
U.S. Treasury	11.875% of November 2003		148.60	6.52
Caterpillar	6.000% of May 2007	(Callable)	93.25	7.45
Dow	8.550% of October 2009	(Putable)	119.34	7.81
Citicorp	8.910% of May 1995	(Floater)	106.84	0.18
GNMA	8.000% issued 1992		104.33	3.49
GNMA	8.000% issued 1992	PO	67.77	18.44
GNMA	8.000% issued 1992	IO	36.56	-24.20

FACTOR COVARIANCE

Given these exposures, we must also estimate the variances and covariances of the fixed-income factors. Here we can use historical analysis, on this significantly reduced set of data. We can also use more sophisticated approaches, including weighting more recent observations more heavily, and scaling the factor covariance matrix **F** up or down based on nonlinear volatility forecasts[3] for overall market volatility.

EXAMPLES

To understand this approach to risk modeling in more detail, we will now apply it to the set of sample instruments shown in Exhibit 1. These include a non-callable Treasury bond, callable and putable corporate bonds, a corporate floating-rate note, a passthrough mortgage, and a PO and IO. The specific analysis date is August 31, 1993, though as you will see, the general pattern of results is typically valid.

To compare magnitudes of risk, we will convert exposures to every risk factor to an equivalent annual movement. (We can impose this definition of the exposures X, as long as we consistently define the covariance matrix **F**.) So, for example, we will interpret the term structure shift exposures as the returns generated by a one-standard-deviation (annual) shift up in interest rates, and the baseline prepayment exposures as the returns generated by a one-standard-deviation (annual) shift up in baseline prepayment rates. For the purposes of this chapter, we will ignore the subtleties of how best to calculate such exposures: based on positive or negative shocks, multiple shocks, and so on.

---

[3] For references on nonlinear volatility forecasts, see Tim Bollerslev, Ray Y. Chou, Narayan Jayaraman, and Kenneth F. Kroner, "ARCH Modeling in Finance: A Selective Review of the Theory and Empirical Evidence, with Suggestions for Future Research," *Journal of Econometrics,* Vol. 52 (1992), pp. 5-59; and Robert F. Engle, "Autoregressive Conditional Heteroskedasticity with Estimates of the Variance of U.K. Inflation," *Econometrica,* Vol. 50 (1982), pp. 987-1008.

Exhibit 2: U.S. Shift/Twist/Butterfly Shapes

Monthly
Movements
in Basis

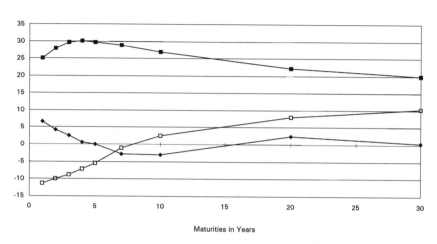

Maturities in Years

—■— Shift —□— Twist —◆— Butterfly

Exhibit 3: Term Structure Exposure Examples

Security	Shift	Twist	Butterfly
Treasury	-7.16%	0.39%	0.61%
Callable Corp.	-8.48%	-0.24%	0.61%
Putable Corp.	-7.86%	-0.27%	0.05%
Corp. Floater	-0.24%	0.10%	-0.04%
GNMA	-4.43%	0.28%	-0.31%
PO	-23.15%	3.12%	3.67%
IO	30.28%	-5.02%	-7.69%

Let's start with interest rate risk. Exhibit 2 shows monthly shift, twist, and butterfly shapes. For this example we have defined these factors using principal components analysis, but we also could have used more intuitive shapes: a parallel shift, linear twist, and others. Exhibit 3 shows the exposures of the sample instruments to each of these shapes — the X's — scaled to an annual positive movement. So most of the shift exposures are negative because a rise in rates negatively affects returns for most bonds. The IO has a positive exposure because of its negative duration.

For each instrument, the shift is the dominant source of interest rate risk. However we cannot ignore the twist and butterfly risk in many circumstances. Active risk relative to a benchmark, for example, will depend on active exposures. For most institutional portfolios, active durations (and similarly active shift exposures) will be near zero. Also note that the twist and butterfly exposures of the IO are comparable in magnitude to the shift exposure of the long bonds.

Exhibit 4: Yield Spread Risk Exposures

Instrument	Spread Risk Exposure
Treasury Bond	-1.15%
Callable Corp.	-3.21%
Putable Corp.	-3.27%
Corp. Floater	-1.20%
GNMA	-1.45%
PO	-7.67%
IO	10.06%

Next consider spread risk: the risk that yield spreads could widen or tighten, independent of any moves in interest rates. Exhibit 4 shows yield spread risk exposures for the sample instruments based on a widening spread shock.

Spread risk depends on yield spread volatility and the duration of the instrument. For almost all these examples, spread risk is smaller in magnitude than interest rate shift risk, but comparable or even larger than twist or butterfly risk. Especially for some corporate bonds, it can be the dominant source of active risk (assuming an active shift risk exposure near zero).

For this example corporate floating-rate note, spread risk dominates interest rate risk. For floaters, the coupon reset mitigates interest rate risk but not default risk. For purposes of interest rate risk, the floater effective maturity is the next reset date. But for spread risk, the relevant cash flows extend all the way out to the true maturity.

Now consider two sources of prepayment risk shown schematically in Exhibit 5, which shows a generic prepayment model with the forecast conditional prepayment rate (CPR) a function of the difference between the mortgage coupon and the current coupon. The movement A denotes baseline prepayment risk and the movement B denotes rate-dependent prepayment risk. Exhibit 6 shows sample instrument exposures to these risk factors. First note that the Treasury bond and the corporate bonds are not exposed to this prepayment risk. If we shock the prepayment model while holding all other parameters fixed, the prices of these bonds will not change. This does not mean that we expect no change in interest rates correlated with a change in prepayments. We account for such effects in the factor covariance matrix, not the factor exposures.

Exhibit 6 also shows that the IO exposure to baseline prepayment risk is comparable to its exposure to interest rate shift risk. If we combine this IO with a Treasury strip to create a zero duration portfolio, we would still be exposed to very significant risks.

In contrast to the IO and PO, the passthrough mortgage has relatively low exposures to prepayment risk. This is because the passthrough is only at a slight premium, so prepayments have only a small impact on price.

Exhibit 5: Prepayment Risk Movements

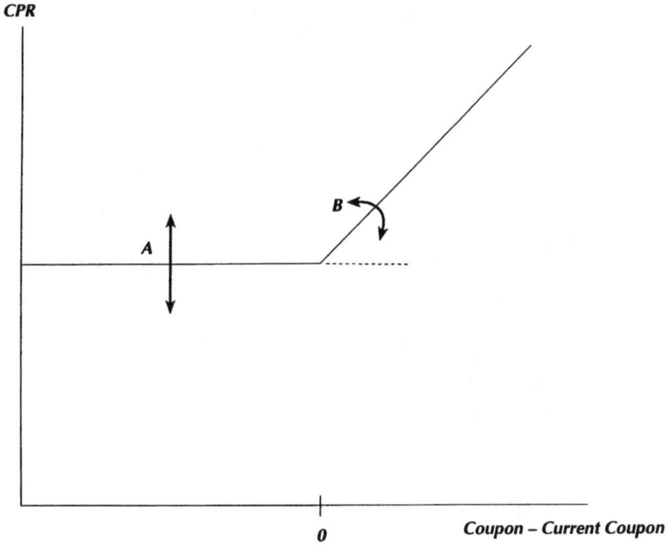

CPR

Coupon – Current Coupon

Exhibit 6: Prepayment Exposure Examples

Security	Baseline	Rate Dependent
Treasury	0.00%	0.00%
Callable Corp.	0.00%	0.00%
Putable Corp.	0.00%	0.00%
Corp. Floater	0.00%	0.00%
GNMA	-0.04%	-0.52%
PO	12.14%	4.72%
IO	-22.58%	-10.20%

To account for volatility risk we can look for shocks to short-rate volatility and/or long-rate volatility. For consistency with our option model, we will parametrize volatility shocks as volatility shifts, where short- and long-rate volatilities move in parallel; and volatility twists, where long-rate volatility moves relative to a fixed short-rate volatility.

Exhibit 7 shows volatility risk exposures for the sample instruments. Since the Treasury bond is noncallable, its volatility risk is zero. Since the floater resets to par at the next reset date no matter what the volatility, its volatility risk is zero. Once again, volatility risk is highest for the IO. Volatility risk in general is smaller in magnitude than other risk sources, but it still may be hard to ignore in some circumstances. For active risk, assuming shift risk exposure near zero, volatility risk is comparable in magnitude to twist and butterfly risk for the callable corporate bonds.

Exhibit 7: Volatility Exposure Examples

Security	Volatility Shift	Volatility Twist
Treasury	0.00%	0.00%
Callable Corp.	-0.22%	-0.32%
Putable Corp.	0.23%	0.39%
Corp. Floater	0.00%	0.00%
GNMA	-0.20%	-0.25%
PO	0.81%	0.45%
IO	-2.08%	-1.54%

Exhibit 8: Annual Risk Forecasts

Security	Total Annual Risk Forecast
Treasury	7.29%
Callable Corp.	9.10%
Putable Corp.	8.54%
Corp. Floater	1.27%
GNMA	4.71%
PO	26.84%
IO	41.41%

Risk Analysis

We have completed the exercise of calculating each sample instrument's exposures to the risk factors. The exposures of a portfolio of these assets would be just the portfolio-weighted average of the instrument exposures.

To complete the analysis of risk, we must combine these exposures with the covariance matrix $\mathbf{F}$, according to equation (18). Only when we combine our risk exposures with the covariance matrix can we see our overall risk.

Equation (18) also includes a contribution from each instrument's specific risk. This risk is idiosyncratic to each instrument and independent of the risk factors.

When we combine these effects, we find the total risk forecasts for the sample instruments listed in Exhibit 8.

The risk rankings aren't surprising — IO's and PO's are riskier than Treasuries, corporates, and straight passthrough mortgages on August 31, 1993 and most other days as well. But the magnitudes of the differences are impressive, and the sources of these differences, as we have observed, are insightful. Significant contributions to IO and PO risk arise from prepayment risks not traditionally analyzed. No combination of Treasuries can hedge out these significant risk factors.

THE USES OF A RISK MODEL

Having now covered in detail the structure of a fixed-income risk model, what are its investment applications? Broadly speaking, there are three. They involve the present, the future, and the past. We will describe them in turn, mainly focusing on uses concerning present risk.

The Present: Current Portfolio Risk Analysis

The multiple factor risk model analyzes current portfolio risk. It measures overall risk. More significantly it decomposes that risk in several ways. This decomposition of risk identifies the important sources of risk in the portfolio and links those sources with aspirations for active return.

One way to divide the risk is to look at risk relative to a benchmark and identify the active risk. Another way to divide the risk is between the model risk and the specific risk. The risk model can also perform marginal analysis: what assets are most and least diversifying in the portfolio, at the margin?

Risk analysis is important for both *passive management* and *active management*. Passive managers attempt to match the returns to a particular benchmark. Passive managers run index funds. But, depending on the benchmark, the manager's portfolio may not include all the bonds in the benchmark, possibly due to the prohibitive transactions costs for holding the thousands of assets in a broad benchmark. Current portfolio risk analysis can tell a passive manager the risk of his portfolio relative to his benchmark. This is his active risk, or *tracking error*. It is the volatility of the difference in return between the portfolio and the benchmark. Passive managers want minimum tracking error.

Active managers attempt to outperform their benchmarks. Their goal is not to track the benchmark as closely as possible. Still, risk analysis is important in active management, to focus active strategies. Active managers want to take on risk only along those dimensions they believe they can outperform.

By suitably decomposing current portfolio risk, active managers can better understand the positioning of their portfolios. Risk analysis can tell active managers not only what their active risk is, but why and how to change it. Risk analysis can classify active bets into inherent bets, intentional bets, and incidental bets:

> *Inherent:* An active manager who is trying to outperform a benchmark will have to bear the benchmark risk. This risk is a constant part of the task that is not under the portfolio manager's control.
>
> *Intentional:* An active portfolio manager has identified bonds that will do well and bonds that will do poorly. The manager should expect that these bonds will appear as important marginal sources of active risk. This is welcome news; it tells the portfolio manager that he has taken active positions that are consistent with his beliefs.
>
> *Incidental:* These are unintentional side effects of the manager's active position. The manager has inadvertently created an active position on some factor that is a significant contributor to marginal active risk. Incidental bets often arise through incremental portfolio management, where a sequence of decisions, each plausible in isolation, leads to an accumulated incidental risk.

The Future

A risk model helps design future portfolios. Risk is one of the important design parameters in portfolio construction, which trades off expected return and risk.

The Past

A risk model helps to evaluate the past performance of the portfolio. The risk model offers a decomposition of active return and allows for an attribution of risk to each category of return. Thus the risks undertaken by the manager will be clear, as well as the outcomes from taking those active positions. This allows the manager to determine which active bets have been rewarded and which have been penalized.

SUMMARY

Portfolio management centers on the trade-off between expected returns and risk. This chapter has focused on risk. We have quantified risk as the standard deviation of annual returns, though by assuming normal distributions we could report standard deviations as value at risk numbers. Institutional portfolio managers care mainly about active risk. Risk models, and structural risk models in particular, can provide insightful analysis by decomposing risk into total and active risk; and by identifying inherent, intentional, and incidental bets. Accurate risk models include all important sources of risk, especially interest rates, spread movements, prepayment and volatility risk, and currency risk. Risk models can analyze the present risks and bets in a portfolio, forecast future risk as part of the portfolio construction process, and analyze past risks to facilitate performance analysis.

TECHNICAL APPENDIX: MARGINAL CONTRIBUTIONS TO RISK

The risk model in matrix notation is written as

$$\mathbf{r} = \mathbf{X} \cdot \mathbf{f} + \mathbf{u}, \tag{A-1}$$

where $\mathbf{r}$ is an N vector of excess returns, $\mathbf{X}$ is an N by K matrix of factor exposures, $\mathbf{f}$ is a K vector of factor returns, and $\mathbf{u}$ is an N vector of specific returns.

We assume that the specific returns $\mathbf{u}$ are uncorrelated with the factor returns $\mathbf{f}$, and that the covariance of specific return u_n with specific return u_m is zero, if $m \neq n$. With these assumptions we can express the N by N covariance matrix $\mathbf{V}$ of bond returns as

$$\mathbf{V} = \mathbf{X} \cdot \mathbf{F} \cdot \mathbf{X}^T + \Delta, \tag{A-2}$$

where $\mathbf{F}$ is the K by K covariance matrix of the factor returns and Δ is the N by N diagonal matrix of specific variance.

Marginal Contributions

Although total allocation of risk is difficult, we can examine the marginal effects of a change in the portfolio. This type of sensitivity analysis allows us to see what factors and assets have the largest impact on risk. The marginal impact on risk is measured by the partial derivative of the risk with respect to the asset holding.

We can compute these marginal contributions for total risk and active risk. The N vector of marginal contributions to total risk is:

$$\mathbf{MCTR} = \frac{\partial \sigma_P}{\partial \mathbf{h}_P^T} = \frac{\mathbf{V} \cdot \mathbf{h}_P}{\sigma_P}. \tag{A-3}$$

The $\mathbf{MCTR}(n)$ is the partial derivative of σ_P with respect to $\mathbf{h}_P(n)$. We can think of it as the change in portfolio risk given a 1% increase in the holding of asset n, financed by decreasing the cash account by 1%.

The marginal contribution to active risk is given by

$$\mathbf{MCAR} = \frac{\partial \psi_P}{\partial \mathbf{h}_{PA}^T} = \frac{\mathbf{V} \cdot \mathbf{h}_{PA}}{\psi_P}, \tag{A-4}$$

where $\mathbf{h}_{PA}$ measures the active portfolio holdings.

Using equations (A-3) and (A-4), and the definitions of total and active risk, we can also show that:

$$\mathbf{h}_P^T \cdot \mathbf{MCTR} = \sigma_P \tag{A-5}$$

$$\mathbf{h}_{PA}^T \cdot \mathbf{MCAR} = \psi_P. \tag{A-6}$$

This means that we could, for example, interpret $\mathbf{h}_{PA}(n) \cdot \mathbf{MCAR}(n)$ as asset n's contribution to active risk.

Chapter 15

Advanced Risk Measures for Fixed-Income Securities

Teri Geske
Vice President, Product Development
Capital Management Sciences

Gunnar Klinkhammer, Ph.D.
Vice President, Quantitative Research
Capital Management Sciences

OVERVIEW

Over the past ten years, the evolution of risk and return measures for fixed-income securities has moved from traditional, static measures such as Macaulay's duration, yield-to-maturity, and nominal spread to option-adjusted values such as effective duration, effective convexity, partial or "key rate" durations, and option-adjusted spreads (OAS). All of these concepts focus on the sensitivity of a bond's (or fixed-income derivative's) price to changes in interest rates, as interest rate risk and the relationship between interest rates and the value of a bond's embedded options is the dominant risk factor in this market. However, there are other sources of risk which can have a material impact on the valuation of fixed-income securities. The presence of these additional risk factors highlights the need for risk measures which define and quantify a bond's (or a portfolio's) sensitivity to changes in other variables. This article describes four such measures: prepayment uncertainty, volatility risk (vega), zero-volatility OAS (ZVO), and spread duration. These measures provide an additional dimension to investment analysis, complementing measures such as effective duration, convexity, and OAS. As with effective duration and convexity, these additional risk measures may be calculated both for individual securities and at the portfolio level, allowing portfolio managers to compare individual investment alternatives and overall portfolio strategies.

The four measures are summarized below and are discussed in detail in the following sections.

Prepayment uncertainty — The sensitivity of a mortgage-backed security's price to a change in the level of the prepayment speeds projected by a prepayment model. To calculate this measure, alternative sets of cash flows for the security are produced by shifting each single monthly mortality (i.e., prepayment) rate (SMM) generated by a prepayment model upward and downward by some percentage, e.g. 10%. Based on the security's current OAS, two new prices are computed for the slower and faster prepayments. The average percentage change in these prices compared to today's price is the measure of prepayment uncertainty. The prepayment uncertainty measure recognizes the fact that although a Monte Carlo simulation incorporates interest rate uncertainty, it does not recognize the uncertainty of prepayment forecasts. Prepayment uncertainty may also be calculated for asset-backed securities.

Volatility risk (vega) — The sensitivity of a security's price to a change in the underlying volatility of Treasury rates. To calculate this measure, volatility is increased and decreased along the entire term structure of volatility by specified amounts, and the security's price is recalculated using these higher and lower volatilities, assuming a constant OAS. The average percentage change in price is the measure of volatility risk, or vega. This measure is important for all securities with embedded options, including callable corporates, step-ups, mortgages, CMOs, and ARMs.

Zero volatility spread (ZVO) — The constant spread over the Treasury spot curve which equates the discounted cash flows derived from today's implied forward curve to the current price of the security. As the name suggests, this is the spread an investor would expect to earn if there was no uncertainty about the future path of interest rates. When an OAS is subtracted from the zero volatility spread the result may be interpreted as the time value of the embedded option, since the ZVO assumes that interest rates, and therefore expected future cash flows, will not fluctuate from levels predicted by today's implied forward yield curve.

Spread duration — The sensitivity of a bond's price to a change in its OAS. To calculate this measure, the security's OAS is shifted up and down by some specified amount and the two resulting prices are computed, holding today's term structure of interest rates and volatilities constant. Spread duration equals the resulting average percentage change from the original price (scaled to a 100 bp shift in OAS) and indicates the sensitivity of a bond's price to changes in the risk premium demanded by the market.

PREPAYMENT UNCERTAINTY

Investors have long been aware that the market consensus on expected prepayment rates can change unpredictably. Such changes occur, for example, when new prepayment data indicate that homeowner behavior is no longer adequately described by existing prepayment models. The effect of revised prepayment expectations on the valuation of mortgage-backed securities thus constitutes an additional source of risk. This risk, which we may call prepayment uncertainty risk, is a model risk since it derives from the inherent uncertainty of all prepayment models.

While effective duration and convexity have gained universal acceptance as measures of interest rate risk, no standard set of prepayment uncertainty measures exists yet. Some proposed measures have been called "prepayment durations" or "prepayment sensitivities."[1] Here, we describe three measures that are readily understood and capture the major dimensions of prepayment uncertainty. We call these measures overall prepayment uncertainty, refinancing ("refi") partial prepayment uncertainty, and relocation ("relo") partial payment uncertainty.[2] Our methodology assumes that a (possibly quasi-random) Monte Carlo interest rate path generator is used in conjunction with a prepayment model to compute OASs for mortgage-backed securities.

Overall prepayment uncertainty measures the price effect of a proportional increase or decrease of all projected prepayment rates that underlie the valuation of a given security. To this end, all single month mortality rates (SMMs) that are predicted along the various Monte Carlo paths used for the security's valuation are scaled up by 10% from what the prepayment model would normally predict. The security's price is then recomputed using the OAS derived from the original market price (and the original prepayment model). The price is also recomputed for SMMs that are scaled down by 10% from their originally predicted levels, holding the OAS constant. The price for faster prepayments is then subtracted from the one for slower prepayments, and the overall prepayment uncertainty measure equals one-half the difference, expressed as a percentage of the original price. Thus, an overall prepayment uncertainty of 0.2 indicates that a security's market price will increase (decrease) by 0.2% if all projected prepayment rates are revised downward (upward) by 10%.

In many situations, investors might be less concerned with the possibility of an overall revision of expected prepayments than of expected refinancings. Therefore, the *refinancing partial prepayment uncertainty* is based on a 10% up and down scaling of the refinancing portion of each predicted SMM. The calculation is otherwise analogous to the overall prepayment uncertainty. To complete the picture, one can also compute a *relocation partial prepayment uncertainty* measure which quantifies the exposure to revisions of the projected baseline prepayment rate (the "demographic prepayment rate").

[1] Andy Sparks and Frank Feikeh Sung, "Prepayment Convexity and Duration," *Journal of Fixed Income* (March 1995), pp. 7-11; and, Gregg N. Patruno, "Mortgage Prepayments: A New Model for a New Era," *Journal of Fixed Income* (December 1994), pp. 42-56.

[2] These measures have been implemented by Capital Management Sciences (CMS) in the BondEdge® fixed-income portfolio analytics system.

Exhibit 1: Prepayment Uncertainty Measures for FNMA 30-Year Passthroughs (June 1995)

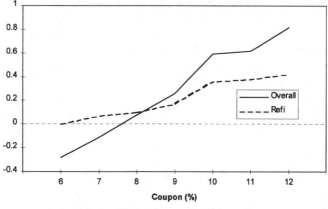

Coupon (%)

Source: Capital Management Sciences

Exhibit 1 shows overall and partial refinancing prepayment uncertainties for FNMA 30-year passthroughs as of June 1995. For discount coupons, the overall prepayment uncertainty measure is negative because a slow-down of prepayments decreases the security's value. Furthermore, the overall prepayment uncertainty for discounts is approximately equal to the relocation uncertainty, since the effect of a revised refinancing expectation on discount mortgages is small. By contrast, premium coupons gain value under an overall slow-down of prepayments and thus have a positive overall prepayment uncertainty. They also have an appreciable refinancing uncertainty. Note that the refinancing uncertainty is positive (or zero) for all coupons since refinancings are projected only for those times and interest rate paths where the coupon bears a premium. For leveraged mortgage securities, such as volatile CMO tranches or mortgage strips, the prepayment uncertainty measures can attain much greater magnitude, both positive and negative, than for passthroughs.

The prepayment uncertainty measures presented here can assist with trading decisions on a single security basis, as differences in prepayment uncertainty may explain why two securities with seemingly very similar characteristics trade at different OASs. On a portfolio basis, these prepayment uncertainty measures allow the user to construct portfolios with controlled exposures to the basic drivers of prepayment uncertainty.

VOLATILITY RISK (VEGA)

Implicit in the valuation of fixed-income securities with embedded options is an estimate of the volatility of interest rates. Obviously, changing one's volatility estimates will affect the value of such securities. The value of an option increases as volatility increases because higher volatility makes it more likely that the option will be in the money on its exercise date (European option) or some time during its exercise period (American option). The investor who holds a security with an embedded option exercisable by the issuer (e.g., a callable corporate bond) therefore faces a drop in value as volatility increases. The opposite is true when the investor is long an embedded option (e.g., in a putable corporate bond). The volatilities implied by the market prices of fixed-income securities with embedded options change over time. These changes are tied to the changing volatility outlook of the markets for interest rate derivatives (caps, floors, swaptions, etc.). If implied volatilities in the markets for callable corporate bonds, mortgage-backed securities and similar assets exhibited large deviations from the volatilities implied by the prices of these derivatives, arbitrage opportunities would arise.

Absent the ability to predict changes in implied volatilities, investors need one or more risk measures to quantify the exposure of their holdings to volatility changes. To value fixed-income securities with embedded options, one needs a dynamic model of the term structure of interest rates. Since different term structure models treat interest rate volatility differently, there is no unique way to measure volatility risk. In particular, models with a term structure of volatility allow the computation of more than one measure of volatility risk, because long-rate volatilities may be changed differently from short-rate volatilities. For simplicity, we present a fundamental measure of volatility risk, which we shall call vega.[3] This risk measure quantifies the sensitivity of a security's price to an overall upward or downward shift of the term structure of volatility. In other words, vega measures the change in a security's value when the volatilities of interest rates of all maturities rise or fall in tandem. In this respect, vega resembles effective duration, which measures exposure to a parallel shift of the term structure of interest rates.

Of course, how one implements the notion of all volatilities rising or falling in tandem may still depend on one's dynamic term structure model. For example, the term structure of volatility in the BondEdge® system is completely characterized by the specification of any two of the following parameters: volatility of the short rate, volatility of the long rate (i.e., the 30-year par bond yield), and mean reversion, which governs the steepness of the term structure of volatility. Building on this term structure model, one can implement a straightforward definition for vega: the percentage change of a security's value under a change in long volatility of one percentage point, with the mean reversion rate and the security's OAS held constant. For example, if the initial long volatility is 11%, vega will involve recalculating a security's price for 10% and 12% long volatility, respectively, holding the security's original OAS constant. The price for 12% long volatility is then subtracted from the one for 10% long volatility, and vega equals one half the difference, expressed as a percentage of the security's original price.[4]

---

[3] Vega is a common name for the volatility sensitivity of options, particularly when the option value is assumed to depend on only one volatility parameter (such as in the basic Black-Scholes option formula).

[4] Since mean reversion is held constant, the volatilities of shorter interest rates also move up and down in this calculation, although typically by more than one percentage point.

Exhibit 2: Vega for 30-Year FNMA Passthroughs (September 1995)

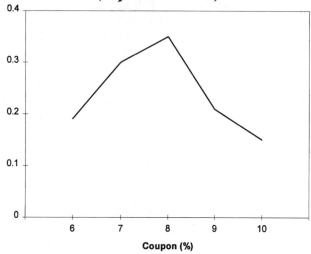

Source: Capital Management Sciences

Mortgage-backed securities provide a good illustration of how a security's characteristics determine its sensitivity to volatility changes. As we discuss in the section on zero volatility spreads, the prepayment options held by homeowners can be thought of as a portfolio of calls and puts. Depending on interest rates, homeowners will prepay faster (thus exercising calls) or slower (thus exercising puts) than expected for a specified base case. Increasing volatility increases the value of the prepayment options and thus reduces the value of a mortgage passthrough. Given our definition, vega should be positive (greater than zero) for passthroughs. Exhibit 2 shows vega for representative 30-year FNMA issues, as computed in September 1995. For example, the 8% issue's vega of 0.35 means that the price of this passthrough would fall by 0.35% if long volatility were to increase by one percentage point. Conversely, the price would increase by 0.35% if long volatility were to fall by one percentage point.

It is not surprising that the near-current coupon issues exhibit the largest vegas. For current coupon mortgages, the prepayment options allow for both accelerated prepayments under falling interest rates and slowed prepayments under rising interest rates. By contrast, for a discount mortgage, homeowners' put options are in the money and gain little additional value under rising interest rates. Similarly, for a premium mortgage, the calls are in the money and gain little additional value under falling interest rates. In other words, the value of the prepayment options in a current-coupon mortgage is most sensitive to changes in volatility because both the puts and the calls are at the money. We see, also, that the volatility sensitivity of the 10% premium collateral is low due to burnout and shorter maturity.

Vega can be negative for some mortgage-backed securities. For example, as of September 1995, a PO backed by 6.50% FNMA collateral maturing in 2024 had a vega of −0.53. This discount collateral hardly has any extension risk, but falling interest rates could cause principal to be returned faster. Thus, volatility creates value for the holder of this PO strip. This last conclusion may seem to conflict with the fact that the prepayment option is still with the homeowners and not with the holder of the PO. The contradiction is solved by considering the third party involved: the holder of the corresponding IO. In our example, the IO backed by the same collateral had a strongly positive vega of 1.65. If one weights the vegas of the IO and the PO by their market values one obtains a combined vega of 0.24 for the IO/PO pair. As we expect, this equals the vega computed for the underlying collateral.

In summary, vega helps to manage the exposure of assets with embedded options to fluctuations of the implied volatility levels in the fixed-income markets.

ZERO VOLATILITY SPREAD

Zero volatility spread (ZVO) is the spread an investor would expect to earn on a bond if there was no uncertainty about the future path of interest rates. It is the spread (in basis points) over the Treasury spot curve which equates the present value of expected future cash flows to the current price of the security, where the "expected" cash flows are determined by today's term structure of interest rates. ZVO is similar to OAS as it is a spread over the entire Treasury curve, unlike nominal spread which is computed relative to a single point on the yield curve. The difference between OAS and ZVO is that OAS incorporates the possibility that interest rates will vary into the future, thereby reflecting the impact of any embedded options under different interest rate environments. The ZVO calculation uses a single set of expected cash flows based on today's term structure to determine whether any embedded options will be exercised. As described below, the difference between ZVO and OAS provides interesting information about the nature of the embedded options in the security.

Intrinsic Value versus Time Value of Options
As discussed earlier, we know that the value of a fixed-income security with embedded options depends on the amount of volatility that interest rates are expected to experience in the future. The greater the volatility, the more valuable the embedded options, and vice versa. When considering the impact of volatility on option value, it is useful to think of options as having both intrinsic value and time value. The intrinsic value is the amount the option holder would realize if the option were exercised today, and in many cases the intrinsic value is zero. A simple example of this is a currently callable corporate bond priced below its call price, e.g., priced at 98 and callable at 102. Although this option's intrinsic value is zero its overall value is greater than zero as long as we assume interest rates can deviate from current levels.

This value which exceeds the intrinsic value is called the *time value of the option*. The longer the time to the option's expiration and the more volatility we assume interest rates will experience in the future, the greater its time value (all other things being equal) because there is more opportunity for the option to end up in-the-money prior to its expiration date. In the example of a corporate bond priced at 98 and currently callable at 102, the option's time value could be considerable (perhaps $2, $3, $4, etc.) depending upon the bond's coupon rate, maturity date, and our expectations for interest rate volatility into the future. If we assume that interest rates will have zero volatility in the future, the time value of this option would also be zero, because there would be zero probability that the call would ever end up in-the-money.

The impact of volatility on an option's time value also applies to the prepayment option embedded in mortgage-backed securities, and to interest rate caps in floating rate CMOs and adjustable-rate mortgages (ARMs). At CMS, we define the intrinsic value of the prepayment option by the level of prepayments which are expected given today's term structure of interest rates. The time value of the prepayment option is derived from the fact that, assuming there is some interest rate volatility going forward the level of prepayments can deviate from current expectations. For those who prefer to think in terms of puts and calls, the prepayment option in a mortgage may be thought of as a combination of a call option and a put option, since homeowners have the right to accelerate prepayments (to call their high coupon mortgages away from investors) when rates fall, and can reduce prepayments below original expectations when rates rise (forcing the investor to hold the mortgage for a longer period when its value has declined) — a put option. As with the example of the callable corporate bond, the time value of the prepayment option depends upon the level of volatility we assume interest rates will experience over the life of the mortgage. If we assume no volatility of interest rates in the future, the time value of the prepayment option drops to zero.

ZVO and OAS

Since the ZVO calculation is equivalent to an OAS calculation with volatility "turned off," the difference between ZVO and OAS expresses the time value of embedded options in basis points. The greater the level of volatility assumed in valuing a security, the greater the difference between the ZVO and OAS. If we turn off volatility, OAS would be equal to ZVO. Therefore, comparing ZVO and OAS tells the investor the cost of future volatility, in basis points. As noted above, for mortgage-backed securities, the difference between ZVO and OAS represents the time value of the prepayment option. For ARMs and CMO floaters, the difference also reflects the time value of periodic and lifetime caps.

CMOs are also affected by the value of the homeowner's prepayment option, with the added complexity of the deal structure. VADM tranches and PACs with short average lives are not particularly sensitive to changes in the time value of the prepayment option because their cash flows are stable. We would therefore expect there to be little difference between the ZVO and the OAS for these instruments, since interest rate volatility in the future will have little impact on the pattern of cash flows received by the investor. We see a greater difference between ZVO and OAS for support tranches which absorb most of the prepayment risk, indicating the cost of future interest rate volatility for these securities.

The difference between the ZVO and OAS for an ARM or CMO floater may be greatly affected by changes in the time value of the lifetime and periodic caps. Even if the bond's coupon is below the cap rate, the cap (which the investor has shorted) has time value because there is a positive probability that the coupon formula will exceed the cap rate during the remaining life of the security. The time value of a cap is also impacted by the slope of the yield curve. For CMO floaters with long average lives, and for ARMs, a positively sloped yield curve implies that a short-term index, such as 1-month LIBOR or the 1-year CMT, will rise into the future. If the curve steepens, the likelihood that a coupon based on one of these rates will ultimately encounter its lifetime cap increases, thereby increasing the time value of the embedded option. The difference between ZVO and OAS measures that value.[5]

Computing ZVO and comparing it to OAS allows the investor to quantify the impact of uncertainty about the future of interest rates. It can be used to compare investment alternatives across different types of fixed-income securities, and to track over time how the time value of embedded options changes.

SPREAD DURATION

Spread duration measures the sensitivity of a bond's price to a change in its OAS. To calculate spread duration we hold the Treasury spot curve fixed at its current level, increase and decrease the security's OAS by some amount and compute two new prices. Spread duration equals the average percentage change from the original price and indicates the sensitivity of the bond's price to changes in the risk premium demanded by the market.

Recall that OAS is the average spread which, when added to the possible future Treasury spot curves, equates the discounted present value of the security's option-adjusted cash flows to its market price. (See Exhibit 3.)

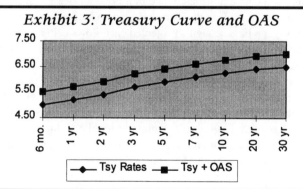

Exhibit 3: Treasury Curve and OAS

---

[5] For ARMs and floating-rate CMOs the difference between ZVO and OAS also reflects the time value of the prepayment option, but this is typically less important than for fixed rate mortgage-backed securities.

OAS may be interpreted as a summary measure of the possible future returns offered by a security based on the expected cash flows across different interest rate paths. OAS allows investors to compare risk/reward characteristics across different types of fixed-income securities with embedded options, such as callable corporate bonds, mortgage passthroughs, and CMOs. Often, investors are just as concerned with the magnitude and direction of changes in spreads as with changes in interest rates, and spread duration allows the portfolio manager to measure the impact of changes in OAS across a variety of fixed-income investment alternatives.

An interesting contrast between corporate bonds and mortgage-backed securities may be observed when analyzing spread duration. With mortgage-backed securities, a change in OAS does not alter the cash flows which the investor expects to receive, as a homeowner's prepayment option is unaffected by changes in OAS demanded by investors.[6] Similarly, a change in OAS for an adjustable-rate mortgage has no impact on the evolution of its coupon rate and therefore would not impact the likelihood of encountering the ARM's reset or lifetime caps. Therefore, spread duration for mortgage-backed securities reflects the fact that a change in OAS affects the present value of expected future cash flows, but the cash flows themselves are unaffected by the change in the OAS.

However, a change in the OAS of a callable (or putable) corporate bond does affect the cash flows an investor receives, since the corporate issuer who owns the call option will decide whether or not to call the bond (or the investor decides to put the bond) on the basis of its price in the secondary market. If a bond's OAS narrows sufficiently a bond's price could rise above its call price, causing the issuer to call the issue (likewise, a sufficient widening of OAS would cause an investor to put a bond to the issuer). Thus a small change in the OAS of an "at-the-money" callable bond could mean the difference between receiving cash flows based on the maturity date or the call schedule.

Consistent with these observations, we see that the spread duration for a mortgage passthrough often resembles its Macaulay's duration, with good reason. Macaulay's duration calculates the change in a bond's price given a change in yield, assuming no change in cash flows. Similarly, spread duration is calculated by discounting the mortgage passthrough's projected cash flows using a new OAS, which is analogous to changing its yield. Spread duration for a mortgage passthrough will not be exactly equal to Macaulay's duration, as spread duration is derived from projected mortgage prepayments along a variety of possible interest rate paths (using a Monte Carlo simulation), whereas Macaulay's duration uses the single set of cash flows generated by a lifetime PSA speed. For CMOs, the difference between the single set of so-called "PSA cash flows" used to calculate Macaulay's duration and the multiple sets of cash flows resulting from the various interest rate paths can cause spread duration to be markedly different than Macaulay's duration.

---

[6] One could argue that changes in the secondary market ultimately affect the interest rate charged on new mortgages, thereby impacting the homeowner's refinancing incentive, but any potential impact is assumed to be negligible for purposes of this discussion.

In contrast, the spread duration for a corporate bond is actually equal to its effective duration.[7] Recall that a corporate issuer will decide whether or not to call a bond based on its price in the secondary market. Since changing a corporate bond's OAS by x basis points has the same impact on price as shifting the underlying yield curve by an equal amount, the calculation for spread duration and effective duration produce the same result. Therefore, either one can be used to estimate the impact of a change in OAS on a corporate bond's price. For example, the impact of a 20 basis point shift in OAS on the price of a bond with an effective duration of 4.37 is estimated by $[0.20 \times 4.37] = 0.874\%$.[8]

Why go to the trouble of calculating spread duration for corporate bonds when it is equal to effective duration? The benefit becomes clear when we consider a portfolio which contains both mortgage-backed securities and corporate bonds. The spread duration of the portfolio measures the portfolio's sensitivity to a change in OASs across all security types, giving the portfolio manager important information about a portfolio's risk profile which no other duration measure provides.

CONCLUSION

The risk measures discussed in this chapter recognize that investment analysis and portfolio management must go beyond interest rate risk measurement and address other sources of risk which impact all fixed-income securities. They can assist with trading decisions on a single security basis, helping to explain why two securities with seemingly similar characteristics have different OASs and offer different risk/return profiles. At the portfolio level, these risk measures allow the portfolio manager to manage exposure to these sources of risk, trading off one type of exposure for another, depending upon one's expectations and risk tolerances.

---

[7] Assuming effective duration is calculated using the same basis point shift used to calculate spread duration.

[8] This assumes effective duration and spread duration are calculated using a 100 basis point shift in the term structure.

Chapter 16

Yield Curve Risk Management

Robert R. Reitano, Ph.D., F.S.A.

Vice President
John Hancock Mutual Life Insurance Company

INTRODUCTION

Yield curve risk management pertains to the general discipline of controlling the sensitivity of a portfolio of fixed-income securities to changes in one or more interest rates or yield curves. In general, the purpose for wanting control can be defensive or offensive, strategic or tactical, but in virtually all such cases, the sensitivity of the given portfolio is being controlled relative to the sensitivity of a second "target" fixed-income portfolio. For example, in asset/liability management, one controls the sensitivity of assets relative to fixed-income liabilities. In total-return fixed income management, one typically controls the sensitivity of the asset portfolio relative to a fixed-income benchmark index which defines the performance objective of the portfolio. Finally, in fixed-income market-neutral portfolios, one manages the sensitivities of a long portfolio of fixed-income assets relative to a short portfolio of fixed-income derivatives, such as interest rate futures contracts.

Defensive yield curve risk management means controlling interest rate sensitivity with the primary objective of protecting against losses relative to the target portfolio; in contrast, the primary objective of offensive or opportunistic management is to capitalize on perceived opportunities for gains. Defensive risk management can be strategic or tactical. A strategic implementation involves risk management in light of longer term models of the behavior of interest rates, while a tactical implementation is in response to shorter term expectations for such behavior. Offensive risk management is by definition tactical.[1] Asset/liability manage-

---

[1] One documented example of a strategic offensive management approach pertains to portfolios at the very short (under 1 year) end of the yield curve, where longer portfolios enjoy a "liquidity premium" relative to shorter portfolios. See for example, Robin Grieves, and Alan J. Marcos, "Riding the Yield Curve: Reprise," *Journal of Portfolio Management* (Summer 1992), pp. 67-76.

The author dedicates this chapter to his mathematics advisor and mentor, Professor Alberto P. Calderón, on the occasion of his 75th birthday.

ment and market-neutral portfolio management tend to be primarily strategic and defensive but with perhaps a tactical leaning, while total-return management tends to be strongly tactical but with perhaps a defensive leaning. Exceptions are not rare.

Independent of the objective of the yield curve risk management program, the first fundamental problem is one of quantifying the interest rate sensitivities of a given fixed-income portfolio. The next fundamental problem is either one of developing defensive risk management strategies from a longer term model of yield curve movements, or developing opportunistic tactics to capitalize on shorter term expectations. The last fundamental problem relates to the development of yield curve models, both strategic and tactical.

The purpose of this chapter is to provide a detailed survey of various approaches to the problem of quantifying interest rate sensitivity, emphasizing both the theoretical merits and practical shortcomings, and to discuss the implications of these approaches for defensive and opportunistic portfolio management. As for models of yield curve movements, useful strategic approaches will be outlined. Tactical models of yield curve expectations will not be surveyed because practitioners are silent both on the methodologies utilized, and especially on all but selective reports of the efficacy of such models.

SINGLE FACTOR YIELD CURVE MODELS[2]

Mathematical Framework

A single factor model is a model for which all of the uncertainty in the future movement of all interest rates is reduced to uncertainty about a single factor, which is typically thought of as a statistical entity, i.e., random variable. There are many such models, as will be seen, because there are many reasonable ways in which this unique factor can be specified. We suspend for now the question of whether or not *any* one factor is sufficient, and simply note that given the assumption of adequacy, many possibilities for a factor can be evaluated. Moreover, independent of any such adequacy assumption, it seems reasonable to expect that there must be a "best" such factor, which might in fact work very well.

Given this factor, which we denote as i even though in some models this variable may not be an interest rate in the usual sense, we can now model the price of the security or portfolio of interest as a function of this variable, $P(i)$, and inquire into the sensitivity of price to changes in this variable. Luckily for portfolio managers, Leibnitz and Newton developed calculus centuries earlier, so this inquiry has a fruitful conclusion. Specifically, it is well known that:

$$P(j) = P(i) + P'(i)(j - i) + 0.5P''(i)(j - i)^2 + \ldots \qquad (1)$$

where $P'(i)$ and $P''(i)$ denote the first and second derivatives of $P(i)$, respectively.

---

[2] For more technical details on these models and their properties, and additional historical references, see Robert R. Reitano, "Multivariate Duration Analysis," *Transactions of the Society of Actuaries*, XLIII (1991), pp. 335-91.

Equation (1), which is recognizable to math aficionados as a Taylor series expansion, states that by knowing the value of a function and its derivatives at a point i, it is possible to determine the exact value of the function at a point j. While this equation is not valid for all functions in theory, it is valid for the fixed-income price functions encountered in practice. Besides providing an identity for the exact value of $P(j)$, equation (1) also provides a basis for approximating $P(j)$: simply stop after the first two or three terms. Just how well a given number of terms works depends on the security and the size of the "shift" implied by the factor shift, $j-i$. In general, the approximation of any given security will deteriorate as $j-i$ increases, while for a given value of $j-i$, a given approximation will deteriorate for securities which are more "exotic;" i.e., contain more embedded optionality.

For finance applications, equation (1) is always restated by factoring out $P(i)$; that way, the units of the derivative terms are relative, so for a given security they are independent of the dollar amount held. Special notation and terminology for these "relative" derivatives have evolved, so that rewritten in the common finance fashion, and omitting terms beyond the second derivative, equation (1) becomes:

$$P(j) \approx P(i)[1 - D(i)(j-i) + 0.5C(i)(j-i)^2] \qquad (2)$$

The "duration," $D(i)$ or D for short, has picked up a mysterious negative sign compared to equation (1), but this is because duration is defined as a negative derivative to be more compatible with the "Macaulay duration"[3] which was developed earlier and outside a calculus context. While apparent by comparison, the definitions of duration and convexity are:

$$D(i) = -\frac{P'(i)}{P(i)}; \quad C(i) = \frac{P''(i)}{P(i)} \qquad (3)$$

Of course, in finance as in any application of mathematics, derivatives must often be approximated since there may be no simple closed formula for the function of interest which allows an exact differentiation. In these cases, derivatives can be approximated by:

$$P'(i) \approx \frac{P(i + \Delta i) - P(i - \Delta i)}{2\Delta i} \qquad (4a)$$

$$P''(i) \approx \frac{P(i + \Delta i) - 2P(i) + P(i - \Delta i)}{(\Delta i)^2} \qquad (4b)$$

In equation (4a), the so-called "central difference" formula is given. An alternative method, though typically biased because of the price function's convexity, is the forward difference formula which uses $P(i)$ in the numerator, instead of $P(i-\Delta i)$, and Δi in the denominator. For any approximation application, there is no

---

[3] Frederick R. Macaulay, *Some Theoretical Problems Suggested by the Movements of Interest Rates, Bond Yields, and Stock Prices in the United States Since 1856* (New York: Columbia University Press, 1938).

useful rule of thumb as to how small Δi must be to give a good numerical approxima-tion. Perhaps using trial and error, the objective is to determine a value so that the approximation produced "stabilizes," and changes little if smaller values are used. This is not as inefficient as it seems, as once the necessary tolerance is calibrated for a given asset class, it tends to remain stable so further testing is unnecessary.

Equation (3) has as a simple consequence the fact that duration and con-vexity have the "portfolio" property. That is, given the durations or convexities of a collection of securities, the corresponding measure of the portfolio is easily calcu-lated as a weighted average of the individual measures, with weights equal to the "relative" prices of the securities, and where relative price is the ratio of security price to portfolio price. Specifically:

$$D^P = \frac{\sum P_j D^{P_j}}{\sum P_j}; \quad C^P = \frac{\sum P_j C^{P_j}}{\sum P_j}$$

These identities have numerous applications. For example, one can calculate measures for surplus given values for assets and liabilities; embedded option charac-teristics can be determined from those of a security with options and its "optionless" counterpart; portfolio effects of a given trade can be predicted, and, desired effects at the portfolio level can readily be translated to the trade required; etc.

Yield to Maturity Approach

The simplest and most natural one factor model is based on the yield to maturity (YTM) of a security. This value, of course, equals the unique interest rate i, so that the present value of the cash flows equals the price, $P(i)$. That is: $P(i)=\Sigma c_t v^{mt}$, where c_t equals the time t cash flow (t is usually denominated in yearly time increments, by convention), and $v=(1+i)^{-1}$ for annual YTMs, $v=(1+0.5i)^{-1}$ for semi-annual YTMs, and $v=(1+i/m)^{-1}$ in general. Equation (3) now produces the familiar:

$$D = \frac{\sum tc_t v^{mt+1}}{P}; \quad C = \frac{\sum t(t+1/m)c_t v^{mt+2}}{P} \tag{5}$$

The Macaulay duration of a security, D^M, equals: D/v. While not actually derived within a calculus context, nor as a result of a pursuit of a measure of price sensitivity, it was soon realized that D^M provided such a measure as long as it was first multiplied by v. Macaulay duration remains popular despite this numerical shortcom-ing because it has the intuitive interpretation as a weighted-average-time-to-receipt of the cash flows: $D^M=\Sigma tw_t$, where $w_t=c_t v^{mt}/P$. Consequently, for a zero-coupon bond, D^M equals the maturity. Interpreting the weights as probabilities, since they sum to one (though need not be all positive), D^M equals the average or "expected" value of t, $E[t]$. Extending the analogy, if we define the Macaulay convexity, C^M, as C/v^2, this measure equals $E[t^2]+E[t]/m$, which can in turn be expressed in terms of the variance of t, and hence has the intuitive appeal as a measure of cash flow dispersion.

Unfortunately, besides the minor inconvenience of having to scale the Macaulay measures to use for an approximation formula given by equation (2), these measures have limited use in securities with embedded options where the basic formulas make little sense. In addition, when the durations of such securities are calculated in terms of equations (3) and (4), and converted into the Macaulay counterpart, the value often defies interpretation in terms of measures of t and implied cash flows. For example, interest-only strips (IOs) have negative durations, and principal-only strips (POs) have duration values far in excess of the time to receipt of the last cash flow. Nonetheless, Macaulay advocates persist and often refer to D and C in equation (3) as "modified" duration and convexity to avoid confusion.

Beyond the Macaulay shortcomings, the YTM one factor formulation itself suffers a fatal flaw. That is, YTMs of fixed cash-flow securities cannot satisfy *any* one factor relationship, except under the most restrictive model for the shape and movement of the term structure of interest rates (i.e., the "yield curve"). This restrictive model is that the yield curve is flat, and can only move in parallel.

For example,[4] the assumption that all YTMs move by equal amounts readily implies this conclusion. However, this result leaves open the possibility that YTMs may satisfy a more complicated one factor relationship. That is, perhaps there is a function, $Y(i,y)$, where $Y(0,y)=y$, or today's YTMs, so that as the factor i changes, each y-value changes according to $Y(i,y)$. For the above classical result, it was assumed that $Y(i,y)=y+i$. As it turns out, even the general one factor model requires the yield curve to be flat and move only in parallel.

Even more generally, it can be shown that the above conclusion also extends to general multi-factor models. That is, if $Y(\mathbf{i},y)$ is a given model with $Y(\mathbf{0},y)=y$, and $\mathbf{i}$ denotes the factor vector, it turns out that the YTM shift model, $y \rightarrow Y(\mathbf{i},y)$, can never be consistent if the yield curve is not flat. The proof of this result is technical and tedious, and beyond the scope of this chapter.

Consequently, even though YTMs are a natural factor framework for single security analysis, they provide a hopeless dead end for portfolio analysis and management. This is because to perform portfolio analysis, one must be able to calculate the one factor sensitivity of the total portfolio from the sensitivities of the individual securities. To do that, one needs in essence a model which specifies how the individual YTMs move as a collective. But as was noted, no such model can in general exist.

Other Single Factor Models

The problem with YTM is that it summarizes too much information; many cash flow structures can have the same YTM. Therefore, based on virtually any example of how the underlying term structure moves, these initially equal YTMs will move to different values. In fact, this observation underlies the proofs of the results noted above. But within this observation of the problem with YTMs lies an alternative potential solution to the single factor problem: simply model the movement of the

---

[4] See Jonathan E. Ingersoll, Jr., Jeffrey Skelton, and Roman L. Weil, "Duration Forty Years Later," *Journal of Financial and Quantitative Analysis* (November 1978), pp. 627-650.

term structure of interest rates directly as a one factor model. The price and price sensitivity of all assets can then be related to today's yield curve and the single factor proposed for its movement.

Of course, there are any number of ways of doing this. First off, one must choose the initial term structure. The most common models are the "par bond" curve, and "spot rate" models, typically denominated in semi-annual equivalent units, although a forward rate model is equally serviceable. The obvious starting points for these models are the "on-the-run" Treasury bond and Treasury strip (i.e., zero coupon bond) curves. Typically, various levels of "quality spreads" are added to these "risk-free" rates to allow the market pricing of securities with default risk.

The next step is to define the manner in which these underlying term structures move, assuming a single factor format. Many models have evolved,[5] among them:

Parallel (Additive) Shift: $i_t \rightarrow i_t + i$
Multiplicative Shift: $i_t \rightarrow i_t (1+i)$
Lognormal Shift: $i_t \rightarrow i_t e^i$
Log-Additive Shift: $i_t \rightarrow i_t + i \ln(1+\alpha t)/\alpha t$
Directional Shift: $i_t \rightarrow i_t + n_t i$

where in each of the above specifications, i_t denotes the initial (pre-shift) value of the term structure utilized at maturity t, i denotes the single factor, α is a parameter, and n_t a maturity-specific shift parameter. The first such model introduced was the additive shift by Fisher and Weil, then multiplicative by Bierwag and Kaufman, log-additive by Khang, who also devised a log-multiplicative model, and directional by Reitano.[6] Of course, many other specifications have been studied as well.

While not initially obvious, the directional shift model is the most general specification possible for the purpose of defining a duration measure. To see this, consider the specification: $Y(i,i_t)$, where $Y(0,i_t)=i_t$. It is easy to check using equation (3) that this specification gives the same duration value as the directional model with $n_t = \partial_1 Y(0,i_t)$, where ∂_i denotes differentiation with respect to i.

Using any single factor specification, it is not difficult to prove the following identity [compare to equation (2)]:

$$P(j) = P(i) \exp\left[-\int_i^j D(s)ds \right] \tag{6}$$

---

[5] In addition to the references in footnotes 2 and 3, see G. O. Bierwag, *Duration Analysis* (Cambridge, MA: Ballinger Publishing, 1987), and the references therein.

[6] Lawrence Fisher and Roman L. Weil, "Coping with the Risk of Interest Rate Fluctuations: Returns to Bondholders from Naive and Optimal Strategies," *Journal of Business* (October 1971), pp. 408-31; G.O. Bierwag and George Kaufman, "Coping with the Risk of Interest Rate Fluctuations: A Note," *Journal of Business* (July 1977); Chulson Khang, "Bond Immunization when Short-Term Interest Rates Fluctuate More Than Long-Term Rates," University of Oregon Working Paper (1977); Reitano, "Multivariate Duration Analysis."

In contrast to equation (2), this identity states that the price on factor value j is completely determined by the price on factor value i and the duration values at all factor values between i and j. On the surface, it indicates that all higher order derivatives of the price function are irrelevant, and to control price, one only needs to control duration. While this observation is formally valid, it does not carry with it the practical significance one might expect for yield curve management. In short, one cannot manage duration with the precision required by equation (6) without also managing convexity.

While this will also be discussed below in the context of time dynamics, it is easy to understand this point in the current context. To determine the "manageability" of duration, we need to understand the sensitivity of duration to changes in the factor. Applying equation (1) to the function $D(i)$, we get:

$$D(j) \approx D(i) + [D^2(i) - C(i)](j - i) \qquad (7)$$

Consequently, even for the smallest of factor shifts, $j-i$, the change in duration will reflect the magnitude of convexity relative to duration squared.

When convexity is relatively large, duration will decrease with increases in the factor; for example, noncallable bonds and insurance and annuity contracts with long embedded put options have this property. When convexity is relatively small or negative, duration will increase with increases in the factor; for example, callable bonds, mortgage-backed securities, and collateralized mortgage obligations have this property. Finally, when convexity equals duration squared, such as is nearly true for zero coupon bonds, duration is relatively insensitive to factor changes.

Equation (6) also provides a new approximation basis for price sensitivity, which in many situations is superior to the approximation basis derived above in equation (2) for a given "order" in terms of $j-i$. For example, the first order approximation:

$$P(j) \approx P(i) \exp[-D(i)(j - i)] \qquad (8)$$

is often superior to the first order approximation implied by equation (2). In addition, these two approximations can often be used together to provide upper and lower bounds for the exact value of $P(j)$.

Beyond the formal mathematics underlying equations (6) and (8), a relatively simple and intuitive explanation can be given. Imagine dividing the factor shift interval, $[i,j]$, into a large number of subintervals, $[t_j, t_{j+1}]$, and on each, approximating the relative change, $P(t_{j+1})/P(t_j)$, by $1-D(t_j)\Delta t$ reflecting equation (2). Of course, the total relative change, $P(j)/P(i)$, is just the product of the subinterval changes. As can be shown, if all the intermediate duration values used are exact, equation (6) is produced in the limit, whereas setting all to $D(i)$ produces equation (8). Approximating the intermediate durations based on equation (7) provides the second order exponential approximation.

Single Factor Yield Curve Management

The opportunistic, i.e., tactical, implications of any one factor model are quite obvious. Given an expectation for the "sign" of the factor change, i.e., positive or negative, one simply trades to the maximum feasible value of duration of the opposite sign. For example, a negative shift expectation motivates a maximum positive duration, as is easily seen from any of the above approximations. Convexity can be ignored for this purpose since in any one factor model, $j-i$ will quite small so the duration effects on price will overwhelm the convexity effects; that is, $j-i$ will be very large compared to $(j-i)^2$. Of course, this aggressive strategy carries the risk that if the realized factor shift has the opposite sign, large losses are possible.

When less certain of the sign of the factor shift, tactical management becomes more subtle. For example, given a likely range for the shift, say: -0.01 to 0.02, a probability distribution, say rectangular, and a personal utility function for wealth, $u(w)$, one would seek a duration value which maximized one's expected utility, $E[u(P(j))]$, which is approximated by: $P(i)E[u(1-D(i)(j-i))]$. Equating the first derivative with respect to D to zero, one must solve: $E[(j-i)u'(1-D(j-i))]=0$, for $D=D(i)$. If the solution exists, it is easy to see that this must be an expected utility maximizing duration value when the manager is risk averse (i.e., $u''(w)<0$). This analysis could be further refined by considering the duration-income relationship over the period modeled.

In defensive yield curve management, one seeks to find conditions which will minimize factor exposure of the managed portfolio relative to a target portfolio. As noted above, asset/liability and market-neutral portfolio management are examples of this, but so is active management of a fixed-income portfolio to match a benchmark index. In each such case, one can create an "objective" portfolio equal to a long portfolio of assets and a short position in the target portfolio. In market-neutral strategies, this objective portfolio is actively managed on both the long and short (i.e., futures, for example) positions, where in general active management only occurs in the long position.

For example, in ALM the objective portfolio is surplus, $S(i)$, and the objective price function is given by: $S(i)=A(i)-L(i)$. Using equation (2), although this result can be derived more formally, it seems apparent that to minimize surplus sensitivity to factor changes, one must have $D^S(i)=0$, since otherwise one will have first order exposure to "unfavorable" shifts. Furthermore, once this is done, one can in theory make surplus favorably exposed to all factor shifts by making $C^S(i)>0$. Using equation (3) to convert these conditions to conditions on assets and liabilities, we get:

$$D^A = \frac{L}{A}D^L; \quad C^A > \frac{L}{A}C^L \qquad (9)$$

While one must assume that $S(i)\neq 0$ to derive these "immunization" conditions, they remain valid if $S=0$.

The conditions in equation (9) can be interpreted in two ways. First, consistent with equation (2), the equivalent conditions $D^S=0$ and $C^S>0$, create a surplus function which has the graph of an upright parabola with equation:

$$S(j) \approx S(i)[1 + C^S(j-i)^2] \qquad (10)$$

where this statement is approximately correct with error magnitude: $(j-i)^3$, which is usually quite small.

Secondly, using equation (7), these conditions assure that the duration of surplus will always have the "right" sign. That is, with error magnitude $(j-i)^2$:

$$D^S(j) \approx -C^S(i)(j-i) \qquad (11)$$

so duration will become positive for negative factor shifts, and conversely. That this is a favorable factor sensitivity for surplus duration stems from the identity in equation (6), since this in turn assures that the exponent of "exp" will be positive, and surplus will always grow.

One of the troubling implications of equation (10) is that perhaps immunization works too well; we have now created a portfolio which is instantaneously riskless, and with real opportunities for a profit due to a change in the factor value. This is, in theory, the holy grail of finance, but in practice, it is usually an indication that a mistake has been made. But has one? Does equation (10) really imply a risk-free arbitrage? On close examination, the answer is an unambiguous not necessarily.

First, the real world is not constrained by our single factor representation of it. If the term structure shifts in a way that is outside that anticipated by the model used, this immunization equation is no longer valid. Second, even if the real world were constrained by our model, what does "instantaneously" immunized really mean? If it means we are immunized against instantaneous factor shifts, what is that? Does anything really happen "instantaneously," without the passage of any time? Of course not! Even within the realm of our single factor world, every shift in the factor corresponds to some shift in time, which the above analysis ignores. This time dynamic will be addressed below, but for now, suffice it to note that equation (10) does not imply the possibility of untold riches.

The above development centered on the objective of immunizating today's surplus value, but can readily be applied to market-neutral portfolios, with $L(i)$ denoting the short portfolio, and to actively managed indexed portfolios, with $L(i)$ denoting the benchmark index. In the surplus context, one may also be interested in immunizing other objective functions, such as the surplus ratio: $S(i)/A(i)$, or the time T forward value of surplus: $S(i)/Z_T(i)$, where $Z_T(i)$ denotes the price of a T-period zero-coupon bond.[7] In these cases, analogous conditions to those in equation (9) can be developed (see equation (34) in the multi-factor development below).

Single (and Multi-)Factor Yield Curve Management Failure

Unfortunately, single and multi-factor yield curve management can fail, and at times fail seriously. Fortunately, these failures are always explainable; indeed, they

---

[7] See Robert R. Reitano, "Multivariate Immunization Theory," *Transactions of the Society of Actuaries* XLIII(1991), pp. 392-438 for more details on these objective functions.

are predictable. Specifically, it is always the case that such failures are traceable to the failure of one or more of the assumptions required in the development of the management strategy. While we illustrate this in the context of single factor models, the validity of these comments in the more general case will be obvious.

As a simple example, it is implicit in the above development that prices, and the associated durations and convexities, are calculated accurately, properly, and consistently. The need for accuracy is self evident. As an example of an improper calculation, consider the pricing of a callable bond or MBS as the present value of noncallable or best-guess callable cash flows at a given spread to Treasuries. Such a spread can always be found, of course, so that today's price is accurately reproduced. However, such a valuation scheme will provide erroneous durations because it ignores the sensitivity of cash flows to changes in the factor. More subtly, even for option-adjusted valuations, it is important that the prepayment model utilized be calibrated as closely as feasible to that underlying traded prices.

Inconsistent calculations occur primarily due to inconsistencies in the manner in which the term structure and shift factor are specified. For example, a yield curve can be specified in par bond, spot, or forward rates; in continuous, semi-annual, monthly, etc., nominal units; and as a credit quality specific curve, Treasuries plus credit spreads, or Treasuries plus option-adjusted spreads. Besides consistency between all valuation yield curves, it is equally important that the shift factor be consistently modeled in terms of both the parameters above, and the manner in which the factor is applied. For example, any multiplicative factor model will provide one set of price sensitivities if applied to the Treasury curve underlying the credit-adjusted valuation curves, and a different set if applied directly to the credit-adjusted curves.

Consistency problems also occur when using stochastic yield curve generators for price valuations. In theory, the exact price is produced only when an infeasible number of "yield curve paths" is generated, where each path is usually generated by first generating a binomial "bit string" of 0s and 1s. To utilize such systems, one typically samples several hundred to several thousand such bit strings, and uses the resulting price as an approximation to the theoretically correct result. The consistency problem occurs in the application of equation (3) which requires three such price estimates. If three sets of bit strings are generated, the resulting D and C values will reflect both price sensitivities and the errors in the estimated prices. To avoid this inconsistency, it is better to generate only one set, and use it for all three valuations.

The major challenge today in achieving correct calculations from practitioner-developed pricing systems stems from the complexity of the finance theory, computer programs, and data manipulations required. For vendor-developed software, assuming correct calculations, the primary challenge is producing valuations which are consistent with the results of practitioner-developed and other vendor supplied systems. In general, when working with more than one system it is better to calculate all price sensitivities directly using equation (4) than use vendor supplied sensitivities, since one can then control consistency through the term structure specifications.

Beyond inaccurate, improper and inconsistent valuations, failure of a yield curve management strategy can also be due to unanticipated higher order effects, model risk, and most importantly, what has been called factor risk or stochastic process risk.

A *higher order effect* means the effect of the first term of the Taylor series in equation (1) that is ignored. For example, it is not uncommon to only partially implement the immunization conditions of equation (9) by balancing durations, but ignoring convexities. This strategy is typically justified by the commitment to rebalance duration frequently, and the belief that this will imply that rebalancing will occur only after small shifts, for which the convexity implications are minor. Unfortunately, the yield curve can occasionally move quickly and significantly, and generate substantial losses.

As a simple example, consider duration balancing mortgage-backed securities and single premium deferred annuities using equation (9). The convexities of these portfolios violate the immunizing condition since as is obvious, MBSs lengthen when rates rises due to the short call option, and SPDAs shorten due to the long put (i.e., surrender) option. Consequently, the duration of surplus moves in exactly the wrong direction — positive for rate increases and conversely. For small shifts, this "tracking" error may seem minor, but large losses have been realized in periods of large shifts.

Model risk means using the wrong pricing model. The simplest example is the improper valuation of a callable bond discussed above. More common examples include using a different option pricing model (i.e., different yield curve dynamics) or most seriously, a different option election behavior function than those used underlying traded prices. The behavior function risk is by far the most serious since it is standard practice to assume, say, that the mortgagors underlying MBSs are relatively inefficient in the election of their call (i.e., refinancing) options. Unfortunately, these assumptions are regularly updated as experience emerges, with major updates not uncommon. In essence, immunization fails because the sensitivity of the prepayment model to a change in factor values was not modeled for the calculated D and C values from equation (3).

Finally, and perhaps most obvious, is *stochastic process risk*. This is the risk that the yield curve shift experienced is inconsistent with the factor assumed.[8] For example, one may immunize against parallel shifts, but experience a steepening shift.

While using a multi-factor model mitigates stochastic process risk more or less, depending on the number and quality of the factors used, the other causes of

---

[8] For theoretical estimates and illustrations of this risk, see Robert R. Reitano, "Nonparallel Yield Curve Shifts and Durational Leverage," *Journal of Portfolio Management* (Summer 1990), pp. 62-7; Robert R. Reitano,"Nonparallel Yield Curve Shifts and Spread Leverage,"*Journal of Portfolio Management* (Spring 1991), pp. 82-7; Robert R. Reitano, "Nonparallel Yield Curve Shifts and Convexity," *Transactions of the Society of Actuaries,* XLIV (1992), pp. 479-507; Robert R. Reitano,"Nonparallel Yield Curve Shifts and Immunization,"*Journal of Portfolio Management* (Spring 1992), pp. 36-43. See also: G.O. Bierwag, G.C. Kaufman, and A. Toevs, "Bond Portfolio Immunization and Stochastic Process Risk," *Journal of Bank Research* (Winter 1983) for the first formal analysis of this risk.

management failure discussed above apply equally well in these more general models, and will not be repeated below.

Single Factor Yield Curve Management: The Time Dynamic

The above discussion ignored the fact that a price function modeled as $P(i)$ can only represent the price sensitivities of a portfolio to an immediate shift in interest rates; that is, to a shift which occurs before the passage of time has a material effect on the portfolio and its price sensitivities. Such shifts are also called *instantaneous shifts*. In reality, price would be better modeled as an explicit function of time, as would the factor value, that is, $P=P(t,i(t))$.

To this end, we use the methods of Ito stochastic calculus.[9] To begin with, we need a model for the evolution of the factor $i(t)$ in time, where this factor will also be denoted i_t. A tremendously important and general model is that of an Ito process, whereby the "instantaneous" change in i_t, denoted di_t, satisfies:

$$di_t = \mu(t, i_t)dt + \sigma(t, i_t)dz_t \tag{12}$$

where z_t denotes Brownian motion. This "differential" expression is shorthand for the notion that i_T, or the value of the factor at time T, is a random variable that is a stochastic integral, and that i_T is given by:

$$i_T = i_0 + \int_0^T \mu(t, i_t)dt + \int_0^T \sigma(t, i_t)dz_t \tag{13}$$

One of the critical contributions of Ito was introducing the manner in which the integrals in equation (13) could be interpreted, and determining properties of the functions μ and σ that were sufficient to make these integrals, and functions of these integrals, well defined in that context.

For our purpose, it is sufficient to think of equation (12) as describing how i_t changes in a very short time increment. Specifically, this equation can be interpreted as stating that $i_{t+\Delta t} - i_t$, or Δi_t for short, is approximately normally distributed with mean (i.e., expectation) and variance given by:

$$E(\Delta i_t) \approx \mu(t, i_t)\Delta t; \ \text{Var}(\Delta i_t) \approx \sigma(t, i_t)^2 \Delta t \tag{14}$$

where the approximations are good to the order of $(\Delta t)^2$. Because of equation (14), $\mu(t,i_t)$ is generally referred to as the "drift" coefficient, and $\sigma(t,i_t)$ as the "diffusion coefficient."

Returning to the subject of primary interest, if the factor i_t is assumed to follow the Ito process defined in equation (12), what can be said about a function of that process; or more specifically, what can be said about $P(t,i_t)$?

Another critically important contribution of Ito, which has come to be known as Ito's Lemma, answers this question. It states that if P is a fairly smooth

---

[9] See John C. Hull, *Options, Futures and Other Derivative Securities* (Englewood Cliffs, New Jersey: Prentice Hall, 1993), second edition.

function (i.e., twice differentiable with continuous second derivatives), then $P_t \equiv P(t,i_t)$ is also a stochastic integral with drift and diffusion coefficients definable in terms of the coefficients in equation (12) and the derivatives of P. Applying this result and dividing the Ito expression for dP_t by P_t produces:

$$\frac{dP_t}{P_t} = \left(\frac{\partial_t P_t}{P_t} - D_t \mu_t + \frac{1}{2} C_t \sigma_t^2\right) dt - D_t \sigma_t dz_t \tag{15}$$

where D_t, C_t, μ_t, and σ_t denote $D(t,i_t)$, etc., and ∂_t denotes differentiation with respect to t.

While initially imposing, equation (15) has a relatively simply interpretation in terms of single factor yield curve management. Before discussing this, let's first look at what equation (15) reduces to for the simply example of a T-period zero-coupon bond, and where i_t denotes the $(T-t)$-period spot rate at time t. For this example, $P(t,i_t) \equiv \exp[-(T-t)i_t]$, and a calculation produces:

$$\frac{dP_t}{P_t} = \left(i_t - (T-t)\mu_t + \frac{1}{2}(T-t)^2 \sigma_t^2\right) dt - (T-t)\sigma_t dz_t \tag{16}$$

These equations state that the relative price change (i.e., dP_t /P_t) has three components of drift at time t. The first component reflects the relative time-derivative, also known as the security's earnings rate, which for time zero is just the $(T-t)$-period spot rate at that time. The second drift component is the "expected" factor gain or loss reflecting the security's duration at that time and the expected change in the factor, and is reminiscent of equation (2). The third component is perhaps unexpected based on the earlier analysis which ignored time drift, and represents the "expected" factor gain or loss reflecting half the security's convexity and the variance of the factor. The surprise is that in these equations, convexity is first order in time as is duration, in contrast to the implication of equation (2), where convexity was a second-order adjustment in factor units. That such a convexity adjustment is appropriate can be inferred by treating j in equation (2) as a random variable and taking expectations. The convexity term then is multiplied by $\sigma^2 + \mu^2$ instead of just σ^2 as in equation (15), but this is a start. Just what happens to the μ^2 term, not to mention all the other terms of the Taylor series, must remain a mystery for now, with a resolution contained in the theory of stochastic calculus.

The diffusion coefficient in equations (15) and (16) is no surprise. Specifically, these terms state, due to the interpretation in equation (14), that the standard deviation of a portfolio equals the standard deviation of the factor times the duration of the portfolio. That is, duration acts like a lever when $|D|>1$, and like a buffer when $|D|<1$, in translating factor volatility into portfolio volatility. Of course, $|D|$ denotes the absolute value of D.

While providing an elegant and complete framework for representing the time dynamic of a portfolio, equation (15) does not generally alter the conclusions developed earlier using the naive, time-static model. For example, applying this equation to the surplus function $S_t = S(t,i_t)$, it becomes clear that the conditions of equation (9), that $D^S = 0$ and $C^S > 0$, are again necessary. These immunization conditions then force dS_t/S_t to have only the earnings rate and convexity drift terms, and *no* stochastic term; but only for an instant! At any time $t+\Delta t$, the D^S and C^S values change (see below) and immunization is certainly lost because the stochastic term in equation (15) depends on D^S. That is, having $D^S=0$ and $C^S>0$ initially does not protect surplus even a moment later as in the static model, where these conditions assured that D^S would move in the right direction relative to the factor move. Here, as soon as D^S strays away from 0, immunization is lost due to the diffusion term in equation (15).

So how can we be sure that duration will immediately drift away from zero? The answer can be found in a second application of Ito's Lemma, this time to $D_t \equiv D(t,i_t)$, the duration of surplus, to get:

$$dD_t = (\partial_t D_t + (D_t^2 - C_t)\mu_t + 0.5[D_t(D_t^2 - C_t) - \partial_i C_t]\sigma_t^2)dt$$

$$+ (D_t^2 - C_t)\sigma_t dz_t \qquad (17)$$

While the drift term in equation (17) is complicated, it need not concern us for the question at hand. Looking to the diffusion coefficient, at time zero this term is equal to $-C_0\sigma_0$, which is strictly negative by the immunization condition and the assumption that the factor is not deterministic (i.e., $\sigma_t >0$). Consequently, even though initially zero, the duration of surplus will immediately change in an unpredictable way due to the non-zero diffusion coefficient, and hence, the immunization property will be immediately lost.

While the above derivation and conclusion was based on the simple model in equation (12), with only one Brownian motion term, dz_t, it holds equally well if it is assumed that the single factor, i_t, depends on several such terms, $dz_t^{(k)}$, $k=1, 2, ...,$ n. Moreover, with still more effort and advanced Ito calculus, this conclusion holds for the general vector valued Ito process, $d\mathbf{i}_t$, where $\mathbf{i}_t$ denotes the vector of factors in the multi-factor model discussed below, and each depends on the collection of Brownian motions above; i.e., on the vector valued Brownian motion, $d\mathbf{z}_t$.

Of course, this does not imply that immunization is not effective in managing yield curve risk. It simply implies that immunization does not create the risk-free arbitrage implied by equation (10), above, or in the multi-factor counterpart in equation (32) below.

Is There a "Best" Single Factor Model?

Before exiting the realm of single factor models, it makes sense to at least consider the question: Is there a best factor to use when you are using only one factor? Before answering this, it makes sense to first contemplate in what way do we mean "best." Of course, the best single factor model is the one which exactly predicts the "nature" of the yield curve shift which occurs over the period of interest. For example, during a period of parallel shifts, one can hardly do better than the Fisher-Weil model. Unfortunely, since such predictions seem to be impossible to make with confidence, we abandon this notion of "best."

At the other extreme, what if we not only did not possess perfect foresight, but we had no knowledge at all? That is, what if it were the case that any yield curve shift that was possible was equally likely and that historical data were of no value in determining shifts to come. In a sense, yield curve shifts were just a random walk limited only to the extent that shifts which allowed riskless arbitrage were "banned." In such a world, it is hard to imagine by what paradigm we could evaluate whether a given single factor model was best.

Consequently, we pose the question and propose an answer within the framework of an informational "middle-ground," as it were, whereby we assume that we have good information on the "necessary" structure of yield curve moves, but that past experience suggests that there are random components in these moves which preclude perfect predictions. That is, using a sample of historical shifts and the assumption that future shifts will be selected from the same statistical "urn," we pose the question: Is there a single shift, which when used to underlie a single factor model, will provide the best predictor of yield curves to come? This model of shifts is also called a "stationary" model, in the sense that all of the statistics of the series are assumed to be fixed in time.

We now investigate an answer to this question under the additional assumption that sequential shifts have no autocorrelation structure and can be assumed to be independent. The approach to be taken is known as the *method of principal components*.[10] To begin, assume that we are given a collection of historical yield curve shifts: $\{\mathbf{Y}_j\}$, where each shift is a vector: $\mathbf{Y}=(y_1, y_2, ..., y_m)$, of changes at selected points on the term structure. Our goal is to find a vector, $\mathbf{P}$, so that its multiples approximate the original shifts as closely as possible. We use multiples of $\mathbf{P}$ because in the context of a single factor model, $\mathbf{P}$ represents the "shape" of the term structure shift, while the multiples equal values of the factor modeled.

One method for simultaneously approximating all shifts is the method of principal components, which seeks to minimize the sum of the squared-lengths of the residual terms: $\Sigma|\mathbf{Y}_j-a_j\mathbf{P}|^2$, where the multiples, a_j, are chosen optimally, and $|\mathbf{P}|^2$ denotes the length of $\mathbf{P}$ squared, $|\mathbf{P}|^2=\Sigma p_j^2$. It is sometimes convenient to express this value in the notation of the dot or inner product of vectors $|\mathbf{P}|^2=\mathbf{P}\bullet\mathbf{P}$, where in general this product is defined as $\mathbf{X}\bullet\mathbf{Y}=\Sigma x_j y_j$, and will also be denoted: $(\mathbf{X},\mathbf{Y})$. In order to simplify the interpretation of results later, it is standard practice to first normalize the yield curve shifts to have a mean of zero. That is, we seek to approximate $\{\mathbf{Y}_j'\}=\{\mathbf{Y}_j-E[\mathbf{Y}_j]\}$ with multiples of $\mathbf{P}$, where $E[\mathbf{Y}_j]$ denotes the mean or average shift vector.

As it turns out, given any value of $\mathbf{P}$ it is straightforward to determine the optimal values for the multiples of $\mathbf{P}$; specifically, $a_j=(\mathbf{P},\mathbf{Y}_j')/|\mathbf{P}|^2$, which geometri-

---

[10] For the traditional derivation of this approach, see Henri Theil, *Principles of Economics* (New York: John Wiley & Sons, 1971), and, Samuel S. Wilks, *Mathematical Statistics* (New York: John Wiley & Sons, 1962). For an application of this method in the multi-factor context to yield curve management, see Robert Litterman and Jose Scheinkman, "Common Factors Affecting Bond Returns," *The Journal of Fixed Income* (June 1991), pp. 54-61.

cally represents the "projection" of $\mathbf{Y}_j'$ onto $\mathbf{P}$. This can be readily derived by defining $f(\mathbf{a})=\sum|\mathbf{Y}_j-E[\mathbf{Y}_j]-a_j\mathbf{P}|^2$, with $\mathbf{a}=(a_1,....,a_n)$, and setting the partial derivatives equal to zero. This derivation is simplified by rewriting the terms in the summation as inner products $|\mathbf{X}|^2=(\mathbf{X},\mathbf{X})$, and rewriting each term as $|\mathbf{Y}_j'|^2-2a_j(\mathbf{Y}_j',\mathbf{P})+a_j^2|\mathbf{P}|^2$. That this value of $\mathbf{a}$ identifies a minimum of $f(\mathbf{a})$ follows from the positive definiteness of the (diagonal) matrix of second derivatives. Below, we assume that $\mathbf{P}$ is a unit vector, i.e., $|\mathbf{P}|=1$, to simplify this expression for a_j.

The problem of identifying the "best" single factor model now becomes:

$$\text{Minimize: } \sum|\mathbf{Y}_j' - (\mathbf{Y}_j', \mathbf{P})\,\mathbf{P}|^2 \tag{18}$$

over all unit vectors, $\mathbf{P}$. Unfortunately, methods of calculus quickly produce a mess here because unlike the search for the a_j, setting these partial derivatives to zero produces difficult nonlinear equations. We need a trick!

Rewriting the terms in the summation in equation (18) as inner products, and rearranging, we get:

$$\text{Minimize: } \sum|\mathbf{Y}_j'|^2 - \sum(\mathbf{Y}_j', \mathbf{P})^2 \tag{19}$$

which is equivalent to maximizing the second summation since the first is independent of $\mathbf{P}$. This second summation can be rewritten as a matrix product $\mathbf{P}^T\mathbf{V}\mathbf{P}$, where $\mathbf{V}$ is $n-1$ times the variance/covariance matrix of the sample $\{\mathbf{Y}_j\}$, justifying the normalization of the sample above; $\mathbf{P}^T$ is the row vector transpose of the column vector $\mathbf{P}$; and n is the sample size. Since this matrix has the special property of positive semi-definiteness (which is in fact usually the stronger condition of positive definiteness in practice), finding the maximum of this "quadratic form" is easy. Specifically, it is well-known[11] that this expression is maximized when $\mathbf{P}=\mathbf{E}_1$, the unit "eigenvector" or "characteristic vector" of $\mathbf{V}$ associated with the largest (eigen)characteristic value, e_1.

As an aside, let's recall some linear algebra. First, an eigenvector of a matrix, $\mathbf{V}$, is a vector, $\mathbf{E}$, so that $\mathbf{V}\mathbf{E}=e\mathbf{V}$ for some constant, e. That is, multiplying by the matrix just "stretches" the vector if $e>1$, "compresses" the vector if $0<e<1$, and zeros it out if $e=0$. If e is negative, matrix multiplication first "flips" the vector $180°$, then stretches or compresses. In general, e can also be a complex number. Because $\mathbf{V}$ is a symmetric matrix, $\mathbf{V}=\mathbf{V}^T$, it is well known that all eigenvalues are real, and that there exists a complete set of orthogonal (i.e., $(\mathbf{E}_i,\mathbf{E}_j)=0$ for $i\neq j$) eigenvectors. Because $\mathbf{V}$ is also positive semi-definite, i.e., $\mathbf{E}^T\mathbf{V}\mathbf{E}\geq0$, for all $\mathbf{E}$, the eigenvalues satisfy: $e_j\geq0$. Finally, for the typical case of $\mathbf{V}$ positive definite, i.e., $\mathbf{E}^T\mathbf{V}\mathbf{E}=0$ only when $\mathbf{E}=0$, the eigenvalues are strictly positive.

Now that we have $\mathbf{P}$, just how good is it? Returning to equation (19), the "total variation" of the original sample $\sum|\mathbf{Y}_j'|^2$ equals $\sum e_j$, where $e_2, ..., e_m$, denote the remaining characteristic values of $\mathbf{V}$ in descending order (all are non-negative

---

[11] See any linear algebra textbook that discusses quadratic forms: for example, Gilbert Strang, *Linear Algebra and Its Applications* (New York: Academic Press, 1976).

because $\mathbf{V}$ is positive semi-definite). This assertion follows from the observation that both equal the "trace," or sum of the main diagonal components, of $\mathbf{V}$. In addition, the second term in equation (19) is easily seen to equal e_1, since it can be rewritten as $\mathbf{E}_1{}^T\mathbf{VE}_1 = e_1|\mathbf{E}_1|^2$, and $\mathbf{E}_1$ has unit length. Consequently, the total variation of the sample *net* of the first principal component is $\Sigma e_j - e_1$, for a relative reduction of $e_1/\Sigma e_j$, which is often 60-80%.

As for the "shape" of $\mathbf{E}_1$, what can be said? As noted by an associate,[12] since $\mathbf{V}$ is a "positive" matrix, i.e., all components are positive, it must be the case by the Perron-Frobenius Theorem that all of the components of $\mathbf{E}_1$ are also positive. Of course, that does not imply that this is a parallel shift, but only that it is a yield curve shift for which all points move in the same direction. In practice,[13] however, the first principal component looks somewhat linear, but decreases from the short to long maturities; that is, short rates have a tendency to move more than long rates.

MULTI-FACTOR YIELD CURVE MODELS

Mathematical Framework

As expected, it is relatively straightforward to generalize the mathematics underlying single factor model risk analysis to its multi-factor counterpart since once again, only calculus is required. Given a collection of factors, $i_1, i_2,..., i_m$, assumed to capture the statistical drivers of yield curve movements, and which will often be denoted as a vector, $\mathbf{i} = (i_1, i_2,..., i_m)$, it is natural to model the price of a security or portfolio as a function of these factors $P(\mathbf{i})$. Generalizing the single factor case, there is a multivariate version of the Taylor series expansion which gives the value of the price function on $\mathbf{j}$, $P(\mathbf{j})$, in terms of the value of the price function and its various derivatives on $\mathbf{i}$. Specifically:

$$P(\mathbf{j}) = P(\mathbf{i}) + \Sigma \, \partial_k P(\mathbf{i})(j_k - i_k) + 0.5 \Sigma\Sigma \, \partial_{kl} P(\mathbf{i})(j_k - i_k)(j_l - i_l) + \ldots \ldots \quad (20)$$

where ∂_k and ∂_{kl} denote first and second order partial derivatives.

Restating equation (20) analogously to equation (2), one identifies natural generalizations of the notions of duration and convexity in this multi-factor framework:[14]

$$P(\mathbf{j}) \approx P(\mathbf{i})[1 - \Sigma D_k(\mathbf{i}) \, (j_k - i_k) + 0.5 \Sigma\Sigma \, C_{kl}(\mathbf{i}) \, (j_k - i_k)(j_l - i_l)] \quad (21)$$
$$= P(\mathbf{i})[1 - \mathbf{D}(\mathbf{i}) \bullet \Delta\mathbf{i} + 0.5\Delta\mathbf{i}^T \mathbf{C}(\mathbf{i})\Delta\mathbf{i}]$$

---

[12] Benjamin Wurzburger, personal communication. See Marvin Marcus and Henryk Minc, *A Survey of Matrix Theory and Matrix Inequalities* (New York: Dover Publications, 1992), for properties of positive matrices.

[13] See Litterman and Scheinkman, "Common Factors Affecting Bond Returns."

[14] See Reitano "Multivariate Duration Analysis" for a more complete treatment of risk analysis based on multi-factor (i.e., multivariate) models.

where $\Delta i = j - i$. In equation (21), the first approximation is in terms of "partial" durations, $D_k(i)$, and "partial" convexities, $C_{kl}(i)$, while the second uses the more compact vector and matrix notation of the "total duration vector," $\mathbf{D}(i) \equiv (D_1(i), ..., D_m(i))$, and "total convexity matrix," $\mathbf{C}(i) \equiv (C_{kl}(i))$, where:

$$D_k(i) = -\partial_k P(i) / P(i), \qquad C_{kl}(i) = \partial_{kl} P(i) / P(i) \tag{22}$$

$\mathbf{C}$ is a "symmetric" matrix, i.e., $C_{kl} = C_{l\,k}$, reflecting a well-known analogous property of second-order partial derivatives.

Just as for the single factor model and equation (4), equation (22) has as a consequence that all of the above duration and convexity measures enjoy the portfolio property, in that the corresponding measure for a portfolio equals the price-, or market-value-weighted average of the component security measures.

Analogous to equation (4), it is also the case that partial durations and convexities can be approximated by finite difference methods. For example:

$$\partial_k P(i) \approx [P(i + \Delta i \mathbf{E}_k) - P(i - \Delta i \mathbf{E}_k)] / [2\Delta i] \tag{23a}$$

$$\partial_{kl} P(i) \approx [P(i + \Delta i(\mathbf{E}_j + \mathbf{E}_k)) - P(i + \Delta i(\mathbf{E}_l - \mathbf{E}_k)) - P(i + \Delta i(\mathbf{E}_k - \mathbf{E}_l))$$
$$+ P(i - \Delta i(\mathbf{E}_k + \mathbf{E}_l))] / [2\Delta i]^2 \tag{23b}$$

where $\mathbf{E}_k$ is a vector with all 0's except for the kth component, which is a 1. Although these equations at first seem imposing, they are easily programmed and simply require calculated prices on the original term structure, i, as well as on a host of term structures where one or two of the factors is shifted up or down by a "small" amount.

In all, given m factors, equation (23a) requires $2m$ calculated prices in addition to the price on the original term structure, or only m additional prices if the "forward" difference approach is taken. Equation (23b) requires a good deal more effort, requiring in addition to the prices used in equation (23a), a total of $2(m^2 - m)$ additional valuations.

Analogous to equation (6), there is an identity for multi-factor models which relates the price on j, $P(j)$, to the price on i, and values of the total duration vector "between" j and i. To this end, let $\gamma(t)$ denote a parametrization of term structures so that $\gamma(0) = i$, and $\gamma(1) = j$. For example, a simple linear shift could be defined as $\gamma(t) = i + (j - i)t$. The identity is then:

$$P(j) = P(i) \exp(-\int \mathbf{D}(\gamma(t)) \bullet \gamma'(t) dt) \tag{24}$$

where the integral is taken over $[0,1]$, and $\gamma'(t)$ denotes the derivative of this vector valued function, which in the case of the above simple example is $\gamma'(t) = \Delta i$. This identity gives rise to an alternative approximation approach, similar to equation (8), which in its first order version replaces the integral with $\mathbf{D}(i) \bullet \gamma'(0)$, in general, or with $\mathbf{D}(i) \bullet \Delta i$ in the linear case.

Multi-Factor Models

With the first general single factor term structure model introduced in 1971 by Fisher and Weil, multi-factor models have been investigated since 1976.[15] The first such model was:

$$\textit{Mixed Additive-Multiplicative Shift:} \quad i_t \to (1 + i)i_t + j$$
$$\mathbf{i} \to (1 + i)\mathbf{i} + j\mathbf{M}$$

where i and j denote the two factors, and i_t denotes the term structure at maturity t. Letting $\mathbf{i}$ denote the term structure in vector notation, and $\mathbf{M}$ the vector with all 1's, this multi-factor model can also be represented as in the second expression above, where the various operations are by convention to be interpreted component by component.

Another model, generalizing the directional model earlier, is the:

$$\textit{Multi-Directional Model:} \quad \mathbf{i} \to \mathbf{i} + \sum j_k \mathbf{N}_k$$

where $\{\mathbf{N}_k\}$ are a collection of fixed vectors, and the various j_k are the factors. One implementation of this model is derived from a principal component analysis, whereby the various direction vectors used represent some or all of the principal components of term structure movements (see below).

Another example of this model is the key (spot) rate model of Ho.[16] Here, $\mathbf{i}$ denotes the risk-free term structure of 360 monthly spot rates from 1 month to 30 years, derived from a procedure which reflects the prices of all traded Treasuries, subject to various smoothness criteria. From this vector, "key" rates are selected at maturities: 1, 2, 3, 5, 7, 10, 20, and 30 years, and each rate has associated with it a "pyramid" direction vector defined to be 1 at the key rate maturity, 0 at maturities equal to or greater than the next key rate, and maturities equal to or smaller than the prior key rate, and with all other values linearly interpolated. Consequently, the collection $\{\mathbf{N}_k\}$ so defined forms a "partition of unity" in that $\sum \mathbf{N}_k = \mathbf{M}$, the parallel shift vector of all 1's.

Another convenient parametrization of the term structure was introduced by Reitano as part of the first general study of these models, and called the "yield curve driver" model.[17] Here, $\mathbf{i}$ denotes the term structure of "on the run" treasury bond yields, at maturities 0.25, 0.5, 1, 2, 3, 5, 7, 10, 20, and 30 years, with other maturities developed using interpolation by spline or other methods, and the entire term structure

---

[15] See G.O.Bierwag, "Measures of Duration," University of Oregon, working paper, 1976. Other historical references can be found in Bierwag, *Duration Analysis*. See also D.R.Chambers, W.T. Carleton, and R.W. McEnally, "Immunizing Default-Free Bond Portfolios With a Duration Vector," *Journal of Financial and Quantitative Analysis* (March 1988), pp. 89-104; T.S.Y. Ho, *Strategic Fixed Income Management* (Homewood, Ill.: Dow Jones-Irwin, 1990); T.S.Y. Ho, "Key Rate Durations: Measures of Interest Rate Risks," *Journal of Fixed Income* (September 1992), pp.29-44; and the various papers by Reitano referred to in this chapter.

[16] See Ho, "Key Rate Durations: Measures of Interest Rate Risks."

[17] See Reitano, "Multivariate Duration Analysis."

is then converted to spot rates for valuations in the usual way. Consequently, these ten or so yields form the "drivers" of the valuation process. The shift model is then:

Yield Curve Driver Model: $\mathbf{i} \to \mathbf{i} + \Delta\mathbf{i}$

where $\Delta\mathbf{i}$ denotes the vector of factors of yield curve driver shifts $\Delta\mathbf{i}=(\Delta\mathbf{i}_1, \Delta\mathbf{i}_2,....., \Delta\mathbf{i}_m)$. Of course, the yield curve driver model can be implemented with an arbitrary number of yield curve drivers, and within any term structure basis.

Relationships Between Single and Multi-Factor Models

Once a multi-factor model is developed, it is only natural to investigate its properties relative to single factor, and other multi-factor models. For instance, assume that partial durations and convexities have been calculated as in equation (22). Next, fix a direction vector, $\mathbf{N}$, denominated in components consistent with the multi-factor model, which specifies the fixed relationship assumed to hold between the various factor movements. For instance, the original factors could be based on yield curve drivers, key rates, or a multi-factor directional model. What then is the relationship between the duration and convexity in the single factor directional model, called "directional" durations and convexities, and the "partials" of the multi-factor model?

As proved elsewhere,[18] denoting by D_N and C_N the directional duration and directional convexity calculated as in equation (3) using the directional shift model:

$$D_N = \mathbf{D}{\bullet}\mathbf{N} \qquad C_N = \mathbf{N}^T\mathbf{C}\mathbf{N} \tag{25a}$$

where $\mathbf{D}$ and $\mathbf{C}$ denote the total duration vector and total convexity matrix of the multi-factor model as defined in equations (22) and (23). That is, the directional duration and convexity of the single factor model is easily calculated by:

$$D_N = \sum D_j\, n_j \qquad C_N = \sum\sum C_{jk}\, n_j\, n_k \tag{25b}$$

where $\mathbf{N}=(n_1, n_2,...., n_m)$.

A simple consequence of equation (25) follows when $\mathbf{N}$ is set equal to the parallel shift vector, $\mathbf{M}$, which has all its components equal to 1. Specifically, the resultant duration and convexity is equal to the sum of the "partials:"

$$D = \sum D_j \qquad C = \sum\sum C_{jk} \tag{26}$$

Equations (25) and (26) are identities between exactly calculated durations and convexities (i.e., identities between the underlying derivatives). Consequently, for durations and convexities approximated using the finite difference equations (4) and (23), these identities will hold only approximately. Similarly, for measures calculated using yield curve scenario sampling techniques, the resultant values will only approximately satisfy these identities, even when the binary bit strings are con-

---

[18] See Reitano, "Multivariate Duration Analysis."

trolled as discussed above. To be certain that the resulting "errors" are the result of such approximations, and not calculation errors, it is important to "stress test" calculations by decreasing the finite difference interval, increasing the sample size, and verifying that the convergence assured by the theory is observed.

It is also important that equation (26) not be too hastily applied in anticipation that the "traditional" duration and convexity measures of Fisher-Weil will be produced from any multi-factor model. This equation simply states that if the individual factors of a multi-factor model are assumed to move "in parallel," that the sum of the partials will reproduce the results of the single factor model where this assumption is modeled explicitly. A few examples will clarify this point.

For the yield curve driver model, the individual factors are defined as the respective shifts of the various yield curve drivers: $\Delta i = (\Delta i_1, \Delta i_2, \ldots, \Delta i_m)$. The associated parallel shift model reflects the assumption that each shift component, Δi_j, is equal to i, say. Is this model now equivalent to the Fisher-Weil parallel shift model where each point of the term structure is shifted in parallel? A little thought reveals that this will be the case only if the interpolation algorithm used converts parallel shifts of the yield curve drivers to parallel shifts of all the interpolated points of the term structure. Linear interpolation has this property, of course. On the other hand, if the Fisher-Weil parallel shift model is "defined" in terms of the yield curve drivers, the resulting duration and convexity will satisfy equation (26), independent of the interpolation method used.

As another example, consider the multi-factor directional model, where the shift is given by $\sum j_k N_k$, and where the $\{j_k\}$ are the factors. Assume next that these factors are modeled to move in parallel; that is, where each j_k equals a given single factor, i. By construction, this single factor model will now be a single factor directional model, where shifts are modeled as $(\sum N_k)i$. Is this parallel shift model that of Fisher-Weil? Only when the sum of the direction vectors equals $\mathbf{M}$, the vector of all 1's. An example of when this condition holds is the key rate model, as noted above. However, it is clear from this construction that any multi-factor directional model for which the direction vectors form a "partition of unity," $\sum N_k = \mathbf{M}$, will enjoy the property that the partial durations and convexities will sum to the corresponding traditional values.

Equation (25) can be generalized to relate the total duration vectors and total convexity matrices of two multi-factor models for which the factors are functionally related. For simplicity, we assume here that this functional relationship is linear. Specifically, consider the above multi-factor directional model with shift $\sum j_k N_k$, and where $\{j_k\}$ are interpreted as the factors, denoted $\mathbf{j}$ for short, and $\{N_k\}$ are interpreted as fixed. Consider next the general multi-factor model whereby each point of the term structure is modeled as a separate factor, and parametrized in terms of the term structure vector $\mathbf{i}$. What is the relationship between the total duration vectors of the two models? Letting $\mathbf{N}$ denote the matrix with the $\{N_j\}$ as columns, we have in matrix notation ($\mathbf{D}$ is interpreted as a row matrix):

$$\mathbf{D(j)} = \mathbf{D(i)N} \qquad \mathbf{C(j)} = \mathbf{N}^T \mathbf{C(i)N} \qquad (27)$$

Equation (27) provides a more formal way of justifying the observations above regarding "parallel" shift relationships. By equation (25), the parallel shift duration in $\mathbf{j}$-space is equal to $\mathbf{D(j)}\bullet\mathbf{M}$, which can also be expressed in matrix notation as $\mathbf{D(j)M}$, where $\mathbf{M}=(1,1,....,1)$. Is this equal to the parallel shift duration in $\mathbf{i}$-space? Using equation (27), we see that $\mathbf{D(j)M}=\mathbf{D(i)NM}$, so the answer is in the affirmative if and only if $\mathbf{NM}=\mathbf{M}$, which is equivalent to $\Sigma\mathbf{N}_k=\mathbf{M}$; i.e., $\{\mathbf{N}_k\}$ form a partition of unity. The careful reader will note that in the above argument, the symbol $\mathbf{M}$ was used with dimension equal to that of $\mathbf{j}$-space, as well as $\mathbf{i}$-space. The transition occurred in the equation $\mathbf{NM}=\mathbf{M}$, in which the $\mathbf{M}$ on the left had dimension equal to the number of columns of $\mathbf{N}$ (i.e., the number of the $\mathbf{N}_k$, or j_k), while the $\mathbf{M}$ on the right had dimension equal to the number of rows of $\mathbf{N}$ (i.e., the dimension of the $\mathbf{N}_k$, or $\mathbf{i}$).

Is There a "Best" Multi-Factor Model?

Without a great deal of thought, the obvious answer to the above question is: Yes, the model with the number of "independent" factors equal to the number of yields on the term structure being modeled. For instance, if the term structure is modeled as a vector in 360-space, describing monthly spot rates from 1-month to 30 years, one such multi-factor model is the general yield curve driver model: $\mathbf{i}\rightarrow\mathbf{i}+\Delta\mathbf{i}$, where the shift vector describes the component by component moves along the curve. Alternatively, one could use any multi-factor directional model with 360 linearly independent direction vectors. This generalizes the above general yield curve driver model which is equivalent to a multi-factor directional model with $\mathbf{N}_k=(0,..,1,0,...0)$, with 1 in the k-th component.

For the yield curve driver model described earlier, with 10 or so yields identified on a par bond curve and the rest interpolated, again it makes little difference whether one parametrizes factors as described, or in terms of a multi-factor directional model with 10 linearly independent direction vectors. While one parametrization may be more convenient to work with than the other, they will be equivalent in terms of their ability to capture all feasible shifts in the given model.

It is also clear that adding linearly dependent direction vectors to a multi-factor model in no way improves the model's descriptive ability or analytic power. More factors are only better if they are independent factors.

Returning to the title of this section, the real question is: Is there a "best" multi-factor model when the number of factors is "small," i.e., small relative to the number of parameters in the term structure model? In the single factor case discussed above, this distinction did not need to be made because all term structure models have at least one parameter, so of necessity, single factor models are relatively "sparse" in their descriptive ability. However, as was shown above, one single factor model was indeed "best" in terms of capturing the largest share of the movement in historical yield curve shifts.

Specifically, if $\{\mathbf{Y}_j'\}$ represents a collection of historical yield curve shifts, denominated in units compatible with the term structure model used, and normalized to have mean $\mathbf{0}$, we saw that the "best" direction vector to use to approximate this collection was $\mathbf{E}_1$, the unit eigenvector of the variance/covariance matrix of these shifts, $\mathbf{V}$, associated with the largest eigenvalue, e_1. In that development, the $\mathbf{Y}_j$ were assumed to have dimension m, so we next consider the generalization of this result to multi-factor models with less than m factors. In actuality, the two factor development provides the template and will be seen to be easily generalized.

To this end, we seek a direction vector, $\mathbf{P}$, so that for optimally chosen $\{b_j\}$, the following is minimized: $\sum|\mathbf{Y}_j'-a_j\mathbf{E}_1-b_j\mathbf{P}|^2$, where as noted earlier, $a_j=(\mathbf{E}_1,\mathbf{Y}_j')$. Not surprisingly, the same derivation shows that the optimizing b_j equals: $(\mathbf{P},\mathbf{Y}_j'-a_j\mathbf{E}_1)/|\mathbf{P}|^2$. Before proceeding, let's simplify this expression by requiring $\mathbf{P}$ to also be a unit vector, and "orthogonal" to $\mathbf{E}_1$, i.e., $(\mathbf{P},\mathbf{E}_1)=0$. Then, mirroring the formula for a_j, we have: $b_j=(\mathbf{P},\mathbf{Y}_j')$.

Another neat consequence of this orthogonality assumption is that the objective function to be minimized reduces to:

$$\text{Minimize: } \sum|\mathbf{Y}_j'|^2 - \sum(\mathbf{Y}_j',\mathbf{E}_1)^2 - \sum(\mathbf{Y}_j',\mathbf{P})^2 \tag{28}$$

because $|\mathbf{X}|^2=(\mathbf{X}, \mathbf{X})$, and all the mixed terms in $\mathbf{E}_1$ and $\mathbf{P}$ disappear. Comparing equation (28) to equation (19), a clear pattern emerges in the problem to be solved. Specifically, the problem is to *maximize* the last term, $\sum(\mathbf{Y}_j', \mathbf{P})^2$, which equals $\mathbf{P}^T\mathbf{V}\mathbf{P}$, subject to $|\mathbf{P}|=1$, and $(\mathbf{P}, \mathbf{E}_1)=0$.

As expected, the solution to this problem is well known to be $\mathbf{E}_2$, the eigenvector of $\mathbf{V}$ associated with the second largest eigenvalue, e_2. Using these first two principal components, $\mathbf{E}_1$ and $\mathbf{E}_2$, in a 2-factor directional model explains $(e_1+e_2)/\sum e_j$ of the total variation of the sample, which is often 80% to 90%.

Generalizing the above derivation, it is apparent that the "best" n-factor directional model uses the first n eigenvectors of $\mathbf{V}$, corresponding to the largest eigenvalues, which need not be distinct. That is, a single eigenvalue can have multiple eigenvectors in theory. In that case, it is irrelevant in which order they are used once the given eigenvalue is brought into the model. This n-factor directional model then explains $\sum'e_j/\sum e_j$, where the sum in the numerator includes only the first n eigenvalues, and each summation includes eigenvalues up to their multiplicity (i.e., number of eigenvectors used).

Multi-Factor Yield Curve Management I

Once a multi-factor model is in place, how do we evaluate and reduce the strategic or tactical risk implied by the portfolio's durational profile, or, how do we evaluate and enhance the tactical opportunities?

To begin with, recall equation (21) which provides an approximation to the value of price on multi-factor value $\mathbf{j}\equiv\mathbf{i}+\Delta\mathbf{i}$, $P(\mathbf{j})$, based on the value of price, durations and convexities on $\mathbf{i}$: $P(\mathbf{i})$, $\mathbf{D}(\mathbf{i})$, and $\mathbf{C}(\mathbf{i})$; and on $\Delta\mathbf{i}$. Using only the durational term, the expression $P(\mathbf{i}+\Delta\mathbf{i})/P(\mathbf{i})$ can be approximated by $R(\Delta\mathbf{i})$:

$$R(\Delta\mathbf{i}) = (1 - \mathbf{D}(\mathbf{i})\bullet\Delta\mathbf{i}) \tag{29}$$

Recalling the well known Cauchy-Schwarz inequality, that: $|\mathbf{X} \bullet \mathbf{Y}| \leq |\mathbf{X}||\mathbf{Y}|$, we have that the absolute variation of this price ratio from 1 is bounded by:

$$|R(\Delta\mathbf{i}) - 1| = |{-}\mathbf{D(i)} \bullet \Delta\mathbf{i}| \leq |\mathbf{D(i)}| \, |\Delta\mathbf{i}| \tag{30}$$

Taking risk assessment first, equation (30) provides an upper bound to risk based on the total duration vector and an estimate of the maximum shift possible. For the yield curve driver model, $|\mathbf{D(i)}|$ is equal to the square root of the sum of the partial durations squared:

$$\sqrt{\Sigma D_j^2}$$

by definition, and an estimate of $|\Delta\mathbf{i}|$ can be made by an analysis of historical yield curve data denominated in the same units as the yield curve driver basis.

Within a multi-factor directional model, such as the key rate model, $|\mathbf{D(i)}|$ again reflects the partial durations under this model, which in turn are directional durations to the direction vectors. For example, if the model used is: $\Delta\mathbf{i} = \Sigma j_k \mathbf{E}_k$, with $\{\mathbf{E}_k\}$ defined from a principal component analysis, each partial duration to j_k, $D_k(i)$, is in fact a directional duration with respect to $\mathbf{E}_k$, $D_E(\mathbf{i})$, which in turn is equal to, by equation (27), $\mathbf{D(i)} \bullet \mathbf{E}_k$, where here $\mathbf{D(i)}$ equals the total duration vector with respect to the yield curve driver model underlying the principal components. The estimate here for $|\Delta\mathbf{i}|$ is again based on historical data, but recognizing that for this multi-factor directional model, $\Delta\mathbf{i}$ is defined in terms of the coefficients of the principal components in the yield curve expansions. That is, since each historical yield curve can be expanded $\mathbf{Y}_k = \Sigma(\mathbf{Y}_k, \mathbf{E}_j)\mathbf{E}_j$, we have $\Delta\mathbf{Y}_k \equiv \mathbf{Y}_{k+1} - \mathbf{Y}_k = \Sigma(\Delta\mathbf{Y}_k, \mathbf{E}_j)\mathbf{E}_j$, and the components of the parameter vector in equation (30), $\Delta\mathbf{i}$, are the $(\Delta\mathbf{Y}, \mathbf{E}_j)$ terms and hence:

$$|\Delta\mathbf{i}| = \sqrt{[\Sigma(\Delta\mathbf{Y}, \mathbf{E}_j)^2]}$$

for each shift, $\Delta\mathbf{Y}$.

Opportunistically, equation (30) can be utilized by investigating the relationship between $\mathbf{D(i)}$ and $\Delta\mathbf{i}$ that assures the most favorable result. Besides providing an inequality for a dot product, the Cauchy-Schwarz derivation identifies the relationship between the two vectors which assures that the largest or smallest value is in fact obtained. Specifically, it turns out that the maximum value of a dot product is obtained when $\mathbf{X}$ equals a positive multiple of $\mathbf{Y}$, denoted $\mathbf{X} \approx \mathbf{Y}$, while the minimum value is obtained when $\mathbf{X}$ is a negative multiple, $\mathbf{X} \approx {-}\mathbf{Y}$.

Consequently, referring to equation (30), to take a maximum opportunistic position on an anticipated factor shift $\Delta\mathbf{i}$, one needs to trade to achieve a total duration vector, $\mathbf{D(i)}$, so that $-\mathbf{D(i)}$ is positively proportional to this anticipated shift; i.e., $\mathbf{D(i)}$ must be positively proportional to $-\Delta\mathbf{i}$. Hence, one wants negative durational exposure to positive anticipated factor shifts and conversely, and the more one anticipates the factor to move, the more durational exposure is sought. This generalizes the one factor opportunistic tactic in a natural way.

However, there are infinitely many vectors positively proportional to $-\Delta\mathbf{i}$, so which should be targeted? Again, the answer is analogous to the single factor case where it was clear that for negative shifts, maximize $D(\mathbf{i})$, and conversely. Here, "larger" multiples are better than smaller multiples since this strategy magnifies the effect. Specifically, if $D(\mathbf{i})=-a\Delta\mathbf{i}$, where a is assumed to be positive, then by equation (30), $|R(\Delta\mathbf{i})-1|=a|\Delta\mathbf{i}|^2$, so the larger a is the better.

When making an explicit assumption about $\Delta\mathbf{i}$ is deemed imprudent, but one wishes to take advantage of beliefs about the probable range of such factor shifts, as in the single factor model, a utility based analysis is possible. To this end, assume that the likely behavior of $\Delta\mathbf{i}$ can be modeled in terms of a probability distribution, however crude, and that a utility function, $u(w)$, has been selected. Consider the expected utility objective function to be maximized: $f(\mathbf{D})=E[u(1-\mathbf{D}\bullet\Delta\mathbf{i})]$. Equating the partial derivatives with respect to the various D_j to zero, the following system of equations is produced:

$$E[\Delta i_j\, u'(1 - \mathbf{D}\bullet\Delta\mathbf{i})] = 0$$

It is easy to see that any solution, $\mathbf{D}$, to this system is a utility maximizing total duration vector for a risk averse investor, because the matrix of second degree partial derivatives $(E[\Delta i_j\Delta i_k u''(1-\mathbf{D}\bullet\Delta\mathbf{i})])$ is positive definite.

To see this, let $\mathbf{X}$ be any vector and consider the matrix product: $\mathbf{X}^T\mathbf{A}\mathbf{X}$, where $\mathbf{A}$ is this second derivative matrix. Using properties of expectations, we get: $\mathbf{X}^T\mathbf{A}\mathbf{X}=E[(\sum\Delta i_k x_k)^2 u''(1-\mathbf{D}\bullet\Delta\mathbf{i})]$, which is positive unless the entire probability mass of $\Delta\mathbf{i}$ is concentrated on a hyperplane. In that case, there is an $\mathbf{X}$ so that $\sum\Delta i_k x_k=0$ for all $\Delta\mathbf{i}$. Of course, in this case, the number of factors can in fact be reduced by 1, and the process repeated.

We next return to a risk assessment perspective, and investigate theoretical risk "elimination" with an immunization strategy. As in the case for single factor models, we in reality eliminate risk only to factor shifts encompassed by the given model, since we can not escape stochastic process risk unless the model is full dimensional (i.e., the same dimension as the number of points on the term structure). However, even in that case, protection is compromised once the time dynamics of the portfolio are taken into consideration.

To this end, consider equation (21). In order to eliminate the risk to all factor shifts encompassed by the model, it is evident that as in the single factor case, we must have $\mathbf{D}(\mathbf{i})=\mathbf{0}$. In actuality, it is only necessary that $\mathbf{D}(\mathbf{i})\bullet\Delta\mathbf{i}=0$ for all feasible factor shifts, $\Delta\mathbf{i}$. However, this equation implies that $\mathbf{D}(\mathbf{i})=\mathbf{0}$, except in the case when all feasible shifts belong to a hyperplane of the factor space. In that case, the number of factors in the model can be reduced to the point where $\mathbf{D}(\mathbf{i})=\mathbf{0}$ is the conclusion. This vector equation is equivalent to $D_j(\mathbf{i})=0$ for all j. When the model is a multi-factor directional model, these equations are equivalent to having the directional durations with respect to the model's directions all zero; i.e., $D_E(\mathbf{j})=D(\mathbf{j})\bullet\mathbf{E}=0$ for all $\mathbf{E}$ in the model. This result follows from equation (27), where here, $\mathbf{D}(\mathbf{j})$ denotes the total duration vector on the yield curve driver model underlying the directional model.

Besides the durational constraint, immunization theory also recognizes the potential for gains and losses from the convexity term, and seeks to make them only gains. Again referring to equation (21), we seek to have: $\Delta i^T C(i) \Delta i \geq 0$, for all Δi. That is, we seek to have the total convexity matrix positive semi-definite, although the purists might require positive definiteness: $\Delta i^T C(i) \Delta i > 0$, except if $\Delta i = 0$. In the multi-factor directional model, this condition on the convexity matrix in units of direction factors, i, can also be translated to a condition on the convexity matrix in units of the yield curve driver model underlying the directional model, using equation (27).

Let j denote the yield curve driver units, $j = \sum i_k N_k = Ni$, where N denotes the matrix with the N_k as columns. Then

$$\Delta i^T C(i) \Delta i = \Delta i^T N^T C(j) N \Delta i = (N \Delta i)^T C(j) N \Delta i$$

so the conclusion is that $C(j)$, the convexity matrix in yield curve driver units, must be positive (semi-)definite on the space generated by the collection of direction vectors used. For example, if the direction vectors used are from a principal component analysis, $\{E_j\}$, the yield curve driver convexity matrix must have this property on all yield curve shifts generated by these components.

Combining the above results, immunization criteria for a general multi-factor model can be easily stated in terms of the price function of interest, $P(i)$. When applied, the general equation (21) becomes the multi-factor counterpart to equation (10):

$$P(j) \approx P(i)(1 + 0.5 \Delta i^T C(i) \Delta i) \tag{31}$$

where $C(i)$ is at least positive semi-definite, so it is always the case that $P(j) \geq P(i)$.

However, as noted above, this price function typically represents a net portfolio such as surplus, a market-neutral account, or an asset portfolio net of a notional index portfolio, so it is more relevant to state these criteria in terms of these underlying price functions. To do this, we need to recall that as a consequence of equation (22), total duration vectors and convexity matrices enjoy the portfolio property. That is, if $\{P_k(i)\}$ are a collection of non-zero price functions with duration vectors, $\{D_k(i)\}$, and convexity matrices, $\{C_k(i)\}$, then if $P(i) = \sum P_k(i)$ is non-zero:

$$D(i) = \sum w_k D_k(i) \qquad C(i) = \sum w_k C_k(i) \tag{32}$$

where $w_k = P_k(i)/P(i)$.

Using equation (32) applied to a surplus portfolio, $S(i) = A(i) - L(i)$, we obtain the following conditions for immunization against yield curve shifts implied by the multi-factor model used:

$$D^A(i) = [L(i)/A(i)]D^L(i) \qquad A(i)C^A(i) - L(i)C^L(i) >> 0 \tag{33}$$

where $X >> 0$ denotes that X is a positive definite matrix.

The conditions of equation (33) provide protection for the current value of surplus against "instantaneous" shifts in the factors. One can also develop conditions which protect the value of the surplus ratio, $(A(\mathbf{i})/L(\mathbf{i}))/A(\mathbf{i})$, which turn out to be identical to those in equation (33) *except* that the values of assets and liabilities are omitted.[19] Another strategy, with applications to surplus as well as to other portfolios discussed above, is the strategy of immunizing the *forward* value of surplus against instantaneous shifts.

To make this notion precise, let $Z_k(\mathbf{i})$ denote the value of a k-period, zero-coupon bond with maturity value \$1, where as always, this value reflects the term structure implied by the factor value, $\mathbf{i}$. If $P(\mathbf{i})$ denotes the price function for a given portfolio, define the forward price function, denoted $P_k(\mathbf{i})$, by:

$$P_k(\mathbf{i}) = P(\mathbf{i})/Z_k(\mathbf{i})$$

Intuitively, $P_k(\mathbf{i})$ represents the value of the portfolio at time k that can be locked-in today by selling the portfolio and buying the zero. Strictly stated, this value is locked-in only if the zero is risk-free, but we assume that this poses no valuation problems and that the necessary term structure is also driven by the multi-factor model used.

Immunization criteria for $P_k(\mathbf{i})$ are:

$$\mathbf{D}^A(\mathbf{i}) = [L(\mathbf{i})\mathbf{D}^L(\mathbf{i}) + S(\mathbf{i})\mathbf{D}^Z(\mathbf{i})]/A(\mathbf{i})$$

$$A(\mathbf{i})\mathbf{C}^A(\mathbf{i}) - L(\mathbf{i})\mathbf{C}^L(\mathbf{i}) - S(\mathbf{i})\mathbf{C}^Z(\mathbf{i}) \gg 0$$

(34)

where $\mathbf{D}^Z$ and $\mathbf{C}^Z$ denote the duration vector and convexity matrix of $Z_k(\mathbf{i})$. Note that the conditions in equation (34) reduce to those in (33) when $k=0$, as expected. Note also that the conditions in equation (34) are equivalent to the requirement that surplus have the same durational structure, and more convexity (i.e., in the sense of positive definiteness), than the k-period zero-coupon bond.

When either equation (33) or equation (34) is utilized in equation (31), it appears that we have constructed conditions which assure a risk-free arbitrage for surplus, on the one hand, or the forward value of surplus, on the other. However, in the same way that this conclusion was overstated in the one factor case using equations (9) and (10), it is again overstated here, and for the same reason. The reason is that the multi-factor immunization conditions were developed without regard for the time dynamics of the portfolio in question. It was explicitly assumed that the portfolio's characteristics did not change as the factor shifted, so as before, the above immunization conditions can only be said to provide protection against "instantaneous" factor shifts.

In the more realistic model which explicitly recognizes the time dynamic, what was modeled as $P(\mathbf{i})$ above, would be modeled as $P(t, \mathbf{i}_t)$, where $\mathbf{i}_t$ denoted the dependence of the factor vector on time. As in the one factor case, when $\mathbf{i}_t$ is assumed to follow a multi-factor Ito process, one discovers that the immunization

---

[19] See Reitano, "Multivariate Immunization Theory" for more details on all the immunization models discussed.

condition on the duration structure can only hold instantaneously, due to the diffusion coefficients, and hence no risk-free arbitrage is created.

Multi-Factor Yield Curve Management II[20]

Once an immunization theory has been developed within a multi-factor context and implemented, two fundamental truisms are discovered: (1) the more factors that are used, the more restrictive the conditions become until virtual cash-matching is required; and, (2) the less factors that are used, the more likely immunization will fail because the model is too sparse to capture the true variability of term structure shifts.

While initially discouraging, these truisms compel a rethinking of the underlying framework for immunization theory. The classical goal of immunization theory is the virtual elimination of downside risk, but in practice, it is only to a subset of feasible shifts that the portfolio is protected. Worse yet, the typical approach completely ignores the potential for loss from shifts outside the model used. As an alternative, rather than seek complete protection from some shifts and have unknown protection from others, perhaps it would be better to have a strategy which provided a minimal amount of risk from all shifts.

The search for such a strategy lead to the development of the theory of "stochastic immunization." Its goal is to minimize the "risk," as yet to be defined, of the relative price function $P(\mathbf{i}+\Delta\mathbf{i})/P(\mathbf{i})$, which is approximated by the linear function, $R(\Delta\mathbf{i})$, defined in equation (29). More generally, its goal is to minimize risk subject to various constraints and objectives of interest.

To develop a measure of risk, first note that since $\Delta\mathbf{i}$ is fundamentally a stochastic variable, it makes sense to follow Markowitz,[21] and consider the variance of $R(\Delta\mathbf{i})$. As it turns out:

$$\text{Var}[R(\Delta\mathbf{i})] = \mathbf{D(i)KD(i)}^T$$

where $\mathbf{K}$ denotes the variance/covariance matrix of the factor change vector, $\Delta\mathbf{i}$ (recall that above, $\mathbf{V}$ denoted $n-1$ times the variance/covariance matrix; i.e., $\mathbf{V}=(n-1)\mathbf{K}$). For simplicity, $\Delta\mathbf{i}$ will be referred to as if its components were in fact changes in the term structure at designated maturities, although the model applies equally well in the general multi-factor case. Recall also that $\mathbf{D(i)}$ is by convention treated as a row matrix, and hence the placement of the transpose symbol above.

Variance is an important measure to minimize because its value determines the likelihood that the random variable under consideration can assume relatively large values. For instance, when normally distributed, only 32% of the distribution is more than one standard deviation away (recall S.D.$=\sqrt{\text{Var}}$), only 5% more than 2 S.D.'s, 0.2% more than 3 S.D.'s, etc. While Ito calculus assumes that factors are

---

[20] For details on the approach developed here, see Robert R. Reitano, "Multivariate Stochastic Immunization," *Transactions of the Society of Actuaries*, XLV (1993), pp. 425-484 and, "Non-Parallel Yield Curve Shifts and Stochastic Immunization," *Journal of Portfolio Management* (Winter 1996), pp. 71-78.

[21] Harry Markowitz, *Portfolio Selection: Efficient Diversification of Investments* (New York: John Wiley & Sons, 1959).

"locally" normal, i.e., over infinitesimal time increments, we cannot assume the same for Δi or $R(\Delta i)$ over finite time interval shifts. So what does variance imply in the general case?

An important result, known as Chebyshev's Inequality, provides the answer in the general case. Specifically, it states that for any constant $a > 0$, the distribution of $R(\Delta i)$ satisfies:

$$Pr(\{\Delta i: |R(\Delta i) - E[R(\Delta i)]|^2 \geq a\}) \leq \mathrm{Var}[R(\Delta i)]/a$$

That is, the probability that the random variable, $R(\Delta i)$, is far from its expected value depends on the variance. Setting $a = n^2 \mathrm{Var}[R(\Delta i)]$, and rearranging, we get:

$$Pr(\{\Delta i: |R(\Delta i) - E[R(\Delta i)]| \geq n(\mathrm{S.D.})\}) \leq n^{-2}$$

which is much weaker than in the normal case. For example, the probability that the random variable is at least 3 S.D.'s away from its mean is no more than about 11% in general, compared with 0.2% for the normal.

Because of this relatively weak general upper bound, and the importance of limiting the likelihood of "outlier" values of $R(\Delta i)$, another risk measure of interest follows from equation (30), which can be restated:

$$|R(\Delta i) - E[R(\Delta i)]| \leq |\mathbf{D}(i)| \, |\Delta i - E[\Delta i]|$$

That is, the difference between the approximate relative price ratio, $R(\Delta i)$, and its expected value, $E[R(\Delta i)]$, is bounded above by the length of the duration vector, $\mathbf{D}(i)$, and the length of the yield curve shift less its mean. Because that last term can be assumed to be bounded, $|\mathbf{D}(i)|$, or equivalently, $|\mathbf{D}(i)|^2$, can be viewed as a risk proxy in that by making it small, outliers in the distribution of $R(\Delta i)$ can be limited, not only in probability as is assured by Chebyshev, but completely.

Both risk proxies above, $\mathrm{Var}[R(\Delta i)]$ and $|\mathbf{D}(i)|^2$, can be weighted and combined into a general risk proxy which provides the user with the option of giving these measures the relative weights desired. Specifically, for a general weighting parameter, w, we define a risk measure, $RM(w)$, by:

$$RM(w) = w\mathrm{Var}[R(\Delta i)] + (1 - w)|\mathbf{D}(i)|^2$$

where we assume $0 \leq w \leq 1$. As it turns out, $RM(w)$ can also be written as a quadratic form in $\mathbf{D}$, similar to the above expression for variance. That is, defining $\mathbf{K}_w \equiv w\mathbf{K} + (1 - w)\mathbf{I}$, we have:

$$RM(w) = \mathbf{D}\mathbf{K}_w\mathbf{D}^T \tag{35}$$

As noted above, $\mathbf{K}$ is at least positive *semi*-definite in theory, although in practice, it will be positive definite for appropriate factor parametrizations. In any case, $\mathbf{K}_w$ is positive definite for $w < 1$, so we assume that $\mathbf{K}_1 = \mathbf{K}$ also has this property.

On a practical note, while the theory only requires $0 \le w \le 1$, in practice, w must be relatively close to 1. This is due to the fact that the units of $\mathbf{K}$ are of the order of magnitude of 10^{-5} or so, depending on the length of the period underlying $\Delta\mathbf{i}$, while the units of $\mathbf{I}$ are magnitude 1. Hence, unless w is close to 1 to offset this unit disparity, the risk minimization problem will effectively reduce to the minimization of $|\mathbf{D(i)}|^2$.

Because $\mathbf{K}_w$ is positive definite, as noted above, it is completely trivial to minimize $RM(w)$ for any w. That is, the minimum of $RM(w)$ is 0, and this value is obtained if and only if $\mathbf{D=0}$, by definition. This conclusion is equivalent to that which is obtained by applying the traditional notion of immunization to this multifactor setting. We have not yet obtained anything of value using this new immunization paradigm.

The payoff for this model is the ability of the portfolio manager to incorporate a host of constraints and strategic objectives into the minimization problem. One such objective relates to the targeting of the term structure shift (i.e., factor shift) return, $E[R(\Delta\mathbf{i})]$. An easy calculation shows that since $R(\Delta\mathbf{i})=1-\mathbf{D} \cdot \Delta\mathbf{i}$:

$$E[R(\Delta\mathbf{i})] = 1 - \mathbf{D} \cdot E[\Delta\mathbf{i}]$$

where $E[\Delta\mathbf{i}]$ is the expected yield curve (i.e., factor) vector shift. Consequently, one can target $E[R(\Delta\mathbf{i})]=r$, using the constraint: $\mathbf{D} \cdot E[\Delta\mathbf{i}]=1-r$.

In practice, this objective can be used strategically or tactically. In the former case, one selects $E[\Delta\mathbf{i}]$ based on an analysis of historical data; in the latter case, $E[\Delta\mathbf{i}]$ represents a personal view of short-term expectations on which one seeks to take a position. Admittedly, the strategic approach has limited applicability because historical values of $E[\Delta\mathbf{i}]$ are so dependent on the period analyzed. Consequently, the selection of a value often involves a process which is fundamentally tactical in nature. As a final point, the strategic choice $E[\Delta\mathbf{i}]=\mathbf{0}$, adds nothing to the problem and can be omitted because this assumption in no way constrains the solution, $\mathbf{D}$, sought.

Another constraint of interest is the targeting of one or more directional durations. That is, based on a principal component or other analysis, or tactically selected direction vectors, one may want to target directional duration values $D_N=\mathbf{D} \cdot \mathbf{N}$, for various values of $\mathbf{N}$. For example, choosing $\mathbf{N=M} \equiv (1,1,..,1)$, allows the targeting of the parallel factor shift duration measure.

In practice, the direction vectors selected and the values of the directional durations targeted will reflect the application in hand. For example, if surplus is the object portfolio underlying the price function, one might simply target traditional duration to 0 or a small value consistent with the traditional theory. More generally, one could limit the directional duration exposures to one or several of the principal component directions. A similar approach might be taken with a market neutral portfolio, or a portfolio actively managed against an index fund where one creates an objective portfolio equal to a long position in the active portfolio and a short position in the index. Alternatively, this last application can be handled by targeting the various directional durations of the actively managed portfolio to those of the index fund.

A final constraint of interest is one which reflects the assets available for trading from the initial total durational structure to that identified as the solution to the constrained risk minimization problem. This asset collection is important since the fewer securities it contains, the less likely one will be able to achieve the desired outcome without specifically providing for the implied limitations. For example, if one can only trade 5-year and 10-year bonds, it is apparent that the portfolio's 20-year partial duration can not be changed. Hence, when developing the constrained minimization problem, it is important to have some constraint so that the solution does not require a change in this value.

In general, it turns out that the asset trading set imposes constraints by defining direction vectors for which the directional durations of the portfolio cannot be changed. That is, it defines a collection $\{\mathbf{N}_j\}$, so that the solution to the problem, $\mathbf{D}$, must satisfy $\mathbf{D} \bullet \mathbf{N}_j = \mathbf{D(i)} \bullet \mathbf{N}_j$, where $\mathbf{D(i)}$ denotes the original portfolio total duration vector. As expected, when the asset trading set is sufficiently large, the above set of vectors is empty, implying that the duration of the portfolio can be changed in any direction.

To determine the constraining direction vectors implied by the given asset trading set, first note that any trade in the portfolio must be "cash neutral;" that is, the totality of purchases must equal the totality of sales. While one may initially reject this notion with the counterexample of a portfolio with excessive cash, a moment of thought reveals that cash neutrality is again obeyed since the purchases must be funded by the sale of short-term securities, such as commercial paper, or the "sale" of cash holdings in a STIF (i.e., short term investment fund) account. In any case, these "cash" positions are part of the initial portfolio value, and this value does not change after a trade; i.e., trades are always cash neutral.

Next, assume that there are n assets available, with total duration vectors $\{\mathbf{D}_k(\mathbf{i})\}$. Form the matrix, $\mathbf{A}$, with $n-1$ columns equal to: $\mathbf{D}_1 - \mathbf{D}_n, \ldots, \mathbf{D}_{n-1} - \mathbf{D}_n$. It is irrelevant which asset is chosen as the nth; while the matrix $\mathbf{A}$ will look different, the same constraints result in the end. Finally, determine a "basis" for the null space of $\mathbf{A}^T$. That is, determine any collection of independent vectors that span the vector space of solutions to $\mathbf{A}^T \mathbf{N} = \mathbf{0}$. This can be accomplished with available software, or with more effort, by reducing this system of equations to upper triangular form. The number of such solutions is called the nullity of $\mathbf{A}^T$, and denoted $v(\mathbf{A}^T)$, or v for short.

The collection of null space vectors: $\mathbf{N}_1, \mathbf{N}_2, \ldots, \mathbf{N}_v$ then represent the directions in which the directional duration of the portfolio can not be changed by trading the given assets. That is, this collection of tradable assets requires the following constraints on the risk minimization problem: $\mathbf{D} \bullet \mathbf{N}_j = \mathbf{D(i)} \bullet \mathbf{N}_j$, for $j=1, 2, \ldots, v$.

In summary, note that every constraint or strategic objective above could be represented by a linear equation for the total duration vector of the form $\mathbf{D} \bullet \mathbf{N} = r$, for some vector $\mathbf{N}$ and value r. Collecting all such constraint vectors as columns of a matrix, $\mathbf{B}$, and the associated values into a vector, $\mathbf{r}$, all such constraint equations can be compactly expressed as $\mathbf{DB} = \mathbf{r}^T$. Consequently, the constrained risk minimization problem of "stochastic immunization" can be expressed:

Minimize: $\mathbf{DK}_w\mathbf{D}^T$, subject to: $\mathbf{DB} = \mathbf{r}^T$ (36)

Before presenting a solution to equation (36) which requires conditions on **B**, let's pause to understand why conditions are needed. First off, no limitation has yet been placed on the number of restrictions allowed in the equation $\mathbf{DB}=\mathbf{r}^T$. Even on an intuitive level this seems problematic since if there are too many constraints, there will likely be no solutions; i.e., we will have an empty constraint set. For example, in 2 dimensions if $\mathbf{D}=(x,y)$, the three constraints: $2x+2y=4$, $2x+3y=4$, and $2x+3y=8$, have no solution, as is easily verified. In general, the number of constraints must be no greater than the dimension of **D**, or m. But is that enough to assure a "consistent" constraint set?

In general the answer is no. Returning to the above example of three equations, any one gives a consistent constraint set of a straight line, as do equations 1 and 2 together, or, 1 and 3, in each case giving a constraint set of a single point. But equations 2 and 3 produce an empty set! In this case the problem is that the constraint direction vectors agree, equalling (2,3), but the constraint values do not, producing an empty intersection. Geometrically, the constraint lines are parallel. If the constraint values also agreed, the constraints would be redundant, and only one needed.

In m dimensions, the constraint set will always be problem free if the set of direction vectors, i.e., the columns of **B**, are linearly independent. Automatically, this condition assures that the number of such constraints is less than the dimension of **D**, but also, that inconsistent and redundant constraints illustrated above are avoided.

Assuming that **B** has linearly independent columns, i.e., that the constraint direction vectors have this property, the solution to equation (36), $\mathbf{D}_o$, is unique and given by:

$$\mathbf{D}_o^T = \mathbf{K}_w^{-1}\mathbf{B}(\mathbf{B}^T\mathbf{K}_w^{-1}\mathbf{B})^{-1}\mathbf{r}$$ (37)

Further, the value of the risk measure for this total duration vector, $RM_0(w)=\mathbf{D}_0\mathbf{K}_w\mathbf{D}_0^T$, is given by:

$$RM_0(w) = \mathbf{r}^T(\mathbf{B}^T\mathbf{K}_w^{-1}\mathbf{B})^{-1}\mathbf{r}$$ (38)

While equations (36) and (37) appear imposing because of the needed matrix manipulations, they are easily evaluated using popular computer software.

Equation (38) can be interpreted as defining an "efficient frontier" in (Risk, r)-space, reflecting the constraint direction vectors assumed in **B**. Specifically, if $\mathbf{D}'$ is any total duration vector satisfying $\mathbf{DB}=\mathbf{r}^T$, then $RM(w) \geq RM_0(w)$. It is not difficult to show that the "shape" of this frontier is a paraboloid in (Risk, r)-space.

For example, if **B** has only one column equal to $\mathbf{M}=(1, 1, \ldots, 1)$, then $\mathbf{DB}=\mathbf{r}^T$ reduces to: $D=r$, where D denotes the traditional parallel factor shift duration measure. Equation (38) then reduces to $RM_0(w)=cr^2$, where $c=(\mathbf{M}^T\mathbf{K}_w^{-1}\mathbf{M})^{-1}=$ $1/\sum\sum(\mathbf{K}^{-1})_{jk}$, and $(\mathbf{K}^{-1})_{jk}$ denotes the jk^{th} element of $\mathbf{K}^{-1}$. Clearly, this efficient frontier is a parabola in (Risk, r)-space.

Once $\mathbf{D}_0$ has been calculated from equation (38), the final problem is to develop the trade that will convert the current total duration vector, $\mathbf{D}(\mathbf{i})=\mathbf{D}$, into the optimum total duration vector, $\mathbf{D}_0$. To this end, let $\mathbf{a}=(a_1, a_2, ..., a_n)$ denote the "trade vector," with a_j corresponding to the amount traded of the jth asset, which as before is assumed to have total duration vector, $\mathbf{D}_j$. By convention, we will interpret $a_j>0$ as denoting a purchase, and $a_j<0$ a sale (of course, $a_j=0$ means "no trade").

If $P(\mathbf{i})=P$ denotes the value of the portfolio pre-trade, then by equation (32), the total duration vector after a trade, $\mathbf{D}'$, is given by: $\mathbf{D}'=[PD+\Sigma a_j\mathbf{D}_j]/P$, since all trades are cash neutral (i.e., $\Sigma a_j = 0$). Of course, the goal of the trade it to make $\mathbf{D}'=\mathbf{D}_0$. Equating expressions, and substituting: $a_n=-\Sigma a_j$, where $j<n$, we get:

$$\mathbf{Aa}' = P[\mathbf{D}_0 - \mathbf{D}]^T \qquad (39)$$

where $\mathbf{A}$ is the matrix used above in connection with the asset trading set constraints (i.e., with columns equal to $\mathbf{D}_j-\mathbf{D}_n$, $j=1, 2, ..., n-1$), $\mathbf{a}'$ is the "truncated" trade vector: $\mathbf{a}'=(a_1, ..., a_{n-1})$, and a_n is implicitly defined by the condition of cash neutrality.

Equation (39) will always be solvable with a sufficient number of assets (i.e., large enough so that $\mathbf{A}$ has "rank" equal to m, the dimension of $\mathbf{D}$), or with fewer assets if constraints are imposed in equation (36) as discussed above. Being solvable, of course, does not mean "uniquely solvable." In general, there will be an infinite number of solutions from which to chose based on criteria outside the scope of the problem so far.

As is well known, if the solution of equation (39) is not unique, then there exists vectors $\mathbf{a}_j'$, $j=0, 1,...v$, so that $\mathbf{a}_0'$ is an arbitrary solution to this equation, and the other $\mathbf{a}_j'$ span the null space of $\mathbf{A}$: $\{a'|\mathbf{Aa}'=\mathbf{0}\}$. It should be noted that here, $v=v(\mathbf{A})$ denotes the "nullity" of $\mathbf{A}$, in contrast to the discussion on asset trading set constraints where this standard notation denoted the nullity of $\mathbf{A}^T$. Consequently, any solution of equation (39) can be expressed as $\mathbf{a}'=\mathbf{a}_0'+\Sigma b_j\mathbf{a}_j'$.

Once this standard expression is derived, the actual implemented solution can be required to satisfy additional constraints on current yield, average quality, amount traded, etc. Many such constraints will in themselves require the solution to a minimization/maximization problem, which can usually be solved with standard techniques.

For example, one might chose to minimize the amount traded to limit bid/asked trading costs. Using linear programming software, the problem is to: Minimize $\Sigma|a_j'|$, summing j from 1 to n, where $\mathbf{a}'=(a_1', ..., a_{n-1}')$ solves: $\mathbf{a}'=\mathbf{a}_0'+\Sigma b_j\mathbf{a}_j'$, and a_n' is defined as: $-\Sigma a_j'$, for cash neutrality. In the absence of such software, one could solve a related problem analytically: Minimize $\Sigma|a_j'|^2$, subject to the same constraints. Note that a_n' can be written as: $-\mathbf{a}'\bullet\mathbf{M}$, where $\mathbf{M}=(1,1,...,1)$ as before. Consequently, $\Sigma|a_j'|^2=\mathbf{a}'\bullet\mathbf{a}'+[\mathbf{a}'\bullet\mathbf{M}]^2$.

Additional Considerations for Multi-Factor Models

Throughout the above development, the intuitive framework for the multi-factor representations was the term structure. That is, it was intuitively assumed that the factors utilized were in one way or another, directly related to the dependence of yield on maturity. This yield could be defined on a par bond, spot, or forward basis, and be denominated in semi-annual or any nominal basis. In general then, the multiple factors related either to movements in these yields directly, as in the general yield curve driver model, or were related indirectly by assuming certain "structural" relationships in the factor movements, as in the general multi-factor directional model.

However, these multi-factor models have much wider applicability. For instance, even in the realm of a term structure, there is not a unique structure but many such structures. Risk-free yields represent the most obvious example of a term structure because of the "real time" availability of traded yields. But at every credit quality another structure exists, although generally less observable across all maturities in real time. Even different sectors of the fixed-income markets often trade at different yields for a fixed given credit quality and maturity, sometimes due to factors such as liquidity and optionality, but equally often not apparently related to any such analytic variable.

Fortunately, such sector differentials are usually relatively small, so it is not unrealistic to ignore them in a strategic model, the goal of which is to develop yield curve management strategies, even though it would be foolhardy to ignore such differentials in a tactical model, the goal of which is to develop cheap/rich insights. Consequently, for a realistic model of "term structure" movements, one needs not only the term structure of risk free rates, but also the term structure of risk spreads for the various credit qualities. Within such a multi-factor model, one could also evaluate "credit spread" durations and partial durations,[22] and evaluate the risks of immunization strategies to shifts among the various spreads. For example, multi-term structure shifts which widen quality spreads would be expected to adversely affect the real value of surplus if assets were of a lower quality than liabilities, although simple single-term structure models would not identify this risk because such models implicitly assume that all spreads move in lock-step.

Naturally, the more general and realistic multi-term structure model can be accommodated in a multi-factor framework by defining **i** to not only reflect risk-free term structure parameters, but also the term structure parameters for credit spreads at the various qualities. While the resulting multi-factor models will have more dimensions than simple single-term structure models, the various risk analyses and immunization strategies are as easily implemented using computer routines.

One real difficulty, however, is the development of statistical assumptions needed for principal component analyses, or for stochastic immunization discussed above, or any application which requires the variance/covariance matrix of the factor vector. For risk-free statistics, of course, this analysis is relatively easy due to the volumes of data on historical Treasury yield curves which are readily available. For credit spreads, available data must first be "scrubbed" for consistency, and

---

[22] See Reitano, "Nonparallel Yield Curve Shifts and Spread Leverage," for more details on the multi-factor framework. See also Martin L. Liebowitz, William S. Krasker and Ardavan Nozari, "Spread Duration: A New Tool for Bond Portfolio Management," *Journal of Portfolio Management* (Spring 1990).

oftentimes holes filled in the series. Even then, spread statistics tend to be more stylistic than risk-free statistics, although still of potential value.

Another extension of the multi-factor framework, but this time beyond the term structure of yields, is to the parameter "yield volatility," or in the more general case, the "volatility term structure." Because of the prevalence of embedded options in fixed-income securities, including liabilities, and because of the dependence of the value of such options on volatility, it is only natural to explicitly model this dependency and seek to manage it, either strategically or tactically.

Recognizing such parameters explicitly as part of the multi-factor structure provides continuity between option management via the "Greeks"(i.e., gamma and delta), and general yield curve management via the notions of "volatility duration" and "volatility convexity." In fact, these latter measures are more convenient in practice for embedded options because they represent measures of the sensitivity of price to changes in the factor directly, in contrast to the "Greeks" which provide option price sensitivities to changes in the underlying security's price, which in turn must be converted to a factor basis. Moreover, even though mathematically equivalent, the volatility duration/convexity analytics are oftentimes far easier to use because in many applications, embedded options can not be easily defined as options on a simple, well-defined underlying security, for which the "Greeks" are easily calculated.

For example, even a callable bond's embedded option has a complicated security underlying it; namely, the callable bond itself. While one can formally perform the decomposition of the embedded option into gamma, etc., it is far more efficient to simply calculate the volatility duration of the bond directly; or better yet, the volatility partial durations.

Chapter 17

Portfolio Risk Management

H. Gifford Fong
President
Gifford Fong Associates

Oldrich A. Vasicek
Senior Vice President
Gifford Fong Associates

INTRODUCTION

Fundamental to portfolio risk management is risk measurement. Risk measurement can be thought of as the quantification of the characteristics of risk. Early attempts at risk quantification dealt with investments in relatively simple security types such as Treasury securities and equities. Risk was characterized by volatility of returns and measured by quantities such as variance, standard deviation, or mean absolute deviation.[1]

The development in risk management techniques introduced additional risk measures. In the case of fixed income securities, the concept of duration became a widespread tool for risk management. For equities, the beta coefficient[2] was introduced to provide further capability in managing the risk of equity portfolios. These analytical paths are indicative of the specialization by asset type since the earlier attempts at risk management. In addition, portfolio-oriented measures such as the concept of shortfall risk have been described.[3]

As derivative securities such as options or swap transactions with embedded options were introduced, the structure of marketable assets has become more complex. Derivative securities exhibit an asymmetric price distribution and, hence,

---

[1] Harry M. Markowitz, *Portfolio Selection* (New Haven, CT: Yale University Press, 1959) and Harry M. Markowtiz, "Portfolio Selection," *Journal of Finance* (March 1952), pp. 77-91.

[2] William F. Sharpe, "Capital Asset Prices: A Theory of Market Equilibrium Under Conditions of Risk," *Journal of Finance*, September 1964, Vol. 19 pp. 425-442.

[3] Martin Leibowitz and Roy D. Henriksson, "Portfolio Optimization With Shortfall Constraints: A Confidence-Limit Approach to Managing Downside Risk," *Financial Analysts Journal* (March-April 1989), pp 34-41.

cannot be adequately analyzed using the more traditional risk measures suitable for simpler investments. A number of recommendations have emerged to address the perceived need for additional risk analysis insight. The Group of Thirty[4] reviewed the derivative product industry practice and suggested value at risk as an appropriate risk measure. The Derivative Policy Group (DPG)[5]recommended stress testing under improbable market conditions.

Value at risk provides a useful summarization under prespecified conditions of the amount at risk given the risk characteristics of the portfolio. Stress testing complements the value at risk analysis by providing the results of extreme scenarios of risk factor changes. These two methods view risk from an overall portfolio standpoint rather than at the individual security level.

The focus of attention in this chapter will be the development of the methodologies appropriate for quantifying the risk of complex investments. The discussion concentrates for illustrative purposes on fixed income portfolios, as these contain typically the largest percentage of derivative securities and transactions. The principles of the analysis, however, apply to portfolios of all asset types.

RISK SOURCES

The total risk of a portfolio is represented by the potential decline in the market value of the portfolio. In order to measure this risk, it is necessary to quantify the possible market value changes, under probable as well as extreme circumstances, resulting from the individual risk sources and from their interplay. By identify individual sources of risk, the total and each component risk of the portfolio can be measured. These sources of risk include market risk, option risk, credit risk, foreign exchange risk, and security specific risk, etc.

In the area of fixed income derivatives, market risk arises from changes in the level and shape of the term structure of interest rates. Option risk results from uncertain future interest rate movement. The uncertainty in interest rate movement can be characterized by interest rate volatility. Credit risk stems from changes in the creditworthiness of issuers and can be quantified as the spreads over the default free government rates. Foreign exchange risk for foreign investments is due to exchange rate movements. Security specific risk is the remaining risk not explained by these principal risk factors.

In recapitulation, the principal risk factors for fixed income derivatives can be described as follows:

1. Interest rate level
2. Rates of benchmark maturities
3. Spreads over government rates

---

[4] *Derivatives: Practices and Principles* published by The Group of Thirty, Washington, DC in July 1993.
[5] See Section 1 of *Derivatives: Practices and Principles*. Appendix I: Working Papers.

4. Volatility of interest rates

5. Exchange rates

The investor may be able to hedge or otherwise compensate for some of these risks. For instance, the interest rate risk of the fund can be easily counterbalanced by short positions in interest rate futures contracts. Foreign exchange risk can be eliminated by forward currency hedges. In addition, the specific risk of the fund may be diversified away by the investor's other holdings. For proper risk management, therefore, it is necessary to measure the exposures to the sources of risk in such a way that these can be reduced or eliminated.

RISK EXPOSURES

An essential basis to risk measurement and management is determining the security and portfolio exposures to their risk factors. Suppose we denote the values of the risk factors by $F_1, F_2,..., F_n$. If P is the value of a security, then the change in the security value resulting from the change in the risk factors can, in the first approximation, be given as

$$\frac{\Delta P}{P} = -\sum_{i=1}^{n} D_i \Delta F_i \qquad (1)$$

The quantities $D_1,..., D_n$ in equation (1) are the exposures of the security to each of the risk factors. They measure the percentage change in the value of the security due to a unit change in the value of the factors.

If we postulate a linear relationship between the changes in the value of the factors and the percentage price change represented by equation (1), then the exposures to the factors are defined by the partial derivatives as

$$D_i = -\frac{1}{P}\frac{\partial P}{\partial F_i} \qquad (2)$$

For example, if F_i is the interest rate level, the expression (2) is the familiar definition of duration. If F_i is the volatility, the expression (2) gives the exposure to changes in volatility, which is sometimes referred to as "vega." It generalizes in the same form to other risk factors as well. Care needs to be taken that the duration and all other exposures are correctly measured on an options adjusted basis. Therefore, the price sensitivities will have already taken into account any embedded options affecting price changes.

Except as a first-order approximation, however, equation (1) is not a satisfactory representation for the price change of a security for several reasons. First, the price change is not a linear function of the factor change, particularly for derivatives. Secondly, the changes in the factors are not instantaneous, so that a change due to the passage of time needs to be incorporated. Third, there may be a specific component in the value of a security, not explained by the market move. And finally, it is more appropriate to characterize the dollar change, rather than the percentage value change, since derivatives such as swaps and other contracts often start with a low or even zero value.

We will therefore assume that the market value of each security is governed by the equation

$$\Delta P = A - \sum_{i=1}^{n} D_i X_i + \frac{1}{2} \sum_{i=1}^{n} C_i X_i^2 + Y \tag{3}$$

where

$$X_i = \Delta F_i \tag{4}$$

are changes in the value of each risk factor and Y is the risk specific to each security. The quantities D_i, C_i are then the *linear* and *quadratic exposures* of the security value to the factors. They are analogous to the dollar duration and dollar convexity measures of interest rate exposure. In order that the non-linear price response is properly approximated, however, D_i, C_i should be measured for a finite factor change, rather than the infinitesimal one given by equation (2). In fact, there are considerations (related to the theory of Hermite integration) that suggest that the exposures should be determined as

$$D_i = -\frac{P_i' - P_i''}{2\Delta F_i} \tag{5}$$

$$C_i = \frac{P_i' + P_i'' - 2P}{(\Delta F_i)^2} \tag{6}$$

where P_i' and P_i'' are the prices of the security calculated under the assumption that the risk factor F_i changed by the amount of ΔF_i and $-\Delta F_i$ respectively, and ΔF_i is taken specifically to be equal to

$$\Delta F_i = \sigma_i \sqrt{3} \tag{7}$$

where σ_i is the volatility of F_i over the interval Δt. With the definitions (5), (6), (7), the exposures characterize the *global* response curve of the security price rather than the local behavior captured by durations and convexities. Finally, the quantity A in equation (3) is equal to

$$A = \mu - \frac{1}{2} \sum_{i=1}^{n} C_i \sigma_i^2 \tag{8}$$

where μ is the expected return,

$$\mu = E\Delta P \tag{9}$$

With this representation of the price behavior, a risk analysis and measurement is facilitated. Both the linear risk exposures D_i and the quadratic risk exposure C_i combine for the portfolio as simple sums of those for the individual securities. Thus, if D_{ik} is the linear exposure of the k-th security to the i-th risk factor (and similarly for C_{ik}), then

$$D_{ip} = \sum_{k=1}^{m} D_{ik}$$

$$C_{ip} = \sum_{k=1}^{m} C_{ik}$$

would be the risk exposures for the portfolio.

A risk management process may then consist of a conscientious program of keeping all the portfolio risk exposures close to zero,

$$D_{ip} = 0 \qquad i = 1, ..., n$$

$$C_{ip} = 0 \qquad i = 1, ..., n$$

to eliminate an undesirable dependence on market factors. This is equivalent to hedging against all sources of market risk. The specific risks $s_k^2 = Var(Y_k)$ which combine by the formula

$$s_P^2 = \sum_{k=1}^{m} s_k^2$$

can only be reduced by diversification.

The overall variability of the portfolio or security value can be calculated from its risk exposures using the formula

$$\sigma^2 = Var(\Delta P) = \sum_{i=1}^{n}\sum_{j=1}^{n} D_i D_j \sigma_{ij} + \frac{1}{2}\sum_{i=1}^{n}\sum_{j=1}^{n} C_i C_j \sigma_{ij}^2 + s^2 \tag{10}$$

which is a consequence of the value change equation (3). Here σ_{ij} are the covariances in the changes of the i-th and j-th risk factor,

$$\sigma_{ij} = Cov(X_i, X_j)$$

To the extent possible, the variances and covariances should be obtained from current pricing of derivatives whose values depend on these variances (these are called the *implicit volatilities*). For instance, quotes are available in the swap market for interest rate volatilities, calculated from market prices of swaptions. These volatilities reflect the market's estimate of the prospective, rather than past, interest rate variability. Only when such implicit volatilities are not available for a given risk factor, a historical variability should be used. In this case, care should be taken that the historical period is long enough to cover most market conditions and cycles.

VALUE AT RISK

The *value at risk* (*VAR*) is a single most useful number for the purposes of risk assessment. It is defined as the decline in the portfolio market value that can be expected within a given time interval (such as two weeks) with a probability not exceeding a given number (such as 1% chance). Mathematically, if

$$Prob(\Delta P \le -VAR) = \alpha \tag{11}$$

then *VAR* is equal to the value at risk at the probability level α.

In order that the *VAR* can be calculated, it is necessary to determine the probability distribution of the portfolio value change. This can be derived from equation (3).

Assume that the factor changes X_i have a jointly normal distribution with mean zero and covariance matrix (σ_{ij}), $i, j = 1,..., n$. Then the first three moments of ΔP are given by equations (9), (10), and (12), where

$$\mu_3 = E(\Delta P - \mu)^3$$

$$= 3\sum_{i=1}^{n}\sum_{j=1}^{n}\sum_{k=1}^{n}D_iD_jC_k\sigma_{ik}\sigma_{jk} + \sum_{i=1}^{n}\sum_{j=1}^{n}\sum_{k=1}^{n}C_iC_jC_k\sigma_{ij}\sigma_{jk}\sigma_{ki} \tag{12}$$

Knowing the three moments, the probability distribution of ΔP can be approximated and the *VAR* calculated. There are theoretical reasons to use the Gamma distribution as a proxy. The resulting formula for the value at risk is then very simple:

$$AR = k(\gamma) \cdot \sigma \tag{13}$$

where σ is the standard deviation of the value of the portfolio or security, obtained as the square root of the variance given in equation (10) above. The quantity γ is the skewness of the distribution,

$$\gamma = \frac{\mu_3}{\sigma^3} \tag{14}$$

calculated using equations (9) and (11). Finally, the ordinate $k(\gamma)$ is obtained from Exhibit 1 (corresponding to the Gamma distribution). (Exhibit 1 only extends to the values $\gamma = \pm 2.83$, since this is the highest magnitude attainable for the skewness of the quadratic form in equation (3).)

Exhibit 1: 0.01 Ordinates as a Function of Skewness

γ	$k(\gamma)$
−2.83	3.99
−2.00	3.61
−1.00	3.03
−0.67	2.80
−0.50	2.69
0.0	2.33
0.50	1.96
0.67	1.83
1.00	1.59
2.00	0.99
2.83	0.71

Note that the value 2.33 in Exhibit 1 corresponding to $\gamma = 0$ is the 1% point of the normal distribution. In other words, if the portfolio value change can be represented by the symmetric normal distribution, the VAR at the 1% probability will be $VAR = 2.33\sigma$. For most derivative securities and portfolios, however, the probability distribution is highly skewed one way or the other and the normal ordinates do not apply. The numbers in Exhibit 1 represent the proper ordinate values.

It may also be noted that equation (13) does not include the expected return μ. This is because the mean is of lower order of magnitude (namely Δt) than the standard deviation σ (which is of the order $\sqrt{\Delta t}$) and can be neglected.

The VARs can be calculated for individual securities, portfolio sectors, and the total portfolio, as well by the sources of risk. Exhibit 2 illustrates a VAR analysis with a global portfolio. This global portfolio consists of US Treasury securities, a floating-rate loan, a short position in an interest rate cap, and German government bonds hedged with a cross currency swap. The cross currency swap is composed of fixed rate DEM payments in exchange for floating rate USD receipts.

The numbers in Exhibit 2 do not necessarily add up, either down or across. The reason that they do not add up for the sectors and the total portfolio is that the value at risk due to, say, foreign exchange risk may come from rising exchange rate for German government bonds while for the cross currency swap, it comes from declining exchange rates. The reason the numbers do not add up across the sources of risk is that events of a given probability (say, 1%) do not add up: an interest rate change that can happen with 1% likelihood when considered alone is not the same as that which would happen together with, say, an exchange rate movement for a joint 1% probability.

Exhibit 2: Value at Risk (USD)

Security	Market Value	Interest Rate Risk	Derivative Risks	Specific Risks	Foreign Exchange Risks	Total Risk
USA						
TB 01/16/97	973,750	2,980	0	310	0	3,000
T 5.5 11/15/98	989,670	13,860	0	1,580	0	13,950
T 8.5 02/15/20	2,314,560	127,480	0	10,650	0	127,920
T 7.5 11/15/24	1,026,050	62,500	0	6,780	0	62,870
Floating rate loan	5,055,630	9,830	0	1,950	0	10,020
Cap sold	−85,790	46,940	5,540	5,510	0	47,590
USA Total	10,273,860	260,420	5,540	24,980	0	261,670
Germany						
DBR 8.5 08/21/00	80,430	920	0	110	3,220	3,350
DBR 9.0 01/22/01	797,260	10,180	0	1,320	31,900	33.510
DBR 8.0 07/22/02	742,100	12,640	0	1,240	29,690	32.290
DBR 6.0 02/16/06	661,130	16,980	0	1,580	26,450	31.470
Cross currency swap	−150,410	28,330	0	3,450	89,870	94,290
Germany Total	2,130,510	12,610	0	1,460	4,330	13,410
Portfolio Total	12,404,370	267,320	5,540	25,030	4,330	268,580

STRESS TESTING

Although value at risk represents a useful assessment of the potential losses from various sources of risk and their interplay, it should be complemented by a series of stress tests. Value at risk is a proper measure of the instantaneous portfolio riskiness. This is all that would be necessary if all securities in the portfolio were perfectly liquid and if the portfolio risk was managed on a continuous-time basis. But in reality this is not the case. Thus, stress simulations of the portfolio's value response to market condition changes that are more extreme or persistent than those likely to occur in a short time interval are in order for comprehensive risk analyses. In this sense, stress tests are less systematic and somewhat ad hoc compared to the value at risk.

A stress test consists of specifying a scenario of extreme market conditions occurring over a specific time interval, and evaluating the portfolio gains or losses under such scenarios. This is useful for a number of reasons. First, such analysis allows for consideration of path-dependent events, such as cash flows on CMO securities. Second, it does not rely on a specific form of the value response curve, such as the quadratic form in equation (3). Portfolio values including derivatives with embedded options will not change in a linear or quadratic form. Depending on the structure of the portfolio, it may change by a large amount under extreme conditions. Third, it has an appeal to intuition that is lost in the VAR alone by showing the situations under which a loss can occur. And last but not least, it is required or recommended by the various oversight agencies and auditors.

Exhibit 3 is a possible stress test output table for the portfolio described in Exhibit 2. Scenarios 1 and 2 represent U.S. term structure movements, which affect USD denominated securities only. Scenarios 3 and 4 represent U.S. interest rate term structure steepening or flattening, which affects the cross currency swap through the floating-rate USD receipts. Scenarios 5 and 6 are exchange rates changes, which influence DEM denominated securities and the cross currency swap through the fixed-rate DEM payments. Scenarios 7 and 8 represent German interest rate term structure movements, which may affect DEM denominated securities only. Scenario 9 is a combination of a DEM/USD exchange rate change and a German interest rate change, which affects both German government bonds and the cross currency swap.

CONCLUSIONS

Risk measurement of fixed income investments is a complex process due to the asymmetry of their return distribution. By utilizing value at risk and stress testing, an ability to evaluate non-symmetric return outcomes emerges. Each of these techniques has an important role. Value at risk is the expected loss from an adverse market movement with a specified probability over a stated time period. For example, value at risk is defined as the dollar amount that the total loss may exceed within 14 days with a 1% probability. On the other hand, stress testing determines how the portfolio would perform under stress conditions.

Exhibit 3: Stress Tests

Number	Scenario	Gain/Loss (USD)
1	USD interest rate up 100 bps	−451,950
2	USD interest rate down 100 bps	481,560
3	USD interest rate: 2 yr up 50 bps, 10 yr down 50 bps	112,490
4	USD interest rate: 2 yr down 50 bps, 10 yr up 50 bps	−103,640
5	DEM/USD up 10%	−9,840
6	DEM/USD down 10%	12,030
7	DEM interest rate up 30 bps	−137,710
8	DEM interest rate down 30 bps	140,300
9	DEM/USD up 10% & DEM interest rate up 30 bps	−2,290
	etc.	

The market characteristics that affect the value of a security or portfolio are called risk factors. Risk factors that affect fixed income derivatives include interest rate level, benchmark maturity rates, spread over government rates, volatility of rates, and foreign exchange rates. To quantify the risk exposure to those risk factors, a quadratic approximation may be used and then a standard deviation may be calculated. The VAR number may be calculated by a Gamma distribution approximation. While value at risk gives a summary risk number, it does not tell the source or direction of the risk. To see the possible loss under extreme or least favorable market conditions, a series of stress tests must be performed. The value at risk and the result of a comprehensive stress test give a better risk picture than either one of them. In combination, they represent a comprehensive risk measurement necessary for portfolios with complex structures and interrelationships.

Chapter 18

Numerical Pitfalls of Lattice-Based Duration and Convexity Calculations

C. Douglas Howard, Ph.D.
Department of Applied Mathematics and Physics
and
The Center for Finance and Technology
Polytechnic University

INTRODUCTION

Duration and convexity are two important tools used to quantify the sensitivity of the value of a portfolio or an individual security to changes in the prevailing interest rate environment. In this chapter we discuss a numerical pitfall associated with using discrete lattice-based valuation models for the purposes of calculating duration and convexity. This pitfall, one of many "lattice effects," has undoubtedly been encountered by many a practitioner.

For ease of exposition we shall assume throughout this chapter a flat term structure, so the prevailing (risk-free) interest rate environment may be specified by one number r. We will allow r to vary, but always retain a flat yield curve. Let $P(r)$ denote the value of a particular fixed-income security when interest rates are at r. (Of course P may depend on other variables such as interest rate volatility, credit risk, etc., but we suppress this dependence since we will hold these variables constant.) Then

$$D = \frac{-1}{P(r)} \times \frac{dP}{dr}(r) \tag{1}$$

and

$$C = \frac{1}{P(r)} \times \frac{d^2P}{dr^2}(r) \tag{2}$$

Research for this chapter was supported by Andrew Kalotay Associates, Inc.

are the familiar duration and convexity calculations. This works perfectly well if we have an explicit formula for $P(r)$ that we can actually differentiate. Unfortunately, for most fixed-income securities there is no such formula. In these cases, $P(r)$ is typically calculated using some kind of numerical algorithm in which r is the input and $P(r)$ is the output. Since there is no explicit formula for $P(r)$, numerical estimates are made:

$$D = \frac{-1}{P(r)} \times \frac{P(r + \Delta r) - P(r - \Delta r)}{2\Delta r} + \text{error} \tag{3}$$

and

$$C = \frac{1}{P(r)} \times \frac{P(r + \Delta r) - 2P(r) + P(r - \Delta r)}{\Delta r^2} + \text{error} \tag{4}$$

If $P(r)$ is sufficiently smooth, the error in equation (3) is of order Δr^2 while the error in equation (4) is of order Δr. In principle, therefore, one can estimate D and C as accurately as desired my making Δr very small.

But this rosy scenario assumes that $P(r)$ is exact where actually the numerical algorithm only produces an approximate $\tilde{P}(r)$. Our numerical estimates of duration and convexity are therefore more properly stated as:

$$D = \frac{-1}{\tilde{P}(r)} \times \frac{\tilde{P}(r + \Delta r) - \tilde{P}(r - \Delta r)}{2\Delta r} + \text{error} \tag{5}$$

and

$$C = \frac{1}{\tilde{P}(r)} \times \frac{\tilde{P}(r + \Delta r) - 2\tilde{P}(r) + \tilde{P}(r - \Delta r)}{\Delta r^2} + \text{error} \tag{6}$$

The additional error introduced by the differences between P and $\tilde{P}$ at r, $r+\Delta r$, and $r-\Delta r$ to the duration and convexity estimates in equations (5) and (6) is potentially of order $1/\Delta r$ and $1/\Delta r^2$, respectively. Suddenly its not such a good idea to make Δr small!

In the next section, we illustrate this effect with a specific example. In our example equations (5) and (6) do, in fact, converge nicely to limits as $\Delta r \to 0$. This is deceptive however, since, at least in the case of equation (6), it is the wrong limit. In fact, letting $\Delta r \to 0$ will actually get the sign of the convexity wrong!

THE CASE OF THE CALLABLE BOND

We consider a newly issued five year bond that pays interest annually at a rate of 7%. Beginning in year two the issuer may call the bond at par. We will use a four period standard binomial lattice with annual time increments and an annual interest rate volatility of 20% to recursively value this bond. (We assume the reader is familiar with this basic methodology.) We assume no credit risk; cash flows are discounted at the risk-free rate. Henceforth $\tilde{P}(r)$ will refer to the estimated value of our callable bond as calculated using a lattice calibrated to explain a term structure that is flat at a rate of r. Note that although we vary the interest rate environment r, we hold the bond's coupon fixed at 7%.

Exhibit 1 shows the callable bond valued in a 7% interest rate environment. Each block of information in this exhibit corresponds to a "node" in the binomial lattice and displays the following node-dependent information: the single-period interest rate; the value of the callable bond (per $100 face amount); and whether the bond is called, not called, or not callable at the particular node. One can confirm the volatility parameter by calculating, for example, ½log(8.403/5.633)=0.20. We leave it to the reader to verify that this interest rate lattice corresponds to a flat 7% term structure, but we will verify several of the callable bond valuation calculations.

In year 4 the bond matures one period later (generating a cash flow of 107) and, for example, at the 14.774% node we have

$$93.227 \ = \ \min[100, \ 107/1.14774]$$

and the bond is not called since this number is less than the call price of 100. At the 6.639% node we see that the bond is called and its value is therefore 100 — the call price. It is called, of course, because 107/1.06639 exceeds the call price.

Exhibit 1: Valuing the Callable Bond

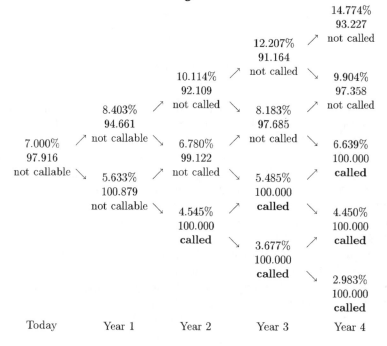

| Today | Year 1 | Year 2 | Year 3 | Year 4 |

In year 2, for the 6.780% node we have

$$
99.122 = \min[\text{call price,}
$$
$$
(0.5 \times (\text{up value} + \text{down value}) + \text{coupon})/(1 + \text{interest rate})]
$$
$$
= \min[100, (0.5 \times (97.685 + 100) + 7)/1.06780]
$$

and the bond is not called.

In year 1, for the 5.633 node the bond is not called even though 100.879 exceeds the call price because the bond is not yet callable.

The value of the bond today is calculated as

$$
\tilde{P}(7\%) = 97.916 = (0.5 \times (94.661 + 100.879) + 7)/1.07 \tag{7}
$$

We note that this means that the call option is worth 100−97.916=2.084 to the issuer since the same bond without a call option would be valued at 100 (the term structure is flat!).

Next, we calculate the estimates in equations (5) and (6) for Δr equal to a very large 100 basis points. Repeating the calculations in Exhibit 1 for $r=6\%$ and $r=8\%$ one finds that $\tilde{P}(6\%)=100.828$ and $\tilde{P}(8\%)=94.717$. Setting these values and equation (7) into equations (5) and (6) yields that

$$
D \approx \frac{-1}{97.916} \times \frac{94.717 - 100.828}{0.02} = 3.12
$$

and

$$
C \approx \frac{1}{97.916} \times \frac{94.717 - (2)(97.916) + 100.828}{0.0001} = -29.31
$$

Blindly letting Δr get smaller and smaller we plot the convergence of our duration and convexity estimates in Exhibit 2 (use the scale on the left for duration and the scale on the right for convexity). The estimates we just calculated are highlighted on the right side. Notice that the duration estimate converges nicely to roughly 3.27 while the convexity estimate converges to roughly 16.40 as $\Delta r \rightarrow 0$.

As indicated, this nice limiting behavior is misleading. Consider Exhibit 3 where we plot $\tilde{P}(r)$. We have highlighted the point corresponding to the calculations of Exhibit 1 and drawn a line through it tangent to $\tilde{P}(r)$. $\tilde{P}(r)$ is visibly negatively convex at $r=7\%$ and our nicely convergent estimate of convexity in fact has the wrong sign. This negative convexity is real and is the typical price/yield behavior of callable bonds at intermediate interest rate levels.

We remark that the magnitude of the negative convexity is small in this example because, for purposes of illustrating the calculations, we chose a bond with a short maturity. The effect is more pronounced for longer-term bonds.

Exhibit 2: Convergence of Duration and Convexity Estimates

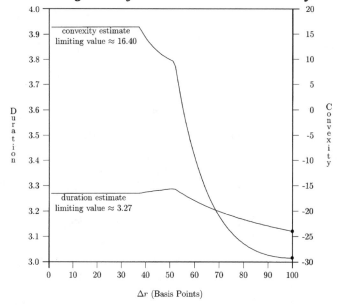

Exhibit 3: The Price Curve of the Callable Bond

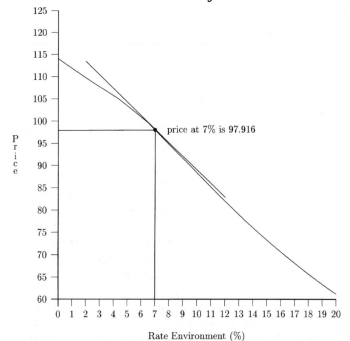

Exhibit 4: The 7% Strategy in a 4% Rate Environment

				8.351%
				98.753
				not called
			6.930% ↗	
			100.103	
		5.761% ↗	not called ↘	5.598%
		102.584		101.328
	4.797% ↗	not called* ↘	4.646% ↗	not called
	105.439		102.884	
4.000% ↗	not callable ↘	3.862% ↗	not called ↘	3.752%
108.289		104.410		100.000
not callable ↘	3.215% ↗	not called* ↘	3.114% ↗	called
	105.803		100.000	
	not callable ↘	2.589% ↗	called ↘	2.515%
		100.000		100.000
		called ↘	2.087% ↗	called
			100.000	
			called ↘	1.686%
				100.000
				called
Today	Year 1	Year 2	Year 3	Year 4

* Should be called.

THE 7% SOLUTION

To understand what is happening we must look closely at what the pricing model does. Referring back to Exhibit 1, we see that when $r=7\%$ it is optimal to call the bond at six different nodes in the lattice in the lower right-hand corner. We refer to this as the "7% strategy" for managing the call option. In Exhibit 4, we value the callable bond in a 4% rate environment assuming that the option is managed with the 7% strategy, i.e., that it is called at the same six node locations. We observe that the rates associated with each node in Exhibit 4 are lower than the corresponding numbers in Exhibit 1 reflecting the lower initial interest rate environment. One can readily verify that, on the 4% lattice, the bond *should* be called at all three nodes in year 2. This is because doing so would produce a price of 105.658 which is lower than the value under any other strategy of option management — including of course the value of 108.289 calculated in Exhibit 4 when the option is managed with the sub-optimal 7% strategy.

Exhibit 5 shows, among other things, the price curve for the callable bond as a function of initial rate environment *assuming* that the option is always managed with the 7% strategy regardless of which strategy is actually optimal — we'll refer to this as the "7% strategy curve." The point corresponding to the calculation in Exhibit 4 is highlighted and lies above the callable bond's actual price curve $\tilde{P}(r)$ for the reason mentioned above. We have indicated the portion of the bond's price curve (roughly where $6.5\% \leq r \leq 7.4\%$) where these two curves coincide. On this portion of the bond's price curve the 7% strategy is optimal. The "I" symbols placed along the price curve correspond to changes in the optimal option management strategy, i.e., to changes in the node locations of optimal calls. As we move from left-to-right along $\tilde{P}(r)$, it becomes optimal to call the bond at fewer and fewer node locations reflecting the increasing interest rate at each node site.

Two extreme strategy curves are also shown in Exhibit 5: the 0% strategy curve where the bond is always called as soon as possible at year 2 (this curve coincides with $\tilde{P}(r)$ until $r \approx 4.3\%$; and the 20% strategy where the bond is never called (which coincides with $\tilde{P}(r)$ after $r \approx 16.0\%$). Many more option management strategies exist; in fact eleven of them are represented along the callable bond's price curve. Since the issurer uses the option management strategy that produces the lowest bond value (hence lowest cost to the issuer), the bond's price curve is the lower envelope of these eleven different strategy curves.

Exhibit 5: The Price Curve as a Lower Envelope

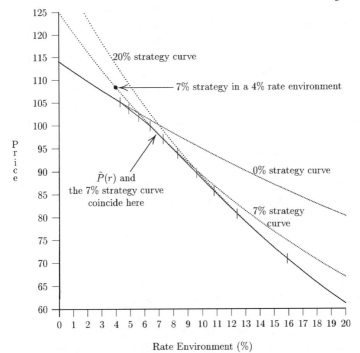

Rate Environment (%)

Now it is clear what is happening: if Δr is less than approximately 40 basis points (so 7%−Δr and 7%+Δr both lie between 6.5% and 7.4% — the region in which the bond's price curve and the 7% strategy curve coincide), then equation (6) is actually providing a very good measure of the convexity of the 7% strategy curve. But we see from Exhibit 5 that all the individual strategy curves, including the 7% strategy, behave like optionless bonds and exhibit *positive* convexity. In order to properly measure the negative convexity of the callable bond we must clearly take Δr large enough so that we cross at least one (and preferably more) of the "|" symbols as we move left from 7%−Δr to 7%+Δr. The convexity estimate of −29 corresponding to Δr=100 basis points is actually a much better estimate than our limiting value of 16.4.

The situation with duration is not quite so perverse. If one envisions the analogous continuous-time valuation model, the bond's price curve becomes the lower envelope of a continuum of strategy curves — each one tangent at one point to the bond's price curve. At this point of tangency the derivative (and hence duration) of the bond's price curve and of the corresponding strategy curve are identical. We see this in Exhibit 5 as well: the 7% strategy curve clearly has roughly the same (first) derivative in the region from 6.5% to 7.4% as must the bond's true price curve $P(r)$.

Exhibit 6 provides further insight into the problem. Here we plot the duration estimate as a function of the rate environment r when we first take Δr=10 basis points (in equation (5)) and then take Δr=100 basis points. The plot points are all separated by a distance of 10 basis points on the horizontal axis. The 10 basis point curve comprises eleven distinct downward sloping segments together with a number of isolated plot points. The eleven segments correspond to the regions of the price curve in Exhibit 5 where the eleven different strategy curves are represented on the lower envelope. They are downward sloping due to the positive convexity of the individual strategy curves. The isolated points correspond to those values of r where r−10 bp, r, and r+10 bp are bridging from one strategy curve to another.

Clearly the duration of the callable bond should not jump radically for small changes in r as it does in the Δr=10 basis point curve. We see quite clearly from this exhibit that when Δr=100 basis points the duration estimate behaves much more appropriately as we vary the interest rate environment.

CONCLUSION

We have shown how discrete-time lattice effects wreak havoc on numerical duration and, more pronouncedly, convexity calculations. Due to these effects, the natural tendency to let $\Delta r \rightarrow 0$ in equations (5) and (6) is exactly the wrong thing to do. While the resulting calculations will converge nicely, in the case of convexity the answer has the wrong sign. Furthermore, this will inevitably happen with a callable bond for sufficiently small Δr, regardless of how refined the underlying lattice is.

Exhibit 6: Duration Estimates for the Callable Bond

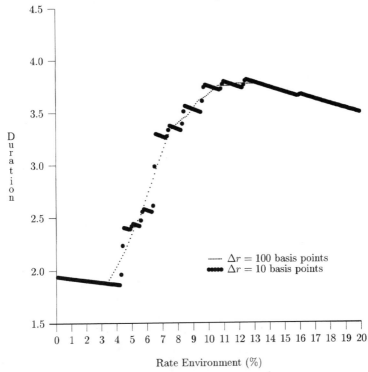

Of course, there is a relationship between the refinement of the lattice (i.e., the frequency of bifurcations in the lattice) and the appropriate choice for Δr. In general, with a more refined lattice one can "get away with" a smaller Δr. As we have mentioned, the key is to ensure that there is a sufficient change in the option management strategy as the rate environment changes from $r-\Delta r$ to r to $r+\Delta r$.

Chapter 19

Price Sensitivity Measures for Brady Bonds

Steven Dym, Ph.D.
President
Steven I. Dym & Associates

INTRODUCTION

Brady bonds are marketable securities created from defaulted bank loans to developing countries, under the auspices of then Secretary of the Treasury Nicholas Brady. These bonds come in a myriad of forms: collateralized and uncollateralized, fixed and floating rate, short and long term. While the bonds are denominated in a number of currencies, the bulk are dollar denominated, which is the concern of this chapter.

As with any non-governmental issue, Brady bonds must yield the U.S. Treasury rate plus a premium for credit risk. Thus, the bond's price will react to changes in the structure of U.S. yields and to movements in the market's perception of the issuing country's creditworthiness. Institutional investors, market makers, and traders need a precise measure of a Brady bond's responses to such changes. Positioning bonds in anticipation of shifts in these underlying variables is an important facet of the market, but becomes unmanageable without a concise measure of price sensitivity to such shifts. A dealer in Bradys may be comfortable with the credit risk of the firm's inventory, but a steep rise in U.S. interest rates will punish the portfolio even though the credit is unchanged. Hedging the U.S. interest rate aspect of the bond requires a measure of the bond's U.S. rate sensitivity. Finally, investors need to quantify their exposure to various markets. Separating a Brady's price sensitivity to U.S. interest rates and to credit risk is crucial in this regard.

This chapter presents such sensitivity measures in the familiar form of duration. By doing so it addresses the foregoing problems, as well as provides a basis for comparing Brady bond risk to that of other bonds. As a by-product of the analysis, the

A substantial portion of this work was developed while the author was a consultant for Brinson Partners, Chicago, IL.

chapter also provides a new way to quantify the duration of floating-rate securities with credit risk. The risk measures developed here, therefore, are relevant to Euro-bonds of developing countries as well, fixed and floating rate.

The format of the chapter is as follows. Formulas for price sensitivities, with corresponding durations, are presented for each of the four forms of Brady bonds: fixed or floating, with or without collateral. In each of the cases, the sensitivity measure is provided both for the U.S. interest rate component of the bond's yield, and for the credit risk component. Thus, there are eight measures in total. The algebraic derivations are tedious, but not complex, and are presented in summary form.

NOTATION

The following notation is used in this chapter:

P	=	price of bond
P_C	=	price of collateralized bond
C	=	coupon
m	=	maturity
y	=	yield to maturity
t	=	corresponding U.S. Treasury yield
tz	=	U.S. Treasury zero rate
r	=	bond credit spread over Treasuries
L	=	LIBOR
s	=	stated spread over LIBOR for floating-rate issues
Dur	=	standard duration measure
Dur_C	=	duration measure in presence of Treasury collateral

Thus, $y = t+r$. (In the context of floating-rate issues, r can be taken to represent the bond's discount margin.)

FIXED COUPON BONDS, NO COLLATERAL

A fixed-rate coupon bond with no collateral is the simplest type of bond, corresponding to the structure of a "plain vanilla" government bond. To review the interest rate-price relationship begin with the promised semiannual cash flows of the bond. (In this chapter we assume full coupon periods; that is, no accrued interest. Accommodating partial periods involves adjusting the maturity and duration by the fraction of the coupon period having elapsed.) The bond's present value is:

$$P = \frac{C/2}{1+y/2} + \frac{C/2}{(1+y/2)^2} + \frac{C/2}{(1+y/2)^3} + \ldots + \frac{C/2+100}{(1+y/2)^{2m}} \tag{1}$$

where $y=t+r$. Notice that each of the cash flows are treated symmetrically in terms of their discount factor — the yield in the denominator equals the sum of the risk-free

Treasury rate plus the risk premium. Thus, the bond's price sensitivity to these two variables will be the same.

First, write the standard duration formula:

$$\text{Dur} = \left[\frac{C/2}{1 + y/2} \cdot 1/2 + \frac{C/2}{(1 + y/2)^2} \cdot 2/2 + \frac{C/2}{(1 + y/2)^3} \cdot 3/2 \right.$$
$$\left. + \dots + \frac{C/2 + 100}{(1 + y/2)^{2m}} \cdot m \right] / P \tag{2}$$

Taking the derivatives of bond price with respect to the two variables — the Treasury rate and the credit spread — we have the following well known price sensitivities:

$$\frac{\Delta P / P}{\Delta t} = - \frac{\text{Dur}}{1 + y/2} \tag{3}$$

$$\frac{\Delta P / P}{\Delta r} = - \frac{\text{Dur}}{1 + y/2} \tag{4}$$

Consider the Republic of Argentina Eurobond of November 1 1999, paying a coupon of 10.95%. In early February 1996 it was yielding 8.55%, for a price of 107.5 (plus 2.85 of accrued interest). The interest rate on the interpolated U.S. Treasury note at that time was 5.08%, for a credit spread of 3.47%. Its duration using equation (3) was 3.11 years. Thus, a 10 basis point increase in either the Treasury rate or the credit spread will cause a 0.30% drop in the bond's price to 107.17.

FIXED-COUPON BONDS, PRINCIPAL COLLATERALIZED

The typical benchmark Brady bond — the "Pars" or "Discounts" — have their principal payments at maturity collateralized by U.S. Treasury zero coupons. This makes the cash flow of 100 in equation (1) riskless from a credit standpoint. As such, it should be discounted by the Treasury zero coupon rate for that maturity, without a premium for credit risk. For a fixed coupon collateralized bond, its present value therefore is:

$$P\_C = \frac{C/2}{1 + (t + r)/2} + \frac{C/2}{(1 + (t + r)/2)^2} + \dots$$
$$+ \frac{C/2}{(1 + (t + r)/2)^{2m}} + \frac{100}{(1 + tz/2)^{2m}} \tag{5}$$

The lack of symmetry in the discount factors for the cash flows implies that were we to calculate yield to maturity in the standard way (as in equation (1)), the yield would be a blend of the credit spread and the Treasury rates, but would not be additive. Market convention is to subtract the last term from the price, which leaves the coupon cash flows to be discounted by the "stripped yield." (The terminology reflects the removal of the Treasury collateral from the bond.) r is then termed the "stripped spread."[1]

For example, Mexico's Par Brady bond, with a coupon of 6.25% and maturing December 31 2019, was priced at 67.375 in early February 1996. The interpolated Treasury bond yield at that time was 5.99%, while the Treasury zero was 6.53%. Solving for r in equation (5) produced a stripped spread of 6.96% and a stripped yield of 12.95%.

Treasury Yield Price Sensitivity

In order to arrive at a price sensitivity measure analytically similar to the standard method which uses duration, we define the duration of a principal collateralized bond, or "collateralized duration," in the following way:

$$\text{Dur}\_C = \left[\frac{C/2}{1+(t+r)/2} \cdot 1/2 + \frac{C/2}{(1+(t+r)/2)^2} \cdot 2/2 + \dots \right.$$
$$\left. + \frac{C/2}{(1+(t+r)/2)^{2m}} \cdot m + \frac{100}{(1+tz/2)^{2m}} \cdot m \cdot \frac{1+(t+r)/2}{1+tz/2} \right] / P\_C \quad (6)$$

Notice that the final term receives more weight. Since it is riskless, it is discounted less heavily. And the "correction factor" $(1+(t+r)/2)/(1+tz/2)$ raises it somewhat more. This is as it should be — a change in Treasury yields will affect the bond considerably, as it is a factor in all the bond's cash flows, in particular the last one. But a change in the credit risk will have less of an effect on the bond's price, as it discounts only the coupon payments. Defined this way, the Mexican Par bond's collateralized duration is 12.51 years. (Duration calculated in the standard way would be 10.30 years.)

Specifying collateralized duration this way produces a very concise price sensitivity measure for the bond with respect to changes in the Treasury yield, exactly parallel to that for a non-collateralized bond, namely:

$$\frac{\Delta P\_C / P\_C}{\Delta t} = - \frac{\text{Dur}\_C}{1+(t+r)/2} \quad (7)$$

For the Mexican Par, a 10 basis point increase in the Treasury yield causes a price decline of 1.17% to 66.58.[2]

---

[1] Technically, another factor enters the "stripped" calculations. The first two or three interest payments may also be collateralized for some Brady bonds, but with high grade money market instruments rather than Treasury zeros. Clearly, their discount factor should contain some sort of risk premium, albeit of lower order of magnitude than the bare coupons. It is a "rolling" guarantee, which means simply assigning the collateral to the nearby coupons is not entirely correct. Further, the precise circumstances which initiate payment of the collateral are complex. Some analysts, therefore, do not "strip" these interest payments from the bond. While not a perfect solution, this is the approach taken here.

The stripped calculations also ignore any "value recovery rights" (a call on the country's oil export revenues), if any.

[2] Implicit in this result is the assumption that the zero spot rate moves one-for-one with the Treasury coupon curve. A minor correction factor (available from the author) is necessary when this is not the case.

Credit Spread Price Sensitivity

The collateralized bond's price sensitivity to changes in the credit spread is not symmetric with its Treasury rate sensitivity. The credit risk premium is only present in the discount factor for the coupon cash flows, so a change will have less of an impact on price. The sensitivity here takes the following form:

$$\frac{\Delta P\_C / P\_C}{\Delta r} = - \frac{\text{Dur\_C} - A/P}{1 + (t + r)/2} \tag{8}$$

where

$$A = m \cdot 100 \cdot \frac{1 + (t + r)/2}{(1 + tz/2)^{2m + 1}}$$

Notice that the presence of the A/P term in the numerator of equation (8) reduces the impact of a change in the risk premium on the bond's price compared to a change in the Treasury yield of the same magnitude. (For the Mexican Par A/P=7.80.) A 10 basis point rise in the risk premium causes the bond's price to decline by only 0.46% to 67.06, well less than half the impact of the same basis point rise in Treasury yields.

FLOATING RATE BONDS, NO COLLATERAL

Calculating duration, hence price sensitivity, of a fixed coupon bond, even with some cash flows collateralized, is relatively simple, as shown above. What about issues with non-fixed coupons? If the bond is priced at par, then the process is again straightforward: duration equals the time until the next interest setting date, so that its price sensitivity is equivalent to that of a money market instrument. But Brady bonds typically trade far from par. The following discussion presents a general method of calculating durations and price sensitivities of floating-rate issues, regardless of their price, and whether they are Bradys or not. The next section adapts the method to collateralized bonds.

Consider first a non-government floating-rate note which pays, every six months, the then current 6-month LIBOR rate, L_i, plus a fixed spread, s. To arrive at the price, the market discounts each expected cash flow by the fixed long-term LIBOR rate, L, appropriate for the bond's maturity, plus the credit risk premium, r, for that point in time. It is important to note that while s is fixed for the life of the floater, r is market determined, and therefore will vary according to market conditions, just as yield to maturity or spot rates do. The bond's price thus reflects all the *expected* future values of L_i, and is determined by:[3]

$$P = \frac{100 \cdot (L_1 + s)/2}{1 + (L + r)/2} + \frac{100 \cdot (L_2 + s)/2}{(1 + (L + r)/2)^2} + \frac{100 \cdot (L_3 + s)/2}{(1 + (L + r)/2)^3}$$

$$+ \dots + \frac{100 \cdot (1 + (L_m + s)/2)}{(1 + (L + r)/2)^{2m}} \tag{9}$$

[3] Operationally, calculating the credit spread, r, requires substituting the prevailing fixed swap rate for LIBOR and solving for the credit spread that produces the market price.

Calculating the effect of a change in LIBOR on the floater's price is complicated because both the cash flows in the numerator and the discount factors in the denominator will change. A way to get around this is by recognizing that if long-term rates, L, are completely determined by expected future rates, L_i, we can substitute L for all the expected L_i. (Alternatively, the cash flows can be "swapped" for a fixed coupon via an interest rate swap paying L fixed.) Doing so, and rewriting each cash flow as $L+s=(L+r)+(s-r)$, the bond's price can be presented as:

$$P = \frac{100 \cdot (L+r)/2}{1+(L+r)/2} + \frac{100 \cdot (L+r)/2}{(1+(L+r)/2)^2} + \frac{100 \cdot (L+r)/2}{(1+(L+r)/2)^3} + \dots$$
$$+ \frac{100 \cdot (L+r)/2}{(1+(L+r)/2)^{2m}} + \frac{100}{(1+(L+r)/2)^{2m}} + \frac{100 \cdot (s-r)/2}{1+(L+r)/2}$$
$$+ \frac{100 \cdot (s-r)/2}{(1+(L+r)/2)^2} + \frac{100 \cdot (s-r)/2}{(1+(L+r)/2)^3} + \dots + \frac{100 \cdot (s-r)/2}{(1+(L+r)/2)^{2m}} \quad (10)$$

Recognizing that the first set of discounted cash flows are simply that of a bond paying a *fixed* coupon of $100 \cdot (L+r)$, the price can be rewritten further as:

$$P = 100 + \frac{100 \cdot (s-r)/2}{1+(L+r)/2} + \frac{100 \cdot (s-r)/2}{(1+(L+r)/2)^2} + \frac{100 \cdot (s-r)/2}{(1+(L+r)/2)^3} + \dots$$
$$+ \frac{100 \cdot (s-r)/2}{(1+(L+r)/2)^{2m}} + \frac{100}{(1+(L+r)/2)^{2m}} - \frac{100}{(1+(L+r)/2)^{2m}} \quad (11)$$

This can be finally simplified as:

$$P = 100 + P^* - \frac{100}{(1+(L+r)/2)^{2m}} \quad (12)$$

where P^* is the price of a bond with coupon $100 \cdot (s-r)$, yielding $L+r$ and maturing in m years. While this bond also has a variable coupon, importantly it does not vary with LIBOR, so that its price sensitivity with respect to LIBOR (as well as its duration) is analytically calculable. This, in turn, means that getting a measure of price sensitivity (and duration) for the original bond is relatively easy. But before we do so, we must adapt this formulation to a Brady bond.

Brady issues trade off the U.S. Treasury curve. This means that the long-term Treasury yield, t, appropriate to the floater's maturity, replaces LIBOR as the yield in the denominator. To arrive at an equation like equation (12) rewrite each cash flow as $L+s=(L-t)+(t+r)+(s-r)$. Let $x=L-t$, the spread between the long-term LIBOR and Treasury yields. Then proceeding in exactly the same manner as above, we can write the value of the floater's cash flows as:

$$P = 100 + P^* - \frac{100}{(1+(t+r)/2)^{2m}} \quad (13)$$

where now P^* becomes the price of a bond with coupon $100 \cdot [x+(s-r)]$, yielding $t+r$ and maturing in m years.

Treasury Yield Price Sensitivity

Price sensitivity with respect to the Treasury yield is simply a matter of taking the derivatives of each of the three terms in equation (13):

$$\frac{\Delta P/P}{\Delta t} = -\frac{\text{Dur}^* \cdot P^*/P}{1+(t+r)/2} + \frac{100/P}{(1+(t+r)/2)^{2m+1}} \cdot m \tag{14}$$

where Dur^* is the duration of an m year, $100 \cdot [x+(s-r)]$ fixed coupon bond, yielding $t+r$.

Consider the Venezuelan FLIRB (Floating Rate Interest Reduction bond), paying 6-month LIBOR plus $\frac{7}{8}\%$, maturing March 31, 2007. In February 1996, it was trading at 59.875. The corresponding Treasury yield was 5.69%. Using the (interpolated) 11-year swap rate of 6.05% for long-term LIBOR, this produced a credit spread of 8.50%. Then $x+(s-r)$ is -7.27%, which produces a bond price (P^*) of negative 18.4232 (without accrued interest) with a duration of negative 2.99 years.[4] Putting all the terms in equation (14) together, an increase of 10 basis point in the Treasury yield causes the floater's price to rise by 0.27% to 60.04.[5]

Credit Spread Price Sensitivity

The effect of a change in the risk premium on the floater's price is simpler, since the risk variable appears only in the denominator of the pricing equation (9). Substitute the fixed swap rate for LIBOR in the numerator to produce a "synthetic" fixed coupon equal to the swap rate plus the floater's spread over LIBOR. Then take the derivative with respect to r. The result is exactly equation (8), but where duration is that of a bond with the floater's maturity, yielding $t+r$ and a fixed coupon of $L+s$. For the Venezuelan FLIRB, duration is 6.62 years so that a 10 basis points rise in the risk premium will result in a 0.62% *decline* in price to 59.49.

FLOATING-RATE BONDS, PRINCIPAL COLLATERALIZED

There are no new complications in the case of floating-rate bonds that are principal collateralized. We already know how to alter the duration formula for a collateral-

---

[4] This bond is only being used to illustrate the methodology for floating-rate issues. In fact, the bond has an amortization schedule which will shorten its average life, hence durations and price sensitivities.

[5] This result assumes no change in the LIBOR-Treasury spread in response to the shift in Treasury yields ($\Delta x/\Delta t=0$). Allowing for changes in the spread results in:

$$\frac{\Delta P/P}{\Delta t} = -\frac{\text{Dur} \cdot P^*/P}{1+(t+r)/2} + \frac{100/P}{(1+(t+r)/2)^{2m+1}} \cdot m + \frac{\Delta x}{\Delta t} \cdot \frac{100}{P} \cdot Z$$

where

$$Z = \frac{1-(1+(t+r)/2)^{-2m}}{(t+r)/2}$$

ized bond. And we have just presented a method for calculating price sensitivity to rate movements for floating-rate issues. Thus, a collateralized floater requires going through the same steps we did in deriving equation (13) for an uncollateralized floater, but recognizing that in the presence of collateral the final term is discounted using only the Treasury zero rate. This leads to:

$$P\_C = 100 + P\_C* - \frac{100}{(1 + (t + r)/2)^{2m}} \tag{15}$$

where P_C* is the price of a *collateralized bond* with fixed coupon $100 \cdot [x+(s-r)]$, credit risk premium r and maturing in m years.

Treasury Yield Price Sensitivity

Taking the derivative for price sensitivity with respect to the Treasury yield we have:

$$\frac{\Delta P/P}{\Delta t} = - \frac{\text{Dur\_}C* \cdot P*/P}{1 + (t + r)/2} + \frac{100/P}{(1 + (t + r)/2)^{2m+1}} \cdot m \tag{16}$$

where Dur*_C is the collateralized duration (as defined in equation (6)) of an m year, $100 \cdot [x+(s-r)]$ fixed coupon bond, with corresponding Treasury yield t and risk premium r.[6]

Brazil's Discount bond is a floating rate, collateralized issue. It pays LIBOR + 13⁄16% and matures April 15, 2024. In early February 1996, this bond was priced at 66.5. The corresponding Treasury was yielding 6.12%, with the appropriate Treasury zero 6.57%, for a stripped spread of 8.37%. Using the (interpolated) 28-year swap rate of 6.63% for long-term LIBOR, $x+(s-r)$ is -7.07%, which produces a collateralized (P_C*) bond price of negative 31.6528 (without accrued interest) and a collateralized duration of negative 4.30 years. Using equation (16), an increase of 10 basis points in the Treasury yield causes the collateralized floater's price to decline by 0.12% to 66.42.[7]

Credit Spread Price Sensitivity

For the effect of a change in the credit spread on the collateralized floater's price, equation (8) can be used, but substitute the swap rate plus the spread for the fixed coupon in calculating collateralized duration. For the Brazil Discount issue, a synthetic fixed coupon consisting of the 6.63% swap rate plus the spread of 13⁄16% produces a bond with a collateralized duration of 11.89 years. A 10 basis points increase in the credit spread causes the floater's price to drop by 0.47% to 66.18.

---

[6] The statement in footnote 3 applies here as well.

[7] Here, too, we need to add the extra term as explained in footnote 5 to recognize any changes in the LIBOR-Treasury spread caused by the movement in rates.

Chapter 20

Modeling and Forecasting Interest Rate Volatility with GARCH

Wai Lee, Ph.D.
Assistant Vice President
J.P. Morgan Investment Management, Inc.

John Yin, Ph.D.
Assistant Vice President
J.P. Morgan Investment Management, Inc.

INTRODUCTION

Interest rate risk management has always been important for financial institutions, corporations, and investors. As use of interest rate derivatives has grown, modeling the short-term risk-free interest rate process is important for pricing and hedging interest rate-sensitive securities such as bonds, bond options, and futures.[1] Such models have to provide a reasonably good description of the historical data during a certain period of time.

Exhibit 1 plots the weekly 3-month U.S. Treasury bill rate from early 1976 to the end of 1993.[2] We use this series as an example throughout the chapter. The most obvious message from the graph is the volatile period during the late 1970s and early

[1] For an extensive survey on the growth and uses of interest rate derivatives, see Eli M. Remolona, "The Growth of Financial Derivative Markets," *Quarterly Review* (Winter 1992-1993), and Charles W. Smithson, Clifford W. Smith, Jr., and D. Sykes Wilford, *Managing Financial Risk: A Guide to Derivative Products, Financial Engineering, and Value Maximization* (New York: Irwin Professional Publishing, 1995), Chapters 1 and 3.

[2] Data are from Federal Reserve Bulletin Statistical Release H15.

The authors thank for support and constructive comments of members of the Capital Markets Research Group of J.P. Morgan Investment Management, Inc., particularly Michael Granito and Michael Kang; and Sanjiv R. Das of the Harvard Business School.

1980s. In 1979, the U.S. Federal Reserve agreed on a money supply target instead of an interest rate target. As a result, U.S. interest rates rose dramatically, and became much more volatile, prompting an exponential growth in trading and uses of exchange-traded and over-the-counter interest rate derivatives. Over the whole sample period, the average interest rate is about 7.5% with a standard deviation of about 2.98%.

In general, volatility measures the intensity of randomness. It is typically measured by standard deviation or variance, although other measures such as absolute change are also used. Exhibit 2 graphs these two measures of volatility of interest rates. The 52-week rolling sample standard deviation is relatively smooth, while the absolute change is erratic. This is because the former is a time-averaging measure of degree of variation, while the latter is a measure at a certain time.

Exhibit 1: Weekly 3-Month Treasury Bill Rate 3/31/76 - 12/29/93

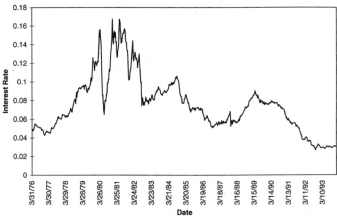

Exhibit 2: Volatility of Weekly 3-Month Treasury Bill Rate 3/31/76 - 12/29/93

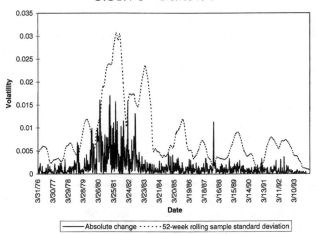

Strictly speaking, there is no best measure of volatility. The value of a measure depends on how it is used. For example, immediately after the stock market crash on October 19, 1987, the Federal Reserve lowered the interest rate by more than 1% in a week. While this gives rise to a spike in the absolute change measure in Exhibit 2, it has little material effect when volatility is measured by the 52-week rolling sample standard deviation, because of the time-averaging effect.

Nevertheless, two clear messages emerge from the graph: (1) volatility is time-varying and (2) episodes of low and high volatility are common.

There is accordingly a strong need for modeling and forecasting volatility. In this chapter, we introduce and discuss probably the most extensively applied family of volatility models in finance, Generalized AutoRegressive Conditional Heteroskedasticity (GARCH) models. It is well known that unconditional distributions of many financial prices and returns series exhibit fatter tails than normal distributions.[3] GARCH models can capture this characteristic under the assumption of conditional normality. We focus on the properties and applications of GARCH in modeling interest rate volatility instead of the underlying statistical theory, although we discuss some basic econometric background, extension, and limitations of the models.[4]

MOTIVATION AND THEORETICAL BACKGROUND OF GARCH

In modern term structure theory, the instantaneous short-term risk-free interest rate is typically assumed to follow a stochastic process, which can be depicted as

$$dr = \mu(r, t)dt + \sigma(r, t)dW \tag{1}$$

where r is the interest rate, t denotes time, $\mu(r,t)$ is the expected instantaneous change, or drift, of interest rate, $\sigma(r,t)$ is the instantaneous standard deviation, and W is a standard Brownian motion such that change in W, dW, is normally distributed with mean zero and variance of dt. Both $\mu(r,t)$ and $\sigma(r,t)$ are functions of the current interest rate r and time t.

To see the insights in equation (1), consider a particular discrete time version as follows:[5]

$$r_t - r_{t-1} = \alpha_0 - \alpha_1 r_{t-1} + \varepsilon_t \tag{2}$$

[3] This property is also known as leptokurtosis. There is evidence that the conditional distributions of some financial series, such as interest rates and exchange rates, also exhibit leptokurtosis.

[4] More advanced treatments include Tim Bollerslev, Ray Y. Chou, and Kenneth F. Kroner, "ARCH Modeling in Finance," *Journal of Econometrics* (1992), pp. 5-59; Robert F. Engle (ed.), *ARCH: Selected Readings, Advanced Texts in Econometrics* (New York: Oxford University Press, 1995); and Tim Bollerslev, Robert F. Engle, and Daniel Nelson, "ARCH Models," Chapter 49 in Robert F. Engle and D. L. McFadden (eds.), *Handbook of Econometrics* (Amsterdam: Elsevier, 1994).

[5] A good reference for the issues of discrete time approximations and convergence to continuous time processes is P.E. Kloeden and E. Platen, *Numerical Solution of Stochastic Differential Equations* (New York: Springer-Verlag, 1992).

where

$$\varepsilon_t = \sigma_t e_t$$

$$E[\varepsilon_t | I_{t-1}] = 0$$

$$E[\varepsilon_t^2 | I_{t-1}] = \sigma_t^2$$

$\alpha_0 > 0$ and $\alpha_1 > 0$ are parameters to be estimated, ε_t is a noise term, e_t is white noise that is normally distributed with mean zero and variance of one, I_{t-1} denotes the information set available up to time $t - 1$, and $E[\bullet | I_{t-1}]$ denotes the conditional expectation based on I_{t-1}, which represents the expectation given the information available up to time $t - 1$. In this chapter, we consider only the case that $I_{t-1} = \{r_{t-1}, r_{t-2}, ..., r_0; \varepsilon_{t-1}, \varepsilon_{t-2}, ..., \varepsilon_0\}$, i.e., our information set is restricted to the history of interest rates and interest rate shocks.

In equation (2), the change in the interest rate, $r_t - r_{t-1}$, is modeled as a sum of a deterministic drift term, $(\alpha_0 - \alpha_1 r_{t-1})$, and a random disturbance term, ε_t. The drift is a linear function of the past interest rate, r_{t-1}, while the random disturbance term is time-varying. Although ε_t has a conditional expected value of zero, its conditional variance, denoted by σ_t^2, is positive and time-varying. A variable with time-varying variance is said to be heteroskedastic. When σ_t^2 is a constant, ε_t is said to be homoskedastic; i.e., it has constant variance.

Before we discuss how to model and forecast volatility, some highlights on the model of the level of interest rates are necessary. Notice that when we add r_{t-1} to both sides of equation (2) and take expectations, it can be shown that the unconditional expectation of r is:

$$E[r] = \frac{\alpha_0}{\alpha_1} \tag{3}$$

Since interest rate levels and averages cannot be negative, the inequality constraints on α_0 and α_1 are justified. A positive α_1 also ensures that interest rate is mean-reverting, which can be illustrated as follows. Equation (2) can be rewritten as

$$r_t - r_{t-1} = -\alpha_1 \left(r_{t-1} - \frac{\alpha_0}{\alpha_1} \right) + \varepsilon_t \tag{4}$$

Since α_0/α_1 and α_1 are positive, equation (4) indicates that when the interest rate at $t - 1$ is above (below) its average, we expect a decrease (increase) in the interest rate at t. This phenomenon, called *mean reversion*, guarantees that interest rates will not go unbounded, while the speed of mean reversion depends on the magnitude of α_1. This is by far the most popular drift model applied in modern term structure theory.[6]

To model time-varying volatility, Engle proposes a process for conditional volatility known as AutoRegressive Conditional Heteroskedasticity model (ARCH),

---

[6] Although a bounded interest rate process is theoretically and intuitively appealing, most empirical work finds that α_1 is slightly above zero, but statistically insignificant. In other words, even if interest rates are mean-reverting, their behavior is close to an unbounded random walk.

which has become one of the most prominent tools in time series econometrics.[7]
Recall that the conditional volatility of r_t is given by:

$$\text{Var}(r_r|I_{t-1}) = E[\varepsilon_t^2|I_{t-1}] = \sigma_t^2 \tag{5}$$

In an ARCH(q) process, conditional volatility is modeled as:

$$\sigma_t^2 = a_0 + a_1\varepsilon_{t-1}^2 + a_2\varepsilon_{t-2}^2 + \ldots + a_q\varepsilon_{t-q}^2 \tag{6}$$

where $a_0 > 0$, $a_i > 0$ for $i = 1, 2, \ldots, q$, $a_1 > a_2 > \ldots > a_q$, and the sum of the $a_i s$ is less than one. Equation (6) says that the conditional volatility at time t depends on realizations of ε in the past periods up to lag q. The conditional volatility in the current period tends to be high (low) when past shocks are large (small), and shocks in the more recent past have more of an impact on conditional volatility than shocks in the more distant past.

A shortcoming of the original ARCH specification is that, in its early applications to financial and economic time series, relatively long lags (large values of q) were found to be necessary. In addition, an arbitrarily declining weights lag structure had to be imposed during estimation.

To tackle this problem, Bollerslev proposes a generalized version of ARCH, known as the GARCH(p,q) model, as follows:

$$\sigma_t^2 = a_0 + \sum_{i=1}^{q} a_i\varepsilon_{t-i}^2 + \sum_{j=1}^{p} b_j\sigma_{t-j}^2 \tag{7}$$

where $a_0 > 0$, $a_i > 0$ for $i = 1, 2, \ldots, q$, and $b_j > 0$ for $j = 1, 2, \ldots, p$.[8] This GARCH specification allows the conditional variance to follow an autoregressive and moving average (ARMA) process, which is a more parsimonious specification to capture the time series properties in volatility.

A little caution is required here to understand the terminology of the lags of AR and MA terms. Although the specification in equation (6) is an autoregressive process, conditional volatility appears to be a moving average of past squared residuals with declining weights. In contrast to the generally accepted terminology of an ARMA(p,q) model, where p is the lag order for the AR components, and q is the lag order for the MA components, p and q in the GARCH(p,q) specification of equation (7) actually denote the lag orders of MA and AR components instead.

---

[7] Robert F. Engle, "Autoregressive Conditional Heteroskedasticity with Estimates of the Variance of United Kingdom Inflation," *Econometrica* (1982), pp. 987-1006.

[8] Tim Bollerslev, "Generalized Autoregressive Conditional Heteroskedasticity," *Journal of Econometrics* (1986), pp. 307-327. To guarantee that conditional volatilities from GARCH(p,q) model are nonnegative, Bollerslev imposes inequality constraints on the parameters. Daniel B. Nelson and Charles Q. Cao, "Inequality Constraints in the Univariate GARCH Model," *Journal of Business and Economic Statistics* (April 1992), pp. 229-235, have shown that these constraints can be substantially weakened while in-sample conditional volatilities are still guaranteed to be positive. Thus, the constraints should not be imposed in estimation.

For clarification, consider a GARCH(1,1) as an example:

$$\sigma_t^2 = a_0 + a_1 \varepsilon_{t-1}^2 + b_1 \sigma_{t-1}^2 \tag{8}$$

which can be rewritten as

$$\varepsilon_t^2 = a_0 + (a_1 + b_1)\varepsilon_{t-1}^2 - b_1(\varepsilon_{t-1}^2 - \sigma_{t-1}^2) + (\varepsilon_t^2 - \sigma_t^2) \tag{9}$$

Recall that the conditional expectation of ε_t^2 is equal to σ_t^2, so that the difference between the two is in fact an error term, or a white-noise sequence. As a result, equation (9) makes it clear that a GARCH(1,1) model is an ARMA(1,1) model in squared form. Moreover, $(a_1 + b_1)$ is the coefficient of the AR term, while $-b_1$ is the coefficient of the MA term.

The GARCH model is popular not only for its simplicity in specification and its parsimonious nature in capturing time series properties of volatilities, but also because it is a generalization of other measures of volatilities. For example, historical sample variance is in fact a T-period rolling sample measure of variance, which can be written as:

$$\sigma_t^2 = \frac{1}{T}\sum_{k=1}^{T}(r_{t-k} - E[r])^2 = \frac{1}{T}\sum_{k=1}^{T}\varepsilon_{t-k}^2 \tag{10}$$

A particular form of exponential smoothing scheme of volatility measure is defined as:

$$\sigma_t^2 = \delta\sigma_{t-1}^2 + (1 - \delta)\varepsilon_{t-1}^2 = \delta\sum_{k=1}^{\infty}(1 - \delta)^k \varepsilon_{t-k}^2 \tag{11}$$

Both measures are weighted averages of past squared residuals. To make a direct comparison of the two measures to the GARCH model, one can recursively apply the GARCH(1,1) specification to the σ_{t-j}^2 in equation (8), and rewrite the GARCH(1,1) equation as:

$$\sigma_t^2 = \frac{a_0}{1 - b_1} + a_1\sum_{k=0}^{\infty}b_1^k \varepsilon_{t-k-1}^2 \tag{12}$$

A comparison of equations (10) and (11) to equation (12) should make it obvious that both measures are in fact special cases of GARCH(1,1), but with different restrictions on the weights assigned to each lagged term, and the first term in equation (12) is restricted to be zero.

Besides being a generalized version of other measures, the GARCH model also captures the concept of mean reversion in volatility. To exemplify the concept, when we take unconditional expectations on both sides of equation (8) and rearrange, it can be shown that:

$$E[\sigma^2] = \omega = \frac{a_0}{1 - a_1 - b_1} \qquad (13)$$

where $(a_1 + b_1) < 1$, and ω is the long run average volatility. Using the definition of ω in equation (13) above, the original GARCH(1,1) model in equation (8) can now be written as:

$$\sigma_t^2 = \omega + a_1(\varepsilon_{t-1}^2 - \omega) + b_1(\sigma_{t-1}^2 - \omega) \qquad (14)$$

Since both a_1 and b_1 are positive, equation (14) says that when volatility is above (below) the long-run average volatility, ω, at time $t - 1$, it will mean-revert downward (upward) toward ω at time t. The speed of mean reversion depends on the magnitude of $(a_1 + b_1)$. Generally speaking, the closer the value of $(a_1 + b_1)$ to 1, the longer it takes for volatility to revert to its mean.[9]

GARCH MODEL FOR WEEKLY 3-MONTH TREASURY BILL RATES

We can illustrate the estimation of a GARCH model using the weekly 3-month Treasury bill rates in Exhibit 1.[10] We model the level of the interest rate as a mean-reverting process as in equation (2), rewritten here for convenience as:

$$r_t - r_{t-1} = \alpha_0 - \alpha_1 r_{t-1} + \varepsilon_t \qquad (15)$$

and the conditional volatility as a GARCH(1,1) process, written as:

$$\sigma_t^2 = a_0 + a_1 \varepsilon_{t-1}^2 + b_1 \sigma_{t-1}^2 \qquad (16)$$

Experience has shown that a GARCH(1,1) specification generally fits the volatility

---

[9] At the extreme case of $(a_1 + b_1) = 1$, we have a process known as integrated GARCH(1,1), or IGARCH(1,1) model, which is discussed in Robert F. Engle and Tim Bollerslev, "Modeling the Persistence of Conditional Variances," *Econometric Reviews* (1986), pp. 1-50, 81-87. The degree of persistence of volatility in this model is as high as a random walk. Technically speaking, we say that there is a "unit root" in the volatility process. Daniel Nelson, "Stationarity and Persistence in the GARCH(1,1) Model," *Econometric Theory* (1990), pp. 318-334, shows that, in contrast to a random walk, volatility is still "strictly stationary." For details on speed of mean reversion, unit roots, and stationarity of time series, see James D. Hamilton, *Time Series Analysis*, (Princeton, NJ: Princeton University Press, 1994).

[10] In the early 1980s when computer technology was not as advanced, estimating an ARCH model was an expensive exercise in terms of computing time. As a result, Engle proposed a preliminary test for the ARCH effect, known as the Lagrange Multiplier test, which was to be performed before one actually estimated the ARCH model. The test was conducted by regressing the square of the residuals from the mean equation on their own lags, and the R^2 of the regression was noted. A large value of $T \times R^2$, which follows a chi-square distribution with degrees of freedom equal to the number of lags in the regression, indicated the existence of ARCH effect. This preliminary test is now rarely performed, as experience finds that most financial time series have GARCH effects, and estimating a GARCH model is no longer as time-consuming.

of most financial time series well, and is quite robust. The appropriateness of a particular specification can be checked using some diagnostic statistics (discussed below).

The unknown parameters in our model, $\{\alpha_0, \alpha_1, a_0, a_1, b_1\}$, can be estimated using maximum likelihood estimators (MLE).[11] When ε_t is assumed to be conditionally normally distributed with mean zero and variance σ_t^2, i.e., $\varepsilon_t | I_{t-1} \sim N(0, \sigma_t^2)$, the log-likelihood function for the sample from $t = 0$ to $t = T$ is:

$$L = -\frac{T}{2}\ln(2\pi) - \frac{1}{2}\sum_{t=1}^{T}\ln\sigma_t^2 - \frac{1}{2}\sum_{t=1}^{T}\frac{\varepsilon_t^2}{\sigma_t^2} \tag{17}$$

This log-likelihood function is then maximized with respect to $\{\alpha_0, \alpha_1, a_0, a_1, b_1\}$.[12] The results are reported in Column A of Exhibit 3.

Consistent with many of the empirical findings in the interest rate literature, the mean reversion parameter of the interest rate level, α_1, is estimated to be 0.0013978, which is statistically insignificant.[13] This result indicates that interest rate levels are highly persistent, with little tendency to revert to their long-run average. In the GARCH(1,1) volatility equation, both a_1 and b_1 are statistically significant at 1%, which indicates that there is a strong GARCH effect in interest rate volatilities.

A closer look at the parameters reveals that $(a_1 + b_1)$ has a value of 0.9930. Again, this finding is consistent with the literature that interest rate volatility is also highly persistent. When interest rate volatility is high (low) this period, it is highly likely that volatility will be high (low) in the following period as well, which seems a good description of the volatility clustering in Exhibit 2.

---

[11] For the details of the efficiency and consistency of the estimators, and how to obtain the covariance matrix of the parameters, refer to the original articles by Engle, "Autoregressive Conditional Heteroskedasticity with Estimates of the Variance of United Kingdom Inflation," and Bollerslev, "Generalized Autoregressive Conditional Heteroskedasticity," or Hamilton, *Time Series Analysis*, Chapters 5 and 21. Alternatively, the GARCH model may be estimated by generalized method of moments (GMM) procedure. See Robert Rich, Jennie Raymond, and J.S. Butler, "Generalized Instrumental Variables Estimation of Autoregressive Conditional Heteroskedastic Models," *Economics Letters* (1991), pp. 179-185. If the distribution function is correctly specified, it is shown that MLE is more efficient than GMM.

[12] The maximization may be initiated with the sample variance as the starting value of a_0. Generally, there is no guarantee that the global, instead of a local, optimum is attained. One may need to do a grid search, i.e., starting with different sets of initial values for the parameters, and compare the resulting maximized likelihood values.

The maximization algorithm used is BHHH, proposed by E.K. Berndt, B.H. Hall, R.E. Hall, and J.A. Hausman, "Estimation and Inferences in Nonlinear Structural Models," *Annals of Economic and Social Measurement* (1974), pp. 653-665.

[13] See, for example, K.C. Chan, G.A. Karolyi, F.A. Longstaff, and A.B. Sanders, "An Empirical Comparison of Alternative Models of the Short-Term Interest Rate," *Journal of Finance* (1992), pp. 1209-1227; and Robin J. Brenner, Richard H. Harjes, and Kenneth F. Kroner, "Another Look at Models of the Short-Term Interest Rate," *Journal of Financial and Quantitative Analysis* (March 1996), pp. 85-107.

Exhibit 3: GARCH (1, 1) Models for Weekly 3-Month Treasury Bill Rates 3/76 - 12/93

Parameter	Column A Conditional Normal	Column B Conditional t
$\alpha_0(\times 10^{-3})$	0.5714^{***}	0.2380^{**}
	(0.1077)	(0.1107)
$\alpha_1(\times 10^{-3})$	1.3978	4.7753^{***}
	(1.4858)	(1.6345)
$a_0(\times 10^{-6})$	0.1374	0.1860^{*}
	(0.0977)	(0.1060)
a_1	0.6150^{***}	0.7170^{***}
	(0.0153)	(0.0274)
b_1	0.3780^{***}	0.2035^{***}
	(0.0326)	(0.0337)
v		3.5351^{***}
		(0.4110)
L^1	5465.58	5222.65
Statistics of ε_t/σ_t		
Kurtosis[2]	3.0724^{***}	2.4754^{***}
$Q(12)^3$	89.5014^{***}	105.4635^{***}
$Q^2(12)^4$	11.9704	16.8508

Note:
1. The log-likelihood function values reported exclude the first constant term in equation (17), which does not play role in maximization.
2. Kurtosis is here defined as

$$Ku = \frac{T^2}{(T-1)(T-2)(T-3)} \frac{(T+1)M_4 - 3(T-1)M_2^2}{s^4}$$

where M_n is the n-th central moment, and s is the sample standard deviation.
3. $Q(12)$ is the Ljung-Box Q statistic for the standardized residual with 12 lags.
   $Q^2(12)$ is the Ljung-Box Q statistic for the squared standardized residual with 12 lags.
   *, **, and *** denote statistical significance at 10%, 5%, and 1%, respectively.
   Standard errors are reported in parentheses.

Some diagnostic statistics are available for checking the adequacy of the model. When the model is adequately specified for the level and volatility, the standardized residual, ε_t/σ_t, and the standardized residual square, $(\varepsilon_t/\sigma_t)^2$, should be independent and identically distributed (i.i.d.) and thus, not exhibit any time series properties such as autocorrelation.[14] The statistic that we use for this purpose is the Ljung-Box Q statistic:

$$Q(m) = T(T+2) \sum_{j=1}^{m} \frac{1}{T-j} \rho_j^2 \qquad (18)$$

where m denotes the number of lags, and ρ_j is the j-th-order autocorrelation coefficient of the variable. The statistic is used to test the joint hypothesis that there are insignificant autocorrelations in the first m lags of the variable. Under the null hypothesis, $Q(m)$ follows a chi-square distribution with m degrees of freedom.

We compute and report in Exhibit 3 the Q statistics for 12 lags of ε_t/σ_t and $(\varepsilon_t/\sigma_t)^2$; the statistics are denoted $Q(12)$ and $Q^2(12)$, respectively. We find that $Q(12)$ is highly significant at the 1% level, which implies that specification of the interest rate level does not entirely eliminate its time series pattern.[15] While it is possible to refine the model further with higher lag order terms, we leave the model in its current form and proceed to inspect it for volatility, which is the main focus of this chapter. A $Q^2(12)$ value of 11.9704 suggests that $(\varepsilon_t/\sigma_t)^2$ does not have jointly significant autocorrelations in the first 12 lags, and thus the specification seems to have captured all the time series properties in the volatility.[16]

As a final model specification check, we note that the unconditional distribution for ε_t in a GARCH(p,q) model with conditional normal errors has fatter tails than the normal distribution, while the conditional standardized residual should not. We report the kurtosis of the standardized residual in Exhibit 3.[17] The result indicates that ε_t/σ_t still exhibits excessive kurtosis relative to a normal distribution.

This raises the question of whether a conditional normal is an adequate distributional assumption in performing maximum likelihood estimation. In fact, research has found that this distributional assumption is often violated, especially in interest rates and foreign exchange rates.[18] To tackle with this problem, Bollerslev suggests using the standardized Student-t distribution with degrees of freedom, v, estimated as an additional parameter. The higher the value of v, the fatter the tails.

---

[14] The rationale is clear when one refers to equation (2) that (ε_t/σ_t) is in fact e_t, which by construction, is a white noise both in level and in square.

[15] Again, this is consistent with the findings of Brenner, Harjes, and Kroner, "Another Look at Models of the Short-Term Interest Rate."

[16] Another diagnostic test that has been applied in GARCH models is the conditional moment test suggested by Jeffrey M. Woolridge, "A Unified Approach to Robust, Regression-Based Specification Tests," *Econometric Theory* (1990), pp. 17-43, which is found to be robust to distributional assumptions and is able to help identify the sources of misspecifications. It is not as easy to compute and is less well understood, however.

[17] The formulas for computing the kurtosis and the test statistic of kurtosis = 0 are taken from M.G. Kendall and A. Stuart, *The Advanced Theory of Statistics*, Volume 2 (New York: Hafner, 1958). According to the formula, an i.i.d. normal distribution should have a kurtosis of zero.

The model is thus reestimated in exactly the same way as before, except that the log-likelihood function for the sample from $t = 0$ to $t = T$ is now replaced by:

$$
L = \sum_{t=1}^{T} \left\{ \ln\left[\Gamma\left(\frac{v+1}{2}\right)\right] - \ln\left[\Gamma\left(\frac{v}{2}\right)\right] \right.
$$

$$
\left. - \frac{\ln((v-2)\pi)}{2} - \frac{\ln(\sigma_t^2)}{2} - \frac{v+1}{2}\ln\left(1 + \frac{\varepsilon_t^2}{\sigma_t^2(v-2)}\right) \right\} \tag{19}
$$

where $\Gamma(\bullet)$ denotes the gamma function. This log-likelihood function is then maximized with respect to $\{\alpha_0, \alpha_1, a_0, a_1, b_1, v\}$.[19] The results are reported in Column B of Exhibit 3.

Overall, the results are similar to those in Column A when a conditional normal is assumed. α_1 is small and positive, but statistically significant at 1% this time. $(a_1 + b_1)$ is 0.9205. Thus, although mean reversion is found in both interest rate level and volatility, it is seen to take place very slowly. Interest rate shocks subside slowly across time, while episodes of low and high volatility are often seen.

Exhibit 4 presents the fitted conditional volatilities (σ_t) based on the results of Column B. Compared to Exhibit 2, the GARCH volatilities seem to capture interest rate volatilities reasonably well.

FORECASTING INTEREST RATE VOLATILITY USING GARCH

After fitting a GARCH model for the interest rate, we can use the fitted model together with the available information at this period to predict volatility in the future. Define $\sigma_{t+k|t}^2$ as the k-period ahead volatility forecast, and $\sigma_{K|t}^2$ as the average volatility forecasted over K periods based on the available information at time t. For example, with weekly interest rate data, $\sigma_{t+4|t}^2$ denotes the current forecast of interest rate volatility four weeks from now, and $\sigma_{4|t}^2$ the average volatility in the next 4-weeks period.

It can be shown that

$$
\sigma_{t+k/t}^2 = a_0 + \frac{a_0(a_1+b_1)(1-(a_1+b_1)^{k-1})}{1-(a_1+b_1)} + (a_1+b_1)^{k-1}(a_1\varepsilon_t^2 + b_1\sigma_t^2) \tag{20}
$$

---

[18] See, for example, Tim Bollerslev, "A Conditional Heteroskedastic Time Series Model for Speculative Prices and Rates of Return," *Review of Economics and Statistics* (1987), pp. 542-547, and Brenner, Harjes, and Kroner, "Another Look at Models of the Short-Term Interest Rate."

[19] Generally, the model should first be estimated with a conditional normal distribution. When excess kurtosis is found in the conditional standardized residuals, one may proceed to reestimate the model with a conditional t-distribution. To be technically correct, the BHHH maximization algorithm is appropriate only if the log likelihood function is correctly specified. In other words, the results reported in Column A of Exhibit 3 have to be interpreted with care.

Exhibit 4: Conditional Volatility of GARCH (1, 1)-t Model of Weekly 3-Month Treasury Bill Rate 3/31/76 - 12/29/93

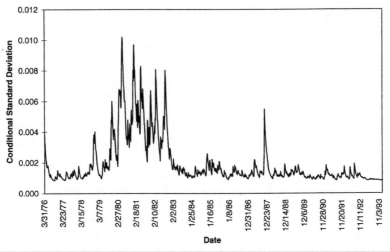

and

$$\sigma_{K/t}^2 = \frac{1}{K} \sum_{k=1}^{K} \sigma_{t+k/t}^2 = \omega + \frac{(\sigma_{t+1}^2 - \omega)}{K} \frac{1 - (a_1 + b_1)^K}{1 - (a_1 + b_1)} \tag{21}$$

where ω is defined as in equation (13) the long-run average volatility. Thus, one can generate a term structure of volatility forecasts for one, two, and to K weeks ahead.

A brief description of the derivation of equations (20) and (21) appears in Engle and Bollerslev.[20] Simply speaking, given σ_t^2, one can obtain $\sigma_{t+1|t}^2$ using the GARCH(1,1) specification, which in turn can be used recursively and inductively to obtain $\sigma_{t+k/t}^2$, and finally equation (21) as well.

In Exhibit 5, we plot the term structure of volatility forecasts (expressed in terms of standard deviation) up to three years ahead based on the GARCH(1,1) model with conditional t-distribution as reported in Column B of Exhibit 3. With the estimates as reported, the long-run average volatility, measured as the square root of ω, is calculated as 0.0015, which is represented by the horizontal line in Exhibit 5.

The average volatility forecasts over one week to three years ahead are shown as increasing and mean-reverting to the long-run average. This is because the conditional volatility at the end of the estimation sample period is found to be below the long-run average.

For a GARCH(1,1) model, the term structure of average volatility forecasts can either be monotonically increasing or monotonically decreasing toward the long-run average volatility, which depends on whether the conditional volatility in

---

[20] Engle and Bollerslev, "Modeling the Persistence of Conditional Variances."

the last period of estimation is below or above average. To generate other shapes of volatility term structure, higher-order models are required.

EXTENSIONS OF GARCH

There are countless extensions of GARCH models. At least several hundred research articles applied some form of GARCH model, and probably another several hundred are forthcoming. We describe some versions of GARCH models that have been proven useful in empirical finance. Other versions of GARCH may be useful under different conditions. Some extensions are complicated and difficult to estimate.

Asymmetric GARCH

There has been some evidence that financial markets exhibit asymmetric responses to good news and bad news. For example, research has found that bad news on stock returns tends to have more of an impact on current stock market volatility than good news, which is generally known as the "leverage effect."

To capture this asymmetric effect, at least four versions of GARCH have been proposed and applied. Here we describe the two most widely applied versions.

Exponential GARCH (EGARCH) Nelson proposes the specification :[21]

$$\ln \sigma_t^2 = a_0 + \sum_{i=1}^{q} a_i \left(\phi \frac{\varepsilon_{t-i}}{\sigma_{t-i}} + \lambda \left(\left| \frac{\varepsilon_{t-i}}{\sigma_{t-i}} \right| - E \left| \frac{\varepsilon_{t-i}}{\sigma_{t-i}} \right| \right) \right) + \sum_{j=1}^{p} b_j \ln \sigma_{t-j}^2 \qquad (22)$$

Exhibit 5: Average Interest Rate Volatility Forecast of GARCH (1, 1)-t Model

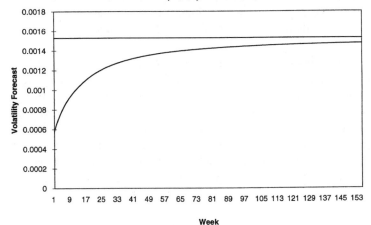

[21] Daniel B. Nelson, "Conditional Heteroskedasticity in Asset Returns: A New Approach," *Econometrica* (1991), pp. 347-370.

The first difference of the EGARCH(p,q) from the GARCH(p,q) is that EGARCH is formulated in logs of conditional volatility. This guarantees that all conditional volatilities will be nonnegative and thus, no restrictions on the parameters are necessary.

In addition, if $a_i \phi < 0$, the conditional volatility will be more sensitive to a negative shock, i.e., $\varepsilon_{t-i} < 0$, than to a positive shock. This asymmetric effect is found in stock series and in some interest rates.

While the EGARCH model is able to incorporate additional time series properties of the underlying variable, applications are considerably more difficult. In particular, it requires a distributional assumption or a numerical simulation in order to compute volatility forecasts.

Glosten, Jagannathan, and Runkle Asymmetric GARCH (GJR-GARCH) To capture the asymmetric GARCH effect, Glosten, Jagannathan, and Runkle propose the GJR-GARCH(1,1) specification:[22]

$$\sigma_t^2 = a_0 + a_1 \varepsilon_{t-1}^2 + a_2 [\min(\varepsilon_{t-1}, 0)]^2 + b_1 \sigma_{t-1}^2 \tag{23}$$

If $a_2 > 0$, a negative shock will give rise to a higher conditional volatility than a corresponding positive shock of the same magnitude. In terms of ease of estimation, the GJR-GARCH model is similar to the original GARCH model. However, volatility forecasting is not as straightforward, as one needs to consider the sign of shocks in the future.

In their comparison of different versions of GARCH models applied to daily Japanese stock return data, Engle and Ng propose using a news impact curve.[23] Their results suggest that the GJR-GARCH is the best parametric model. The EGARCH model is found to lead to a series of conditional volatility that is slightly too volatile, although it captures most of the asymmetry. While there is a theoretical rationale behind an asymmetric GARCH effect in stock returns, it is still unclear why a negative shock in interest rates should have more of an impact on interest rate volatility than a positive shock of the same magnitude.

GARCH Models and Changes in Regime

Experience has shown that GARCH models tend to be very sensitive to sudden changes, which in turn leads to relatively erratic conditional volatility series. A good example is the spike in Exhibit 4 in the week after the 1987 stock market crash, when the Fed lowered the interest rate by more than 1 percentage point. It is unclear whether this should be treated as a random noise effect rather than a regularity to be captured in the model. This property of GARCH may provide for good in-sample descriptions of volatility, but it is uncertain whether it will also produce good out-of-sample volatility forecasts.

---

[22] L.R. Glosten, R. Jagannathan, and D.E. Runkle, "On the Relation Between the Expected Value and the Volatility of the Nominal Excess Return on Stocks," *Journal of Finance* (1993), pp. 1779-1801.

[23] Robert F. Engle and Victor K. Ng, "Measuring and Testing the Impact of News on Volatility," *Journal of Finance* (1993), pp. 1749-1778.

To investigate this issue in weekly stock returns, Hamilton and Susmel introduce a new Markov-switching ARCH model, which is denoted as SWARCH(S,q), where S is the number of possible states, or regimes.[24] In this model, the parameters of the ARCH process are allowed to come from one of S different regimes, with transitions between regimes governed by an unobserved Markov chain.[25] Under this framework, exceptional periods such as the October 1987 crash are allowed to arise from different regimes.

The results indicate that most of the persistence in stock volatility can be attributed to the persistence of low-, moderate-, and high-volatility regimes. The SWARCH also provides both better in-sample statistical fit and better out-of-sample volatility forecasts.

Given the success of the SWARCH model applied to stock returns, and the historical volatility of interest rates in Exhibit 2, it may be fruitful to examine whether the sudden increases in interest rate volatility during the late 1970s, the early 1980s, and October 1987 arise from different regimes. As usual, more advanced modeling comes at the expense of simplicity, and both estimation and forecasting are also considerably more difficult using SWARCH.

Other Exogenous Variables

In the original specification of the ARCH(q) model in Engle, exogenous variables other than the underlying variable itself are allowed.[26] For example, in equation (1), interest rate volatility can be a function of interest rate level as well as time. To explore this more flexible specification, Brenner, Harjes, and Kroner estimate some versions of the model:[27]

$$\sigma_t^2 = a_0 + a_1 \varepsilon_{t-1}^2 + b_1 \sigma_{t-1}^2 + c_1 r_{t-1}^{2\gamma} \tag{24}$$

which allows the conditional volatility at time t to depend on the level of interest rates at time $t - 1$. This dependence is supported by empirical evidence. A similar specification is also used by Lee in studying stock market volatility.[28] Again, volatility forecasting becomes more difficult.

Multivariate GARCH and Volatility Spillovers

So far we have considered only GARCH models applied to univariate time series. In fact, there has been some success applying GARCH specifications to multivariate time series as well as modeling volatility spillovers from one market to the others.

---

[24] James D. Hamilton and Raul Susmel, "Autoregressive Conditional Heteroskedasticity and Changes in Regime," *Journal of Econometrics* (1994), pp. 307-333.

[25] An introduction to Markov chains and changes in regime is Hamilton, *Time Series Analysis*, Chapter 22.

[26] Engle, "Autoregressive Conditional Heteroskedasticity with Estimates of the Variance of United Kingdom Inflation."

[27] Brenner, Harjes, and Kroner, "Another Look at Models of the Short-Term Interest Rate."

[28] Wai Lee, "Market Timing and Short-Term Interest Rates," unpublished manuscript (1996), Harvard Business School.

One difficulty in multivariate GARCH models is a convergence problem in estimation. When too many assets are involved, and specification of volatilities becomes too complicated, it is usually found that parameter estimates tend to be sensitive to initial values, and are unstable when only minor changes in specification are made.

A good reference for specifications, estimations, and properties of multivariate GARCH is Engle and Kroner.[29] Others, such as Engle, Ito, and Lin, and Fung, Lee, and Pan study volatility spillovers with univariate GARCH models by treating volatilities in the other markets as exogenous.[30]

OTHER VOLATILITY MODELS

Although GARCH models are by far the most widely applied models for volatility, they are by no means the only possible class. GARCH models assume that volatilities are observable. More important, volatilities are assumed to be deterministic, although time-varying. This can be illustrated with the GARCH(1,1) model in equation (8). Given an interest rate shock and conditional volatility at time $t - 1$, the model assumes that conditional volatility at time t can then be determined.

Technically speaking, the GARCH specification does not have a random noise term, such as the one in a typical linear regression. Multivariate GARCH models are also difficult to estimate and interpret.[31] To deal with these shortcomings, a relatively new class of volatility models, known as "stochastic volatility (SV)" models, has been proposed. A good reference is Harvey, Ruiz, and Shephard.[32]

In the class of SV models, volatility is treated as an unobservable variable whose logarithm is modeled directly as a linear stochastic process, typically as a low-order autoregressive process. This class of volatility models is related more closely to the continuous-time counterparts than is the discrete-time class of GARCH models. The stochastic volatility is modeled as an unobservable component, and the system of equations can then be estimated by generalized method of moments (GMM), or maximum likelihood method with a Kalman filter.

---

[29] Robert F. Engle and Kenneth F. Kroner, "Multivariate Simultaneous Generalized ARCH," *Econometric Theory* (1995), pp. 122-150.

[30] Robert F. Engle, Takatoshi Ito, and Wen-Ling Lin, "Meteor Showers or Heat Waves? Heteroskedastic Intra-Daily Volatility in the Foreign Exchange Market," *Econometrica* (1990), pp. 525-542; and Hung-Gay Fung, Wai Lee, and Ming-Shuen Pan, "International Interest Rates Linkage: Evidence from the Money Markets of the United Kingdom" *Journal of Multinational Financial Management* (forthcoming in 1997).

[31] Daniel B. Nelson, "ARCH Models as Diffusion Approximations," *Journal of Econometrics* (1990), pp. 7-38, introduces the idea that a discrete-time GARCH model with short enough frequency may be considered an approximation for the continuous-time stochastic diffusion process.

[32] Andrew Harvey, Esther Ruiz, and Neil Shephard, "Multivariate Stochastic Variance Models," *Review of Economic Studies* (1994), pp. 247-264. Also see Torben G. Andersen, "Stochastic Autoregressive Volatility: A Framework for Volatility Modeling," *Mathematical Finance* (April 1994), pp. 75-102; and Stephen J. Taylor, "Modeling Stochastic Volatility: A Review and Comparative Study," *Mathematical Finance* (April 1994), pp. 183-204.

Recently, however, it has been shown that such an estimation can be inefficient. Other estimation methods, such as simulated method of moments, are being explored.[33] The successfulness and usefulness of SV models still needs to be studied.

CONCLUDING REMARKS

The search for a good model of interest rate volatility is by no means closed. Although many versions of GARCH models are relatively easy to estimate with widely reported success, they are still subject to some limitations. Generally, GARCH models tend to outperform other volatility models in short-horizon volatility forecasts, but their performance at longer horizons is not as clear.[34] It is also unclear whether one should fit a monthly GARCH model to forecast volatility in the next month, or fit a weekly GARCH model and use the average volatility forecast over the next four weeks.[35] Thus, some practitioners are still in favor of simpler models such as exponential smoothing, which give more weight to recent periods, are less sensitive to period-to-period changes, and are relatively much easier to apply.

When more advanced estimation methodologies are studied, it may be worthwhile to explore stochastic volatility models, which treat volatility as stochastic and thus allow random noise to affect the underlying volatility patterns. It is possible that such models may be able to provide good forecasts for longer horizons, and thus become good complements for GARCH.

Modeling and forecasting volatility still remains a difficult empirical task and an amount of judgment is needed. Instead of relying on a general rule, it may be better to treat each application as an individual case, and more extensive investigations have to be done before sound decisions can be made.

---

[33] See, for examples, Esther Ruiz, "Quasi-maximum Likelihood Estimation of Stochastic Volatility Models," *Journal of Econometrics* (1994), pp. 289-306; Torben G. Andersen and Bent E. Sfrensen, "GMM Estimation of a Stochastic Volatility Model: A Monte Carlo Study," working paper (1994), Northwestern University; A. Ronald Gallant and George Tauchen, "Which Moments to Match?" working paper (1994), University of North Carolina; and Eric Jacquier, Nicholas G. Polson and Peter E. Rossi, "Bayesian Analysis of Stochastic Volatility Models," *Journal of Business and Economic Statistics* (October 1994), pp. 371-389. For specific application to interest rates, see Torben G. Andersen and Jesper Lund, "Stochastic Volatility and Mean Drift in the Short Term Interest Rate Diffusion: Sources of Steepness, Level and Curvature in the Yield Curve," working paper (1996), Northwestern University.

[34] There are many articles that evaluate different volatility forecasting techniques applied to various asset classes. The relative ranking of these techniques on volatility forecasting accuracy seems to depend on the sample period, specific asset classes, and specifications of the models. See Timothy J. Brailsford and Robert W. Faff, "An Evaluation of Volatility Forecasting Techniques," *Journal of Banking and Finance* (1996), pp. 419-438; Theodore E. Day and Craig M. Lewis, "Forecasting Futures Market Volatility," *Journal of Derivatives* (Winter 1993), pp. 33-50; Ronald C. Heynen and Harrry M. Kat, "Volatility Prediction: A Comparison of the Stochastic Volatility, GARCH(1,1), and EGARCH(1,1) Models," *Journal of Derivatives* (Winter 1994), pp. 50-65; and Kenneth D. West and Dongchul Cho, "The Predictive Ability of Several Models of Exchange Rate Volatility," *Journal of Econometrics* (1995), pp. 367-391.

[35] It has been shown that, theoretically, GARCH models do not allow time aggregation. For example, if daily data follow a GARCH model, data of all other frequencies cannot be exactly GARCH. See Feike C. Drost and Theo E. Nijman, "Temporal Aggregation of GARCH Processes," *Econometrica* (1993), pp. 909-927.

Index

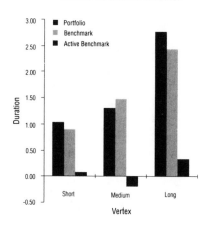

INSIGHT

BARRA'S FIXED INCOME ANALYTICS ASSIST INVESTMENT PROFESSIONALS BY PROVIDING INSIGHT INTO RETURN AS WELL AS RISK.

Situation
You want to assess the risk/return tradeoffs over a six month horizon based upon your forecast of future market conditions.

Solution
BARRA's scenario analytics will perform a total return analysis on your portfolio and benchmark based on the "what if" scenarios you have created. The scenarios can include yield curve movements, sector and quality spread changes.

Situation
Your marketing department and clients want to understand how you outperformed the benchmark.

Solution
Analyze your portfolio with the BARRA performance attribution module. Performance attribution decomposes returns into components like duration and yield curve reshaping bets, sector and quality spreads, and specific issue selection. The performance analysis incorporates transactions and tabulates returns on both an absolute basis and relative to your benchmark.

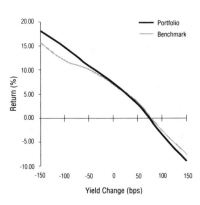

Annualized Return (6 Month Horizon)

	Return %		
	Portfolio	Benchmark	Active
Rolldown	0.46	0.46	0.00
Interest Rate			
Shift	1.30	1.15	0.15
Twist	0.10	0.13	-0.03
Other	-0.07	-0.09	0.02
Sector	-0.14	-0.21	0.07
Quality Rating	-0.02	-0.02	0.00
Specific	0.02	0.00	0.02

⑥ BARRA

Internet http://www.barra.com
BERKELEY 510.548.5442 • LONDON 0171.283.2255 • YOKOHAMA 045.451.6161

COMPARED TO BONDEDGE,™ OTHER SOFTWARE IS JUST SOFT.

If you're not using BondEdge, your current fixed income portfolio system isn't giving you everything you need to respond to changing market conditions. Here are **20** reasons why more institutional bond managers choose BondEdge than any other system.

CMS FOCUSES ON BOND ANALYTICS AND ONLY BOND ANALYTICS

1. Option-adjusted risk measures that capture changes in interest rates, volatility estimates, prepayment speeds

2. Specialized regulatory reports that quickly meet ever-changing requirements

3. ARMs, municipal bonds and a local database to model specialized securities

4. Tax-exempt bonds fully incorporated in all your portfolio analytics

5. Ability to price private placements and include credit, option and liquidity risk

FEATURES THAT SET INDUSTRY STANDARDS

6. Integrated security and portfolio analytics right on your PC

7. A true Windows® format with multi-user, multi-tasking capabilities

8. Presentation graphics that save you hours of explanation

9. Daily performance measurement results through AIMR-compliant system

10. Taxable and tax-exempt bond indices from all the leading providers modeled in their entirety

BONDEDGE STREAMLINES INVESTMENT MANAGEMENT

11. Inventory management to quickly identify where securities are held

12. What-if analytics to fully understand the implications of proposed trades

13. Custom report writer for simplified management and client reporting

14. Electronic trade tickets that eliminate time-consuming, hand-written forms

15. Connectivity with other systems to easily import data and export calculations

WE'RE THERE WHEN YOU NEED US

16. Keep your costs down by subscribing only to the applications you need

17. Independent, unbiased research that lets you consider the facts without the sales pitch

18. Choose between a flexible 30-day contract or an annual contract

19. Frequent enhancements help you keep up with new market developments

20. Full training and continual support makes using BondEdge productive and cost effective

CAPITAL MANAGEMENT SCIENCES

A DATA BROADCASTING CORPORATION COMPANY

Get on the Leader Board.

Why use a putter in a sand trap?

With GAT Decision™, even the longest shots get legs. Callable corporates? Birdie. Floating rate notes? Eagle. Swaptions? Hole in one. Analyzing re-REMICs is a chip shot. Because of our extensive database of everything from treasuries to asset-backed securities, you don't need extra strokes to analyze your entire portfolio.

With Decision, you'll drive farther off the tee than you ever thought possible. Analyze portfolio risk using OAS duration and convexity. Perform scenario analysis with your viewpoint on rates, spreads and volatilities. Structure portfolios using immunization, enhanced index strategies, cash flow analysis. Windows-based analytics make it easy, so you'll produce down the stretch like a seasoned pro.

Don't risk slicing or hooking with inferior models. GAT's research is rigorous, consistent and accurate. We have an ongoing effort to examine, refine and enhance our work. Whether it's interest rate lattice generation, term structure modeling, path sampling, prepayment modeling, advanced risk measures like Key Rate Durations, or performance attribution, you'll always be pin high.

GAT's technology allows you to shape your shots to the circumstances. Integrate Decision with your own database and run it on your own hardware; it's ODBC-compliant and runs on multiple platforms. The flexible architecture of our object-oriented design ensures that you'll keep pace with the financial markets as new innovations appear. With our commitment to leading edge technology, you'll never find yourself facing an unplayable lie.